This is Deb's book, in many senses.

THE LEGAL MIND
ESSAYS FOR TONY HONORÉ

THE LEGAL MIND

ESSAYS FOR TONY HONORÉ

EDITED BY

NEIL MacCORMICK

AND

PETER BIRKS

CLARENDON PRESS · OXFORD

1986

Oxford University Press, Walton Street, Oxford OX2 6DP
Oxford New York Toronto
Delhi Bombay Calcutta Madras Karachi
Kuala Lumpur Singapore Hong Kong Tokyo
Nairobi Dar es Salaam Cape Town
Melbourne Auckland
and associated companies in
Beirut Berlin Ibadan Nicosia

Oxford is a trade mark of Oxford University Press

Published in the United States
by Oxford University Press, New York

British Library Cataloguing in Publication Data
The Legal mind: essays for Tony Honoré.
1. Legal reasoning
I. MacCormick, Neil II. Birks, Peter
III. Honoré, Tony
340'.1 K290
ISBN 0-19-876196-1

Library of Congress Cataloging in Publication Data
The Legal mind.
Bibliography: p.
Includes index.
1. Law—Adresses, essays, lectures. 2. Jurisprudence —Addresses, essays, lectures. 3. Honoré, Tony, 1921— —Addresses, essays, lectures I. Honoré, Tony 1921- . II. Birks, Peter. MacCormick, Neil.
K160.L44 1986 340 86-870

ISBN 0-19-876196-1

Set and printed by Butler & Tanner Ltd, Frome and London

Editors' Preface

FEW contributors to legal thought have contributed on so broad a front as Tony Honoré, Regius Professor of Civil Law in the University of Oxford since 1971. No less energetic and productive than the great Roman jurists whom he has interpreted to the modern world, he has influenced the development of Roman-Dutch law, has altered perceptions of the form and content of Roman law, and has shown how comparative law can generate fresh insights and stimulate research. As if this were not enough, his work in analytical jurisprudence, and in moral and political philosophy, is continually cited in the writings of other scholars in those fields. In the study of texts, his sensitivity to the Latin language, to the habits of the legal mind in general, and the individuality of legal minds in particular, has combined with a determined numerate empiricism to produce revolutionary new methods, as stimulating as they are controversial. Nor has depth been sacrificed for this astonishing breadth. For sharpness of insight and boldness of legal imagination, few have been his equals.

It is fitting that for his sixty-fifth birthday friends and colleagues, some of them former pupils in the technical sense, all of them acknowledging the inspiration they have found in his thought, should seek to honour Honoré. To do it, how better than to explore at least some aspects of the legal mind? With only the lightest editorial guidance, this exploration has diversified itself into topics which include much that is of the essence of legal thinking whenever and wherever it has flourished. The essays are loosely grouped: it is hard to draw lines. The first five papers investigate the soundness and unsoundness of legal reasoning, not only its logical and practical strength but also its tricks and pretences. The sixth, re-exploring Tony Honoré's concern with justice within a framework of procedural fairness, forms a bridge between the group of essays concerned with reasoning and a series of papers which is given over to analysis of and reflection upon institutions and concepts of fundamental importance in most legal systems, major categories of the legal mind. Next the thirteenth and fourteenth of the essays address questions about the nature of sanctions, punishment, and obligations; these dig down to the roots of the concept of law. The approach of the fourteenth paper then leads into the final group reflecting on the place of history and tradition in law and on the significance of intellectual and juristic traditions in the formation of the legal mind.

It will be seen that the range covered by these essays is a broad one. Yet, broad as it is, it does not, and within one volume could not, cover the whole array and richness of Honoré's own contribution. If in any one particular respect it succeeds in reflecting his achievement it is perhaps in the way its ordering has sought to overcome traditional barriers between specialized subjects of academic study. In honouring Honoré in his sixty-sixth year, we honour him not least for brilliantly transcending academic categories. And in wishing him well for the future we thank him for celebrating the richness and diversity of the serious study of law: *etenim sine controversia et magna est et late patet et ad multos pertinet et summo in honore semper fuit.** And, more personally, we are grateful for his devotion to reason and toleration, moderate lawyerly virtues evident in all his work.

P.B.H.B.
D. N. MacC.

* Cicero, *de Oratore*, 1.55.235.

Contents

I

Fraud No. 3

DAVID DAUBE

I

As I am going to inspect a certain dodge, I had best start by declaring what I understand by the term: the attempt to thwart an irksome restriction by means which will stand up to judicial scrutiny. It is an attempt. Strictly, my dodge is a dodge only so long as the courts have not spoken, have not put 'objective' truth in the place of 'subjective' groping, testing. Once upheld—as 'avoidance' in today's nomenclature—then, though it was aimed against a law, it has always been within it, a tenable construction, not essentially different from any other courses open. Once rejected—'evasion'—it has always been off, a misinterpretation, essentially like any other courses ruled out. (Why not enliven the vocabulary a little and add the pairs 'strategy' *v.* 'stratagem', 'circumnavigation' *v.* 'circumvention', 'adjusting' *v.* 'twisting'?) One is reminded of hope in Greek myth, right at the rim of Pandora's box, alive only till either realized or disappointed. A dodge indeed by my definition involves a peculiar hope—that it will pass muster when challenged. The retrospective judicial determination of legality or illegality ushers in an entirely new phase.

There is about a dodge something entrepreneurial—of a special nature: a champing at the bit and risk-taking on the one hand, a wary underhandedness on the other. In a paper 'Dodges and Rackets in Roman Law'[1] I pointed out that, by and large, dodges are the preserve of the haves (which is corroborated rather than contradicted by the fairy-tales where the little guy gets the better of the big guys by using one). The have-nots break the law, the haves skirt it. The former steal and perjure themselves: in order to obtain a handout offered to starving families, they will swear they are married though they are not. The latter, under less pressure, and with access to expert advice, aspire to eat their cake and have it too, set the law at naught while keeping on the right side of it: if you are entitled to a legacy provided you are married and you loathe marriage, you marry—on the understanding that divorce is to follow without delay. Now and then a statute expressly nullifies its circumvention (a clause not quite futile though,

[1] Summarized in *Proceedings of the Classical Association*, vol. 61, 1964, pp. 28 ff.

obviously, whoever was trying on a dodge would deny that it was covered by it). The *lex Fufia Caninia*, limiting the number of slaves that may be released by will, is one example,[2] the part of the *lex Tarentina* laying down property qualifications for councillors another.[3] Neither is addressed to the street people.

No wonder an enormous amount of ingenuity goes into the thinking up of ploys from hoary antiquity. My previous paper, however, suggested that the countless forms assumed by them are reducible to a few basic models and their combinations. I discussed two. (1) Where a law prohibits a certain transaction—sale or gift or interest—an alternative transaction is substituted which will produce the nearest effect—gift plus countergift for sale, sale at a nugatory price for a gift, a late-repayment-penalty with an impossibly early repayment-date for interest. (2) Where a law debars a certain group from a transaction—a governor from money-lending in his province—an *interposita persona* is used—he does business through his cousin. Here I propose to look at a further scheme: (3) Where a law attaches an advantage or disadvantage to a certain quality, this is indeed acquired or shed but in a fashion that drains the change of substance.

II

The punishment for adultery introduced by Augustus was not meted out to professional whores:[4] in olden times, we hear from Tacitus,[5] to figure on the aediles' list of them was considered punishment enough. However, early in Tiberius's reign, he narrates, one Vistilia, highborn and highwed, inscribed herself in that list. Whereupon the senate decreed that no woman whose father, grandfather or husband was a knight might take up this occupation. So far, so good. What is puzzling is that she was tried, convicted and exiled to Seriphos, 'the island having everything one doesn't need'.[6] On what ground, seeing that her indiscretions preceded the decree? C. S. Rogers comments:[7] 'Probably no defence was possible; her conduct was a matter of record on the aediles' books'. Not satisfactory. It is this record which, far from explaining the verdict, creates the problem. In its absence, there would be none; whereas, at first sight at least, the orderly advertisement of her doings ought to have afforded immunity.

The answer lies in the authorities' refusal to recognize her registration,

2 Gaius, *Institutes* 1.46.

3 *Lex Tarentina* 29 ff.

4 See T. Mommsen, *Römisches Strafrecht*, 1899, pp. 691 ff.

5 Tacitus, *Annals* 2.85.1 ff.

6 Plutarch, *On Exile* 7, *Moralia* 602B; see L. Bürchner, art. 'Seriphos', in Pauly-Wissowa, *Real-Encyclopädie der classischen Altertumswissenschaft*, 2nd ser., vol. IIA2, 1923, col. 1732.

7 See C. S. Rogers, *Criminal Trials and Criminal Legislation under Tiberius*, Middletown, Conn., 1935, p. 31.

which was a blind. She never meant to provide the indiscriminate, base, paid services of her co-registrants. She chose a lover, or lovers, like any lady of her standing. The sole purpose of her entry was to ward off the criminal sanction she deserved. In short, she was not a *bona fide* prostitute, and the judges pronounced accordingly. Additionally, in order once for all to close this loophole, the senate passed the resolution already mentioned: a woman of rank must not trade in her body. What about an untitled one? No need to bother *de minimis*.

Support is furnished by Suetonius.[8] To go by him, a fair number of women in that epoch avowed themselves madams or procuresses, the point being that these facilitators were no more punishable for adultery than outright sluts. No doubt in this case, too, the members of the *haut monde* in question were selective, not at all like the brothel-keepers or lessors of rooms by the hour at Sankt Pauli. They would have their friends over for wild parties and the like. And in this case, too, exile was the consequence, though exactly who inflicted it is not made clear. The women's aim, we are told, was 'to escape the penalties of the laws'. It is tempting to translate *evitare* by 'to evade' and, conceivably, it does in this passage carry a trace of the crooked. But generally, the verb as such is still neutral in this period. (So is *evadere*—in contradistinction to *eludere*, as we shall see further on. It would be interesting to pursue the development of these and related terms leading up to their present roles.) However, Suetonius goes on to report that the government reacted so fiercely 'lest such fraud should provide shelter to anyone'. A direct reference to fraud on law, of the sort I am postulating: they were 'madams' or 'procuresses' in inverted commas, it was not real. He assigns to the same category those youngsters of the senatorial and equestrian orders who, chafing under a regulation which kept them from the stage and the arena, deliberately got themselves defeated in a court case of the kind where defeat brought with it infamy—and thereby removal from the higher orders and their shackles. Once again, they did not genuinely leave their class. On the contrary, they would earn the admiration of their dissolute clique. Tiberius did not put up with the sham. If they became actors or gladiators, their ruse did not make them any less accountable. A recently unearthed inscription with more detail will be briefly introduced below.

In Republican Rome, as in many cultures, an adulterous wife was dealt with by her husband or father, who might be assisted by other male relations. They had ample discretion and could be brutal or friendly.[9] Augustus's ordinance, oppressive and male-chauvinist as it was, by bringing her before a public tribunal did inch towards her treatment as a person rather

[8] Suetonius, *Tiberius* 35.2.

[9] See D. Daube, *Juridical Review*, vol. 90, n.s. 23, 1978, pp. 177 ff. Tiberius restored the *iudicium domesticum* for cases which the new one did not cover: Suetonius, *Tiberius* 35.1.

than as an object. Plainly, for those who would have managed well under the old dispensation—with Helen of Troy as patron saint, lovingly re-installed by Menelaus, *un mari épique*—the price of progress was high. Vistilia was unwilling to pay it. She resorted to a dodge—wanting to have it both ways, be accounted law-abiding and defy the law. To be more concrete, the system so far prevailing reckoned with an élite faithful to the tenet *noblesse oblige*. She was not, but neither had she any inclination to mingle with the rabble. Her nominal enlistment was meant to safeguard the *noblesse* unencumbered with the obligation. From a slightly different angle: the hookers were enjoying a *privilegium odiosum*, a liberty that is really a disability.[10] (One may think of a court jester's licence to speak out or a medieval Jew's to practise usury.) Vistilia craved the privilege without the *odium*.

We can now say a little more about the sensatusconsult Tacitus mentions. So long as matrons of rank were practically all of them jealous of their reputation, an occasional misuse of the exemption from prosecution granted to professionals would not be alarming. From Suetonius it is evident, however, that at a certain juncture indifference to official censure became widespread among the jet set. Quite apart from general, moral considerations—to have to investigate in each case whether the label of prostitute did or did not correspond to lifestyle was too much. A complete exclusion from this trade of females belonging to the aristocracy cut the Gordian knot. Time was, in the USA, when to be kept out of the army because of homosexuality or schizophrenia constituted a fearful disgrace. During the war with Vietnam that changed. Strange no one thought of a senatusconsult prohibiting men from being homosexual or schizophrenic. The Roman lawmakers cannot have been happy being forced into explicitness as to the reservation of the aediles' list for the lowly majority. At the time, whenever possible—for example, in getting more progeny out of the well-to-do minority—less overt means of discrimination were preferred. (Which did not prevent Pliny, under Trajan, from noticing it: 'Massive rewards and corresponding penalties urge the rich to rear children'.)[11] Only in many cases, as in the present one, plain language was unavoidable. I cannot here enter into the tangled fortunes of this distinction.

Women, it appears, bravely continued wrestling with the spoilsports. Justinian's Digest contains an excerpt from Papinian[12]—around AD 200—to the effect that she who, 'in order to escape the penalty of adultery', goes in for procuring or hires herself out to the theatre can still be charged under that head and sentenced. A few details may be noted. First, the text presupposes that, like a harlot and a procuress, in principle, a professional

[10] See D. Daube, *Harvard Theological Review*, vol. 68, 1975, pp. 371 ff., *Zeitschrift der Savigny-Stiftung*, vol, 99, 1982, *Rom. Abt.*, pp. 27 ff.

[11] Pliny, *Panegyric* 26.5. See D. Daube, *The Duty of Procreation*, 1977, p. 32.

[12] Digest 48.5.11.2, Papinian II *de adulteriis*.

actress is exempt from the Augustan reform; hence, here is yet another opening for a fake alibi. It is arguable that this part is interpolated: the subjunctive *fecerit* is followed by the indicative *locavit*. I prefer to ascribe the switch to abbreviation. Secondly, here as in Suetonius, *evitare* as such may be free of any derogatory connotation. The phrase 'to escape a penalty' recurs in quite different fields in the Digest,[13] not once alluding to trickery. That we have to do with it in the fragment before us is shown by the accompanying data; the verb itself is not needed for it. Thirdly, Papinian says that where procuring or acting is intended to neutralize the legislation, the latter will none the less operate 'by virtue of a senatusconsult'. Possibly, he has in mind the decree cited by Tacitus, which may have done more than deal with a pseudo-whore, or at least have been rendered more widely useful by a vigorous exegesis. Or, possibly, he is thinking of a supplementary measure. Anyhow, his *evitandae poenae adulterii gratia* and Suetonius's *ad evitandas legum poenas* are similar enough to warrant the guess that some such expression was employed by the first-century senate.

A tablet found near Larino, south of the Abruzzi, preserves a senatusconsult of AD 19, the very year of the Vistilia scandal, combating public performances by nobles. Its edition by Barbara Levick is provided with so magnificent a commentary, philological, legal, historical and cultural, that I may confine myself to some selective observations.[14] On the whole, the decree does the same about these deviations that Tacitus's does about adultery: it makes them illegal even where a noble has lost his or her status as a result of becoming infamous. The motivation, too, is no doubt analogous. The senate is perturbed by a fashion of advisedly incurring infamy—for example, by getting oneself condemned in a *famosum iudicium*,[15] a method we came across in Suetonius. In default of a countermeasure, each time an ex-noble acts or fights, there will have to be a preliminary inquiry as to whether he or she is truly disreputable—entitled to perform—or only a pretender—having engineered the infamy and therefore not entitled. The solution: a once-for-all debarment, outlasting the loss of status. The lawgiver is indeed aware that the daredevils in question might not be overly impressed. That is why a major portion of the pronouncement is addressed not to them but the impresarios: henceforth they must hire no one who ever belonged to the upper classes.[16] Parallels abound through the ages. At this very moment, there is controversy over here about a paragraph in a

[13] See *Vocabularium Iurisprudentiae Romanae*, ed. Preussische Akademie der Wissenschaften, vol. 2, 1933, p. 619. I had been unable to locate 325, 11 when Alan Rodger informed me that it ought to read 315,11: = Digest 10.2.25.13.

[14] See B. Levick, *Journal of Roman Studies*, vol. 73, 1983, pp. 97 ff. When first writing this paper, I was unaware of the discovery. I am greatly indebted to Alan Rodger, whom I asked to comment on my draft, for drawing my attention to it.

[15] Line 13.

[16] Lines 7 ff.

proposed Immigration Act which would penalize not only the permitless alien employee but also—and more effectively—the employer.

Suetonius, we saw, notes that, in the eyes of the powers-that-be, both the fake madams and the youths sacrificing their name for stage or arena were seeking 'shelter in a fraud', in a reprehensible dodge. In conformity with him, the senatusconsult from Larinum charges the latter group with 'applying fraud by which they impair the majesty of the senate': they deceitfully get out from under an anti-performances regulation of this body.[17] Several lines after this, the purpose of their dodge is said to be 'to elude the authority of their order'.[18] In the Digest *eludere* invariably signifies 'to ward off an obligation or punishment by misuse of the law'[19]. Tacitus informs us that exile was the fate of one who planned by procedural finesse and deals with the prosecution 'to elude the retribution' threatening friends of his for the forgery of a will.[20] The senatusconsult, then, is characterizing the culprits as disengaging under a pseudo-legal cover from the demands of their position.[21]

Vistilia's husband, Titidius Labeo, we gather from Tacitus, narrowly missed being engulfed. The statute concerning adultery reserved the husband the exclusive power of arraignment for the first sixty days. The senate demanded an explanation from Labeo why, though his wife had displayed conspicuous indications of the offence,[22] he made no move. His plea that the sixty days—'granted for deliberation', he emphasized—had not yet gone by in the end got him off the hook. Since K. L. Nipperdey,[23] the consensus is that the senate exceeded the bounds set by the statute. In C. S. Roger's words, owing to 'the public indignation, the husband's sixty-day privilege was transformed into an obligation'. I am not sure. In the circumstances, his passivity may have seemed to be the tip of the iceberg indicative of actual aiding and abetting. Thus the interrogation would be designed to find out whether the evidence sufficed to proceed against him for this—not at all for the waiving of the right itself. We are in the dark about other particulars. C. S. Rogers considers it 'a little more likely' that Labeo did finally prosecute than that he did not. I like to think that, notwithstanding his peril, he left it to others though I am aware that people, men with a

[17] Line 6.

[18] Line 12.

[19] Digest 4.8.30, Paul XIII *ad edictum*, 9.4.26 pr., Paul XVII *ad edictum*, 42.8.10.8, Ulpian LXXIII *ad edictum*, 49.5.12.9, Papinian *singulari de adulteriis*, 48.19.1.3, Ulpian VIII *disputationum*, 49.19.6 pr., Ulpian IX *de offico proconsulsis*.

[20] Tacitus, *Annals* 14.41.

[21] See B. Levick, op. cit., p. 103; 'the burdens imposed by membership of a high class'.

[22] This is what *delicti manifesti* signifies. It does not mean 'to be caught in the act'. Compare 'displaying recognizable signs of distaste or fear' in Tacitus, *Annals* 4.53, 'displaying clear signs of life' in 12.51, 'displaying obvious indications of ambition' in 14.29.

[23] K. L. Nipperdey, *Tacitus*, vol. 1, 11th edn., p. 226.

position to guard especially, will do a great deal to save their necks—and weep when the cock crows.

The elder Pliny, writing in the seventies AD, in a chapter of his *Natural History* which treats of art, introduces a Titedius Labeo, possibly Vistilia's ex-husband.[24] He is described as recently deceased at an advanced age, which would fit: if he was, say, thirty-five when she acted out, he would now be well into his eighties. He had once been a praetor, we learn, and then governor of Narbonne. It is not divulged when, but it was hardly after the rumpus though, who knows?, perhaps he worked his way back like politicians in our century. Pliny is silent on the affair which he must have remembered. Nevertheless Labeo does get a black mark: he painted miniatures—a contemptible specialty, *contumeliae erat*. How different cultures or individuals rate miniatures would make a fascinating study. The buyers of miniatures at a London or Munich auction are not mainstream, those at a Tokyo or Kyoto auction are. In the former places, as at Rome, this interest does not quite befit a self-respecting male. Labeo, despite his frightening experience, remained a maverick.[25]

He has, of course, nothing to do with the famous jurist. Yet by an odd coincidence, a striking idea which Tacitus voices in outlining the case, and to which I have already called attention, is reminiscent of Marcus Antistius. When Vistilia sought freedom from the anti-adultery enactment by enrolling as a harlot, she was relying, Tacitus observes, on a practice established by the ancients: they regarded the shameless as sufficiently punished by this very publicity of their wretchedness. In other words, the overall degradation made it superfluous, illogical, to come down on any specific lapse. With this we may compare a statement in the Digest[26] with respect to the problem how far money paid out for an illegal or immoral purpose may be reclaimed. Labeo refuses such an action against a whore 'on a new ground, namely not on the ground of immorality on the part of both (the customer and the whore) but on the ground of immorality on his part alone: for though she is acting immorally in being a whore, once she is a whore her acceptance of money is not immoral'. It is the same distinction as above: the abject condition *in toto* is a bar to the enforcement of purist directives in each single incident. The authenticity of the text has been attacked.[27]

[24] Pliny, *Natural History* 35.7.20. See M. Fluss, art, Titidius Labeo, in Pauly-Wissowa, vol. VIA2, 1937, cols. 1536f.

[25] I am not the only Oxford professor to indulge in fantasies about the characters in this drama. Vistilia had an aunt who married several times (without having to do so under the levirate as the woman in Matthew 22) and R. Syme wonders (*Tacitus* (Oxford, 1958), vol. 1, pp. 373f.) whether the niece's conduct was 'perhaps a paradoxical protest against the matrimonial adventures of her aunt'.

[26] Digest 12.5.4.3, Ulpian XXVI *ad edictum*.

[27] See P. Heck, *Archiv für die Civilistische Praxis*, vol. 124, n.s. 4, 1925, pp. 42ff., G. v. Beseler, *Studia et Documenta Historiae et Iuris*, vol. 3, 1937, p. 377.

But at least the portion here relevant is, in the main, exceptionally trustworthy. As for form, it is enough to single out the accusative and infinitive in the stretch 'for though she is acting immorally', typical of the classical handing-on of an earlier teaching. And as for substance—surely, Labeo is applying by analogy a notion much talked of in his day in connection with Augustus's pioneering promulgation.[28] In fact, his method is precisely that which Peter Stein has demonstrated to be characteristic of him.[29] The very term *ratio* is significant: 'It is almost certainly he', says Stein, 'who added *ratio* to the list of sources of law'. In this instance, he approves of the prevalent opinion *nova ratione*. I have argued elsewhere[30] that, over a century later, Simeon ben Yohai, a leading Rabbi, seems greatly indebted to him. He displays enormous concern with the wherefore of a provision, and even the new ground crops up when he agrees with somebody else's decision 'but the reason is not according to his words'.[31] Maybe, after all, it is not a one hundred per cent coincidence to come into touch here with M. Antistius Labeo. The name Titidius Labeo might cause Tacitus to think of the jurist whose ethos he admired[32] and to recollect some pertinent reflections of his on the adultery statute.

Yet another fluke allows me to grant a walk-on to Labeo's rival Capito: having been honorary consul in AD 5, he appears as senior witness in the Larino decree.[33] One more illustration of his eager playing along with the new bosses.

Naturally, dodges such as depicted in these sources, with the object of earning infamy, are a rarity. The reverse object is the rule, and we do hear, for example, of pimping under the guise of managing an inn.[34] On the other hand, when I first came to England in the thirties, I met husbands striving to be branded as adulterers. Divorce (in old-fashioned lingo, revealingly, 'matrimonial relief') was then not obtainable by agreement. When a couple resolved to split, the rational course was for him to enable her to allege adultery. He spent a night at a hotel with a call-girl and, as the law presumed that an adult man and an adult woman sharing a bedroom had sexual commerce—except if they were married—the expedient mostly worked. Mostly: not, that is, before a judge too upright to play ball.

28 *Eine der eingreifendsten und dauerndsten strafrechtlichen Neuschöpfungen, welche die Geschichte kennt*: T. Mommsen op. cit., p. 691. But not a patch on Deuteronomy 22: 22 (see my article quoted above, n. 9) with an impact on life and letters—for better or worse—extending from biblical era (Susannah, the pardoning of an adulteress in John 8: 22 ff.) right into the present.

29 See P. Stein, *Cambridge Law Journal*, vol. 31, 1972, pp. 14 ff.

30 See D. Daube, *Jewish Law Annual*, Suppl. 2, 1980, pp. 59 f.

31 Siphre on Leviticus 23: 20, Mishnah Menahoth 4.3.

32 Tacitus, *Annals* 3.75.

33 Line 2; see B. Levick op. cit., p. 100.

34 Digest 3.2.4.2, Ulpian VI *ad edictum*, 23.2.42.9, Ulpian I *ad legem Juliam et Papiam*. See L. Friedlaender, *Sittengeschichte Roms*, 9th edn. G. Wissowa, vol. 1, Leipzig, 1919, p. 348.

Few novels can have been as effective in helping on a law reform as A. P. Herbert's *Holy Deadlock*.

Why some dodges pass and others do not, or why the same dodge succeeds at a certain time and place and not at another, I leave unexplored. Under a luckier star, Vistilia's scheme might have prospered. Indeed, it might have grown into an acknowledged, formal transaction available to couples desiring an 'open marriage'. (Fiduciary *coemptio* comes to mind—to be touched on in the following section.) It was not to be. For all that, she may merit a niche in a pantheon of female resisters. She did fight back, in her way.

III

Fiddling with time, more precisely, the substitution of a flash in the pan for solid duration, distinguishes not a few exploits of the variety here examined. Here is a selection.

The *lex Tarentina*, already adverted to,[35] required a councillor to be owner, 'without evil machination', *sine dolo malo*, of a house roofed with at least 1,500 tiles; and imposed the same fine on one who did not own such a house and one who did but had bought it and taken it over by mancipation 'in a manner doing fraud to this statute', *quo hoic legi fraudem faceret*. An aspirant to office unable to afford a good enough building might acquire one from a wealthy friend pro forma, paying nothing or very little, with a fiduciary clause accompanying the transfer to the effect that at the end of the councillorship the building was to be re-transferred. Pacts empowering each of the parties to rescind the sale would do the same trick.[36] The legislator wanted councillors of dependable substance and—doubtless wised up by experience—issued a warning that fleeting appearance would not be accepted in lieu of reality.

In the same chapter in which Suetonius relates the discomfiture of those who reckoned they could circumvent the dictates of virtue, he tells us about two more jugglings, the first, it seems, designed, like this one, to hide inadequate funds. A senator whose fortunes declined risked being deprived of his seat by the emperor.[37] The one in question had to give up the superior house he owned at Rome and be content with renting a cheap one; and he sought to cover up the operation by a short withdrawal to the country just before 1 July, the general moving day, planning to take up his new abode a little later on. Tiberius expelled him from the senate.

[35] 29 ff.; see above, n. 3.

[36] On *fiducia cum amico*, see W. W. Buckland, *A Text-book of Roman Law*, 2nd edn. by P. Stein, Cambridge, 1963, p. 432, on pacts attached to sale, pp. 495 ff.

[37] Suetonius, *Tiberius* 35.2. See T. Mommsen, *Römisches Staatsrecht*, vol. 3, pt. 2, 3rd edn., repr. Basel, 1952, p. 883, n. 3, not quite finding his way through this text. Mine is admittedly somewhat speculative.

The second subterfuge was provoked by Augustus's *lex Papia Poppaea* which, if of two magistrates running for the administration of two provinces one was married and the other unmarried, allowed the former to choose instead of submitting to the lot.[38] A quaestor took a wife the day before the appointment and divorced her the day after. Not only did he not get his province: he was stripped of his quaestorship. The Loeb translator's footnote, 'The reason for his divorcing his wife is problematical',[39] dates from the eve of World War I, the last moment it could have been penned.

In the Digest it is affirmed[40] that 'a simulated marriage is of no force'. This, from Gaius' work on *lex Julia et Papia*, originally had regard to just the type of phantasma produced by that quaestor—or, indeed, other victims of the anticelibatarian policy of the two statutes. For instance, a bachelor or spinster was prohibited from taking a legacy,[41] so when your uncle died you married, to resume your old ways as soon as the legacy was yours. Justinian, as often,[42] by dropping the limiting context, gains a comprehensive, over-comprehensive, rule. How undogmatic the statement was in its original setting, how narrowly oriented towards the Augustan legislation, may be seen from the fact that, in a different area, virtually the same dodge enjoyed the status of an institution. From the later Republic on, *coemptio*, primarily a mode of establishing *manus* marriage, admitted of a fiduciary arrangement to have it immediately undone—by which tactics a woman might get out of an expensive family cult or achieve a change of guardians.[43] The casting off of the *sacra* is indeed given by Cicero—half-banteringly, to be sure—as an example of the corruptive ingenuity of the jurists;[44] and in expounding the change of guardians, Gaius speaks of *evitare tutelam*, 'to escape from the existing tutelage'.[45]

J. Partsch claims[46] that, as a Roman marriage was concluded by the setting up of a joint life, it could never be 'simulated' in the sense of publicly going through one transaction while privately intending another. Hence the fragment must envisage a case such as where an alien woman was misrepresented as a citizen—not really 'simulation'. But it is difficult to see why at any time, classical or post-classical, it should have been necessary solemnly to point out that a downright lie will not do. Whereas the quaestor's procedure did pose a problem. One can imagine a huge wedding celebration

[38] See T. Mommsen, *Römisches Staatsrecht*, vol. 2, pt. 1, 3rd edn., repr. 1952, pp. 254, 534.
[39] See J. C. Rolfe, *Suetonius* with an English translation, vol. 1, 1914, repr. 1920, pp. 344 f.
[40] Digest 23.2.30, Gaius V *ad legem Juliam et Papiam*.
[41] See W. W. Buckland, *A Text-Book of Roman Law*, pp. 292 f.
[42] See D. Daube, *Zeitschrift der Savigny-Stiftung*, vol. 76, 1959, Rom. *Abt.* 175 ff.
[43] See W. W. Buckland, *A Text-book of Roman Law*, pp. 119 f.
[44] Cicero, *Pro Murena* 12.27.
[45] Gaius, *Institutes* 1.114.
[46] See J. Partsch, *Zeitschrift der Savigny-Stiftung*, vol. 42, 1921, *Rom. Abt.*, pp. 253 ff.

(with the unmarried colleague as guest of honour), to all appearances, and indeed in respect of all tangible data at this hour, a perfect start; yet when its premeditated, short-lived nature emerged, a fake. I am far from denying that *simulare*, ripened or decayed into a highly technical concept, is frequently interpolated. But it looks all right here; and we shall soon come across further early evidence—not only from the Digest but also from Tacitus—for this application of the word.

Like marriage, divorce might be for a while only, an intermezzo staged with a view to meeting the demands, statutory or unwritten, of an austere regime. Domitian, we read in Suetonius,[47] removed a knight from the list of jurors for taking back his adulterous wife after dutifully divorcing and charging her. Marcian, in the Digest,[48] calls him who remarries the divorced adultress guilty of 'fraud'. The excerpt has suffered at the hand of revisers but definitely enshrines a genuine nucleus. G. v. Beseler holds that Marcian spoke, not vaguely of 'fraud', but more trenchantly of 'fraud on law', *fraus legi*:[49] not implausible, though the shorter phrasing is clear enough. 'Fraud' unqualified, we shall presently see, serves in an analogous case (a transitory adoption) in Tacitus—not to mention its occurrence in connection with the flight into infamy in Suetonius and the Larino inscription.[50] Domitian's own shenanigans can fortunately be distinguished. When his wife (whom he had snatched from her former husband) committed adultery, he had her paramour killed and almost killed her as well but then only divorced her and, in fact, shortly took her back.[51] This divorce, however quickly remedied, was serious, not a dodge. How far the resumed relationship would or would not be looked on as continuing the old one may be left open.

A temporary 'divorce' was opportune also where the spouses felt they must beat the ban on gifts between them.[52] This ban was quite possibly incorporated somewhere in Augustus's enactments, so its circumvention may have sprung up in the same climate as the cases just discussed. Anyhow, the Digest contains an extract from a work by Javolenus—around AD 100—on Labeo's posthumous writings,[53] with an opinion by Trebatius, Labeo's teacher, in a dispute between Maecenas and Terentia. As he was ageing, she—much younger and having a liaison with Augustus (yes, Augustus)—led him a dance. 'She kept divorcing him', Seneca writes,[54]

[47] Suetonius, *Domitian* 8; see T. Mommsen, *Römisches Strafrecht*, p. 700, n. 4.

[48] Digest 48.5.34.1, Marcian I *de publicis iudiciis*.

[49] See G. v. Beseler, *Beiträge zur Kritik der römischen Rechtsquellen*, vol. 3, 1913, p. 90.

[50] Suetonius, *Tiberius* 35.2, Line 7 of the senatusconsult from Larinum; see above, n. 17. I am not certain whether the same nuance attaches to *fraus* in Tacitus, *Annals* 13.26.1, cited by B. Levick, op. cit., p. 101.

[51] Suetonius, *Domitian* 3.1, Dio Cassius, *Roman History*, *Epit.* 65.3.4, 67.3.1.

[52] See W. W. Buckland, *A Text-Book of Roman Law*, pp. 111 f.

[53] Digest 24.1.64, Javolenus VI *ex posterioribus Labeonis*.

[54] Seneca, *On Providence* 3.10: *cottidiana repudia*.

obviously to return on her conditions: 'he married a thousand times, all the while having one wife'.[55] On one occasion she left him,[56] came back on receipt of a satisfactory inducement and then left him again. This time, he lost patience and sued, or prepared to sue, for restoration, on the ground that they were in fact husband and wife when he bribed her. It was Trebatius who first enunciated the idea that a leaving need not be taken at face value: 'if it was a true divorce, the gift was valid, if a simulated one, the contrary', *si verum divortium fuisset, ratam esse donationem, si simulatum, contra*. That is to say, if her running away, the present and her rejoining were one manœuvre, that was a foiling of the law, the divorce was 'simulated' and the present void. Jurists later than Trebatius set down criteria of the genuine article: entry into another marriage or the lapse of a lengthy period—here we find a conscious grasp of the time factor referred to at the beginning of this section.

J. Partsch labels 'if a simulated one, the contrary' as spurious and E. Levy follows him:[57] 'this passage utterly distorts the Roman problem', he holds, in making everything dependent on the subjective will of the parties instead of their objective conduct. But this censure is based on the premiss that 'simulated' here has the same meaning as hundreds of years later in Byzantine doctrine. There is no evidence for this; and we are free to assume that Trebatius, Javolenus, and Gaius all judged the verb appropriate where a certain conduct—primarily objective though not devoid of pointers to the subjective attitude behind it—makes it look as if something had happened, yet before long the magic evaporates. As for style, J. Partsch finds fault with the clause as 'superficially patched on'.[58] To my ear, without it, the rest would sound lame: we want to hear, above all, that play-acting will not be accepted for real. At any rate, here are two *responsa* similarly structured in two parts, both found in the same work of Javolenus as that under review. The first[59] is from Servius, transmitted by his disciple Ateius. Somebody bequeathed 'the silver which he would have been keeping on his country seat at the time of his death'. Servius advised that 'that silver also was owing which prior to his death was transferred from the city to the country seat at his, the testator's, bidding; the contrary would be the case if it was transferred without his bidding'. No reason to cross out 'the contrary' etc. The second parallel[60] goes back to none else than Trebatius. A testator

[55] Seneca, *Epistles* 114.6: *uxorem milliens duxit cum unam habuerit.*

[56] Not, of course, a *gerichtliche Scheidung*, 'court-pronounced divorce', as A. Stein, thinking in modern terms, has it: see art. Maecenas, in Pauly-Wissowa, *Realencyclopädie der classischen Altertumswissenschaft*, vol. XIV, 1, 1928, col. 215.

[57] See E. Levy, *Der Hergang der römischen Ehescheidung*, Weimar 1925, pp. 86ff., 100f.: 'in der letzteren Stelle verschieben die Worte *si simulatum, contra* vollkommen das römische Problem'.

[58] *Oberflächlich genug angeflickt.*

[59] Digest 34.2.39.2, Javolenus II *ex posterioribus Labeonis.*

[60] Digest 40.7.39.4, Javolenus IV *ex posterioribus Labeonis.*

freed his slave provided he paid Attia a certain sum. Attia died in the testator's lifetime. Labeo and Ofilius declared that the slave could not be free. Trebatius: 'if Attia died before the will was made, the same (the slave could not be free), if later, he would be free'.

Not surprisingly, under the pressure of Augustus's regulations, people posed not only as married or divorced but also as parents. In the reign of Nero, according to Tacitus,[61] complaints about this mischief expressly invoked the time element, expanded on the contrast between the momentary and the lasting. In order to share in the advantages accorded to competitors for high office with children, childless candidates adopted children just before an election or distribution of provinces and emancipated them immediately after. Authentic fathers were enraged by these 'fictitious adoptions' and opposed 'the right founded on nature and the toils of rearing' to the 'fraud, artifice and brevity of adoption'. (Note 'fraud' in the sense of 'fraud on law' discussed above.) They, the true fathers, 'waited years for the promises of the law'; and it was wrong if those others could 'by a quick stroke catch up with their long cherished expectations'. The senate thereupon decreed that 'a simulated adoption should be of no avail', *ne simulata adoptio iuvaret*, anywhere in the public sphere, nor indeed—this was a rider going beyond the particular grievance voiced—in connection with inheritances, where the law also penalized the childless. So firmly has J. Partsch set his face against 'to simulate' in healthy jurisprudence that he doubts the accuracy of Tacitus's quotation. As far as the tenor of this essay is concerned, the classicality or otherwise of the notion matters not. Still less (can that be?) whether it figured in the actual senatusconsult or only in Tacitus. None the less, for the record: the combined testimony of Gaius, Trebatius and Tacitus, all three treating of topics central since Augustus, and all three affixing the designation to the identical charade, strikes me as unshakeable.

A few more illustrations may indicate the enormous range of this variety of model 3. Alan Rodger has just gone into one of those maxims in the Digest which were much narrower in their native context:[62] 'Things are not deemed to be given which do not become the property of the recipient at the time they are given.' Paul, he shows, was discussing the *actio aquae pluviae arcendae* available where, as a result of a construction on your neighbour's land, yours was exposed to rainwater coming from there. In classical law, your remedy was stronger so long as he who erected the construction still owned the land. Hence, if he made a gift of it to someone, it was important to determine whether ownership had fully passed: it is this

[61] Tacitus, *Annals* 15.19. See T. Mommsen, *Römisches Staatsrecht*, vol. 2, pt, 1, p. 216.

[62] Digest 50.17.167 pr., Paul XLIX *ad edictum*; see A. F. Rodger, *Law Quarterly Review*, vol. 100, 1984, pp. 77 ff.

specific situation Paul has in mind.[63] Rodger goes on to transfers made for the very purpose to impede the action and calls attention to another Pauline disquisition mentioning 'a simulated sale'[64]—manifestly, with an arrangement for re-transfer when the stormclouds have passed. I have nothing to add to his comment: 'The particular clause is widely regarded as interpolated, and this may well be correct, or else the clause may reflect a somewhat more elaborate treatment of the same topic in the original Paul.'

An altruistic dodge belonging here was invented to spare an insolvent debtor infamy.[65] We hear of the following debate among Republican lawyers. Owing me 1000, you hand me 100. I at once return it to you by way of a gift. You hand me 100 again, again to get it back as a gift. And so on, till you have handed me ten times 100—of which I keep only the last instalment. Question: have you paid me 100 or 1000? When I first came upon this conundrum, I could not make head or tail of it; suddenly it became clear. In ancient Rome, infamy befell not only a debtor whose goods were auctioned off but also one who got his creditors to be satisfied with a percentage. By the procedure here described, it was hoped to forestall the consequences of such an arrangement: formally, payment was in full—once more, a substitution of the vanishing for the enduring. To begin with, legal reaction seems to have been hostile, but Servius decided in favour. He saw through it no less than his predecessors. However, what is misinterpretation one day may be tenable the next. By his time, the views about insolvency had become generally less harsh; and, probably, he considered that a man for whom his creditors were willing to do that much despite the loss he caused them deserved remaining a member of the club.

The primitive *fideicommissum*, i.e. before being legalized and tamed in the Principate, exemplifies a combination of the three patterns sketched above, in section 1.[66] Say, in the age of Cicero, when an alien could not be an heir, a testator, wishing his possessions to go to his Greek teacher, instituted a Roman friend, adjuring him to pass them on to the Greek. In so far as this was a replacement of an invalid transaction by the nearest hopefully effective one, it was pattern 1. Actually, an extreme variant, since the alternative resorted to altogether dispensed with the power of law in favour of religion. It was also pattern 2: the Roman friend, though nominally heir, was really a mere stand-in for the Greek, a *persona interposita*. In so far as he was to play his part for the minimum time only, just long enough to project an image, we have to do with pattern 3.

[63] It will be noticed that, as in many other instances, Justinian creates his maxim with the aid of a 'free' text, i.e. a text which, because of changes in the law, is no longer valid in its original sense; see my article cited above, n. 42, pp. 261 ff.

[64] Digest 39.3.12, Paul XVI *ad Sabinum*.

[65] Digest 46.3.67, Marcellus XIII *digestorum*. See, in addition to the summary cited above, n. 1, D. Daube, *Roman Law*, Edinburgh, 1968, pp. 93 f.

[66] See in addition to the summary, D. Daube, *Roman Law*, pp. 96 ff.

IV

From outside Roman law, an instruction by Jesus concerning the temple tax is surely worth adducing.[67] On the one hand, he and his, he contends, are subject to it no more than the sons of an earthly monarch are to tribute. On the other, he stresses the importance of giving no offence. To solve this dilemma, he must find a path around the imposition contemptuous of their unique freedom. He sends Peter out to cast a hook: the first fish to be caught will have in its mouth the appropriate coin with which to satisfy the authorities. Thus, they manage at the same time to pay and not to pay. From a narrowly formalistic point of view, the ownerless coin miraculously brought along does become their property, so can be used for a valid discharge—preserving some *modus vivendi*. But, plainly, it is theirs just for this very purpose, during a tightly circumscribed interval. Substantially, that is, by handing it over, they give up nothing of their own, they do not submit, they remain sons of the King. In this case, it is payment of a debt which is simulated (to draw on Roman terminology) in order to prevent hostility. The Talmud records an occasion when a Rabbi, in order to prevent hostility, simulates acceptance of a gift.[68] No need here to elaborate on it.

In conclusion, some personal reminiscences. Prior to 1933, a marriage entered into solely with an external aim and on the understanding that, as soon as that was attained, it would terminate was a pretty academic topic for me. That changed overnight when it became common, say, for an American to marry a German who badly needed to get out of Germany or into the States. From a talk with Auden, at Oxford around 1960—not world-shaking but unforgettable for revealing his wit, responsiveness and truly good nature—I received the impression that his marriage with Erika Mann was of this description. Others no doubt have precise information. Sad that the need for this dodge did not come to an end with the end of World War II. In fact it has hardly diminished.[69]

A less heavy item goes back to about the same time. Pensions began to be paid by West Germany to refugees in England. At first, though some tax was deducted at source, the Inland Revenue taxed them too. A few years later this stopped, maybe partly in view of the plethora of dodges

[67] Matthew 17:24 ff. See D. Daube, *New Testament Studies*, vol. 19, 1972, pp. 13 ff.

[68] Babylonian Abodah Zarah 6b.

[69] A fortnight after completion of this paper I came upon the following report in the *San Francisco Chronicle* of August 4, 1984, pp. 1, 10: 'As many as 500 American disciples of guru Bhagwam Shree Rajneesh married foreigners solely to enable them to become citizens, according to an Immigration and Naturalization Service investigation of the sect. An Immigration service memo ... says the government is cracking down on the marriage ploy ... The sect's top attorney, Swami Prem Niru ... said it is natural for members of a religious group to intermarry, and he accused the government of launching a systematic program to destroy Rajneesh and his church.'

that sprang up. One of them made use of a provision according to which a pension was not taxable if paid directly to a needy dependant (directly, that is, without ever reaching the pensioner). This was easily arranged: the German authorities did not mind making out their cheques to whoever those entitled named. There can have been few epochs in civilisation when aged parents and grandparents were shown so much solicitude as when knowledge of this method spread. Of course, whether the dependant retained what was addressed to him was of no concern to the Inland Revenue. An acquaintance of mine, a lawyer in general sternly moralistic, when I called it a farce, defended it by pointing out that, for however briefly each month or quarter, the dependant did in fact have the money and, suppose he had a falling-out with the pensioner, might refuse to transmit it. Well, it is the mark of a good dodge that some defence can be thought up.

However, my earliest memories of the flash in the pan dodge date from age 5 or 6. They are linked to Passover and Tabernacles. The sages took very seriously the biblical ban on leaven during Passover.[70] (Meticulous observance is presupposed by Paul's metaphorical warning of the danger of even 'a little leaven'.[71]) You might neither eat it nor have it in your possession nor derive any benefit from it; and their definition of 'leaven' was extremely wide. However, in certain circumstances, they did condone a pre-Passover sale to a non-Jew, to be followed by a post-Passover resale.[72] How the dodge developed, who sponsored it, who disliked it, is not here material. My father and his youngest brother carried on an import trade including goods which were, or conceivably might be, classifiable as leaven. So regularly, two or three days before the festival, they made over their business to a non-Jew, with all the traditionally requisite formalities; and, of course, kept strictly aloof from it till re-acquisition. For the buyer, it was just a rigmarole, except that he received a gratuity. Let us pray that the heavenly academy will approve of the construction.

As also of a similar one, having regard to the biblical precept that, on Tabernacles, 'you shall take you an Ethrog (a citrus), a Lulab (a palm-branch), myrtle and willow-twigs and rejoice before the Lord'.[73] For the sages, the phrasing 'take you', 'take for you', instead of simply 'take', implies that the plants over which joyful benediction was to be recited must be your own—not stolen, not borrowed etc.[74] An *exemplum* of how to mitigate this requirement, however, was set towards the end of the first

[70] E.g. Exodus 12:15. See L. I. Rabinowitz, art. Hamez, in *Encyclopaedia Judaica*, 1971, cols. 1235 ff., and H. Rabinowicz, art. Hamez, Sale of, cols. 1237 ff.

[71] I Corinthians 5:6, Galatians 5:9.

[72] E.g. Tosephta Pesahim 1.24.

[73] Leviticus 23:40. See D. J. Bornstein, art. Laubhüttenfest, in *Encyclopaedia Judaica*, 1934, vol. 10, cols. 692 ff., A. Kass, art. Legal Person, in *Encyclopaedia Judaica*, 1971, vol. 10, col. 1570, L. Jacob, art. Sukkot, vol. 15, col. 501.

[74] Mishnah Sukkah 3.13, Babylonian Sukkah 41b.

century AD by an illustrious quartet: Gamaliel II, Joshua ben Hananiah, Eleazer ben Azariah and Akiba. They were travelling on a ship and only the wealthy Gamaliel had a Lulab, bought at 1,000 zuz. He could afford procuring one well ahead of the festival when the price would be exorbitant; the others had no doubt hoped to reach port in time, but voyages often took longer than expected. After reciting his blessing, he made a present of the branch to Joshua; Joshua in due course gifted it to Eleazar; and Eleazar did the same for Akiba who returned it to Gamaliel. What they did in an emergency in course of time became routine. In our little orthodox community at Freiburg, whenever anyone was without a Lulab, this ritual of transfer and re-transfer was scrupulously performed. Why do I not remember it in connection with the other three plants? For the simple reason that they were much cheaper—not 1000 zuz—therefore everybody had them: even small children brought their Ethrog along, the willow-twigs we usually gathered ourselves. In the evolution of juristic personality in Jewish law, by the way, some interesting reflections take off from a Lulab purchased by a congregation or—more recently—by a Kibbutz: may a member use it as his own?

The fourth model, Tony, I reserve for your seventy-fifth birthday.

2

Form and Substance in Legal Reasoning: the Case of Contract[1]

P. S. ATIYAH

ONE of the advantages of academic life is that many of us are able to combine work and pleasure; the advantage is heightened and the pleasure doubled when we are able, as on the present occasion, to take the opportunity of paying tribute to an honoured friend and colleague. As a close colleague of Tony Honoré's during the period when we were both Fellows of New College, Oxford in the second half of the 1960s, I constantly marvelled at the extraordinary breadth of his knowledge of, and interest in, all things legal: English law, Roman Law, modern European law, legal philosophy, whether classical or modern—all these and other were subjects in which Tony Honoré was a master. I will not enlarge on his achievements here; it is not my role, and the time has not yet arrived, for Tony is still productive, and long may he continue so. But I will venture a few words of thanks to him for providing me with the opportunity to return to Oxford and the academic world in 1964. At that time I had been out of academic life for nearly five years and I was on the verge of settling into a career in the Civil Service when, out of the blue, I received a letter from the Warden of New College asking me whether I was interested in a law fellowship at that College. I have never regretted my decision to accept that invitation which I assume (though of course one does not pry too closely into such matters) had something to do with the simultaneous migration of Tony Honoré from Queen's to New College. For that service, Tony, I owe you my most heartfelt thanks.

I

Throughout the varied areas of law it is apparent that we encounter two different types of legal reasoning. There are, on the one hand, reasons of

[1] This is a revised version of the Eighth Annual Viscount Bennett Lecture delivered at the University of New Brunswick on 11 October 1984, which is also being published in the *New Brunswick Law Journal*.

substance.[2] If we are, for instance, considering what rule should be formulated to govern a particular situation, we may weigh up a variety of arguments bearing on the desirability or the rightness of this rule, or that rule. If we are asking whether one person ought to pay damages to another we shall weigh up a variety of considerations, some pointing in one direction and some in another, but these will mostly be reasons of substance bearing directly on the question. Did the defendant, for instance, commit a wrong against the plaintiff? Did his actions cause the plaintiff's injuries? And so on. Or again if we are trying to construct a procedure for the resolution of disputes, we can weigh up reasons for allowing the parties to adduce such and such evidence, or for allowing them to have such and such opportunities for appeal, reasons of substance bearing directly on the goals we are trying to achieve.

On the other hand, we often find ourselves giving effect to reasons of a different character, which I shall call formal reasons. In the paradigm case, a formal reason is a requirement for writing, or sealing, or perhaps for registration or attestation of some kind. When a document fails to comply with stipulated forms, the law may declare the document to be legally ineffective. A will, for instance, or a contract required to be in writing, may be declared void or unenforceable if the formalities are not observed. In such cases we do not stop as a rule (though there may be exceptions) to ask whether the failure to comply with the formal requirements is outweighed by some other substantive reason in favour of giving legal force to the will or contract. Once the legal rule of ineffectiveness for lack of form is clearly established, the application of that rule shuts out from consideration the substantive arguments in favour of validity or enforcement. These formal reasons are typically thought of as associated with writing and written documents. But there are many other examples of similar kinds of reasons in the law even though we would not perhaps normally refer to them as formal reasons. For example, a judge who follows a binding precedent may do so without examining the substantive arguments in favour of the principle for which that precedent stands. If the precedent is truly binding on him, and if he loyally accepts the principle of *stare decisis*, he will not even pause to consider what substantive reasons may be given for an opposite decision. So far as he is concerned, the question cannot be properly considered at all. There is no question of weighing one set of factors against the other, no question of balancing the authority of prece-

[2] See R. S. Summers, 'Two types of Substantive Reasons: The Core of a Theory of Common Law Justification', (1978) 63 *Cornell Law Rev.* 707. The distinctions I am drawing cut across those drawn by Professor Summers in this paper; however, elsewhere Professor Summers distinguishes between two working conceptions of the law as 'rules' and 'reason'. See 'Working Conceptions of the Law', (1982) 1 *Law and Philosophy* 267. This distinction is closer to that which I draw in this paper.

dent against the weight of the reasoning to be found in the particular precedent. The formal reason—that the precedent binds him—simply excludes from consideration any countervailing reason. Or again, take a case where a claim is defeated by the statute of limitations. Here also, if the statute is properly pleaded and is properly applicable, it shuts out of consideration all other factors. Prima facie at least, the court does not weigh up the strength of the plaintiff's case against the strength of the limitation plea. If the plea is good, all other argument is irrelevant.

The nature of reasons of this kind has been discussed and illuminated in an important series of works by Joseph Raz, but Dr Raz calls them 'second-order' reasons[3] or pre-emptive or protected reasons[4] rather than formal reasons as I intend to call them. Nothing of course turns on mere matters of terminology, but it is understandable why Dr Raz eschews the term I have chosen to use. Formal reasoning today has a bad name among lawyers; indeed, it is often treated as the same thing as formalistic reasoning, as though these were both examples of bad reasoning ranging merely from the bad to the very bad. I do not deny that there are many examples, both in law and elsewhere, of formalistic reasoning which is indeed deplorable. But in my view we ought to distinguish between formal reasoning and formalistic reasoning. Formal reasoning is not *per se* unjustified or wrong, though formalistic reasoning is. Where reasons of substance ought to be considered by the decision-maker, and he refuses to consider them, any formal reasons he gives for his decision will be out of place and unjustifiable, and hence can fairly be called formalistic. A judge, for instance, who claims that he is bound to make a particular decision because of a prior precedent, even though the precedent is clearly distinguishable according to the accepted rules and practices governing these matters, is giving a formal reason which is not merely bad, but out of place. He is being formalistic. Similarly, a judge who woodenly applies a rule without even pausing to consider whether it is possible or justifiable for him to create an exception to the rule is reasoning in a formalistic manner. Nobody can deny that the law books are full of examples of formalistic reasoning of this kind. But the fact that formalistic reasons are always bad does not justify us in jumping to the conclusion that all formal reasoning is bad. Indeed, it is quite apparent that the law uses, and, I will argue, correctly uses, formal reasons in all sorts of situations.

Once we start looking at the law and legal reasoning in detail, we find a great many examples of formal reasons which cannot be condemned as bad or formalistic. Statutes, precedents, judgments, jury verdicts, and administrative decisions by statutory bodies all give rise to questions of this character;

[3] See Joseph Raz, *Practical Reasons and Norms* (London, 1975) especially at pp. 35–48 and 58–62; *The Authority of Law* (Oxford, 1979), pp. 30–3.

[4] Ibid.; 'Authority and Justification', in 14 *Philosophy and Public Affairs* 3 (1985).

so too do marriage and contracts though in rather different ways. Although the case of contract is the one to which I mainly want to direct my attention, I shall try to set the issues in context by looking first at some of these other illustrations.

Let me take first some relatively simple examples about the sources of law. The simplest example of a formal reason for a decision is that it is required by a clear statutory provision. Where this is indeed the case, a judge who applies the statute has no cause to consider the substance or merits of the arguments. Within certain limits—and I shall come back to the question of limits in a moment—it is clear that the application of a simple statutory provision just excludes from consideration arguments which would be relevant in a purely common-law inquiry, at least where no binding authority exists. It would be pointless to adduce arguments to suggest that the statute leads to unfair results, or odd results, or anomalous results. Again, within limits, it is pointless and impermissible to suggest that the application of the statute may not produce the result that the legislature intended. Still less is it permissible to argue that, whatever may have been the position when the statute was first passed, conditions have so changed, or even the composition of the legislature has so changed, that to give effect to the Act would be to decide contrary to present-day social or moral views, or contrary to the views of the majority in the present legislative assembly.[5] In all ordinary cases the statute is, and is intended to be, a formal source of law in the sense that it is intended to exclude from consideration countervailing arguments against the result which the statute dictates. The statute is not just one additional reason to be taken account of by the judge, which may tip the scales in one direction, or be overridden by contrary arguments. The statute shuts out contrary arguments.

Of course, as I have said, all this is only the case within certain limits. If a statute seems ambiguous, or unclear, or if it produces results which seem grossly anomalous or utterly absurd or perhaps even seriously unjust, then courts may avoid applying the statute. The limits within which judges do this vary from country to country, from time to time, and no doubt even from judge to judge. They have been much discussed by judges and writers. I do not propose to add to this discussion. For my purpose it is enough that there are some limits, and that everyone recognizes that there are such limits. If a statute could be disregarded by a judge whenever he felt that it led to a result which he would not have reached in the absence of the statute, then a statute would cease to be a formal source of law in the sense in which I am using the term. The reasons underlying the statute would simply be additional arguments to be considered along with all the other reasons of substance bearing on the case. But the fact that these

[5] But see G. Calabresi, *A Common Law for the Age of Statutes* (Cambridge, Mass., 1982).

reasons had been enshrined in a statute would not give them any primacy over other reasons.

Much the same is true of the system of precedent. According to the theory of the common law, some precedents are binding on some courts in the sense that the judges in the subsequent case are bound or obliged to follow the principle of the first case without examining the substantive arguments for and against the principle. Here, however, there tends to be rather more scepticism than there is with regard to statutes. As we all know, not everything that is said in a case is regarded as part of the *ratio decidendi* which is binding on subsequent judges; further, the subsequent court may be able to distinguish the earlier case; and in any event, there are often rules and practices about the relative hierarchy of courts which entitle one court to declare precedents binding on another. Again, practice on these matters varies from country to country, time to time, and even judge to judge; and I would not underestimate the significance of these variations in practice. Moreover, I think it is probably true to say that, especially in well-tilled fields of law, a precedent is often treated as an additional reason for deciding in a certain way, rather than as a different kind of reason which shuts out of consideration all other reasons. But still, at the end of the day, wherever the common law operates, there must, I think, be some cases where a court feels obliged to follow a precedent of a higher court, solely and simply because that precedent is regarded as a formal source for decision, excluding from consideration all reasons of substance. Of course, if we turn away from the effect of precedents on lower courts, and consider their effect on other officials, or even on the citizens at large, it seems still more clear that precedents are habitually treated as formal sources of law binding on every one, unless and until other courts pronounce on the issues. Once again, I do not forget the limits. Precedents are meant to be used intelligently. Counsel advising a client, even the ordinary citizen who reads a case—if that ever happens—may well say: 'Clearly this precedent is not going to be applied in this particular situation; the result is too absurd, and the judges never had that sort of case in mind.' But still, no matter within what limits the doctrine of precedent operates, it clearly amounts in some cases to a formal reason for subsequent decision-making.

In the case of precedents, many lawyers have rebelled at the implications of the doctrine. Bentham, for instance, condemned the system of precedent as 'acting without reason, to the declared exclusion of reason and thereby in opposition to reason'.[6] And in more modern times, lawyers without number have protested—particularly perhaps in the United States—at the slavish following of precedents as an abdication of reason. In the case of statutes, the arguments tend to take a different form. Because the

[6] See F. Rosen and J. H. Burns, edd., *Collected Works of Jeremy Bentham, Constitutional Code*, vol. i, 434.

relationship between the legislature and the court is usually a constitutional datum or starting-point, there are few lawyers who protest at the abdication of reason required of a judge when he gives effect to a statute, at any rate, perhaps I should add, in England. But there are those, of course, who would press the argument that at least the application of a statute is designed to give effect to the intentions of the legislature, and that therefore a statute should never be interpreted in a way which seems plainly contrary to what the legislature intended. Yet this certainly happens on occasion. Is this also be be condemned, as Bentham condemned the following of precedent, as 'acting ... in opposition to reason'? At first sight it might indeed seem to deserve such condemnation. If a friend writes me a letter requesting me to do something for him, but, interpreting the letter in the manner of a Parke B., I do something quite different *even though my declared objective is to carry out his intention*, my action may seem indefensible, indeed incoherent. Yet surely this is *not* true of the action of a judge who sticks somewhat rigidly to the apparent meaning of a statute, even though he may think that the result is not what the legislature intended. Indeed a not unsophisticated defence of this approach was offered by Lord Simon of Glaisdale in the House of Lords in 1975 in the *Black-Clawson* case[7] which concerned the interpretation of a statute giving effect to the report of a committee.

The true function of the court interpreting a statute, said Lord Simon, is *not* to ascertain what Parliament intended, but what is the meaning of the words used by Parliament. Conceding that this was not a self-evident juristic truth, Lord Simon nevertheless offered a spirited defence of this procedure. First, he insisted that if the courts were permitted to search for the intentions of Parliament outside the words of the statute itself, a great deal of time and cost would be wasted in the ransacking of additional material as to the intentions of Parliament. 'By concentrating on the meaning of what has been said, to the exclusion of what was meant to be said, the material for scrutiny is greatly reduced.'[8] Secondly, interpretation is concerned not merely with the intentions of the legislature but with the reasonable understandings and expectations of the citizen. Citizens, with or without their advisers, are entitled to look to an enactment as the source of the law, and to base their conduct on it, without having to concern themselves with questions about the intention of Parliament behind and beyond the words used. Thus the statute operates as a sort of barrier; it is the final expression of Parliament's intentions, and the reader and interpreter must confine himself in principle[9] to the words of the Act. Thirdly, Lord Simon went on

[7] *Black-Clawson International* v. *Papierwerke Waldhof-Aschaffenburg A. G.* [1975] AC 591.
[8] Ibid. at p. 645.
[9] Of course exceptions are admitted. In the *Black-Clawson* case reference to the Report of

to point out that if the draftsman has done his job properly, the meaning of the words used should coincide with the intentions of the legislator. The last point is, of course, one of general application whenever the construction of a document is in issue. It is a reasonable starting-point—indeed, the only possible starting-point—that words mean what they mean, and that those who use words intend to convey what the words normally convey. In the great majority of cases this is almost certainly true; and we are likely to achieve more accurate results if we refuse to depart from this assumption than if we open it to question in all cases. We may, of course, occasionally go wrong if we always insist that people mean what they say; but we are far more likely to go wrong if we always question whether they mean what they say. Indeed, it is arguable that we are more likely to go wrong even if we confine ourselves to the more moderate course of questioning whether they mean what they say only where there is some ground for thinking that perhaps they do not mean what they say.

Lord Simon's first two points are especially important to the very nature of formal reasons for decisions. The first is the question of cost. Even if we assume that there is such a thing as a parliamentary intention, even leaving aside the theoretical and practical difficulties in knowing what intentions to attribute to a legislative body of several hundred members, the fact is that it would take a great deal of valuable time to search for a true or real parliamentary intent, different from that ascertainable from the face of a statute. Suppose it is suggested, however, that this search need only take place where a statute is ambiguous or where the intent is not clear on its face? This would certainly reduce the force of the argument from cost, but not very much. For, after all, that still leaves all the cases where the court is today asked to decide a point of statutory construction, and there are enough of those in all conscience. Of course, in some of these cases, the extra cost devoted to a search for parliamentary intention outside the text of the Act might be repaid. Clear signs of intention may be found. But as Lord Simon also pointed out, the American experience, here is not encouraging. The extra cost is likely to produce rare and dubious benefits.

But the second argument is also important. A statute is, and is intended to be, a formal expression of Parliament's will. Statutes are not drafted hastily, nor are they passed lightly or easily, at least in Britain. A great deal of effort goes into the drafting, and the parliamentary scrutiny of important bills is no formality. The whole purpose of this procedure is to present to the public and to the legal profession a document which is designed to be

a Committee was permitted though there was disagreement as to whether this was only permissible to identify the 'mischief' being aimed at, or also as a direct aid to the interpretation of the Act.

read as a formal document. It is not an argumentative document, nor a discursive document. It rarely states reasons. It is assumed in the British parliamentary process that the arguments and the reasons are to be discussed first by those officials responsible for preparing the bill, and second, in Parliament itself. Once the bill is passed it is intended to be treated as a formal piece of law.

Now whether these arguments are found to be convincing may be a matter on which reasonable persons may differ; it may also be relevant to enquire into the procedures and practices regarding the drafting and passing of legislation in different jurisdictions before deciding how far courts should be permitted to look at extraneous material when interpreting a statute. But what is surely not open to question is that these arguments of Lord Simon's for the formal treatment of statutes are *reasoned* arguments. There are, in other words, *reasons* for treating formal reasons as overriding or exclusionary reasons, which shut out other sorts of reasons from consideration.[10]

When we turn to the case of binding precedent we find the situation is much the same. Here again, to say that a system of precedent involves an abdication of reason, as Bentham said, seems an absurd exaggeration. There are *reasons* why it seems right to treat questions of law as having been conclusively settled by earlier decisions—within limits, of course. These reasons are to some degree the same as those which apply in the case of statutes. First, it saves time and trouble. Secondly, it saves us from having to worry about reasons and arguments for a rule. If the rule has been clearly laid down, then, like a statute, it makes for greater simplicity and certainty, if we can be confident that future courts will apply that rule without inquiring too closely into the results, or into the reasons for its application. But there are, in the case of the system of precedent, additional reasons for this rather formal approach which are inapplicable in the case of statutes. In the case of statutes—at any rate in Britain and other countries where there is no judicial power over statutes—lawyers do not question the ultimate power of Parliament to impose on the courts a law which the judges might regard as contrary to all reason. They have no power to set up their judgment on controversial questions in opposition to that of Parliament. But when precedents are in question, it is usually accepted that there are no final answers to many problems. Policy judgments and value judgments are involved in much judicial law-making. In the absence of a system of precedent it is difficult to see how finality would ever be achieved if judges were always entitled to decide a case in the way they think it ought to be decided, regardless of prior decisions.

Once again I must beware of appearing to adopt a position about the

[10] See J. Raz, *Practical Reason and Norms*, esp. at p. 36.

precise way a system of precedent should work, and about the extent to which judges should accept the call to modernize the law and keep it up to date by jettisoning old and obsolete precedents. All that I am saying is that no system of precedent could work if a judge was entitled to disregard a precedent just because he disagreed with it, merely because he thought it wrong. The concept of a system of precedent is that it constrains judges in some cases to follow decisions they do not agree with. This is no more contrary to reason than it is contrary to reason for a military commander to expect his subordinates to obey orders without asking themselves whether the orders are reasonable or sensible.[11]

Let me now turn to some other illustrations of formal reasoning in the legal system. Consider first the principles concerning the finality of judgments. If an issue has been properly litigated, and properly decided, and if appeals have been exhausted or are not available, then the judgment is a formal reason for deciding the rights and obligations of the parties. Once that judgment has been rendered, and become final, it shuts out from consideration any further argument on the merits. Even if, in some objective sense, the judgment is fallacious, or based on an incorrect finding of fact, it will no longer avail to adduce contrary arguments of substance. Once again, it is not a matter of the judgment outweighing the substantive arguments; it simply renders them irrelevant. In this connection I should like to refer to two striking decisions of recent years.

The *Ampthill Peerage* case[12] was not strictly a judicial decision of the House of Lords, but was a recommendation of the Committee of Privileges in which the leading opinion was given by Lord Wilberforce. The facts were somewhat unusual, and it is unnecessary to set them out in great detail. The case concerned the legitimacy of Geoffrey Russell, who claimed to be the legitimate son of John Hugo Russell, later third Lord Ampthill. When Geoffrey was born Lord Ampthill denied paternity and indeed petitioned for divorce on the ground of the adultery of his wife. After a long trial a jury found in his favour, but the decision was reversed by the House of Lords in the case of *Russell* v. *Russell*[13] on the ground that evidence of non-access by the father was inadmissible to bastardize his son. Following the divorce proceedings a petition for a declaration of legitimacy was brought on behalf of Geoffrey Russell and there being no evidence against him other than that declared inadmissible in *Russell* v. *Russell* a declaration was made. Fifty years later, Lord Ampthill died and Geoffrey Russell laid claim to the peerage. The claim was contested and the conclusiveness of the declaration of legitimacy was challenged on a number of grounds, including the legislative reversal of the decision in *Russell* v. *Russell*, and

[11] Ibid., p. 38.
[12] *Ampthill Peerage Case* [1977] AC 547.
[13] [1924] AC 687.

the unwillingness (so it was alleged) of Geoffrey Russell to submit to blood tests. The Committee of Privileges upheld the finality of the legitimacy declaration even though, as Lord Wilberforce conceded, this might be said, in a sense, to prefer justice to truth. Perhaps the truth was in some objective sense that Geoffrey Russell was not the legitimate son and heir of Lord Ampthill. Nevertheless, insisted the House of Lords, there was no adequate ground for going behind the declaration of legitimacy issued by a competent court so many years before. They stressed the fact that the parties must have relied upon the declaration and planned their lives accordingly.

So here we have, in rather striking circumstances, an affirmation of the value of finality in judicial proceedings. The declaration granted by a competent court was treated as a formal and conclusive reason for acknowledging Geoffrey's right to the peerage. Contrary arguments of substance, from which reasonable persons might have inferred that Geoffrey was not legitimate, were not considered and rejected: they were simply shut out from consideration. The judgment was final. In this case we find yet further justifications for upholding the formal nature of a reason. In addition to arguments about cost—relevant, of course, but not stressed here—there were arguments about reliance, and about the need for peace and repose and security in human affairs.

The second decision I want to mention in this context is the Privy Council decision in *Chokolingo* v. *Attorney General of Trinidad and Tobago*.[14] This was an appeal from Trinidad and Tobago, which has a written constitution incorporating an American-style provision against deprivation of liberty without due process of law. The appellant was convicted of contempt of court and sentenced to twenty-one days in prison. He did not appeal and served his sentence; but two and a half years later he sought to challenge his sentence as a deprivation of liberty without due process of law on the ground that the alleged contempt had been based on a publication itself protected as a fundamental freedom under the constitution. This was thus the kind of collateral attack which is familiar under the American system of federal *habeas corpus*, but the Privy Council found the whole concept of such attack utterly irrational and subversive of the rule of law. The guarantee of due process of law, said the Privy Council, is a guarantee of a proper trial before a court of competent jurisdiction. If no appeal is brought against such a conviction, or if appeal is brought and dismissed, then the accused has had due process of law, and no further attack on the decision can be launched. Here, then, is another striking affirmation of the importance of finality in judicial decisions, all the more striking for involving such a decisive rejection of a large body of American jurisprudence. It is, moreover, an excellent illustration of the importance and indeed justifi-

[14] [1981] 1 All ER 244.

ability of formal reasoning in the law. For of course the Privy Council decision was reached without any inquiry into the merits of the original conviction. The judgment of the original court was not just one reason for the decision, to be weighed against other reasons. It was a conclusive or overriding reason—a formal reason in my sense.

As I have indicated, the law makes a great deal of use of such formal reasoning in its own procedures and processes. Apart from the cases I have already mentioned, there are many other types of case in which formal reasons are or may be conclusive reasons which exclude substantive reasons from consideration. To mention just a few, there are rules of jurisdiction—so that application to the wrong court or tribunal must be dismissed irrespective of the merits; there are rules of procedure and pleading under which courts may in the last resort (and I accept of course that this often is a last resort) dismiss a claim or a defence without any consideration of the merits.

Particularly relevant for my purposes is the fact that in criminal procedure, a plea of guilty is normally regarded as a formal and conclusive reason for recording a conviction against the accused. In the common-law adversarial procedure we do not investigate at the trial level a criminal case in which the defendant pleads guilty, though such investigation may of course take place at the police level, where an admission of guilt does not have the same formal consequences. But at the trial level we do not proceed any further. We do not look for corroborative evidence, nor for evidence which casts doubt on the guilty plea. Of the many possible reasons for this, I need only mention two—reasons sufficiently obvious and compelling to require little elaboration. The first is that we are unlikely to go far wrong if we treat guilty pleas as conclusive. Very rarely this may result in the wrongful conviction of an innocent person; but if we required independent proof in all cases in which a guilty plea is today accepted as conclusive, it is almost certain that we should go wrong far more frequently in the opposite direction—that is, we should acquit many more guilty persons than the number of innocent persons wrongly convicted today. The second reason, of course, is the question of cost. Contested trials cost money. At present over 90 per cent of criminal trials in England are resolved by pleas of guilty. The cost of administering the criminal justice system would obviously be magnified manifold if all these cases were tried out. And delay—which is itself a source of further costs—would also become a far more serious problem.

Of course, there are limits on the formal effect—on the conclusiveness—of a plea of guilty, as there are limits on the conclusiveness of all, or nearly all, formal reasons. If there are any indications that the accused is unfit to plead, or does not understand the charge, or if he pleads guilty and then adds qualifying words which cast doubt on the plea, it may be rejected, and further inquiry made; or perhaps a plea of not guilty may be entered. But until very recently it has been uniformly held in England that an unequivocal plea of guilty by a sane adult defendant who understands the charge and the plea is a conclusive reason for a conviction. Indeed, until the recent decision in *R.* v. *Lee.*[15] It was always held that a plea of guilty in such circumstances also precludes appeal. But in that case, for the first time, it was held that an appeal could be entertained and evidence admitted, even where the accused had been convicted on a plea of guilty. This was a remarkable case in which the accused had pleaded guilty to eleven counts of arson and manslaughter, and a subsequent newspaper investigation had revealed facts from which it was manifest that some of these crimes simply could not have been committed by the accused. Yet it was accepted on all hands that the accused was fit to plead, knew what he was doing, intended to make the pleas he did, and pleaded guilty without equivocation after receiving proper advice. One feels, as the Court of Appeal clearly felt, that the case was somehow aberrant. Criminal procedure is based on the assumption that normal sane adults do not plead guilty to crimes which they have not committed. Yet here, it seemed, was manifest proof that this had actually happened. I shall return to this case later because it seems to me not irrelevant to the remarks I want to make about contract law.

II

I turn from these examples of formal reasoning in the judicial process to consider the same phenomena in private law. But again I defer the subject of contract because I want first to look at an area which seems to raise closely analogous problems—namely, matrimonial law. The analogy of marriage may help to illustrate and make more plausible some of the suggestions to be made later about contract.

Now marriage is, of course, a legal status which can only be created in most sophisticated legal systems by actually going through certain formal procedures. But I want to focus not on the forms required to create the status of marriage but rather on the sense in which marriage is itself a formal reason for making many decisions. In order to understand this point, it is only necessary to ask what would happen if the legal institution of marriage were abolished—a proposal which has been seriously canvassed in certain quarters.[16] Plainly this would not prevent or perhaps even discourage men and women from living together just as they do now, in a variety of ways, and for varying lengths of time. Some periods of cohabitation would no doubt be lifelong; others, very short. But why, it is asked, do we need the formality of treating some cohabiting partners in the special

[15] [1984] 1 All ER 1080.

[16] See E. M. Clive, 'Marriage: An Unnecessary Legal Concept?', in *Marriage and Cohabitation in Contemporary Society*, J. M. Eekelaar and S. N. Katz (ed.) (Toronto, 1980), ch. 8.

way signified by marriage? It is, after all, no longer possible to answer that the purpose of marriage is to indicate to the world that the partners have committed themselves to a lifelong union, when we know and they know that the law permits them fairly easy and painless ways of escape. Those who advocate the total elimination of the marriage status as an unnecessary legal formality do not deny that decisions will have to be made about property rights and maintenance obligations on separation and divorce or death. But, they urge, since these decisions already have to be made, especially on separation and divorce, by having regard to all the circumstances of the case—the length of the marriage, the relative income and behaviour of the parties, the number and ages of any children, and so on—it really makes very little difference whether the formal status of marriage is acknowledged or not. The argument, it will be seen, is tantamount to asserting that marriage is no longer a good formal reason for recognizing obligations of the cohabitating partners, whether in regard to the continuance of the cohabitation or to what happens after it ends. These questions, it is implied, can only be settled by looking at reasons of substance, and not at purely formal (and hence, within limits, conclusive) reasons.

Challenging and unfamiliar though this argument may seem to the typical conservative lawyer, it has a certain plausibility, particularly in relation to property rights and questions of maintenance such as arise on separation and divorce, where it is now the practice, in England at least, to treat the answers as depending very much on the general weighing of substantive reasons. But there are, as it seems to me, many other legal questions, questions involving both public and private law, which would not be so easily disposed of if we eliminated the formal status of marriage. What about, for instance, rights of action under the Fatal Accidents Acts and similar legislation? No problem, say the supporters of this proposal. We can simply base such rights on *de facto* dependency, not on the legal tie. Well, that might work for dependency claims, but of course many countries have other types of legal rights to sue on the death of a spouse, where some compensation is payable by way of *solatium* for the bereavement itself. It is not so easy to see how such compensation could be paid if there were no formal reason like marriage to justify it. At the least one might find it necessary to enquire into whether the cohabitation was successful or not if one was going to award a *solatium* to a bereaved cohabitant. But we will let that pass and go on to ask what would happen on intestacy. Here again, it is said, the law could work on the basis of cohabitation rather than the formal marriage status. How would this work? I suppose we could draw up a tariff under which, say, twenty years of cohabitation would entitle a surviving cohabitant to maximum rights of succession on intestacy, and benefits would be reduced proportionately for shorter periods of cohabitation. But that does not seem quite right. Suppose one cohabitant dies after a very short period of cohabitation, the other partner would then receive very little on intestate succession. Surely, it might be argued, the *intentions* of the parties ought to count for something. Casual cohabitation, not intended to involve a permanent or long-term commitment, ought surely to be distinguished from serious cohabitation, planned and entered upon as a life-time commitment? Indeed, if marriage were abolished, it seems that we should have to recognize the rights of the cohabitants to express their intentions in some other way which could be taken account of by the law. But, say the proponents, such methods already exist. A cohabitant has only to make a will to give effect to intentions of such a character. The trouble with that, of course, is that it fails to take into account the simple fact that getting married enables one to avoid having to make a will if one does not wish to do so, or postpones doing so until it is too late, as so many people do, without producing totally unacceptable results on intestacy.

But then, it may be objected, what about the relationship of cohabitants to other parties, to the state, for example, or to employers' pension funds? Social security laws commonly want to know if someone entitled to benefits has a spouse, though it is true that a *de facto* dependant may sometimes have similar rights. Pension funds could, I suppose, be taken care of by appropriate declarations of intention. But then there are yet other problems, including that of trying to define what *is* cohabitation.[17] Suppose a man and a woman live in different houses but spend their weekends together? Suppose they do this for ten years? Suppose they live under one roof but do not have normal sex relations? How is the law to decide whether such parties ought to be treated as cohabitants for this or that purpose? One answer, of course, is to enable them to make some appropriate declaration whereby they should be treated as cohabitants for all legal purposes. But then we have, in effect, restored the status of marriage and it might be simpler not to abolish it in the first place.

The purpose of this discussion should now be clear. Marriage is surely an excellent illustration of a formal reason for making many decisions. So many different questions arise about how we are to treat two parties in some sort of relationship that it is exceedingly convenient and cost-effective to make the answers turn uniformly on one simple formal proposition. Are they married or are they not? Marriage thus becomes, within limits, a conclusive formal reason, for instance, in defining social security entitlements or intestate succession rights. We could, of course, abolish marriage as a legal institution, and answer all these questions by looking behind the formal tie for substantive reasons. Indeed, in some circumstances we do already do this; in particular, we tend to do it as regards property and

[17] See S. M. Cretney, 'The Law Relating to Unmarried Partners From the Perspective of A Law Reform Agency', in Eekelaar and Katz, op. cit., ch. 36.

maintenance rights on divorce. But to do the same thing for all the other circumstances in which we wish to have special rules for long-term cohabitants and also for *intending* long-term cohabitants would be an immensely costly and troublesome business. Formal reasoning thus has great advantages.

III

It is time to turn to the case of Contract, and its relationship to the distinction between formal and substantive reasoning. We can start by considering the place of formal reasons in the relatively straightforward case where a contract is required to be, or to be evidenced, in writing. Consider, for instance, those contracts declared to be unenforceable by the Statute of Frauds if they are not evidenced in writing. What is the function of writing in such a case? We must note, first, that in this situation, the absence of writing is a formal and conclusive reason for deciding *against* (rather than in favour of) the creation of a legal obligation. As with other cases of formal reasons, we do not in principle weigh up the reasons in favour of recognizing the obligation, and balance them against the lack of writing.[18] If there is no writing, the case for recognizing a legal duty is simply excluded from consideration. It does not arise at all. But there is no distinction in principle between a formal reason for excluding a liability and one for recognizing a liability. So we should expect the reasons for the recognition of such a formal rule here to be similar to those we have already identified, such as the saving of cost, and the minimization of the risk of error. In the particular case of the Statute of Frauds there may be grounds for doubting whether these reasons are today adequate except in the case of the requirements relating to the transfer of interests in land. These reasons—the saving of cost and the minimization of error—may well have been more powerful when the Statute of Frauds was first passed in 1677 than they are now. But even in 1825 Bentham protested at the effect of the statute. If, he said, there are grounds for suspecting that the alleged contract is fraudulent or untrue, or fabricated, then the statute is unnecessary. A fabricated contract obviously ought to be found to be fabricated and will give rise to no legal rights. If, on the other hand, there are no such grounds for suspicion, he continued it is simply unjust to treat the contract as unenforceable.[19]

This became the standard argument against the Statute of Frauds and the argument largely carried the day in England in 1954. But the argument

[18] Though it is true that part performance or reliance is increasingly recognized as a substantive reason for recognizing liability, such reliance does not *outweigh* the absence of writing: it merely means that the rule requiring writing is increasingly confined to unrelied-upon (executory) contracts.

[19] *Treatise on Judicial Evidence*, pp. 121–2 (1825); *Rationale of Judicial Evidence*, ch. xxv (Bowring ed., vol. vi, 1843).

is mistaken. It fails to take account of one of the principal purposes of formal reasons in the law. It is easy enough to deal with cases where the facts are known, or indisputably point to the contract either having been made, or not having been made. But one of the main points of formal reasons is that they are designed to save the time and trouble of, and to minimize the risk of errors involved in, discovering the truth. So to require certain contracts to be in writing saves us from having to investigate whether an alleged oral contract was ever truly made or not; and because it saves us that trouble, it eliminates the risk that we may find a contract existed when none was in fact made. Of course it only does this at the price of excluding the possibility of an oral contract when there was indeed such a contract. Consequently we have to make up our minds which of these two errors seems more likely. The fact that in England we repealed most of the relevant provisions of the Statute of Frauds in 1954 for the wrong reasons does not mean that the result was not correct from a policy point of view.[20]

Let me now consider another aspect of formal reasoning in contract law. Ever since the decision in *L'Estrange* v. *Graucob*,[21] it has been accepted that within certain limits, a signature on a contractual document is a conclusive reason for holding the party who has signed to the terms of the document. Subject to proof of fraud, misrepresentation, or *non est factum*, the signature is conclusive. Some ten years ago, Mr J. R. Spencer, in an interesting article in the *Cambridge Law Journal*,[22] challenged this result as in conflict with the fundamental theory of contract law. Contracts, he said, are supposed to be based on agreement; but the rule in *L'Estrange* v. *Graucob* may bind a person who has not agreed to (because he has not read or not understood) the document which he has signed. Mr Spencer certainly put his finger on an important and interesting question. *Why* do we treat signatures as conclusive? Surely it is because a signature is a formal reason of the kind I have been discussing. A signature is, and is widely recognized even by the general public as being a formal device, and its value would be greatly reduced if it could not be treated as a conclusive ground of contractual liability at least in all ordinary circumstances. As in the other cases, we do not pause to examine the underlying reasons of substance, nor do we weigh the substantive reasons against the fact that the document has been signed. The signature is, at any rate within limits, a conclusive reason, a formal reason, for treating the party who has signed as bound by the

[20] However, this assumes that it is desired to create liability for purely executory contracts—which is what the Statute was designed to prevent as regards contracts within its scope. I have argued elsewhere that in 1954 the tide was running against such liabilities, so that repeal at that date was almost anachronistic: *The Rise And Fall of Freedom of Contract* (Oxford, 1979), p. 691.

[21] [1934] 2 KB 394.

[22] 'Signature, Consent and the Rule in *L'Estrange* v. *Graucob* (1973) 32 *CLJ* 104.

document. However, what is, I think, less clear is what is the underlying reason of substance in this kind of situation. The usual explanation for holding a signature to be conclusively binding is that it must be taken to show that the party signing has agreed to the contents of the document; but another possible explanation is that the other party can be treated as having relied upon the signature. It thus may be a mistake to ask, as H. L. A. Hart once asked, whether the signature is merely conclusive evidence of agreement, or whether it is itself a criterion of agreement.[23] But this is something we can leave aside as it does not affect the distinction between formal and substantive reasons.

There was another problem which worried Mr Spencer. The objective rules of interpretation may lead the courts to construe a contract in a way which does not comply with the actual understandings or intentions of either party. This offends Mr Spencer. 'It may be acceptable', he says, 'for the law occasionally to force upon *one* of the parties an agreement he did not want; but surely there is something wrong with a theory which forces upon *both* of the parties an agreement which *neither* of them wants.'[24] I cannot myself see anything very wrong with this result so long as we remember that the law is not so much forcing the parties into a relationship—although it may sometimes do even that—but determining their obligations in a relationship which they have chosen to enter. Indeed, if the parties are in dispute as to what their obligations are, it seems to me a priori much more likely that the reasonable and just view is somewhere between the two parties' contentions, than that one or other party is wholly in the right. Thus it is perfectly natural, indeed, commonplace for the court to hold that the contract imposes obligations on the parties which are not exactly what either of them intended.

The point was made with his usual clarity and vigour by Holmes.

Nothing [he says] is more certain than that the parties may be bound by a contract to things which neither of them intended, and when one does not know of the other's assent. Suppose a contract is executed in due form and in writing to deliver a lecture, mentioning no time. One of the parties thinks that the promise will be construed to mean, at once, within a week. The other thinks that it means, when he is ready. The court says that it means, within a reasonable time. The parties are

[23] See H. L. A. Hart, 'The Ascription of Responsibility and Rights', (1948–9) *Proc. Arist. Soc.* 171.

[24] See 32 *CLJ* at p. 113. Spencer, indeed, contends that this particular version of the 'objective' rule of interpretation is not followed by the English courts except for Lord Denning. Certainly the theory of the law may be doubtful (and clearly if one party knew what the other meant, the latter's intentions might govern) but it seems to me that in construing written contracts English courts habitually follow this version of the objective method of construction. See also W. Howarth, 'The Meaning of Objectivity in Contract' (1984) 100 *LQR* 65.

bound by the contract as it is interpreted by the court, yet neither of them meant what the court declares that they have said.[25]

The point next to be made was also once touched on by Holmes, though on this occasion with less than his accustomed clarity. 'I think', he wrote in a letter in 1896, 'that in enlightened theory, which we now are ready for, all contracts are formal ... I do not merely mean that the consideration of the simple contract is as much a form as a seal, but that in the nature of a sound system of law (which deals mainly with externals) the making of a contract must be a question of form, even if the details of our law should be changed.'[26] I confess that I am not entirely sure what Holmes meant by saying that 'the making of a contract must be a question of form', but there is one way in which these remarks can be understood. Just as in the case of marriage I distinguished between the formalities used to create the marriage tie and the marriage status itself, which also constitutes a formal reason for making various decisions, so also we can distinguish between the formalities (if any) used for the creation of a contract and the contract itself as a formal source of obligation. It is formal in the sense that the mere making of a promise, or even an agreement, the mere act of reaching agreement, the mere act of expressing intention, seems by itself hardly to reach the level of a substantive reason for doing anything. I have argued elsewhere[27] that contractual obligation rarely rests on the bare intention of the parties. In the great majority of cases, I have suggested, a party who is held liable on a contract has received a benefit from the other party, or has induced the other to rely upon him to his detriment. But the receipt of benefits from another is not only a source of contractual liability; it can also give rise to liability even in the absence of an agreement or promise. The law of restitution, or unjust enrichment, deals with these unpromised benefits. Contract law, supposedly, deals with promised benefits; but the line between contract and unjust enrichment is blurred at the edges, if they are to be regarded as distinct doctrines at all, especially when one starts to analyse the case of the implied promise. In any event it is not obvious why we need to draw a line between contract and unjust enrichment in the way that traditional theory teaches. For many an action on a contract is an action for the price of goods supplied or benefits rendered to the other party, and in the absence of any remedy the defendant would plainly be unjustly enriched. Yet this is a paradigm case of contractual liability in ordinary theory.

So too liability through induced reliance is not confined to the area of contract. In tort, and with the aid of estoppel in all its varied forms,

[25] 'The Path of the Law', (1897) 10 *Harv. Law Rev.* 457, at 463–4.

[26] Letter to E. A. Harriman of Northwestern University Law School, cited in M. DeW. Howe, *Justice Oliver Wendell Holmes* (Cambridge, Mass., 1963), vol. ii, p. 233.

[27] 'Contracts, Promises and the Law of Obligations', (1978) 94 *LQR* 193; *Promises, Morals and Law* (Oxford, 1981).

reasonable reliance is itself often a justifiable ground for complaint in law, even where a promise has not been given.[28] So in most cases contractual liability arises out of something—in part at least—which lies behind the actual agreement or intention of the parties. Just as in the case of marriage it is sometimes necessary to see how the parties have behaved, how long the relationship has lasted, and so on, rather than confine attention to the formal status itself, so also in the case of contract it is sometimes relevant to see what has actually happened before or *after* the making of the promise. Indeed, it could be said that these are the real reasons of substance for the enforcement of most contractual obligations. It is a good reason for making *A* pay £100 to *B* that *A* has received goods from *B* worth approximately £100 under a contract of sale. The fact that *A* promised or agreed to pay that precise sum, £100, is perhaps a purely formal reason for arriving at the same conclusion. It shuts out of consideration the substantive reasons. We do not pause to ask, anyhow within certain limits, whether the goods were indeed worth £100. Similarly, where a person is induced to rely on another's promise, we do not ask whether his reliance was reasonable or justifiable. That question is largely ruled out as irrelevant by the express promise. It is conclusively determined by the promise—it is reasonable to rely upon a promise.

Because these formal or exclusionary reasons only operate within certain limits, and because today these limits seem to be narrowing so that courts often seem to be more willing than they were formerly to open up for examination the value of benefits received, or the justifiability of reliance on a promise, I have argued on a previous occasion that a promise or agreement operates rather like a presumption which is sometimes irrebuttable, but sometimes rebuttable.[29] That a person agrees to pay £100 for this item is, I suggested, good evidence that it is indeed worth £100; and the fact that a person made a promise to another is at least prima facie evidence of the justifiability of the promisee's actions in reliance on the promise. It has been objected by Professor Eisenberg that my account is faulty because in fact such evidence is not treated as rebuttable.[30] Apart from established defences, no evidence is admissible to show that the price agreed was too high or too low. The agreed price is treated as conclusive. Of course, as a matter of black-letter law this is correct, though it is not clear why we should brush aside established defences like fraud and misrepresentation as irrelevant to the issue. They do, in a sense, define precisely the limits within which the agreed price is to be regarded as conclusive. But apart from that,

[28] See Barry Reiter in B.J. Reiter and J. Swan (edd.), *Studies in Contract Law* (Toronto, 1980), Study No. 8.

[29] See *Promises, Morals and Law*, ch. 7.

[30] See Eisenberg, 'The Bargain Principle and its Limits', (1982) 95 *Harv. Law Rev.* 741, 785, n. 121.

the objection to my way of putting the matter simply fails to understand the way in which formal or conclusory reasons work in the law. The fact that a presumption is irrebuttable is often treated as demonstrating that the so-called presumption is really a rule of law, and not a presumption at all. But this is a mistake. The *effect* of an irrebuttable presumption is of course the same as the *effect* of a rule of law. But the reason for it may be entirely different. If it is the case, as I have argued, that contractual obligations ultimately derive, at least in the normal case, from benefits received, or acts of detrimental reliance, then it is still possible to explain why we generally treat promises and agreements as formal and conclusive reasons for the establishment and delimitation of those obligations. As is the case with other formal reasons, the obvious reasons for treating them as conclusive are that this saves the cost of more detailed investigation and that it minimizes the risk of error.

It will be helpful at this stage to give a couple of simple illustrations to show how very powerful these reasons can be, so that to call them formal reasons should not be regarded as in any way belittling their significance. Let me take first of all an illustration of the importance of treating promises and agreements as conclusive in the matter of reasonable reliance. Time was, when, in building contracts, the builder was expected to consult the contract documents, study the site, and then decide how much he would tender for the contract. Contract documents customarily provided quite expressly that the builder had no right to rely upon any information given to him by the client but was to make his own examinations and studies, and rely upon these rather than upon the other party to the contract. For a very long time this had been regarded as conclusive of the respective rights and duties of the parties.[31] However, following the *Hedley Byrne*[32] decision, and suggestions that a tort duty of reasonable care might arise even between contracting parties, it came to be asked whether a builder might not be able to sue the client for negligence if the client had failed to disclose this or that piece of information to the builder. Such an allegation implies, of course, that the builder did reasonably rely on the owner, rather than on his own enquiries, even though the contract told him quite clearly that he was not to do so. One might have thought, therefore, that the contract ought to be treated as a conclusive reason for refusing to enquire into the possibility of reasonable reliance by the builder in such circumstances. The contract, it might be said, simply defines in advance what sort of reliance ought to be regarded as reasonable, and there is no room for any factual inquiry in the particular case. Yet in 1972 the High Court of Australia held that this was not the case, and that a duty of care might

[31] See *Thorn* v. *London Corpn.* (1876) 1 App. Cas. 120.
[32] [1964] AC 465.

arise between the parties in such a relationship;[33] but of course the existence of such a duty could only be shown by a careful and detailed examination of all the facts. Following that case, another Australian case, *Dillingham Construction Pty Ltd.* v. *Downs*,[34] actually proceeded to try out such an issue in a negligence claim. The result was a lengthy trial in which all the facts had to be minutely investigated: what knowledge did the client have about the special conditions of the site, whether that knowledge could reasonably have been collected and sifted and made available to the builder, what knowledge the builder had, who reasonably relied on whom, and so on. In the result no liability was established, but the fact that the builder's reliance on the client was not reasonable or justifiable (if indeed there was any reliance at all) was only established at enormous cost. If the traditional view of the effect of a contract on this relationship had been upheld, all these costs could have been saved by treating the contract as a conclusive reason for shutting out these facts as irrelevant. I am not saying that the procedure adopted in this case was unjustified, or even undesirable. I am merely pointing out how costly it was. Broadly speaking, treating matters as settled conclusively by agreement is cheap and simple; determining them by the standards of reasonableness is neither cheap nor simple. Still, sometimes this is necessary and the price must be paid. Justice is often an expensive commodity.

Let me now observe that exactly the same thing can happen with regard to benefits. The whole law of restitution or unjust enrichment stands testimony to the difficulty of establishing, in many circumstances, whether one person has benefited from an act of another. I shall offer just one particularly striking illustration of the extra costs which come from disregarding contractual provisions. It comes from a group of late nineteenth- and early twentieth-century English cases on the *ultra vires* doctrine. After it was finally established that a company could not validly enter into a contract outside the scope of the powers conferred by the memorandum of association, a number of cases came before the courts in which companies had borrowed money under *ultra vires* transactions. The courts were naturally reluctant to see such companies retain the benefit of moneys thus borrowed without having any obligation to repay or restore them, so they resorted to various shifts and devices to overcome this result. If, they held, a company borrowed money under an *ultra vires* contract, but the money was used to pay off debts owed by the company to a third party, then the lender might be able to claim repayment of the money to the extent that this had actually benefited the borrowing company.[35] In so far as the money had actually

[33] *Morrison-Knudson International* v. *Commonwealth* (1972) 46 ALJR 265.

[34] (1972) NSWR 49.

[35] See *Re Cork & Youghal Rly Co.* (1869) LR 4 Ch. App. 748; *Re National Permanent Benefit Building Society* (1869) LR 5 Ch. App. 309.

been used to discharge valid debts of the borrowing company, it was an easy conclusion that a benefit had thereby been conferred. Unfortunately, there were some circumstances in which this conclusion was not so simple as it seemed. How could anyone be sure that the company had really benefited by the money received under the *ultra vires* loan? Suppose, for instance, that the money had been paid into one bank account with the company's own money, and some paid out to third-party creditors, while some was used for other purposes? Who could say whether the company had actually been benefited, or was, in the actual result, better off because of the receipt of the *ultra vires* loan?[36] More generally, it will be seen how arguments that a person has been benefited by something that happened in the past involve an enquiry into what would have happened, if he had not received that particular benefit; such enquiries involve hypothetical explorations into what would have happened if the course of events had been different from what it actually was. Like the analogous enquiries which sometimes have to be made in personal injury actions in tort when collateral benefits have to be probed, these hypothetical enquiries are very troublesome indeed. Consider how much simpler these cases would have been if the contracts in question had not been *ultra vires*. Then the companies borrowing the money would have been liable to repay the loans without any questions arising as to whether they had benefited from the loans or not. The gain in simplification and the saving of cost would be immense. Once again, it should be made clear that we cannot always avoid these enquiries as to whether a person has been benefited by the actions of another. All I am concerned to point out is that allowing people to decide whether something done for them is indeed a benefit which they should be required to pay for leads to a great simplification and improvement in cost-effectiveness in the law. Here again, therefore, the arguments in favour of treating the formal reason as conclusive, and not allowing any enquiry into the underlying reasons of substance, are very strong; even though, on some occasions, justice may require that we disregard them.

IV

It would not be difficult to multiply examples of the great advantages which derive from the fact that contract law normally treats many of the matters lying behind the contract as irrelevant to the obligations of the parties. At the same time, everyone must be aware of the fact that the power of formal reasons in contract law, and indeed, perhaps in all of the law, has been declining in recent years. More and more often the courts seem willing to unpick the transaction, to open it up, as it were, and go behind the formal

[36] See, e.g., *Bannatyne* v. *D. C. MacIver* [1906] 1 KB 103.

reasons, and look at the substantive reasons for the creation or negativing of obligations. In some instances, these developments in the law might seem to amount to a mere narrowing of the limits within which formal reasons are treated as conclusive. But in other cases it is hard to avoid the conclusion that the formal reasons themselves have been jettisoned, and the issues treated as though they were completely at large. The virtual disappearance in modern English law of the parol evidence rule seems one clear example of the emasculation of a formal reason in contract cases. When it is argued that a written contract is not conclusive of the obligations of the parties, the courts seem simply to balance the arguments for and against imposing an orally-derived obligation on a party, rather than treat the writing as conclusive, even within the narrowest limits. Similarly, the statutory discretions now conferred on the courts by the Unfair Contract Terms Act 1977 and other similar enactments involve the elimination of the conclusory or formal effect of various contractual clauses. Such a clause does not become irrelevant, but whether it is to be treated as effective depends on a balancing of the substantive arguments for and against the clause.

This movement away from the use of formal reasons in the law seems to me to be evident in many areas besides contract law. I have already referred to the case of *R.* v. *Lee*[37] in which the Court of Appeal admitted an appeal from a plea of guilty, as another remarkable example of the abandonment of a formal type of reason in criminal procedure. So too the modern English Limitation Act,[38] which gives the court a complete discretion to override the time-limits in a personal injury action is another illustration of the abandonment of a formal reason for disposing of a case. Today, time-limits and other reasons of substance have to be weighed together in deciding whether to allow such an action to proceed after the normal time-limit has expired. In other countries, and especially the United States, it seems to me that formal reasons have been waning in scope and conclusiveness for many years; for example, the doctrine of collateral attack in American Federal criminal procedure is an extraordinary illustration of the destruction of the formal weight attached to the finality of judgments of state courts.

Why has this been happening? In order to answer this question we must, I think, go back a little, and renew our enquiry into the purposes and reasons underlying the use of formal reasons. In this paper I have identified a number of different purposes or reasons. I have laid stress on cost, and on the minimization of the risks of error as the two most important reasons of a general character. But these are by no means the only reasons. Thus I have suggested that in some cases a variety of other factors underlie the use of formal reasons. In contract law, especially, there is the value judgment

[37] [1984] 1 All ER 1080.
[38] See the Limitation Act 1980, s. 33.

that the parties to a contract are the most appropriate persons to decide what the benefits are worth, and that the courts should not prevent parties making their own decisions on such matters. This differs from the argument that it would be very costly for the courts to investigate whether a person has benefited from a contract, and if so, by how much. Then other reasons apply to other cases. For instance, some formal reasons concern the appropriate person to make a decision—matters of jurisdiction arise here—*when* a decision should be made, and by what procedure a question should be raised. Then also there is the value of repose and finality and security in human affairs. The search for justice is important to all lawyers, as well as the public of course; but even that search must be brought to a halt in particular cases when we have eventually done the best we can. Many of these reasons, of course, will overlap in various circumstances.

Now the widespread use of formal reasons for decisions seems to me to presuppose that substantive reasons either will be, or have been, or at least could have been, more appropriately and satisfactorily dealt with another time, or in some other manner, or by some other person. When we bar an action under the limitation period, for example, we do so in the belief that the action could and should have been brought within the proper period, and then adjudicated upon on its merits. If that assumption is unfounded, for example, because the statutes of limitation may bar an action before the plaintiff could possibly have been aware that he even had a cause of action,[39] then something is very wrong indeed. Or again, when an action is dismissed for want of jurisdiction, the normal presumption is that someone else will have jurisdiction. Even if no other court or tribunal can hear the case, so that the applicant remains remediless, automatic dismissal for want of jurisdiction presupposes that the matter could at least receive the attention of the legislature. But here too, if the question at issue could not be considered by any other court, and if there were reasons for supposing that the legislature would never deal with the matter, the formal jurisdictional reason for a decision would come to look thin and eventually perhaps, quite unacceptable. No doubt this is one of the main reasons that led the American Supreme Court eventually to intervene in the apportionment cases when it was evident that the legislatures would not right the matter themselves.

Or again, literal, that is formal, interpretation of a statute, ignoring the result and perhaps even the intentions of Parliament, is more likely to be justifiable if it can be assumed, first, that statutes are drafted and enacted with care, so that the presumption that the literal meaning correctly represents the intentions of Parliament is a strong one; and secondly, if it can be

[39] See *Cartledge* v. *Jopling & Son Ltd* [1963] AC 758, which led to immediate legislative reversal; see now Limitation Act 1980, ss. 11–14.

assumed that Parliament is likely to act reasonably promptly to remedy any deficiencies in the law caused by such a decision. If the drafting of statutes was constantly done with appalling ineptitude and obscurity, and if Parliament refused ever to do anything about it, then surely it is certain that the courts would no longer try to interpret statutes in such a formal and literal manner. It was, after all, only after the present manner of drafting and enacting legislation became standard practice in England that the present methods of interpretation were adopted. Similarly again, the principle of finality of judgments, still adhered to pretty rigidly in England, is only justifiable if we can generally assume that most judgments are carefully considered, and rendered with competence and integrity, and that opportunities for appeal are available. If these conditions did not obtain—if, for instance, appellate courts could not trust lower courts to observe the law with reasonable competence and integrity—and if, for some reason, there were obstacles in the way of bringing appeals against such decisions, it is hard to believe that the finality of judgments we so much prize today would not become undermined.

To make a decision by reference to a formal reason, after all, is to refuse to consider the reasons of substance bearing on the issue. But if these issues of substance are never to be considered at all, still more, if there never has been an opportunity to consider them, then to make the decision by purely formal reasoning is to shut out the possibility of that decision ever being based on the factors most directly relevant to it. Rational institutions, and a rational legal system, demand that we do not do this if we can avoid it. Now it seems to me that one of the reasons why formal reasons are today less favoured in contract law may stem from increasing doubts as to whether the reasons of substance which bear most directly on the result have ever been properly weighed by anyone. If parties have not in fact anticipated the events which have occurred, it is unsatisfactory to claim that the literal words of the contract can be stretched to cover these events, because that is to use a formal reason where the reasons of substance have not been and will not be considered by the parties or by anybody else. Perhaps, too, increasing doubts about how far consumers read or understand printed contracts is one of the principal reasons underlying the introduction of statutory discretions to deal with unfair exclusion clauses. Here again, to give effect to the clause is to dispose of the case with a formal reason when the reasons of substance have perhaps never been considered at all, and of course cannot now be considered because it is too late.

No doubt, in the area of contract and perhaps also elsewhere, there are factors of this kind which help explain why so many formal reasons of the sort I have been discussing have recently been abandoned or whittled down in the law. Without necessarily condemning all manifestations of these trends, this process seems to me one against which we should be on our guard. Formalism, of course, has a bad name; and to make a decision for formal reasons requires a degree of self-discipline; it requires that we should admit that some other person, some other time, some other place, some other procedure, may be the right one for this decision. But that is often true of decisions in a legal system in which, by and large, everyone can be trusted to play his proper part. When it is true, we should not be afraid to recognize that to decide a case for formal reasons is to decide it for good reasons.

3

The Acceptability of Legal Arguments[1]

JOHN BELL

I. INTRODUCTION

PROFESSOR HONORÉ has argued that one of the major contributions of Roman civilization to law was the development of a canon of acceptable arguments proper to legal discourse.[2] Whereas the Greeks had laws and constitutions, their mode of argument was determined by rhetorical and not specifically legal considerations, persuasion of the jury or whatever being the principal objective. With the Romans came a limitation of the range of arguments which were acceptable in justifying a legal conclusion. While I do not deny the continuing place of rhetoric in law, it seems to me that this notion of a canon of acceptable legal arguments developed by the legal profession has a valuable, though somewhat limited, place in a proper understanding of legal reasoning today. Indeed, the two components—an objective canon of arguments, and its development by a specific legal community—bring together a number of varying strands within the literature on legal reasoning.

The purpose of this paper is to consider the structure of legal reasoning in relation both to current analyses of the logic of legal argument and to current studies of the practice of legal reasoning, particularly in the judicial process. Much of the former has been developed in continental Europe and Scandinavia, whereas much of the latter has taken place in the Anglo-American world. A study of Honoré's notion of 'canons of acceptable arguments' brings together not merely logical and sociological studies of legal reasoning, but also approaches from different traditions of jurisprudence.

II. ISSUES AND APPROACHES

My central problem can be stated briefly as follows: what determines whether an argument used in court, in a solicitor's office, or in a law class is sound or not? By 'sound' I do not necessarily mean 'correct', but rather

[1] I wish to thank Neil MacCormick, Zenon Bankowski, Alan Paterson, and other members of the seminar in Edinburgh at which the first draft of this paper was presented.

[2] A. M. Honoré, 'Legal Reasoning in Rome and Today', (1974) 91 *South African Law Journal* 84, 92.

the weaker sense of 'legally arguable'. Lawyers frequently disagree about the correctness of a result, and each lawyer may claim to be presenting the right legal answer. Without some criteria of what is at least arguable and possible as a correct solution, one cannot begin to discuss whose view is right. In the practical world of legal reasoning, one cannot always expect that there will be agreement on the right answer to ever legal problem;[3] but criteria of soundness do provide the basis for discussions about the correct interpretation and application of law. While this may not provide a basis for affirming that an answer is legally right, it can at least provide the basis for saying that some answers are legally wrong. Such an idea, which seems to be articulated in the notion of canons of acceptable arguments, can provide a basis for explaining the limits within which legal reasoning has to take place, and consequently of judicial discretion.

The discussion of the limits on legal reasoning can be treated conveniently from two approaches. The first looks at the logic of the reasoning process itself: to what extent does a judge or legal reasoner find himself constrained by the logical requirements of the process of justifying a decision according to law? The second considers the social practice of legal reasoning: to what extent does a judge find himself constrained by the way in which he is expected to carry out the task of justifying a decision according to law in his society?

III. CANONS AND THE LOGIC OF LEGAL REASONING

Starting with legal logic, I shall try to show that legal reasoning takes place within a framework of canons of legal argument which determine what may count as a justification for a conclusion of law. Furthermore, the logic of the reasoning process reveals that justification involves the persuasion of a particular group, the legal audience, about the rightness of such a conclusion, and this also sets limits on what may count as a legitimate legal justification.

The problem of setting the limits on idiosyncrasy in legal reasoning can be illustrated by the following, extreme example. In *Junior Books Ltd* v. *Veitchi*,[4] the House of Lords held that a warehouse owner could recover in negligence from a subcontractor, who had negligently installed a defective floor in the warehouse, despite the fact that there was no privity of contract between them, and that the loss was purely economic. Now let us suppose a case at first instance soon afterwards which concerns the defective installation of electrical wiring. The judge seeks to distinguish *Junior Books* on

[3] See N. MacCormick, *Legal Reasoning and Legal Theory* (Oxford, 1978), pp. 259–64; cf. R. M. Dworkin, 'No Right Answer?', in P. M. S. Hacker and J. Raz (ed.) *Law, Morality and Society* (Oxford, 1977), ch. 3.

[4] [1983] 1 AC 520.

the ground that, while that case concerned negligent floor-laying, this one concerns electrical wiring, and so all the statements on liability in the precedent case are *obiter* and need not be followed. Accordingly, he holds that the subcontractor in this case is not liable to the warehouse owner in negligence.

Now such a line of reasoning would obviously be criticized by all lawyers and others as not merely wrong in its result, but unsustainable in its justifications. But why is that so? When one considers that the binding part of a case is the ruling based on the 'relevant facts' which leads to the result in the case[5] then how is this narrow view unsustainable? As Montrose pointed out,[6] the 'relevant facts' of a case can be pitched at a variety of levels of generality, from the detail of *wooden* flooring up to the general level of reasonable reliance on the skill or judgment of another. As a matter of (formal) logic, it is not impossible for the judge to limit the binding part of the case to rules about floor-layers. As long as the precedent decision can still be justified by the newly-stated legal rule, then there is logically possible scope for distinguishing as *obiter* statements of general principle in that previous case.[7]

However, mere formal logical possibilities do not provide acceptable legal arguments in the real world. Even a fairly elementary understanding of the purposes of tort law would reveal that there is no tenable distinction between the rules of liability governing floor-layers and those governing electricians, and so the judge's arguments do not amount to reasoning according to law. Even within formal logical possibilities, the judge or lawyer cannot make use of any argument he pleases. The process of legal reasoning can only be properly understood when account is taken of the limits imposed by standards of what counts as an acceptable legal argument.

As has long been noted and as the illustration brings out, the logic of legal reasoning cannot be adequately explained in terms of deduction from settled premisses. It may be that, in some circumstances, such a process may adequately characterize the legal arguments.[8] But there are limits to this. More often this will not be adequate. In most instances, findings and inferences from fact, and the determination and application of legal rules will require value-judgments to be made. The process of reasoning is then not a smooth deduction of what is entailed in a premiss, but what Peczenik has aptly described as a series of 'jumps' or 'transformations'.[9] The reading of the *Junior Books* judgment is taken as supporting a rule which will make

5 A. Goodhart, *Essays in Jurisprudence and the Common Law* (Cambridge, 1931), pp. 9–11.
6 'The *Ratio Decidendi* of a Case', (1957) 20 *MLR* 587, 591.
7 J. Raz, *The Authority of Law* (Oxford, 1979), p. 189.
8 See MacCormick, *Legal Reasoning*, ch. 3.
9 'Rationality of Legal Justification', (1982) 68 *Archiv für Rechts- und Sozialphilosophie* 137, 141.

the electrical subcontractor liable to the warehouse owner. Other readings of the case are logically possible, so the connection between it and the electrical wiring case is not simply one of entailment. A 'transformation', albeit a minor one, has occurred. Once legal reasoning is seen in this way, then the central question becomes what 'transformations' can be justified, and by what criteria they can be judged.

The theses advanced, both individually and collectively, by Aarnio, Alexy, and Peczenik have sought to demonstrate the rational character of such 'transformations' in legal reasoning.[10] They argue that legal reasoning is a specific kind of social activity. It is a language-game or a form of life, to use Wittgenstein's terminology, which is distinguished from other forms of social activity by its specific rules and practices. Now, any social activity will require a body of understandings and conventions which enable individuals to participate in it. People need to know the meaning of specialized terminology and when to use it—who 'silly mid-off' is and when it is appropriate to describe someone as occupying that position on a cricket field. Equally, they need to know what counts as an action within that activity—when a ball has been legitimately bowled and when it has not. Legal discourse is no different. The successful functioning of the activity of justifying decisions requires understandings about appropriate legal terminology, about the sources from which justifications should be drawn, and the kinds of argument which will count as justifications. Because legal discourse is a form of life with the ultimate purpose of enabling law to act as a regulator and guide within society, the conventions will concentrate not just on the technical and procedural aspects of the correct use of legal terminology and the sources from which arguments must be adduced, but also the decisions, values, and commitments to which an interpretation or application of the law must be related. These conventions go to define the process of justifying decisions according to law. The authors describe such conventions as 'rules' of legal discourse. 'Transformation rules' will specify the conditions under which transformations are justified.[11] Alexy has gone far in elaborating the kinds of logical rules which can be said to govern legal discourse, covering the requirements of rationality, rules of argumentation, such as the burden of proof, and rules of justification, such as the requirement of universalizability.[12] These rules of discourse provide a framework lying outside the power of the reasoner within which he has to operate if his arguments are to count as legal justifications. Yet, however

[10] See especially A. Aarnio, R. Alexy and A. Peczenik, 'The Foundation of Legal Reasoning', (1981) 12 *Rechtstheorie* 133, 157, 423.

[11] Ibid., p. 138.

[12] *Theorie der juristischen Argumentation* (2nd edn., Frankfurt, 1983). For a review see N. MacCormick, 'Legal Reasoning and Practical Reason' (1982) 7 *Midwest Studies in Philosophy* 271.

intricate and sophisiticated the elaboration of this rule-governed nature of legal reasoning may be, the authors do not deny that these rules will not always yield a determinate result, either because of their own indeterminacy, or because of the leeway which they permit. The rules of such a non-deductive logic are not of themselves thought to provide the whole explanation of the limits within which legal reasoning operates. No more than the rules of grammar can adequately explain what is good English style can these rules of legal discourse explain what are good legal justifications. Nevertheless, they do provide some limitations and points of reference for decision-makers.

However, this exposition of legal logic is expanded by an analysis of what is meant by legal justification. As has been shown, this involves more than simply demonstrating the entailment of an argument from certain premisses. Equally, it does not mean detailing the psychological reasons which led a person to a decision. That the neighbour dictum in *Donoghue* v. *Stevenson* was the product of conversations between Lord Atkin and his family would not have been a justification for introducing the idea into law.[13] As Perry and Perelman have suggested,[14] legal justification essentially involves providing reasons capable of convincing others of the rightness of one's conclusions. One succeeds in justifying a decision by providing reasons which are more cogent in favour of one's viewpoint than those which tell against it. To the extent that such intersubjective reasons are proffered for the result, justification can be seen to be an appeal to reason, rather then merely to emotion, or to the authority of the decision-maker.

Such a notion of justification requires the provision of convincing reasons for views or actions. The reasons required are not of a particularistic kind, but attempt to be universally applicable. In justification, one seeks to provide reasons which anyone would be bound to accept. It is this idea which is conveyed by Perelman and Olbrechts-Tyteca's notion of the 'universal audience'.[15] Justifications can be considered as attempts to convince all reasonable people, the ideal universal audience, of the rightness of a result. Starting from points held in common with that audience, justification seeks to persuade the universal audience to accept the result proposed.[16] However, even to explain the logic of the process of legal reasoning, this is too abstract.[17] Just who is the addressee of legal justification, and what kinds of premisses can be taken as given for the process of justification?

[13] See J. Salmond and R. F. V. Heuston, *Law of Torts* (18th edn., London, 1981), p. 185 n. 47.

[14] T. Perry, *Moral Reasoning and Truth* (Oxford, 1976), p. 102; Ch. Perelman, *Logique juridique* (Paris, 1976), p. 7.

[15] *The New Rhetoric* (Notre Dame, 1968), pp. 31–3.

[16] Ibid., p. 14.

[17] See P. Goodrich, 'Rhetoric as Jurisprudence: An Introduction to the Politics of Legal Language', (1984) 4 *OJLS* 88, 116.

I think one can explain legal reasoning best by suggesting that legal arguments are addressed to a 'legal audience', provisionally defined as those skilled and knowledgeable in the law. The social activity of legal justification is carried on and defined by this group. If one is to participate in this activity, one has to work within the framework of premisses and criteria of what constitute acceptable legal arguments which it defines. To count as legal justifications, arguments must fit within these limits, and the process of justification seeks to demonstrate, *inter alia*, that these have been satisfied. Thus, in concrete terms, the legal audience is the primary addressee of legal arguments, and one finds concrete limitations on legal reasoning in what this audience takes to be an argument which could legitimately be convincing. Such limitations will not only be based on what the legal audience sees as 'irrational' or 'illogical', but also on the values which it perceives the legal system as serving.

This is not to say that I am substituting convincing a particular section of society for the requirement that justification should be of a universal kind. Rather, to be comprehensible at all, argument has, in practice, to be directed at someone. Legal discourse is addressed to the legal audience not because it is the only relevant body, but because that is the way in which the reasons can be made available to all who wish to inspect them. To take an analogy, you would expect those knowledgeable about cricket to be best able to say whether it was right to describe a batsman's stroke as a 'cut' or a 'glance', or to judge whether one placing of fielders was more likely to save runs than another. An outsider can only judge whether a comment on a cricket match is sensible or fair by taking account of this cricketing expert's point of view. In a similar way, the wider community has to take account of the understanding of the legal audience in order to judge whether an argument constitutes a justification according to law, even if they ultimately disagree with its analysis. Those who are knowledgeable in the law are best placed to evaluate what counts as reasoning according to law, and it is to them, in the first place, that legal arguments are addressed. To this extent, as Perelman says, the particular audience may count as the universal audience.[18]

In summary, it can be said that legal reasoning takes place within a specific context. It constitutes a field of discourse which has its own rules regulating the situations requiring different kinds of legal justification, and what might count as a legal justification in such circumstances. However sophisticated the analysis of these rules becomes, they will, for the most part, be able to show only what is legally possible or impossible, rather than determining conclusively results for all cases. All the same, they do set the parameters which limit the kinds of argument which can be brought

[18] *The New Rhetoric*, p. 34.

forth to justify a particular result. A fuller understanding of the process of legal reasoning needs also to take account of the body to whom legal argument is addressed, and whose practice develops the conventions of legal discourse. This body develops the rules of legal discourse, and by argument addressed to it the legal reasoner seeks to provide justifications of universal acceptibility. The notion of canons of acceptable legal argument is able to capture both these aspects of the logic of legal reasoning.

IV. CLARIFICATIONS

The foregoing analysis of the logic of legal reasoning still requires elaboration. In particular, a couple of major questions remain to be resolved: how far is a canon of acceptable arguments a substantive or merely a procedural constraint on legal reasoning? and is it adequate to define the audience for legal arguments as simply all who are skilled and knowledgeable in the law?

(*a*) *The Notion of a Canon*

The notion of a canon involves a set of criteria against which the acceptability of legal arguments can be judged. Anything which does not fit into the canon is ruled out as a valid legal argument. To some extent, such a canon is integral to a rule of recognition, in that it stipulates what kinds of argument are permissible in legal discourse, and what are not. At the same time, it goes beyond conventional elaborations of such a rule in not confining itself to specifically 'legal' rules or reasons. As Honoré points out, among the permissible arguments will be 'open arguments', reasons based on moral or political values.[19] The canon will regulate their use. In this way, the notion captures the idea that, just because a policy discussion is necessary in some cases to resolve a dispute, it is not true that any policy argument at all will do. For example, arguments about the impact of a decision on national inflation might be thought relevant to the issue of the validity of a gold clause, but not to the liability of a subcontractor in negligence for causing economic loss. The canon sets the framework for what is seen as the appropriate role of legal discourse. The limits are external to the user of the system, and provide constraints within which he is supposed to operate.

A canon cannot adequately be conceived as a list of rules. One can try to set out a number of axioms, as Alexy does in his book, *Theorie der juristischen Argumentation*,[20] but the list is unlikely to be exhaustive. Indeed, as

[19] *Legal Reasoning* at p. 88.
[20] Above, n. 12 at pp. 361–7.

Alexy has more recently admitted,[21] we are more likely to be able to work out many of the appropriate criteria only in concrete circumstances, rather than in advance. At best, a canon is an articulation of a sense of arguability which, though refined and developed in many of its particulars, remains to some degree flexible and open to change.[22] However, to say that one cannot produce a complete list is far from saying that there are no agreed criteria for what is acceptable and what is not.

Unlike Alexy's logical rules of discourse, a canon of legal arguments is not confined simply to the 'grammatical' or 'procedural' aspects of legal reasoning—whether cases must be cited or whether one must put forward arguments in good faith. These have a place. However, if law is to achieve specific social purposes in a society, canons must also have the effect of orienting decision-makers in certain specific directions, and providing substantive limits on what can be justified. Some authors have realized this. For example, Alexy has suggested that we need to develop a 'model of principles', in which the hierarchy between values and principles within the legal system is established, and Dworkin suggests that the judge needs to work out a political theory justifying the rules and principles of the legal system.[23] Both are idealized characterizations of what is required. However the process is described, the search for coherence and consistency in the law represents an attempt to discover the framework of social values within which a decision has to take place. In this way, the elaboration of canons of acceptable argument is an integral part of the practice of legal reasoning, and to the extent that these constitute substantive limits they are important constraints on legal reasoning.

Explained in this way, the notion of canons of acceptable argument is not easily established, nor is it uncontroversial. It would perhaps be fair to suggest that those who have tried to develop precise rules and procedures for legal reasoning on the Continent are likely to be over-ambitious in their endeavours. A concentration on the grammatical or procedural aspects of the rules of discourse is likely to reveal only limited constraints on what can be said by way of a legal argument. Once one moves into the substantive aspect of the work, the results are likely to be more strongly contested, and will be relative to a particular system and its values. The notion of a canon of acceptable arguments has to embrace both these aspects, but suffers in precision as a result.

[21] *Rechtsregeln und Rechtsprinzipien* (World Congress for Legal and Social Philosophy, Helsinki, 1983), p. 23.

[22] J. Esser, 'Motivation und Begründung', in Ch. Perelman and P. Foriers (edd.), *La Motivation des décisions de justice* (Brussels, 1978), p. 152.

[23] R. Alexy, 'Zum Begriff des Rechtsprinzips', *Rechtstheorie*, Beiheft 1 (1979), 68; R. M. Dworkin, *Taking Rights Seriously* (rev. edn., London, 1978), pp. 116–18.

(b) The Notion of 'the Legal Audience'

The idea of conventional rules about what is acceptable, and the centrality of persuasion within the concept of legal justification, brings us on to the community within which these conventions exist.

As I have mentioned, while Aarnio and Perelman talk about the 'universal audience', I think it is best to consider legal argument as addressed to the legal audience. Such a body might be best described as those skilled and knowledgeable in the law. Any writing or argument is addressed, in some sense, at an audience, though its precise nature may be ill defined. The audience for legal reasoning is no exception. While, as Paterson has shown, judges might be at a loss to explain exactly for whom they are writing, that is not to say that they do not write for an audience.[24] You only have to listen to legal argument or read it to appreciate that legal reasoning is a specialized activity which is likely to be understood only by the in-group.[25] The bewilderment of clients noted by sociologists and others bears witness to that. Legal reasoning is a specialized language-game played by a particular linguistic and social community, which develops the necessary conventions to further its practice. To understand the law, you have to view it from the perspective of this community. Only then does the legal material become comprehensible. Legal justifications become accessible and comprehensible, and hence criticizable, by getting on to the same wavelength as the community to which they are primarily addressed. The members of this legal community would be judges, practitioners, commentators, teachers, and students of law, to whom such reasoning is at least comprehensible.

Now it might be said that there is more to legal justification than persuading just the legal audience about the acceptability of a decision. As Touffait and Tunc suggest, the job of the judge is also to present his 'excuses' to the losing party and show that he has not acted out of personal malice, but legal necessity.[26] Clearly, in the way reasons are given in civil, appellate, and, some sociologists would argue, in criminal cases,[27] this is not done directly in most cases. Rather it is the job of counsel to translate the judgment afterwards for the benefit of his client.

The language of the arguments and the subtleties of legal issues hide a decision not merely from the parties to a case, but also from other citizens. It can be forcibly argued that legal argument is ultimately about the exercise of power by the State and that judges and others are participating in this activity to varying degrees in the work they do. As a result, a degree of

[24] *The Law Lords* (London, 1982), pp. 9–11.

[25] J. Maxwell-Atkinson and P. Drew, *Order in Court* (London, 1979), p. 9.

[26] 'Pour une motivation plus explicite des décisions de justice' (1974) 72 *Revue trimestrielle de droit civil* 487, 491.

[27] See Z. Bankowski and G. Mungham, *Images of Law* (London, 1976), p. 58.

political responsibility to the wider community attaches to legal decision-making. The giving of reasons demonstrates that the power so entrusted has been properly exercised. On the whole, answerability to the ultimate political sovereign is tenuous, since ordinary citizens will usually require explanations from legal journalists and experts to be able to understand what has happened, though a degree of direct appeal to the public can be seen in some cases, particularly in sentencing.[28] There is a more direct relationship to the legal sovereign, Parliament, in that it, through its legal advisers, will be able to exercise an appropriate degree of scrutiny.

Thus, although one might be able to identify a number of audiences of the judge: the legal community, the parties, citizens, and Parliament,[29] the legal audience plays a central role. It determines the language of debate and acts as the agency for explaining legal arguments to the outside audiences. It is the centrality of the legal audience which helps the development of a canon of legal arguments. Indeed, continental legal systems recognize the importance of such an audience in shaping the law by ascribing high esteem to *la doctrine*, legal writings, criticism, and analysis of law. If doctrine is hostile to a particular view, the law cannot easily be treated as settled, whatever the courts say.

The traditions of each legal community will differ, so different styles and kinds of argument will be treated as persuasive. The rather brief and cryptic style in France might almost be seen as not an attempt at persuasion at all, yet, within the tradition, its evocation of the right phrases draws forth agreement or dissent similar to that of longer judgments in Britain, as can be seen by looking at the notes on cases.[30]

The notion of the legal audience has two aspects. The first, emphasized here, is its epistemological character: legal reasoning is only possible as justifications directed to a particular legal audience. The audience provides a focus for argument, a way of making it accessible to all, and thus of making the claim to universality which is characteristic of justification. However, it also has a technical character.[31] In the real world of practical discourse, the criteria for whether a legal argument is acceptable may well be the reactions of the actual legal community. The connection between Greek rhetoric and Roman justification is the convincing of an audience of the rightness of an argument. The difference between the two lies in the fact that for the former the persuasion of a concrete audience is a sufficient test of the rightness of an argument. For the latter, actual conviction is neither

[28] See P. Goodrich, 'Rhetoric as Jurisprudence' (above, n. 17), at 92; P. S. Atiyah, 'Judges and Policy', (1980) 15 *Israel Law Review* 346, 355–60.

[29] Cf. E. Pincoffs, 'The Audiences of the Judge', in H. Hubien (ed.), *Legal Reasoning* (Brussels, 1971), pp. 337, 338–9.

[30] R. David, *French Law* (Baton Rouge, 1972), pp. 189–93.

[31] A. Peczenik, *The Basis of Legal Justification* (Lund, 1983), p. 110.

sufficient nor necessary, since the actual conviction may be mistaken or ill-judged. At best, the views of the concrete, legal audience provide criteria for what would count as a good argument, but those criteria are revisable. This provisionality is particularly important when one considers that the conviction of the legal audience is only a method of providing arguments which should be accepted by any rational person. To that extent, the social determination of the canons of acceptable argument can be a handicap, as well as a concrete means of providing limits to legal reasoning.

V. CANONS AND SOCIAL PRACTICE

The development of the logic of legal reasoning in the previous two sections has demonstrated the way canons of acceptable legal argument arise out of a social practice among the legal community. It is only in exploring the nature and cohesion of the social practice that the reality of the limits such canons impose on legal reasoning can be appreciated. As Honoré points out, the development of such canons arose out of the professionalism of lawyers and the development of their role.[32] An enquiry into the social practice supporting such canons of arguments must therefore look at both the composition of the social group from which they arise, and the cohesion of the role-perceptions generated by it.

(*a*) *The Legal Audience*

A crucial aspect of any analysis of the social practice is the identification of the legal audience. A number of sociologists have identified the specific social practice of law as dealing in a particular technical way with ordinary situations according to a specialized linguistic terminology.[33] Analysing society from the legal point of view provides a unifying element in the social practice. To be able to use legal tools, a process of socialization and introduction to the skills and knowledge of the profession is required. The social processes by which such learning is acquired and then put into practice may help to provide a degree of cohesion in outlook among the performers of the task of reasoning according to law. Certainly, writers of very varied perspectives have pointed to this feature in the operation of legal practice,[34] and Llewellyn suggested that the 'law-conditioned' attitudes of officials

[32] *Legal Reasoning* at p. 88.

[33] M. Cain, 'The General Practice Lawyer and the Client' (1979) 7 *Int. Jo. Sociology of Law* 331, 335; Z. Bankowski and G. Mungham, above, n. 27 at p. 99.

[34] e.g., A Paterson, *Law Lords* at p. 197; P. Devlin, *The Judge* (Oxford, 1979), p. 8; R. Pearson, 'Popular Justice and Lay Magistracy', in Z. Bankowski and G. Mungham (edd.), *Essays in Law and Society* (London, 1980), pp. 73, 87–8.

provide one of the steadying factors in the predictability of law.[35] In addition, the common practice of reasoning according to law could be expected to generate conventions to deal with recurrent problems, and these would form the framework for the activity of legal practitioners.

Inherent in the notion of a common social practice is a set of common objectives or purposes which unite the activity and the participants. Reasoning according to law may certainly have the objective of trying to identify what the law prescribes, or even the more lofty ideal of upholding the rule of law. One of the difficulties in giving more precise content to the purposes of the activity lies in the varying concerns of the constituent elements of the legal profession.

As state-appointed arbiters of disputes, judges have constitutional concerns about their role and a sense of responsibility for the reputation and functioning of the legal process, as well as concerns for achieving a fair result, and these will colour their perception of what is an acceptable argument.[36] Practitioners have concerns about being able to advise clients correctly, seeking what is predictable and easy to operate, as well as securing a victory for their client in litigation. In this perspective, maintaining and promoting what is good for the system as a whole has a lesser place among objectives than for the judge.[37] Teachers and students of law, analysing the system away from the pressures of the forensic process, will seek order, coherence, and systematization as well as a correspondence between legal standards and outside values of what is right and just. By contrast, judges and practitioners may be happier with a predictable mess of rules, and may feel constrained in what they can achieve by interpreting the law so as to approximate it to outside standards of justice. These different practices of judging, advising clients, and winning cases in court, and teaching and criticizing the law, produce different objectives and priorities between objectives connected with the common practice of reasoning according to law. Any set of conventions which may be said to be common to this social practice as a whole will be limited to the broad purposes of the activity and leave a great measure of flexibility, so as to give freedom to the diverse objectives of the various constituent groups. To provide worthwhile limitations on the operation of legal reasoning, it is important not to leave the social practice loosely described as 'reasoning according to law', but to specify the particular sub-practice which is under discussion. What is acceptable as a doctrinal argument in the context of law-teaching may not be so in the context of judging a particular dispute.

If one thus specifies the particular aspect of legal practice, it might seem that one should look to the conventions of the particular part of the legal

35 *The Common Law Tradition* (Chicago, 1960), pp. 53, 214.

36 e.g., Lord Keith, *Duport Steels Ltd* v. *Sirs* [1980] 1 WLR 142, 168.

37 Cf. A. Paterson, *Law Lords*, at p. 65.

profession which carries on the sub-practice in order to find the limits of what are acceptable arguments. Other parts of the legal profession may be taken to provide the major criticism of the practice of a particular sub-group, and these may feed into the conventions of the sub-group, but will not provide the primary reference point for a member of that group who is trying to formulate arguments for a particular legal conclusion.

Such studies as there have been on the judiciary suggest that fellow judges, both on the same bench and outside, form the principal reference group for criticism and comment, both in the formulation and in the reaction to decisions made.[38] Other groups may well take their lead on what are acceptable arguments to raise in court from the judges,[39] so that the judicial role-perception dominates the process. Thus, within a particular aspect of legal practice, there may be sufficient commonness of purpose to provide concrete canons of argument and a specific legal audience to which arguments can be addressed.

All this does not imply that there cannot be significant variations within a particular sub-group of the legal profession about the objectives of its activity. One only has to think of the contrast between a Viscount Simonds and a Lord Denning, or between various political groupings among solicitors and barristers, or among academics of the economic-analysis and critical-legal-studies persuasions, to be aware of the possible range of diversity on the purpose of each aspect of legal practice. The result will be that one cannot always expect the commonness of understanding which could generate conventions sufficient to provide criteria of what is to count as an acceptable legal argument in all cases. Nevertheless, if the effective legal audience for arguments is confined in the way suggested, then significant agreement on what is to count as an acceptable legal argument could be expected to emerge.

(*b*) *Role-Perceptions*

Understood in the way I have suggested, a canon of acceptable legal arguments reflects the perception of a particular sub-group within the legal profession of its function. The canons developed will give effect to the objectives of reasoning according to law by that sub-group and enable them to be realized. The group itself will formulate these for its members in the light of the pressures exerted on it both from the rest of the legal profession and from the other audiences for legal reasoning. Role-expectations of this kind provide points of orientation for a judge or legal reasoner which can secure a degree of uniformity in the performance of the legal practice in

[38] Ibid., ch. 5; L. V. Prott, *The Latent Power and Culture of the International Judge* (Abingdon, 1979), pp. 34–5; R. Pearson, loc. cit., above, n 34.

[39] A. Paterson, *Law Lords*, pp. 60–1.

which he is engaged.[40] In this way, social analysis can support and refine the assumptions of legal logic about the way legal reasoning operates.

All the same, the diversity even within a particular sub-group of the legal profession, which was noted above, will limit the extent to which a particular legal reasoner is expected to respond to a coherent set of role-perceptions in the performance of his task. Studies of role-perceptions among judges do not suggest that a uniform view is held of their job description.[41] Historical studies like those of Stevens[42] demonstrate the difficulty of finding a uniform view even among a very small number of Law Lords at any one epoch. At best what can be presented is a 'period style', from which individual judges diverge to a lesser or greater extent. Such a dominant trend may create pressure for conformity and for the justification of divergence, but it falls short of a strong limitation on the performance of the judicial task.

Diversity in role-perception can in part be attributed to the inevitable diversity of people. Given different backgrounds and beliefs developed in other situations, it is inevitable that the members of a group will not all perceive their task in quite the same way. Furthermore, the role-perceptions will be developed in response to a variety of pressures. The variety of audiences, for instance for a judge, will result in a variety of expectations as to what his role is, and what he is to do. Such role-expectations are transmitted by the varying interests within the rest of the legal profession, in Parliament and government, and in the community at large. Those able to determine whether the judge's role continues and those with most voice and power are likely to receive special attention and to play an important part in transmitting role-expectations to the judges.[43] Group understandings will help to sort and sift the influences so that a role-perception is developed. However, the variety of these different influences will result in a role-model which is an amalgam of various expectations. In consequence, the precise configuration and balance of factors are capable of divergent formulation among the members of the group. Given that the content and strength of the influences brought to bear on the judges will vary over time, any statement of a role-model to which they have to conform will also change. As a result, the canons of legal argument will reflect the vagueness and flexibility of the role-perceptions they are to serve.

It would be wrong to imagine that the interaction between the judge and the audience is simply a matter of the former responding to role-expecta-

[40] T. Parsons, *The Social System* (Glencoe, 1951), pp. 38–42.

[41] e.g., K. Vines, 'The Judicial Role in the American States', in J. B. Grossman and J. Tanenhaus, edd., *Frontiers of Judicial Research* (New York, 1969), p. 461; A. Paterson, *Law Lords*, *passim*.

[42] *Law and Politics* (London, 1979).

[43] L. V. Prott, *Latent Powers*, at p. 137.

tions made upon him. It is equally clear from judicial practice that judges can have a formative influence on the expectations of the judicial role. To take a concrete example, Lord Denning in *Davis* v. *Johnson*,[44] arguing that the Court of Appeal (Civil Division) should not be bound by its own previous decisions, was not so much responding to the constraints imposed by a canon of acceptable arguments as actively seeking to change the canon. As Llewellyn pointed out, tradition may shape and guide lawyers, but it is also true that lawyers make use of it, reshape it, and mould it for the future.[45] The way in which the House of Lords was able to change its practice on not departing from its own previous decisions bears witness to the revisability of canons of legal argument from within the group constrained by them.[46]

(*c*) *Summary*

An examination of the social basis out of which canons of legal argument are expected to emerge by theories of legal logic provides adequate grounds for believing that they exist. However, it is clear that such a social background will not be able to generate strong canons which can regulate and determine the acceptability of arguments in all or even nearly all cases. To obtain that, one would need a static and agreed conception of the function of the practice of legal reasoning, which is not forthcoming.

The analysis of legal reasoning undertaken here has emphasized both the logical and the social aspects of the notion of a canon of acceptable arguments generated by the legal profession. As Simpson pointed out,[47] law is not just a system of rules or even a model of principles, but also a set of social practices observed and ideas received by a caste of lawyers. The constraints within which legal reasoning, for example in judging, has to operate are defined not merely by the structure of the logical procedures adopted for performing the task, but also by the socially developed criteria of what is acceptable. Canons of acceptable arguments embrace both rules defining the logical character of legal discourse and standards of acceptability developed by the principal group within the legal audience to which reasons are addressed.

VI. THE UTILITY OF THE NOTION OF CANONS

Even if one can draw from the logic of legal reasoning and from the social practice of the legal profession a place for the notion of canons of acceptable

[44] [1979] AC 264 at 278–83.

[45] *Common Law Tradition* at p. 53.

[46] A. Paterson, *Law Lords*, ch. 6.

[47] A. W. B. Simpson, 'The Common Law and Legal Theory', in ibid. (ed.), *Oxford Essays in Jurisprudence* (2nd series, Oxford, 1973), 79, 94.

arguments, it remains to be seen how far this is able to provide an adequate explanation of the limits on legal arguments. Once the simple deductive model of legal reasoning has been abandoned and the true place of value-judgments in the characterization of facts and the interpretation of rules is appreciated, then an explanation has to be provided of how the decisions reached are not just at the whim of the decision-maker and his idiosyncratic perceptions of what is right. The explanation of such limits turns on three issues: the rationality of legal decisions, the predictability of their outcomes, and the accountability of those taking the decisions.

(*a*) *Rationality*

The inadequacy of the deductive model of legal reasoning has led some to suggest that decision-making is a matter of 'hunch', rather than of deliberation, and that reasons are found thereafter to rationalize the conclusion reached.[48] The importance of psychological factors in the explanation of judicial decisions, even if not taken to the lengths of 'gastronomic' jurisprudence—that everything is a result of what the judge had for breakfast—would reinforce doubts about the rationality of legal argument. Add to this picture the doubts cast by some philosophers on the rationality of value-judgments, and we seem to lose hope that there can be rational debate about what is legally correct.

The non-deductive logic suggested by Aarnio, Alexy, and Peczenik (discussed in Part III), which is captured in the notion of canons of acceptable arguments, offers a way out. It may be that the kind of empirical proof or logical deduction available to the natural sciences or mathematics is unavailable to test the validity of legal arguments. However, the reasoner has to operate within the rules and conventions which define the practice of legal discourse, if he is to participate in the activity of justification according to law at all. The lawyer appeals to what he conceives to be the right legal answer, but has to do so within the canons of legal discourse. Such canons are developed within the legal community not on the basis that truth is to be found wherever the consensus lies, but that criteria of what possibly could be true are needed before any discussion or argument becomes meaningful. These canons make it possible to provide justifications. What the audience accepts as limits on rational argument provides the limits for this practical exercise of justifying decisions. The test of rationality is whether, within this framework, an argument is capable of providing a justification for a decision according to law.

Seen in this way, the lawyer cannot simply proffer some whim of his own to justify a decision. He is trying to convince an audience, and what that audience accepts as the criteria for rational debate provides the limits

[48] J. C. Hutcheson, 'The Judgment Intuitive', (1929) 14 *Cornell L. Q.* 274.

to how he can approach his justification. Such intersubjective criteria do provide controls on the rationality of the process. All the same, the extent of these controls must not be exaggerated. What might be accepted as rationally arguable could still be substantively unacceptable as an interpretation of the law. Rules of legal discourses, as Alexy has explained, essentially define a *procedure* within which justification can take place.[49] Such a procedure can satisfy the formal requirements of rationality, but will inevitably fall short of providing strong limitations on what can count as legally correct.

(*b*) *Predictability*

Even within the range of what is rational, considerable scope is left for divergence of opinion about what is legally correct. The need for value-judgments and the recognition that lawyers will differ in interpreting legal standards give rise to the nightmare of unpredictability. Even if the ideal of total predictability is abandoned, the value of certainty in planning social affairs necessitates at least some criteria of a substantive kind as to what is legally correct.

In response to these problems, two approaches have been offered in the literature. The first, particularly popular with German authors, but also with Dworkin, has been to concentrate on what is meant by law as a system of standards.[50] Looking at legal practice and methodology, they note the use of rules and other standards of varying generality to justify legal arguments. The suggestion seems to be that, the more precisely one can present the structure of these standards and the way they fit together, the more one is able to appreciate that the solution to legal questions can be found within that system, rather than from the multiplicity of value-perspectives which lie outside it. Such an approach develops further the methodological and procedural aspects of legal reasoning seen in connection with rationality, and grafts on to them requirements as to the substantive values which any acceptable legal argument must satisfy. Such an approach does fit in with the objective of finding canons of acceptable legal arguments which are capable of providing substantive criticism of legal reasoning. The approach does seem, albeit in a not very explicit way, to be articulating the conventions about such substantive limits which exist in the legal audience. However, it would be wrong to exaggerate the strength of these limitations. Such system-building only becomes successful if it leaves a good deal of ambiguity about what is contained in the system itself. As Canaris and Esser

[49] 'Die Idee einer prozeduralen Theorie der juristischen Argumentation', *Rechtstheorie*, Beiheft 2 (1981), 177.

[50] See especially C.-W. Canaris, *Systemdenken und Systembegriff in der Jurisprudenz* (Berlin, 1969); K. Larenz, *Methodenlehre der Rechtswissenschaft* (3rd edn., Berlin, 1975), ch. 5; R. Alexy, above, n. 23; Dworkin, *Taking Rights Seriously*, chs. 2 and 4.

point out,[51] some general values such as 'justice' have to be incorporated into the system, and Dworkin admits that judges will disagree in making the important political value-judgments necessary to determine what rights people have.[52] Thus the content and the limits of the system remain to some degree open and flexible. The notion of canons of acceptable arguments can only provide limits on reasoning to a certain extent. The existence of disagreements as to what is within the system, and its changing needs over time, will ensure that a degree of vagueness and flexibility must exist in any attempted formulation of such canons.

The second approach has been to look for 'steadying factors' within the legal tradition itself. Llewellyn saw factors such as law-conditioned officials, legal doctrine, and a general 'period style' as significant psychological forces towards more predictable decisions.[53] The tradition of the profession moulds thinking and so promotes psychological barriers among legal reasoners to idiosyncratic perceptions of what is legally correct. To some extent, the discussion of the legal audience does show the way in which the operation of canons of acceptable arguments rests upon prevailing, and often ingrained, aspects of legal practice. The process of socialization reinforces acceptance of the role-perspectives and the canons which these generate. At the same time, the notion of canons is something more than simply a psychological fact. They are capable of conscious development and justification as rational ways of achieving the purposes of legal reasoning. The transmission of the role-perceptions they articulate may be often psychological, but the canons represent objective and objectively justifiable standards to which legal reasoning must conform. Indeed, to the extent that the reasoner can mould and influence these standards, the psychological approach loses a degree of its attraction, in that it, in fact, offers less of a limitation than might at first appear.

(c) *Accountability*

Underlying the two previous criticisms of legal reasoning is the suggestion that the subjective aspect of decision-making gives the reasoner, particularly the judge, power which is uncontrollable. The account of legal reasoning as justification to a legal audience helps to dispel this idea of irresponsibility in that the exercise of power has to be justified by the giving of reasons.

In the first place, the act of justification is intended to encourage the decision-maker to question the views to which he wishes to give effect in

[51] Ibid., pp. 49–53; J. Esser, *Vorverständnis und Methodenwahl in der Rechtsfindung* (Frankfurt, 1970), pp. 22–4.

[52] *Taking Rights Seriously* at p. 117.

[53] *Common Law Tradition.*

the light of their acceptability to the legal audience. The decision has to be fitted into the framework of its canons of acceptable arguments, and this process may force the judge to revise his views of the result that could be treated as in accordance with law. Some may, however, argue that the process does not always succeed in weaning judges from their prejudices.[54]

Beyond this rather psychological aspect of justification, the canon of acceptable reasons provides criteria for the proper exercise of political power to which the judge should respond. The provision of reasons opens up the decision to scrutiny and criticism, so that members of the legal audience and others can evaluate the way a decision matches up to the criteria of what is acceptable. The account of legal reasoning given here explains how a decision is made open to scrutiny and the criteria against which it can be judged. Of course, the extent to which this process is successful in providing adequate scrutiny will vary. In France, judgments are brief and deductive in form, so that commentators have complained that they do not adequately provide the kinds of justifications which can be scrutinized.[55] The traditions of each system and profession will affect the degree of control which can really be achieved.

Perhaps the most difficult aspect for ensuring the proper accountability of legal reasoning lies in the narrowness of the group which is the principal audience for legal arguments. The account of the legal audience has had to be refined from the lofty assertion that justification involves the provision of arguments which any rational person would accept to the recognition that, in the practical world, this process of justification passes through the stage of providing arguments acceptable to the sub-group which practises that aspect of legal activity which is under consideration. If judicial arguments must pass through the framework of acceptability to fellow judges, then there is the considerable danger that they will be inadequately universal. Meeting the judges' notions of what is acceptable may not even provide arguments which the rest of the legal community is able to share, let alone the wider community, which constitutes the ultimate body to which political power has to be justified. Lawyers' concerns for legal stability, order, and coherence, may be shared less by the wider community, which is interested in justice for particular cases.

This problem can be illustrated by the reaction to the Court of Appeal decision in *Mandla* v. *Lee*. This concerned a rather intricate point about the policy of the Race Relations Act 1976 and whether this made unlawful discrimination the refusal of a headmaster to allow his pupils to wear turbans rather than school caps. The problem was addressed in terms which may have been acceptable to the legal audience, but failed to take

[54] See J. A. G. Griffith, *The Politics of the Judiciary* (3rd edn., London, 1985).

[55] See A. Touffait and A. Tunc, above, n. 26.

account of the sensibilities of the wider audience, particularly of the Sikh community.[56]

Equally, the values which are perpetuated by the legal community may fail to correspond to the expectations of how the law should develop held by the community as a whole. Lawyers' perceptions of what is 'charitable' may be well out of line with those of the wider community.[57] Accountability to the small group of judges and lawyers in the first instance may not ensure the legitimacy and acceptability of the decisions rendered. The objectivity which a canon of legal arguments provides can only be satisfactory if the standards which it embodies adequately incorporate the role-expectations of those whom the law is to serve.

VII. CONCLUSION

The idea of a canon of acceptable arguments elaborated in the practice of the legal community has obvious attractions. Firstly, it can, I think, capture the way in which legal arguments are couched and structured, their orientation to the legal community. Secondly, it helps explain the special nature of the social practices of reasoning according to law, how it differs from rhetoric or other kinds of practical reasoning. Thirdly, it captures the structure of limitations within which lawyers are accustomed to work. Legal reasoning is not a system of cadi-justice, at the whim of the decision-maker. There are external constraints on the way in which the law can be interpreted. The notion of a canon is not confined to matters of legal logic, but includes the substantive limitations as to values to which legal reasons have to relate.

On the other hand, it is a notion with which lawyers may be tempted to be too comfortable. It may over-stress the constrained nature of legal reasoning and underplay the degree of its overlap with moral and political reasoning in general. For instance, it may be used to hide the fact that, in easy cases, judges are carrying out particular political policies, and, in hard cases, they are making value-judgments substantially similar to those of other branches of government. The degree of freedom which the canons leave, and the ease with which changes can be negotiated in them, may be almost as worth stressing as the limitations within which lawyers operate. Finally, the fact that judges have to respond to the expectations of their part of the legal audience and create a consensus of support has misled some judges into thinking that their decision is based on consensus values.[58]

[56] [1983] QB 1; *The Times*, 30 July 1982.

[57] See J. Hackney, 'The Politics of the Chancery', (1981) *Current Legal Problems* 113, 121–2.

[58] e.g. P. Devlin, *The Judge*, at p. 5.

The consensus among lawyers about what is arguable is neither proof of a consensus among lawyers about the right answer, nor that such a consensus exists in the wider community. In other words, the special limitations within which lawyers have to work are not such as to make legal reasoning self-contained, or capable of self-limitation.

4

Democracy and Adjudication

HUGH COLLINS

WHAT is the law on a particular point? How does legal reasoning work? How do judges reach decisions on questions of law? Each of these questions demands a reply in the form of a description of the behaviour of lawyers. We wish to identify the procedure by which questions of law are answered, and that procedure involves reasoning and decision-making. At first sight, legal theory, when grappling with these problems, embarks upon an empirical science involving the testing of hypotheses against observable behaviour. Yet Honoré insists correctly that the competing theories of the procedure for determining questions of law are not in fact descriptive claims subject to falsification. Instead, the rival schools of jurisprudence present different interpretations of the procedure for answering questions of law both as part of a general moral and political theory of the state and as reasons or justifications for obedience to the rules of the state. 'Legal theory is a form of practical reason, not a science. In contrast with law-making and law reform, which can in theory be scientific to the same extent as other goal-determined techniques like medicine, legal theory is in the end an elaborate form of exhortation or an elaborate display of commitment.'[1]

When we consider modern theories of legal reasoning and adjudication bathed in the floodlight of these candid sentences, we discover that the rival schools share much common ground. The objective is to present a description of the procedure for answering questions of law which claims implicitly the legitimacy of this procedure by reference to a general theory of the state. This general theory asserts the natural division of responsibilities between the various organs of government. In particular, the duty of the democratic legislature is to enact laws designed to further the common good, and the duty of the judiciary is to uphold those laws, and more generally to uphold the constitutional framework and the Rule of Law. Corresponding to this division of labour, each institution of government adopts its own style of practical reasoning: the democratic legislature weighs policies and trades off conflicting interests, the judiciary merely applies and elaborates the existing law by means of a discrete and non-instrumental

[1] A. M. Honoré, 'Groups, Laws, and Obedience', in A. W. B. Simpson (ed.), *Oxford Essays in Jurisprudence (Second Series)* (Oxford, 1973), ch. 1, at p. 1.

style of reasoning. In this institutional arrangement, the forces of social change must channel their efforts into the forum of a democratic legislature, and the courts must defend the existing political settlement as it is represented in the body of the law. The institutions of adjudication can fulfil this task of upholding the Rule of Law without relying upon democratic, popular, or influential opinion. They do so by following the procedure for elucidating and applying the settled law.

Of course, important differences of political philosophy divide the rival schools which expound this general theory. In the first place, some schools concede that the purity of the separation of powers is unworkable because in some cases the existing law provides scant guidance. Consequently judges must assume a modified legislative role to deal with these gaps in the law.[2] On the other hand, some schools regard this subversion of the separation of powers as not only improper, because it accords a paternalistic role to the judiciary, but also unnecessary because the legal materials, when properly analysed, are inexhaustible and can always guide judicial decisions.[3]

A second division between the schools of legal theory derives from divergent understandings of the ideal of the Rule of Law. Whilst the theorists agree that the legitimacy of judicial decisions depends upon fidelity to the ideal of the Rule of Law, their contrasting conceptions of that ideal provoke distinctive approved styles of legal reasoning. On the one hand, legal positivists identify the ideal of the Rule of Law as one requiring strict observance of established legal rules.[4] Their corresponding description of legal reasoning is formal logical rationality,[5] which is the application of rules according to their established or obvious meaning, whilst ensuring that inconsistencies do not arise. On the other hand, legal idealists (or natural lawyers) conceive of the Rule of Law as a substantive principle which embodies the liberal political settlement, with its allocation of institutional responsibilities and a distribution of rights to individual citizens.[6] In accordance with this political philosophy, legal idealists describe legal reasoning as a type of substantive rationality[7] distinguishable in form from other styles of practical reasoning by the duty not to upset the established order of power and wealth. This duty may be expressed as the requirement that

[2] e.g. H. Kelsen, *The Pure Theory of Law* (Berkeley, 1970), ch. VIII; J. Austin, *The Province of Jurisprudence Determined* (1832), ed. H. L. A. Hart, (London, 1954), p. 191; N. MacCormick, *Legal Reasoning and Legal Theory* (Oxford, 1978); J. Bell, *Policy Arguments in Judicial Decisions* (Oxford, 1983).

[3] e.g. R. Dworkin, *Taking Rights Seriously* (London, 1977), ch. 4.

[4] e.g. J. Raz, *The Authority of Law* (Oxford, 1979), p. 217.

[5] This term is coined by Max Weber, *Economy and Society*, ed. G. Roth and C. Wittich (Berkeley, 1978), vol. ii, pp. 656–7. The leading modern exposition of this style of reasoning is found in H. L. A. Hart, *The Concept of Law* (Oxford, 1961), ch. 8.

[6] R. Dworkin, 'Political Judges and the Rule of Law', (1980) 64 *Proceedings of the British Academy* 259.

[7] Weber, *Economy and Society*, vol. ii, pp. 656–7.

all decisions fit into a coherent moral pattern or that the courts should strive to protect existing rights.

Honoré likened the contest between these competing schools to an international soccer tournament. 'Decade after decade Positivists and Natural Lawyers face one another in the final of the World Cup (the Sociologists have never learned the rules). Victory goes now to one side, now to the other, but the enthusiasm of players and spectators alike ensures that the losing side will take its revenge.'[8] If I were scorer today, I could conclude that the positivists are paying the penalty for a purely defensive game and that the idealists, led by their creative striker R. M. Dworkin, are ahead. The idealists benefit from their more elaborate conception of the Rule of Law, which, by virtue of the inclusion of a defence of individual rights, presents a more attractive scheme of institutional responsibilities for the judiciary than the rule-applying tasks advocated by legal positivists. Indubitably, however, Honoré is right to suggest that, when the membership of the teams changes over the next decade, the result may be quite different.

But what of that jibe that sociologists have never learned the rules? Perhaps the sociologists thought that the game was what it pretended to be: a game of descriptive skill, rather than a disguised form of ideological warfare. Certainly this is true of 'positivist sociologists', whose accounts of judicial reasoning look for regularities of behaviour and patterns of cause and effect.[9] But another field of sociological theorizing, which has proved remarkably fertile in recent years, has always recognized the intimate relation between ideology and description, and between criticism and explanation. Since Honoré threw down his jibe, a new team, from the traditions of Marxism and critical social theory, has banded together to challenge the hegemony of the positivists and idealists in the field of legal reasoning.

From the perspective of critical theory, we immediately challenge one of the conventional rules of the game. This rule holds, in its broad outlines, that only one possible distribution of labour between state institutions can satisfy our commitment to individual liberty and respect for individual dignity. More specifically, the separation of powers, responsibilities, and modes of practical reasoning between the legislature and judiciary is in its essential aspects unalterable. Of course, controversy surrounds the identification of the essential elements of this scheme. One of the exciting features of the game is the opportunity to cry 'foul' against the opponents at any time on the ground that they have broken the essential elements of the scheme of the liberal state. But this rule of the game—that the separation of powers in its conventionally interpreted form must be preserved at all

[8] Honoré, 'Groups, Laws and Obedience', p. 1.

[9] e.g. G. Schubert (ed.), *Judicial Behaviour, A Reader in Theory and Research* (Chicago, 1964); cf. R. Cotterell, *The Sociology of Law* (London, 1984), pp. 228–34.

costs—is, in the last resort, only a convention which is agreed and acted upon by positivists and idealists alike.

When we examine this convention closely, it turns out to be rather curious. From our concern for individual liberty and respect for individual dignity, we prefer a democratic legislature since it is the institutional framework which best combines those values by maximizing opportunities for self-determination within a stable social order. Yet these values are immediately supplanted when we examine the judicial branch of government. The legitimacy of judicial power depends entirely upon whether its exercise conforms to the Rule of Law. Why has the value of self-determination suddenly been eclipsed?

The traditional answer is both pragmatic and principled: as a practical matter, the courts are poorly equipped to survey public opinion; as a point of principle, the judicial duty must be to apply the existing law, for those rules already embody the product of democratic self-determination expressed through the legislature. These arguments should be scrutinized carefully.

The principle that courts should apply democratically selected laws must always remain an ideal which cannot be realized in practice. The common law was created by judges rather than the legislature. Even where legislation governs the issue, the courts must still unravel obscurities, ambiguities, and conflicts, and fill in gaps between the provisions. Furthermore, the common law provides uncertain guidance on many issues, and periodically undergoes important transformations through the recognition of new causes of action. No one suggests that these hard cases and common-law decisions may be resolved mechanically without important choices, albeit circumscribed choices, about the distribution of wealth and power. When such choices have to be made without legislative guidance, why not imitate as far as possible the democratic process? Why insist that the judicial form of reasoning must be distinct from that of the legislature?

At this point the pragmatic argument takes over.[10] The courts are not equipped to survey public opinion on every issue. Nor do we wish the process of adjudication to be delayed by lengthy enquiries into conventional standards. On the other side of the coin, however, the democratic legislature also avoids many of these enquiries. The system of representative democracy at best ensures a rough convergence of legislation with public opinion. Apart from the input of periodic elections, which alter the composition of the legislative body, the major source of impact upon legislative decisions lies in pressure groups. Those interest groups with the necessary resources and skills succeed in moulding and modifying legislative programmes to suit

[10] The most influential version is presented by H. Hart and A. Sachs, *The Legal Process* (Cambridge, Mass., Tentative Edition, 1958).

their preferences. Without such pressure groups, which can articulate and advocate specific demands, the needs and aspirations of individuals are unlikely to be met with a direct response from the legislature. This routine subversion of the ideals of democratic government should not be greeted as a virtue,[11] but equally we should recognize that in modern nation states practical considerations inhibit the full realization of democratic self-determination. Given that the legislature lacks credibility as a pure system of democratic control, it becomes acceptable to recognize that other institutions of government, like the courts, may equally claim authority derived from a democratic input, even though that input is weak and incomplete. In other words, the courts may respond to democratic choice without carrying out surveys of public opinion. They can listen to the views of pressure groups and other sources of informed opinion, just like members of the legislature. Merely because the democratic input is bound to be incomplete and therefore unreliable, there is no reason to abandon it altogether.

One of the major errors of our political tradition has been the failure to take this possibility seriously. We have been blinded by the dogma of the separation of powers and unable to see that judicial power need not be legitimated solely by reference to the ideal of the Rule of Law. Adjudication provides another forum for the introduction of self-determination, for the adjustment of the laws to the values of those persons to whom they apply. Far from constituting a challenge to democratic government, this novel description of the responsibilities of the judiciary provides expanded opportunities for democratic self-determination.

The critical legal theory seeks to reverse this trend by reintroducing democratic ideals into adjudication. Instead of the courts being exclusively directed by the ideal of the Rule of Law to maintain the existing order of power and wealth, they should recognize that their decisions should also be legitimated by the consent of the community, and this requirement has the potential to disrupt the established distributive patterns. Legal reasoning should exhibit a constant dialectic between two forms of practical reasoning: one concerned with maintaining a coherent pattern of distribution and the other imagining reconstitutions of this pattern in accordance with democratic choice.

Like other theories of legal reasoning and adjudication, this critical theory presents at once a normative vision and a descriptive claim. In this latter respect, the claim is that judges already canvass public opinion before making choices which have been left undetermined by the legislature. I am not suggesting, of course, that judges conduct surveys in the streets or by telephone to discover public opinion. That might not be such a bad idea, but

[11] See the critique of pluralist theories in S. Lukes, *Essays in Social Theory* (London, 1977), ch. 2.

it does not happen. The process of consultation which permeates adjudication is both more selective and more penetrating than the typical opinion poll. We find evidence of the process of consultation in a variety of guises and contexts. To begin a necessarily brief survey, we look at appeals to public opinion in two judgments of ordinary courts in contractual disputes.

In 1969 Olga Monge was dismissed from her job at the Beebe Rubber Company in New Hampshire. She claimed that the underlying reason for her discharge was that she did not accept an invitation of her foreman to go out with him. She alleged that various forms of harassment resulted from her refusal, including downgrading, abusive remarks, and annoying telephone calls. The legal question was whether Monge had any cause of action against her employers. New Hampshire courts had long recognized the prevailing American common-law rule that an employer could terminate a contract of employment at will, for any reason, without paying compensation. Yet the Supreme Court of New Hampshire declined to follow these precedents. Comparing the case to changes in the law governing the relations between landlord and tenant, they said,

> The law governing the relations between employer and employee has similarly evolved over the years to reflect changing legal, social and economic conditions. 3A A. Corbin, Contracts n. 674 at 205, 206 (1960) In this area '[w]e are in the midst of a period in which the pot boils the hardest and in the process of change the fastest.' *Id.* Although many of these changes have resulted from the activity and influences of labor unions, the courts cannot ignore the new climate prevailing generally in the relationship of employer and employee. *See* Comment, Contracts—Termination of Employment At Will—Public Policy May Modify Employer's Right to Discharge, 14 Rutgers L. Rev. 624 (1960): Blumrosen, Employee Discipline, 18 Rutgers L. Rev. 428, 431–33 (1964).[12]

The court immediately concluded that Monge had a cause of action based upon a duty to terminate a contract of employment in good faith. 'Such a rule affords the employee a certain stability of employment and does not interfere with the employer's normal exercise of his right to discharge, which is necessary to permit him to operate his business efficiently and profitably.'

In 1967 the Ford Motor Company reached a collective agreement with representatives of all the unions at its plants in Britain governing the procedures by which changes in the terms and conditions of employment were to be achieved. The procedural agreement provided that it could only be terminated on three months' notice in writing. Almost certainly in contravention of the agreed procedure, a strike broke out following a dispute about proposals to change the terms of employment. The question for decision was whether or not the collective agreement was legally enforceable, so that an injunction could be issued to prohibit the strike. The court

[12] *Monge* v. *Beebe Rubber Company*, 316 A. 2d 549 (1974) at p. 551.

found that the agreement was enforceable, if that was the intention of the parties, but in the absence of any clear expression of intent, the court chose to infer intent from the general climate of opinion.[13] The opinion was that collective agreements were not legally enforceable. This view was gleaned from articles by Professor Kahn-Freund, a Report of a Royal Commission, evidence submitted to the Commission by trade unions and employers' associations, a government inquiry, and miscellaneous official publications. We should recognize that references to the intention of the parties comprise merely a doctrinal mechanism whereby difficult questions of enforceability of contracts may be adjudicated according to popular opinion. At bottom the court declined to enforce the collective agreement because of the weight of opinion against the use of injunctions in labour disputes.

Having considered these two cases of private contractual disputes, we should now turn to a constitutional court in the process of determining fundamental constitutional rights in order to see the consultative approach at work. Although the following decision has been presented as a model of idealist adjudicative theory by R. M. Dworkin,[14] illustrating how a coherence test of legal materials may afford results without appeals to social goals, we will see the same express appeals to public opinion forming the linchpin of the judgment.

In 1973, a pregnant single woman, known for the purposes of litigation as Roe, brought a class action before the Supreme Court of the United States challenging the constitutionality of the Texas criminal abortion laws, which proscribed procuring or attempting an abortion except on medical advice that it was necessary for the purpose of saving the mother's life.[15] Of course, the constitution provided no explicit guidance about abortion. Yet the court held that a right of privacy was implicit in the Fourteenth Amendment's concept of personal liberty and restrictions upon state action. Furthermore, this right of privacy encompassed, up to a certain point, a woman's decision whether or not to terminate her pregnancy.

In order to reach this conclusion the court found it necessary to survey the history of attitudes towards abortion. The court points out that it is 'doubtful that abortion was ever firmly established as a common-law crime'. But in the nineteenth century, the public's (and particularly the medical profession's) attitude towards abortion hardened and numerous statutes made it a serious criminal offence. The court then notes that in the period of a few years before the case, attitudes and practices had been modified. The American Medical Association, instead of formally opposing abortion, advised its members in 1970 to perform abortions if this was consistent

[13] *Ford Motor Company* v. *Amalgamated Union of Engineering and Foundry Workers* [1969] 2 QB 303.

[14] *Taking Rights Seriously* at p. 125.

[15] *Roe* v. *Wade* 410 US 113 (1973).

with their personally held moral principles after consultation with two other physicians and in conformity with state law when the action was in the best interests of the patient. More radically, the same year the Executive Board of the American Public Health Association urged that rapid and simple abortion services should be readily available through state and other health organizations. In 1972 the American Bar Association joined the tide of opinion towards legalizing abortion when a continuance of the pregnancy would impair the physical or mental health of the mother.

In addition to these surveys of opinion and practice the court discussed the origins and nature of the constitutional right to privacy. For this purpose the opinion refers to earlier decisions of the Supreme Court and other Federal courts, which demonstrate the uncertain basis of the right (since it is not specifically mentioned in the text of the Constitution) and its limits.

From these decisions we can begin to grasp how courts gather opinions and the role they play in determining results. The courts seek a climate of opinion, the dominant informed view. The courts are especially interested in the prevailing attitudes of participants in the relevant activity, for example trade unions in the case of dismissals and doctors in relation to abortion. These attitudes are then tested against a broader climate of opinion to be found in legal scholarship and considered views of professional bodies in order to check that they correspond to a consensus of opinion. In this sense, each decision is the product of a democratic consultation.

In a few instances, the opinions of the participants in the activity clash with other informed opinions. The clearest instance arises in cases of tortious liability for defectively manufactured products. Courts are unwilling to permit manufacturers to set standards of reasonable care in the manufacture of products, for fear that the safety and hygiene standards will be set well below levels acceptable to public opinion.[16] One method to avoid delegating the setting of standards to manufacturers is to insist upon strict liability against the wishes of manufacturers. On the other hand, the medical establishment is normally permitted to set the standard of care of doctors, and other professional bodies through expert witnesses determine the criteria of liability for their own members. The difference in treatment meted out to manufacturers compared to professionals is partly explicable because manufacturers' wishes are out of step with the informed opinions of many other groups. But a further inference which we should draw from these examples is that, in the last resort, the guiding opinion will be derived from the professional groups concerned. The courts weigh the opinions of lawyers, doctors, and other professionals more heavily than those parties with

[16] J. G. Fleming, *The Law of Torts* (6th edn., Sydney, 1983), pp. 113–14; J. A. Henderson, Jr., 'Judicial Review of Manufacturers' Conscious Design Choices: The Limits of Adjudication', (1973) 73 *Col. LR* 1531.

commercial interests at stake. In the case of conflicting opinions, the commercial interests give way to the informed attitudes of the professions.

We should now turn to another source for evidence of the democratic input to adjudication. Essentially we shall consider procedural techniques whereby the formal rationality demanded by liberal theories of adjudication is subverted by reliance upon popular sentiment.

Originally, of course, the jury ensured that the common law did not deviate from the standards of bourgeois conscience. Ironically, however, as the membership of juries has become increasingly representative of the public as a whole, under the influence of the dominant conception of the separation of powers and the Rule of Law, courts and legislation have drastically pruned the powers of juries. In a criminal case, a judge will tell the jury that its job is to determine the facts, not the law. The power to mould the law has been clutched by the judge, who in turn disclaims any responsibility on the ground that his or her role is merely to enforce the existing law.

Modern interpretations of how to include a democratic input to adjudication have become mingled with a faith in the capacity of technology and expertise to achieve rational solutions to social problems. When this faith is combined with the desire to incorporate popular opinion, it results in the creation of specialized tribunals with experts presiding. These tribunals occupy an uncertain territory between neutral adjudicators, bureaucratic administrators with expertise, and embodiments of popular sentiment. Look, for example, at British industrial tribunals composed of a lawyer as chairperson, and then two wingpersons representing management and union perspectives. Their decisions crave legitimacy from three sources: their role as neutral judges, applying known law (hence the legally qualified member); their specialized knowledge of industrial relations attracts the legitimation provided by successful instrumental decisions; their balanced representation from both sides of industry inviting the description of an 'industrial jury',[17] that is, a form of democratic adjudication in which all interest groups are represented. The democratic dimension of these tribunals weighs heavily with courts engaged in judicial review of the legality of their decisions. Judgments exhibit the tension arising from using arguments derived from the Rule of Law to thwart democratic sentiment by invalidating the decisions of specially constituted tribunals.[18] Indeed, this tension explains the source of many of the unsolved problems of administrative law, which perhaps can only be resolved when the courts acknowledge more

[17] *Per* Sir John Donaldson, *Earl* v. *Slater & Wheeler (Airlyne) Ltd* [1972] *ICR* 508, at p. 513; cf. the 'jury function' of the Restrictive Practices Court: see J. Bell, *Policy Arguments*, ch. 5 at p. 138.

[18] Hence the judicial unwillingness to interfere with decisions of industrial tribunals discussed in H. Collins, 'Capitalist Discipline and Corporatist Law', (1982) 11 *ILJ* 78, 170.

openly the importance of popular opinion in the process of adjudication, including judicial review of inferior tribunals and executive decisions.[19]

Another way in which procedures introduce a democratic input to adjudication lies in the rules governing standing before a court. The opportunity to present arguments before a court permits a party to influence the outcome. To the extent that courts permit a wide range of persons to make representations, the decision process ventures closer to a consultative model of adjudication. The acceptance of class actions and *amicus curiae* briefs by the United States Supreme Court brings the adjudicative process close to a canvas of public opinion. In Britain, class actions are not accepted as such, but in English public law the rules governing standing have been liberalized to accommodate a similar form of action.[20] We are edging towards the position advocated by Craig that:

> a citizen should be entitled at the discretion of the court to bring any action alleging invalid public activity, except where it can be shown from a consideration of the statutory framework that the range of persons with standing was intended to be narrower than this. In this latter instance standing should be as of right and limited to the protected class, with the qualification that there may be cases where those with a protected legal interest do not adequately represent a wider group affected by the legislation; this wider group should be admitted at the discretion of the court.[21]

The British rules governing the admission of representations from an *amicus curiae* also appear less broad than the practice of American courts, but in a few cases parties who were not directly involved in the litigation have been permitted to present arguments concerning the public interest. For example, in *Wallersteiner* v. *Moir* (*No. 2*)[22] the Law Society argued before the Court of Appeal that contingency fees for legal services should not be permitted. By a majority, the Court agreed, relying also on the conclusions of two official reports on the subject—a Monopolies Commission Report and a Law Commission Report—thereby ensuring concordance with a wide range of informed opinion.

In concluding this brief survey of the consultative process at work in the system of adjudication common-law jurisdictions, let me stress that I am not suggesting that ordinary courts ignore the established rules and principles of the law and decide the case solely according to their perception of informed opinion. On the contrary, statutes and precedents present an im-

[19] For a critique of this pluralist interest model of judicial review, see R. B. Stewart, 'The Reformation of American Administrative Law', (1975) 88 *Harv. L.R.* 1667 and G. E. Frug, 'The Ideology of Bureaucracy in American Law', (1984) 97 *Harv. L.R.* 1277.

[20] Supreme Court Act 1981, s. 31 (3) and *R.* v. *Inland Revenue Commissioners, ex parte National Federation of Self-Employed and Small Businesses Ltd* [1982] AC 617.

[21] P. P. Craig, *Administrative Law* (London, 1983), pp. 459–60.

[22] [1975] 1 QB 373.

portant set of guides, and sometimes conclusive determinants, towards results. But where choices have to be made, because the law comprises broad standards, or because the normative guides conflict, or even because the law is out of touch with generally held moral standards, then courts appeal to informed opinion to guide and to justify the result. Opportunities for the consultative process to take place are often provided by the creation of specialized tribunals or the rules governing standing before a court. Where both the idealists and positivists have been mistaken is in their failure to notice the prevalence and significance of judicial appeals to public opinion in order to settle controversial claims.

But are they mistaken? Can idealists and positivists not allege that these surveys of public opinion contained in judicial decisions are either so rare that they are insignificant or, in any case, merely surplus baggage irrelevant to the real forces at work guiding the decision? On this question of significance, we only have to examine the cases without wearing the spectacles of conventional theories of the separation of powers in order to rebut the claim that surveys of opinion are rare. Suddenly we are swamped by references to informed opinion, as collected in treatises and learned articles, or evidenced by expert testimony, government pronouncements, and commercial practice. Furthermore these appeals to consensus opinion are not relegated to footnotes or tailpieces in judgments, but make their presence felt precisely at the watershed of the judgment. If anything appears to be surplus baggage, it is not the references to opinion, but the endless citation of precedents which so often prove inconclusive or unpersuasive.

A second reason for believing that these references to public opinion are significant is that in these hard cases the courts wish to reach a decision which is widely perceived to be legitimate and acceptable. The liberal theories of adjudication insist that this aim may only be achieved by ensuring that the decision accords with the ideal of the Rule of Law. Yet the evidence from the cases of constant references to public opinion indicates that the courts do not share this narrow view of the methods by which their decisions should be presented as legitimate and acceptable. After all, any decision-maker is inclined to elicit advice in order to improve his information before reaching a conclusion. Moreover, a decision-maker who seeks to enforce his views will find the job much easier if the standards are accepted by at least some of the persons concerned. These common-sense observations are not forgotten by the courts, despite their absence from liberal theories of adjudication. The courts are naturally anxious to discover public opinion in order to increase the chance that their decisions will be accepted and acted upon.

One further reason for thinking that references to public opinion are significant stems from our sociological understanding of the needs of lawyers. The legal profession, from whose ranks judges are drawn, prides itself upon its distinctive style of reasoning. It makes knowledge of the law and legal reasoning a prerequisite of membership of the profession. It defines its exclusive zone of competence by reference to this technical discourse. Lawyers have a strong incentive to preserve the importance of legal expertise since it provides the *raison d'être* of their profession. It is all the more striking, therefore, to find that legal judgments are littered with references to the opinions of other groups. Such deference to the opinions and modes of discourse of other professions runs against the grain for a lawyer. This strongly suggests that references to public opinion are not present in legal judgments haphazardly or irrelevantly. These opinions are introduced because they form the backbone of the process of legitimation of judicial decisions and are therefore inescapable despite the reservations of lawyers.

In sum, once we abandon the misleading assumption that judges are trying to operate a complex autonomous procedure for determining questions of law, then suddenly we notice a much wider range of materials at work in nearly every disputed case. We see courts regularly referring to what businessmen do and what they want to guide decisions. The attitudes of labour unions, a Royal Commission, and academic lawyers proved decisive in determining whether or not collective agreements should be legally enforceable in Britain. Courts defer to the practices and standards of government agencies even where there is no legal requirement to do so. Standards of reasonableness, fairness, and good faith, which freckle legal rules, are given content and specificity by investigating the practices and norms of those involved in the activity: a doctor is negligent when he fails to do what is normal for doctors to do; an employer dismisses an employee unfairly when he acts in a manner which departs from the normal standards of employers.[23] These references to social norms constitute the key step in the judicial reasoning towards a determination of the relevant legal requirements and prohibitions.

So far this critical theory of legal reasoning may not appear so radically different after all. It certainly resembles a number of theories of adjudication which hold that, once the legal rules no longer provide clear guidance, a judge should look to the consensus of opinion to guide his decision. Yet there are two important differences, which we must examine closely in order to grasp the radical message of critical theory.

In the first place, critical theory denies that consensus exists or is discoverable. When conventional theorists like Lord Devlin in appeal to a

[23] *Saunders* v. *Scottish National Camps Association* [1980] *IRLR* 174 (EAT); affirmed [1981] *IRLR* 277 (CS).

consensus of opinion, in order to guide legal reasoning,[24] they posit a shared set of values among the whole community which, once carefully distilled, reveal a consensus or agreement about the standards of justice. This consensus may then be relied upon to elaborate the law, thereby avoiding the charge that the courts are invading the proper realm of the legislature. The argument runs that the legislature has insufficient time to deal with all matters, so it leaves to the courts uncontroversial points to be settled according to the consensus. Whatever the merits of this theory as a variant of the liberal model of adjudication, it clearly fails as a description of legal reasoning.

Although courts refer to public opinion, they do not look widely enough to discover a consensus, even supposing one exists. Instead the courts examine the views of groups directly involved in the relevant activity. In relation to the case of sexual harassment, for example, the court did not consult the public at large, or even the whole group of women, or women's groups formed to combat sexual harassment. We saw that the court preferred to draw upon the opinions of specialists in the law of contracts and labour law. From these writings the court extrapolated a new climate of opinion about the proper relation of power between an employer and an employee. Similarly, in connection with the abortion issue, the Supreme Court examined closely the attitudes of the medical profession, other professions involved with health care, and the legal profession. Far from canvassing public opinion generally in order to discover a consensus of opinion about the legality of abortion, the court restriction its opinion poll to organized professional groups directly concerned with the operation of the law of abortion.

The pattern which emerges from these cases is one of courts canvassing the opinions of organized groups. Their opinion poll is highly biased in favour of groups which combine to advocate particular policies. Furthermore, in weighing conflicting opinions, the courts are influenced by the relative social prestige of the groups. Professional groups are accorded greater deference than others. Within the same type of employment, one group may have greater cachet than the others, and is looked to for setting the standards to be adopted by the law. For example, in *Miranda* v. *Arizona*,[25] the views of the FBI upon the rights of suspects when arrested were relied upon in preference to the opinions and practices of the less prestigious state police.

In sum, the first distinction between this critical theory of adjudication

[24] P. Devlin, *The Judge* (Oxford, 1979), Ch. 1; cf. Bell, *Policy Arguments*, ch. 7.

[25] 384 US 436 (1966). The practices of the FBI were described in a letter from the Solicitor-General in response to questions from the court. The Supreme Court also relied upon the English 'Judges' Rules', as described in [1960] *Crim. L. Rev.* 298–356, and [1964] *Crim. L. Rev.* 166–70.

and more traditional accounts is that the courts use a selective mechanism for determining public opinion which encourages organized professional groups to set the standards of the law. Far from relying upon a consensus of public opinion, the courts seek a measure of agreement between the organized professional groups which actively participate in the matter concerned in the case. In effect, the courts follow the opinions of the established élites.

This account fits into a broader analysis of the exercise of power. Unlike the traditional radical theories which, following Marx, emphasized the dominant position of owners of the means of production,[26] modern critical theory suggests that the most important exercises of power are those carried out by professional groups who, through organization and articulate exposition of their views, are able to set the standards of normal behaviour and assign the label of deviant behaviour to activities which are disapproved.[27] At the same time, they determine what is feasible, and suppress questions which might challenge their whole system of reasoning. Experts of all kinds rely upon their professional reputation and specialized technology to claim the insight necessary to set public standards of safety and propriety. The courts, by following these standards, both acknowledge the effectiveness of this exercise of power, and indirectly tend to confirm and legitimate it.

The second distinction between the critical theory of legal reasoning and the traditional consensus theories is that the critical theory also contains a radical programme of practical political action in order to democratize the institutions of adjudication. For once we realize how vital the input of professional groups is to the content of the law, we can see that legal standards may be challenged by the creation of rival organizations. These organizations should question the paradigms of the existing experts, and undermine their standards of common sense and reasonableness by pointing out the contingency of these standards upon the interests of these same professional groups. These rival organizations must seek to achieve the levels of technical competence and accomplished advocacy of the more established groups so that court are forced to give their attention to these alternative viewpoints. At all costs, these rival groups must avoid the labels of 'quacks', 'subversives', and the other epithets attached to deviants. Marginalization is the greatest danger, for once the court senses that it can afford to ignore the radical perspective because it lacks authority and good sense, then the struggle for power is both over and lost.

This political programme could be misinterpreted as an endorsement of

[26] S. Lukes, *Power: A Radical View* (London, 1974); H. Collins, *Marxism and Law* (Oxford, 1982), ch. 3.

[27] e.g. M. Foucault, *Power/Knowledge* (Brighton, 1980); cf. B. Fine, *Democracy and the Rule of Law* (London, 1984), pp. 189–202.

the shallow version of democracy contained in pluralist ideals. My argument, however, points in the opposite direction. Given that one element of any conceivable state apparatus suitable for a modern society will include institutions for adjudication over matters of private interest and public right, then this essay contains a plea for the maximum democratization of the process of adjudication. In urging the participation of organized groups in adjudication, I seek to expand the existing opportunities for popular sentiment to influence the outcome. At best these opportunities create a pale imitation of the ideal of democracy, but they comprise the kernel of a restructuring of institutional responsibilities with respect to adjudication which proposes a significant though feasible shift toward the realization of the values of equality, liberty, and self-determination.[28] In consequence, the claim of existing legislatures to superior authority by virtue of their responsiveness to interest groups appears largely unfounded and our critique of adjudicative institutions may provoke further criticism of the weaknesses of parliamentary democracy.

To discover that the pattern of institutional responsibilities is contingent upon our choices rather than upon an inevitable fact of politics liberates our imaginations to explore other institutional schemes. Far from shocking our intuitive notions of the right and the good, a style of democratic adjudication is merely a radical extension of the values of self-determination and consensual government, which already shape the form of legislatures. As a vital part of their practice, the courts already explore the dialectic created between the practical reasoning generated by appeals to democratic choice and the practical reasoning circumscribed by the ideal of the Rule of Law. At present, however, the value of democracy is distorted by an unwritten code which sytematically disvalues the contributions of unorganized, unprofessionalized groups and individuals. Critical theory suggests that marginal groups may transform the content of the legal order, and thus of the constitution of society itself, by imitating the professional advocacy of the existing generators of wisdom and norms of behaviour.

Indirectly, through this democratic theory of adjudication, critical theory challenges our standard conceptions of law. We must reject the pessimism which preaches that law necessarily involves a scheme of ranks and entitlements imposed from above by the established élites. In its daily application, the law is subject to critical review through practical reason, which is not shaped exclusively by the conservative ideals of the Rule of Law. The law is an open system, capable of receiving and endorsing any standards which have proved acceptable to the community. Although professional and technical élites enjoy considerable advantages in influencing the judicial

[28] Cf. R. M. Unger, 'The Critical Legal Studies Movement', (1983) 96 *Harv. L.R.* 561.

reasoning, the door is ajar for alternative conceptions of social norms to be presented. The élites exercise power through law, but their rules are vulnerable to renegotiation, and their powers subject to resistance. The open texture of legal norms makes the legal system a focus of struggle rather than an exclusive implement of the powerful. Instead of law being imposed from above under the guise of neutrality, it is a neutral form of social organization waiting to be seized and directed by the democratic wishes of the community.[29]

[29] I am indebted to Mary Stokes and Ken Simons for their criticisms of earlier drafts of this essay.

5

Fictions Ancient and Modern

PETER BIRKS

DEXTERITY with words is an essential characteristic of the legal mind. The popular view is that lawyers carry their verbal skill to unreasonable extremes. In lay usage the phrase 'legal fiction' often enough recalls this diabolic tendency. The worst excesses are brought on by the pressures of adversarial conflict, and in the past the rationality of the common law has undoubtedly suffered from its being worked out in court. However, textbooks, written for the most part by academic lawyers, have in the last hundred years become ever more important in shaping the law. This has been a gradual revolution in the English legal system, and it means that one lawmaking function, the production of textbooks, is now carried on in an atmosphere in which there is no longer any excuse for language which is other than lucid and honest.

I. FICTION AND FALSEHOOD

There are limits to the abuse of words which neither lawyers nor legislators should transgress. One such line is drawn by Gaius in his discussion of theft. Having described the consequences of manifest theft and the space of time and place within which a thief could still be described as having been caught red-handed, he observes that, even outside those limits, a ritual search for stolen property would, if successful, impose a liability as for manifest theft. That was due to a provision of the Twelve Tables. Gaius is then led to a forceful criticism of a classification engendered by the decemviral rule; some lawyers had made it the basis for saying that manifest theft was of two kinds, either natural or constructive, actual or deemed.

The habit of mind exemplified by those lawyers is instantly familiar even today. It consists in aligning under the same generic term not only facts within the ordinary meaning of that term but also others which are outside that ordinary meaning but which the law nevertheless finds it convenient to attract into the same category. When this is done, terms such as 'constructive' or 'implied in law' partially conceal the genesis of a fiction. A man can be said to have actual or constructive notice of a fact. Constructive notice is notice which he would have had if he had been reasonably alert.

We barely observe the fiction, but in truth the man who knows a fact constructively does not know it at all. Similarly, the term 'constructive trust' indicates at first sight a kind of trust. Only on closer inspection does the phrase concede that there is in truth no trust at all: the event of reposing trust has not happened, neither expressly nor impliedly, and not even by presumption; but another unnamed event has happened, to which important consequences must be attached just as though trust had indeed been reposed. In this example the fiction is doubly concealed, not only by the word 'constructive' but also by a certain ambivalence in the word 'trust', which properly denotes the event of reposing trust but easily slips from event to consequence, so as to denote the condition, however caused, of divided beneficial and bare title. This habit of mind creates false genera and prepares the way for divisions into species which are unsound. It thus builds error into the foundations of legal thought.

That is why Gaius responds to it with great and deliberate emphasis, making it plain that something fundamental is at stake, a methodological truth which transcends the immediate context. In the quotation which follows, the word 'law' in the translation is *lex* in Latin, and the specific reference is to the law of the Twelve Tables. Gaius' point is put very strongly: not even statute can so abuse words as to impose false classifications:

> However, the fact that the law provides that in these circumstances (sc. after ritual search) the theft should be manifest has led some writers to say that theft can be manifest either by nature or in law; in law in the case of which we are speaking, by nature on the facts which we discussed earlier. But it is more true to say that theft can only be manifest by nature. For the law cannot turn someone who is not a manifest thief into a manifest thief any more than it can turn someone into a thief who is not a thief at all, or take a man who is not an adulterer or a murderer and make him an adulterer or a murderer. What the law can indeed do is to make a man liable to the same penalty just as if he had committed theft or adultery or murder, even though in fact he has committed none of these.[1]

Gaius here takes it for granted that words have a proper meaning, at least to the extent that some attempted applications can be, and should be, condemned as contradictory. Red is red, and green is green. Convenience may sometimes suggest that red might be deemed green. But that would be an outright falsehood, and the temptation must be resisted. On the other hand there is no objection to attaching the consequences of green to red. You cannot say that red is green, but you can declare your intention to proceed as though red were green. This is the line between falsehood and fiction. The passage is characteristic of Gaius' mind. Tony Honoré, in the

[1] G. 3.194.

first of this pioneering biographies, introduced him as the jurist with some claim to be '*parens ac princeps* of the profession of academic lawyers' and rightly said of him 'in lucidity he is unrivalled'.[2] Gaius' lucidity is not merely a matter of style in expression. Nor would good Latin and self-effacing *moderatio* suffice to account for the sympathy between the jurist and his biographer. 'Tough, lawyerly, and independent' and also mentally equipped with the methods of philosophy,[3] he was committed to accurate legal cartography,[4] invaluable to understanding and attainable only by patient logic and careful classification.[5] Verbal falsehoods, rooted in confusion and likely to yield further errors, are anathema to lawyers of his cast of mind. Had Gaius been confronted with Holmes's famous aphorism—'The life of the law has not been logic; it has been experience.'[6]—he might not have been unduly shocked, since the jurists were well aware of the non-logical elements in legal development, which they called, compendiously, *utilitas*. But he would certainly have added that the life of legal science could not be long sustained if ever the search for verbal errors and fallacies was given up.

As a matter of observable history Anglo-American common law has in its development been less firmly committed to formal rationality. Indeed the sentence with which Holmes follows the famous statement which has just been quoted recognizes the role of the very forces—intuitions, feelings, and prejudices—which verbal reasoning seeks to control and which the Gaian mentality, and no less the rule of law itself as opposed to the rule of judges, require to be curbed: 'The felt necessities of the time, the prevalent moral and political theories, intuitions of public policy, avowed or unconscious, even the prejudices which judges share with their fellow-men, have had a good deal more to do than the syllogism in determining the rules by which men should be governed.'[7]

With whatever combinations of logic and experience, the substantive law of both systems developed in large measure within the context of forms of action. In simple terms this means that there was a list of claims claimable by plaintiffs and that detailed answers to legal questions built up as expositions of the texts of those claims. It was necessary to say what facts would substantiate them. The answers were not born whole but were worked out slowly, and at different times for different actions. Stripped down to essentials, the Roman *vindicatio* said 'That *res* is mine!' and the *condictio* said

[2] A. M. Honoré, *Gaius* (Oxford, 1962).

[3] Ibid., pp. 97 ff.

[4] For logic as a source of intellectual 'geography', see A. G. Guest, 'Logic in the Law' in id. (ed.), *Oxford Essays in Jurisprudence*, (Oxford, 1961), 176 at pp. 178, 197.

[5] e.g. G. 2. 14; 3. 88–91; 3. 131; 3. 183.

[6] O. W. Holmes, *The Common Law* (Boston, 1881) p. 1. That logic might have to be defended, Gaius would have found beyond belief. Cf. Guest, op. cit.

[7] Holmes, loc. cit.

'You ought to give me that *res*!'[8] It is not to be supposed that any but obvious substantiating facts could at first be listed.[9] Similarly stripped down, the English action for money had and received said 'You are indebted to me in £100 for so much money had and received to my use!' We know that it was not till 1760 that the substantiating facts were listed.[10]

Innovation in a system dominated by forms of action can happen in two ways: either by extending the list of facts which will substantiate an established claim (innovation behind the form of action) or by admitting a new or modified claim (innovation in the form of action). Both types of innovation can entail recourse to fictions. But fictions behind a form of action are concealed falsehoods which offend Gaius' principle that words must be used honestly. On the other hand fictions in a form of action are are neither concealed nor dishonest. They do not offend Gaius' principle. English pleading fictions are of the former kind, Roman of the latter. In the next section one detailed English example is set out.

II. FICTIONS BEHIND 'MONEY PAID'

In the common law fictions were generated behind the forms of action whenever judges held that the propositions recited by plaintiffs in the familiar forms of claim could be substantiated by proof of facts other than those actually recited. The mechanism itself is easy to understand even if the forces and intellectual assumptions behind its use are complex: the plaintiff advances a routine claim which recites A, B, C, and D; he is allowed to win on proving only B and C, or perhaps B, C, and Z. The substance of the matter is a judicial determination that B and C, or B, C, and Z, ought in law to give rise to the same consequences already attributed to A, B, C, and D. However, because this determination is reached behind the recitation of A, B, C, and D, and because plaintiffs in subsequent cases continue to make the old recitation even when intending to advance the new facts, the form of the development is fictionalization of A and D. The contradiction between the facts as recited and the facts as proved can, if it is questioned, be resolved by 'implication in law'; that is, by deeming. Many examples could be given. Ejectment and trover are famous. Money paid is

[8] The abbreviations state the effect of the *intentiones* only, and in direct speech. For the full formulae, O. Lenel, *Das Edictum Perpetuum* (3rd edn.), (Leipzig, 1927, repr. 1956), pp. 185–6, 237–40.

[9] *Pro Roscio Comoedo* proves the scope of 'You owe me' still unfixed for Cicero, whose speech would be largely unintelligible against the closed list of later *causae debendi*. A priori, it is obvious anyhow that people began to make such claims before they or the list could enumerate all the constitutive facts. It is an advanced, not a primitive, jurisprudence that can close the list. Watson, however, makes *mutuum* the only original *causa debendi*: Alan Watson, 'The Evolution of Law: The Roman System of Contracts', (1984) 2 *Law and Hist. Rev.* 1; cf. Liebs below, p. 165, who, however, makes an exclusive link with *stipulatio*.

[10] *Moses* v. *Macferlan* (1760) 2 Burr. 1005; 1 W.Bl. 219.

less well known, but it provides an excellent model, not only because its fictionalization is easily described but also because it has a curious civilian twist, which brings the common law and Roman law into immediate contact and, as it happens, joins the ancient and the modern part of this essay. It comes, moreover, from an area which Dr Baker has described as providing 'the most striking example of the way in which the common law could be developed, whatever the formal procedural restaints, and however devious the subterfuges needed to evade them, in order to achieve equity'.[11] That is a compliment of which Gaius could not have approved.

The action for money paid to the use of the defendant was a species of *indebitatus assumpsit*. Within the category of actions on the case, *assumpsit* was the action on a promise, *indebitatus assumpsit* was the same action when brought to recover a debt, and the action for money paid was an *indebitatus assumpsit* brought where the particular cause of the defendant's indebtedness was that the plaintiff had paid out money to a third party on his behalf ('to his use'). It is important to grasp first its 'natural' scope: according to its wording as recited, it lay where the defendant had (*a*) requested the plaintiff to pay the money to the third party, and (*b*) promised to repay him. Late in the eighteenth century it was none the less held that a plaintiff could win on facts which included neither request nor promise.

Before going further we must set out the words under discussion. It is tempting to abbreviate, but the few moments saved are not worth the loss of authenticity. With the minimum of excisions, therefore, the plaintiff's proposition was as follows:

> Thomas Eeles complains of Thomas Stiles in the custody of the marshall, etc. for this, to wit, that ... whereas the said Thomas Stiles afterwards, to wit, the 29th September in the eighth year of the reign of the now Queen, at London aforesaid in the parish and ward aforesaid, was indebted to the same Thomas Eeles in another £80 of lawful money of this kingdom, for so much money by the said Thomas Eeles for the said Thomas Stiles, and at the special instance and request of the said Thomas Stiles, before then expended, laid out and paid; and the said Thomas Stiles being so therein indebted, the said Thomas Stiles in consideration thereof afterwards, to wit, the same 29th day of September in the eighth year abovesaid, at London aforesaid in the parish and ward aforesaid, assumed upon himself, and then and there faithfully promised, that he the said Thomas Stiles the said £80 last mentioned to the same Thomas Eeles, when he should be thereto afterwards required, would well and faithfully pay and content: nevertheless the said Thomas Stiles his promise and assumption aforesaid not regarding, but contriving and fraudulently intending the same Thomas Eeles in this behalf craftily and subtilly to defraud, the same £80 or any penny thereof to the same Thomas Eeles hath not yet paid, nor him for the same hath hitherto any ways contented, although to do it he the same Thomas Stiles afterwards, to wit, the 2nd day of October in the year abovesaid

[11] J. H. Baker, *An Introduction to English Legal History* (2nd edn. London, 1979), p. 300.

by the same Thomas Eeles was required; whereby the same Thomas Eeles says that he is prejudiced and has damage to the value of £80. And thereof he produces suit, etc.[12]

This can be broken down into its three principal parts; (*a*) the plaintiff paid out money at the defendant's express, which is what is meant by 'special', instance and request; (*b*) the defendant promised to pay; (*c*) the defendant wickedly refused to pay. It is convenient to take out first, because we shall not dwell on them, the fictions in the last of these three parts. The words recite a fraudulent breach, but the plaintiff actually only has to show non-payment. This is a vestige of an early exercise in fictionalization. It goes back to the fifteenth century and is common to the allegations of breach in all actions of *assumpsit*. It belongs to the story by which *assumpsit* came to lie for all types of breach of undertaking, both for misfeasances and non-feasances. The plaintiff's fear was that he might be driven back to the nominate action of covenant if he could allege nothing more than a bare breach of promise, that being the very wrong for which the writ of covenant existed, and the law being that in order to sue for that wrong you had to show a covenant in writing. Hence, the plaintiff in *assumpsit* had to allege a more elaborate wrong. When it was finally accepted that the younger action on the case, innominate in origin and therefore dangerously boundless but gradually settling down and acquiring names and limits,[13] would lie, without dispute, even for the very wrong for which covenant lay, the allegations of deceit were not dropped but simply denatured by the courts. The allegations of fraud could not be traversed. In other words, there was no defence to the effect that one had indeed failed to pay, but not with crafty and subtle intent.[14]

We can now turn to the promise and the request. Some causes of indebtedness include at least a genuine implied promise to pay, and others do not. 'Will you sell me this book for £10?; or 'Will you lend me £10?'; or 'Will you pay John Doe £10 for me?' In all these cases, even though no word of promising may have been used, there is no fiction in saying that, if you comply, I have promised to pay you. On the other hand, if an event happens which triggers a feudal or customary imposition such that I am obliged to pay you £10, or if I intercept £10 by usurping the profits of your

[12] This example is taken from Lilly, but it is compounded from two of his precedents: John Lilly, *A Collection of Modern Entries* (3rd edn. London, 1758), pp. 24 and 43.

[13] The generality of the action on the case, feared by the Common Pleas as subversive of the acquired structures of the legal mind, is thus quaintly caught by William Fulbecke: 'Indeed as D. Stephens his water was fit for many diseases, and yet never had any special name but was generallie tearmed Doctor Stephens his water: so likewise an Action upon the case stretcheth as a remedic against many offences: yet it hath no other name than Action upon the Case' *Parallele*, bk. 2, 16^{r}. For this work see further below, at n. 33.

[14] J. H. Baker, *Spelman's Reports*, vol. ii (1977) 94 *Selden Society* 255–75; *Introduction*, cit. n. 11 above, pp. 275–9: S. F. C. Milsom, *Historical Foundations of the Common Law*, (2nd edn. London, 1981), pp. 322–38.

office, or if I receive £10 for a consideration which fails, my duty to pay you is imposed on me willy-nilly: to say that I have promised to pay in such circumstances could only be a fiction. We can therefore distinguish promissory from non-promissory causes of indebtedness.

So far as concerns the promissory causes, *Slade's Case*[15] marked the triumph, in 1602, of the Queen's Bench view that *assumpsit* could be brought on such 'contracts executory' without the need to prove any promise other than the promise impliedly inherent in the transaction itself. The opposing view, of the Common Pleas, had not been that the promise implicative was unreal or fictitious but that, without some fact additional to the minimum debt facts, the action on the case could not be brought, and the plaintiff would have to use the old nominate action of Debt.[16] It followed from the triumph of the Queen's Bench view that, from the beginning of the seventeenth century, a plaintiff who could establish a promissory cause of indebtedness did not have to prove that the debtor defendant in addition *assumpsit super se* to pay his debt. But the *assumpsit* which such plaintiffs recited was none the less not a fiction: the promise was proved in and with the debt facts. According to its natural tenor, the action for money paid falls into that category of *indebitatus assumpsit*. In requesting the plaintiff to pay on his behalf, the defendant impliedly, but genuinely, promises to reimburse him. Hence the natural scope of the action entails no fictionalization of the promise or the antecedent request.

However, we have at this stage to note that, in relation to non-promissory causes of indebtedness, the courts of the Restoration period held that even plaintiffs who could prove such debts could claim them in the action of *indebitatus assumpsit*. Although the facts giving rise to such indebtedness necessarily included no trace of a promise to pay, the courts accepted that nothing but the indebtedness had to be shown. That is, they fictionalized the allegation of a promise. Thus, in these cases of non-promissory debt, *indebitatus assumpsit* began to be brought on the basis of a fictitious promise.[17] However, this development, important as it was in other sectors of *indebitatus assumpsit* and especially in money had and received, had, on the face of things, no relevance at all to the action for money paid, because the cause of indebtedness recited in that action was, and seemingly could only be, promissory: the indebtedness arose because the defendant expressly requested the plaintiff to pay and, at least impliedly, promised to repay.

[15] *Slade* v. *Morley* (1597–1602) 4 Co. Rep. 92; J.H. Baker, 'New Light on Slade's Case', [1971] *CLJ* 51; D. Ibbetson, 'Sixteenth Century Contract Law: Slade's Case in Context', [1984] *OJLS* 295.

[16] J.H. Baker, *Spelman*, vol. ii, pp. 297–8 and [1971] 30 *CLJ* 213; A.W.B. Simpson, *A History of the Common Law of Contract* (Oxford, 1975), pp. 281–315.

[17] e.g. *Howard* v. *Wood* (1679) Show. K. b. 21, 2 Lev. 245, Freeman 478; *Shuttleworth* v. *Garnett* (1688) 3 Mod. 20; *City of London* v. *Goree* (1677) 2 Levinz 174; *Martin* v. *Sitwell* (1691) 2 Show. K. B. 156; *Lamine* v. *Dorrell* (1701) 2 Ld. Raym. 1216.

However, the courts fictionalized the request in the action for money paid and thus made the action available to plaintiffs who had had no communication with the defendants on whose behalf they claimed to have paid out money. That is, the fictionalization of the request made the action reach into the area of non-promissory indebtedness and thus brought with it the need to rely on the Restoration doctrine that *indebitatus assumpsit* could be brought for any debt, whether or not the defendant could be shown to have promised to pay. Fictionalization of the promise in the action for money paid thus flowed immediately from fictionalization of the request.

This type of development can be illustrated clearly and shortly from a case at the very end of the eighteenth century, *Exall* v. *Partridge* (1799).[18] The true facts were that the plaintiff had left his carriage on the defendant's premises to be repaired. The defendant's landlord had then taken the carriage into his possession in exercise of his right to distrain for arrears of rent. In order to redeem his carriage, the plaintiff had therefore had to pay to the landlord the amount of the rent owed by the defendant. There was a further complication which need not concern us, namely that there were actually three defendants, of whom two had assigned their interest to the third before the landlord levied this distress. The example can be more clearly presented if that issue is cut out and we simply say that the plaintiff had paid the defendant's rent in order to obtain the release of property lawfully siezed by the defendant's landlord. He had undoubtedly paid out money to the use of the defendant, but not at the latter's 'special instance and request' and not in circumstances supporting any inference of a promise to repay.

Nevertheless the court held that the plaintiff's action for money paid was entitled to succeed. One argument was that the necessary request and promise could be implied if the plaintiff had conferred a benefit on the defendant. That failed. But a narrower proposition was upheld: the plaintiff could substantiate the allegations of request and promise by proving not only that by his payment out he had benefited the defendant but also that he had not done so voluntarily. And on these facts he could show that he had not conferred the benefit voluntarily by pointing to the lawful compulsion brought to bear on him by the landlord.

III. HIDDEN RATIONALITY?

Isolation of a single example draws attention to the bizarre nature of this mode of legal development. It breaks the Gaian rule against falsehoods in

[18] (1799) 8 TR 308; 3 Esp. 8. Cf. *Jenkins* v. *Tucker* (1788) 1 H.Bl. 90.

lawyers' use of language, and there is no denying that it is not admirable. With hindsight we can see that what was done in *Exall* v. *Partridge* was an extension to the action for money paid of what *Moses* v. *Macferlan*[19] had already consolidated in another department of *indebitatus assumpsit*, within the action for money had and received. The defendant in *Exall* had received a different kind of benefit—not money but the product of money paid to a third party—and the plaintiff had responded to a different kind of factor negativing voluntariness—the seizure of his carriage. But, at a higher level of generality, the principle is indeed the same. Whether the judges were aware of that analytical consistency is a difficult question. Indeed it is part of the criticism of this curious mode of law-making that it tends to conceal the answers to questions of that kind. At all events, to explain the fictionalization of money paid as an extension of what had already happened in money had and received only pushes the question one stage further back: what rationale if any did the courts have for allowing plaintiffs to pursue by the action on promises claims which had nothing to do with promises? Was the fiction merely an example of bizarre empiricism, or did it in fact have some intellectual justification?

By 1799 the courts had the support of Blackstone's published doctrine that it was right to impute promises which ought in justice to have been made.[20] Whether Blackstone perceived this as convenient, and therefore recognized it as fictitious, or as a philosophical truth, in which case he would have resisted its being described as a fiction, is not clear and cannot be investigated here. Where did this doctrine of Blackstone's come from? It is certainly not a reflection of a special sensitivity, overt or intuitive, to the notion of benefit-based liability—that is, to the efficacy of 'benefit received' as a source of obligation[21]—because it extends to involuntary obligations which have nothing to do with such receipts.[22] It seems on the contrary to have been borrowed directly from the continental civilians, many of whom interpreted the Roman category of obligations *quasi ex contractu* as a category of constructive contract, and some of whom, to be followed in this by Blackstone himself, carried those constructive contracts back to the 'social contract' on which the institution of property, and society itself, were deemed by some to rest.[23] If there was an intellectual backing for the pragmatic extension of *assumpsit* into the field of involuntary obligations, it was this civilian doctrine that the genus 'contract' divided between 'true

[19] Above, n. 11.

[20] W. Blackstone, *Commentaries on the Law of England* (London, 1765–9) Bk. 3, pp. 155–66.

[21] As in P. S. Atiyah, *The Rise and Fall of Freedom of Contract* (Oxford, 1979), pp. 181ff.

[22] Cf. *Shuttleworth* v. *Garnett* and *City of London* v. *Goree* cit. n.16 above. Atiyah, loc. cit., dismisses these too summarily, with *Starke* v. *Cheeseman* (1699) 1 Ld.Raym. 538.

[23] As Blackstone himself, loc. cit. n. 20 above; cf. Pufendorf, *Of the Law of Nature and Nations*, trans. Kennet, 3rd edn. (London, 1717) 4. 4. 4; 3. 6. 2. See also following note.

contracts' and 'constructive contracts'.[24] Most of the civilians who subscribed to that doctrine exhibited another common feature of the legal mind, namely the extreme and genuine difficulty of escaping the language and the categories which have been sanctioned by earlier authority, even when change is demonstrably necessary. The most powerful force which held them in its grip was that the authority of the *Institutes* asserted the existence of the category of obligations *quasi ex contractu* and gave it that perplexing name.

IV. A LARGER FICTION EARLIER EXCLUDED

We saw that in *Exall* v. *Partridge* the court rejected the more extreme proposition that if the plaintiff had benefited the defendant that alone would justify the 'implication' of the request and promise. A contrary decision on this point would in effect have made the action for money paid do the work of the *actio negotiorum gestorum contraria*, by which one had voluntarily done something beneficial for another without any mandate to do it could recover the expenses of his intervention. We know, of course, that two hundred years earlier the common law decided, in *Hunt* v. *Bate*[25] and *Lampleigh* v. *Braithwaite*,[26] that an unrequested 'voluntary courtesy' would not be a good consideration to support a subsequent promise to pay something for it. That is the rule against past consideration. There is a fine line between the question whether one should pay the expenses of an intervention on one's behalf and the further question answered by these cases whether one should pay something for such an intervention if one subsequently promises to do so. And the line is especially fine where, as in *Hunt* v. *Bate*, the something allegedly promised is an indemnity against the expenses. It is therefore interesting to ask whether people at the time actually perceived the rule against past consideration specifically as the exclusion of the quasi-contractual *actio negotiorum gestorum contraria*. There are some indications that they did.

First, there is a hint in *Hunt* v. *Bate* itself. The defendant's servant had been arrested and imprisoned for a trespass. The plaintiff and another stood bail for him. Thereafter the defendant allegedly promised to indemnify the plaintiff against any damages and costs that should be adjudged against

[24] For the civilian doctrine see P. Birks and G. McLeod, 'The Implied Contract Theory of Quasi-Contract: Civilian Opinion Current in the Century before Blackstone', (1986) *OJLS* 1ff, which shows that, *inter alios*, Grotius, Pufendorf, Vinnius, Huber, Voet, and Heineccius subscribed to this teaching; that Stair, Domat, Pothier, and, in England, Wood did not. Simpson, op. cit. n. 16 above, p. 489, dismisses civilian influence on the common law much too swiftly.

[25] (1568) Dyer 272a, pl. 31; cf. also pl. 32, and *Oneley* v. *Earl of Kent* (1576) Dyer 356. Simpson, op. cit. n. 15 above, 450–8.

[26] (1616) Hob. 105; 1 Brownl. & Golds. 7; 7 Moo. K. B 866.

him. In the end the plaintiff had had to pay £31. Apart from the alleged express promise after the event, this was a paradigm case of *negotiorum gestio*. The hint that it was perceived to be such is found in the reason given for the plaintiff's intervention: he did it in order that the affairs of the master should not be neglected,[27] which is the very same reason which is given in Justinian's *Institutes* for allowing the *actio negotiorum gestorum contraria*: 'ne absentium ... deserentur negotia; quae sane nemo curaturus esset, si de eo quod quis impendisset nullam habiturus esset actionem.'[28] Undeniably, this could have been a coincidence, but it looks like a deliberate preparation to argue that the defendant was already bound to indemnify the plaintiff before he promised to do so.[29]

Secondly, John Cowell's *Institutiones Juris Anglicani* in 1605 seems to indicate debate between common lawyers and civilians on this point. Under the Justinianic heading 'De obligationibus quae quasi ex contractu nascuntur',[30] which in the 1651 translation significantly became 'Of Obligations which arise from Implyed Contracts',[31] he observes that in English law the *gestor* is remitted to the conscience and honour of the person whose business has been managed. But he is obviously surprised by this, for he interjects a qualification, 'si verum mihi dixerunt nonnulli iurisperiti'. And then he goes on to express even more surprise—'quod magis videtur mirandum'—that sometimes a man can incur liability in trespass by doing a good deed for another, as by entering another's land to drive off a neighbour's cattle or to save a rector's tithe.[32]

Finally, while Cowell indisputably evidences actual communication between common lawyers and civilians on this point at the beginning of the seventeenth century, from the same period William Fulbecke gives us an actual example, albeit imaginary, of a dialogue between a gentleman of inquiring mind, a civilian, a canonist, and a common lawyer.[33] The evidence of this fascinating but erratic work is not easy to assess. It is certain that *negotiorum gestio* was present in Fulbecke's mind and that he looked to the action of account to do the work of the *actio negotiorum gestorum*

[27] Dyer 272a, tr.: 'in consideration that the business of the master should not go undone'.

[28] J. 3. 27. 1.

[29] As the forensic tactics fell out, the defendant traversed the *assumpsit* and lost before the jury (no sure indication that he actually promised); he then moved in arrest of judgment, taking the consideration point. It is not impossible that the plaintiff never intended to base himself on an express promise but only on the *negotiorum gestio*.

[30] *Institutiones Juris Anglicani* (London, 1605) 193 (=3. 27). The author was Regius Professor of Civil Law at Cambridge, 1594–1611. See B. P. Levack, *The Civil Lawyers in England, 1603–41* (London, 1973), pp. 20, 103–6, 221.

[31] Published in London 'by order of Parliament', 1651, at p. 203. This edition not only translates (sometimes very poorly) but also adjusts governmental references to the altered times.

[32] Ibid., citing *Malverer* v. *Spinke*, Dyer 36, pl. 38.

[33] William Fulbecke, *The Parallele or Conference of the Civill Law, the Canon Law and the Common Law of this Realme of England*, in two parts (London, 1601 and 1602).

directa, the action against rather than by the *gestor*.[34] There is in this part of the discussion an important passage which foreshadows the later use of money had and received (itself drived directly from that sector in the action of debt in which debt was brought in lieu of account) as the vehicle for recovering the proceeds of usurpation of office and waiver of tort. Thus the gentleman Nomomathes asks: 'I praie you let me know whether anie persons be accomptable by the mere and sole operation, and enforcement of Law.' To which part of the answer of Anglonomophylax, the common lawyer, is: 'And the same Law seemeth it to be to Mast. Brooke[35] where a man presumptuouslie and of his owne head undertaketh to be my bailie, a writ of Accompt will lie in a such a case: But if he enter to his owne use, there it seemeth (saith he) that a writ of Accompt will not lie: for there Ne unques son Receivor pur accompt render, is a good plea.' This evidence of reflection on the *actio neg. gest. directa*, against an intervener, encourages one to hope for an unequivocal address to the question of the action to be brought by the gestor for his expenses. However, although Fulbecke, in the debate on the action on the case, does cite *Hunt* v. *Bate* to support the proposition by Anglonomophylax that 'our law meddleth with no contractes, but such as you have tearmed proper contractes',[36] the context disappointingly makes it impossible to do more than suspect that what he had specifically in mind was that *Hunt* v. *Bate* had excluded the gestor's claim under 'improper contract' of *negotiorum gestio*. Codicgnostes, the civilian, had advanced a division between contracts, improper contracts, and most improper contracts, apparently distinguishing only between bilateral obligations, unilateral obligations, and discharges (i.e. no obligations). It is not clear, however, whether the *condictio indebiti*, and with it the other quasi-contractual obligations, were intended to be included within one or other of the two 'improper' categories.[37]

V. FICTIONS WITHOUT FALSEHOOD

We have been looking at the action for money paid as a typical example of the common law's use of fiction in legal development. The characteristic feature has been willingness to press words beyond their natural limits, so that an allegation of A can be satisfied by proof of B. Behind the specific

[34] Ibid., Part 2, 49ff. To confirm the presence of *negotiorum gestio*, it is necessary to see that from p. 43 Fulbecke is treating an appointed bailiff or receiver as a mandatary, hence the unappointed as a *gestor*.

[35] Citing Brooke's 'Abridgement,' 1573—published after his death—s.v. 'Accompt', pl. 8.

[36] Fulbecke, op. cit., Part 2, 17^{v}.–19^{v}.

[37] Construed strictly A's answer would even deny an English liability for *mutuum*, but this cannot have been intended. For the continuing link between *mutuum* and *indebitum*, Cowell, op. cit. 3. 15, adapting J. 3. 14. 1.

example we have identified a flimsy rationale: here the 'implications' could be justified to a certain extent because there was learned authority teaching that involuntary obligations arising without wrongdoing could be referred to a quasi-contract, understood in the sense of constructive contract or 'improper contract'. That was what the continental civilians thought. Although Theophilus was responsible for coining the substantive 'quasi-contract'[38] in his *Paraphrase* of Justinian's *Institutes*, which he himself helped to prepare,[39] there is no evidence that he or anyone of his time or earlier used that term or the adverbial phrase from which he coined it—*quasi ex contractu*—to mean 'sort of contract' or 'deemed contract'. On the contrary, it meant 'as though upon a contract' and asserted that there was none. In other words the Roman term did not affirm the deemed existence of something non-existent but simply said that the consequences of one type of event were the same as the consequences of another. Thus, there is no falsehood in saying that the consequences of a mistaken payment are the same as if a loan had been made[40] or that the consequences of *negotiorum gestio* are the same as if a mandate had been acted on.[41] It is only when the further step is taken of inferring identity of substance from symmetry of consequence that the boundary is crossed between fiction and falsehood. Roman fictions do not cross that line, exemplified as it is in the distinction between '*quasi ex contractu*' and 'quasi-contract'.

Roman fictions are common in two contexts, in pleadings and in legislation. Their function is the same in both, namely to extend a parcel of knowledge which is fixed and safe: we know exactly what happens when X is the case; now that Y is the case, we will proceed in exactly the same way, 'as if the case were X'. This is economical, cautious, and rigorous. For the legislator it is a weapon against what we can nowadays identify as Road Traffic Act mentality, the ruthless pursuit and exploitation of verbal accidents. The style of Republican statutes attests not merely respect for words but an undefeated will to control their power—the legal mind, some might say, at its verbal best. Fictions in legislative drafting are not so eye-catching as in pleadings. They occur as convenient abbreviations, often using one or other variant of the form 'siremps ius lexque esto quasi . . .' (let right and law be the very same as if . . .).'[42] Two examples will be given.

[38] *Paraphrase*, 3. 27. 3, 5; 4.5 pr. This is noted by Nicholas, *Introduction to Roman Law* (Oxford, 1962), p. 224, n. 2.

[39] Tony Honoré, *Tribonian* (London, 1978), pp. 187ff.

[40] J. 3. 27. 6; D. 44. 7. 5. 3, Gaius 3 *aureorum*.

[41] J. 3. 27. 1; D. 44. 7. 5 pr., Gaius 3 *aureorum*.

[42] Apart from the examples in the text, instances occur in *FIRA*, v. i. p. 83 (*lex Latina tabulae Bantinae*), 100 (*lex Acilia repetundarum*), 109 (*lex agraria*), 133 (*lex Cornelia de XX quaestoribus*), 175 (*lex Rubria*), 188 (*lex Ursonensis*), 201 (*lex civitatis Narbonensis de flamonio provinciae*).

The energetic and practical Frontinus, anxious to set down the legal framework for the safekeeping of the city's water-supply,[43] gives the full text of the *lex Quinctia de aquaeductibus* of 8 BC. This first deals with damage to the system. On one who 'sciens dolo malo foraverit, ruperit, foranda rumpendave curaverit peiorave fecerit', the *lex* imposes a fine of 100,000 sesterces together with an obligation to make good: 'id omne sarcire, reficere, restituere, aedificare, ponere, et celere demolire', all to the satisfaction of the *curator aquarum* or, him failing, the *praetor peregrinus*. The *lex* then deals with the case where the miscreant is a slave. It imposes the fine of 100,000 sesterces on the master, without mention of any obligation to make good, precisely the kind of doubt-engendering omission avoided where a fiction is used to keep consequences symmetrical. Presumably this omission was indeed deliberate.

The *lex* then turns to obstruction: 'ne quis in eo loco post hanc legem rogatam quid opponito, molito, obsaepito, figito, statuito, ponito, conlocato, arato, serito, neve in eum quid immittito praeterquam eorum faciendorum, reponendorum causa, quod hac lege licebit, oportebit.' Here we see the legislator's mind on evasive verbal arguments. He even feels bound expressly to save the right to do repairs. In the problems he foresees with a cavilling bar, we can instantly recognize the kind of arguments which necessitated a firm generalization of the Aquilian triplet, *urere*, *frangere*, and *rumpere*—not without some surprise that the *veteres* got away with it.[44] Out of court, reason evidently prevailed, with sufficient authority then to prevail in court as well.

Here, once the legislator has sufficiently described the obstructions against which he is aiming, he proceeds to attach the consequences by means of an economical fiction: 'qui adversus ea quid fecerit, siremps lex, ius causaque omnium rerum omnibus esto, atque uti esset esseve oporteret, si is adversus hanc legem rivum, specum rupisset forassetve.' The consequences, attached with perfect symmetry and without the least opportunity for last-minute cavilling, are to be the same as for *forare* and *rumpere*.[45] This is wonderfully determined craftsmanship, albeit the draftsman is on the defensive. That is to say, he knows that he himself must meet the challenge of later fierce attacks by advocates upon his work and cannot rely on the law itself to impose a standard of reasonableness upon them.

One further example, in outline, to confirm the regularity of the technique: the *lex Rubria*[46] deals with a man who confesses a money debt *in*

[43] *De Aquis Urbis Romae*, 2. 129. Frontinus, consul three times, in AD 74, 98, and 100, was *praetor urbanus* in 70 and became *curator aquarum* in 97.

[44] D. 9. 2. 27. 14, Ulpian 18 *ad edictum*: 'inquit lex ruperit. rupisse verbum fere omnes veteres sic intellexerunt corruperit'.

[45] Further provisions save certain rights and privileges and confer jurisdiction of the *curator*: *De Aquis*, 2. 129 fin. = *FIRA*, i. 154.

[46] 49 or 41 BC: F. J. Bruna, *Lex Rubria* (Leiden, 1972), p. 322.

iure and does not pay, or who does not answer at all. The *lex* provides;

Let the law, right, and legal condition for all persons and in respect of all matters then be the same as it would be or ought to be if he who confessed or failed to answer to that matter, or did not defend himself by *sponsio* or *iudicium* as he ought, was or had been rightly and lawfully condemned in that sum to the plaintiff suing in his own name or to the person to whom the money ought to have been paid.[47]

Here the technique is the same as in the previous example, but less admirable because more neurotic. You can see how, in the draftsman's mind, for each gap he closes two more open. Moreover, he cannot even quite bring himself to trust the logical economies which the technique offers.[48]

These statutory *siremps* clauses are a far cry from the English fictions exemplified in 'money paid', so far indeed that they are barely recognizable as fictions at all. Yet the fictions in Roman formulary pleadings are of the same kind as in the *siremps* clauses, and no less different from the English falsehoods. They do not direct the *iudex* to find false facts but simply arrange a symmetry of consequence between the case to be tried and other facts already understood. The minds behind the formulary fictions operate on the same assumptions and with the same skills as produced the legislative style which we have just been looking at.[49]

So much is this true that, though the exercise would of course spoil the careful duality between civil and praetorian law, one could for every formulary fiction construct a *siremps* clause by which the same innovation would have been introduced had it been introduced by *lex* and not by argument *in iure* before the praetor. Take, for example, the *actio Publiciana*, of which Gaius says, giving a shortened example of the formula:

This action is given to a person who has not yet usacapted a *res* which was delivered to him *ex iusta causa* and who, being out of possession, makes a claim for it. He cannot advance an *intentio* to the effect that the *res* is his by Quiritary title. The fiction is therefore used that he has usucapted the *res*, and he thus advances an *intentio* which proceeds as though he had become owner *ex iure Quiritium*, in this way: 'Let the judge be appointed. If Aulus Agerius had possessed for a year the slave whom he bought and had delivered to him, then if that slave, the subject of this action, ought to be his by Quiritary title,' and so on.[50]

Gaius says that there is a fiction of *usucapio*—fingitur rem usucepisse—which is certainly too sweeping, since it would carry the plaintiff to immediate

[47] Cap. 21, 11. 10–15, *FIRA* i. 173.

[48] Much more extreme, cap. 20, 42–52.

[49] This is especially brought home by the formulae of the *Tabula Contrebiensis*, which see below, n. 57; also by the inclusion of model *formulae ficticiae* in the *lex Rubria*, cap. 20, 11. 20–40 (= *FIRA* i. 171–2).

[50] G. 4. 36, an abbreviated example. See Lenel, *Edictum*, pp. 169–73.

victory. At the most there is a fiction of the period of time. But even the notion of a fiction is a figure of speech, since nothing is deemed or constructed contrary to truth. This is only the praetor saying, in effect: *Si quis hominem emit et is ei traditus est, siremps lex, ius, causaque omnium rerum omnibusque esto atque uti esset esseve oporteret si is eum hominem anno possedisset*. But this version is somewhat too strong, since it allows the recipient to defeat the *dominus* in all cases and not only in the case where the *dominus* himself delivered. It has to be limited, as for instance in this way: *Si quis hominem emit et is ei traditus est, de eo qui emit deque eo qui tradidit, siremps*, etc. A draftsman as anxious as the one who worked on the *lex Rubria* would certainly go further. He would want to qualify *omnibus* in the next line, to exclude the owner not party to the delivery from the effect of the fiction. This exercise, the primary aim of which is to show that the formulary fiction is not essentially different from a statutory *siremps* clause, shows that the Publician action matches the cast of mind evidenced in the Republican statutes. It thus tends to support the traditional date of 67 BC.[51]

Our last example, or family of examples, includes a bold, and early, variation. One group of fictions is used to direct the *iudex* to consider one party to litigation as though he were another person or, at least, enjoyed another personal status. The simplest case is the fiction of citizenship which Gaius illustrates in conjunction with the *actio furti*: 'Let the judge be appointed. If it appears that a theft of a golden bowl was committed against Lucius Titius by Dio son of Hermaeus or with the help of Dio son of Hermaeus, on which account he ought, if he were a Roman citizen, to settle the loss as a thief, etc.'[52] There is no necessity for seeing this as an attempt to deem Dio a Roman. The formula simply expresses, without the concealment characteristic of English fictions, the success of an argument to the effect that the consequences of theft for Romans should be applied to non-Romans. It is interesting that it is not the notion of theft that has to be transferred—'quod lege naturali prohibitum est admittere'[53]—but only the consequential *oportere*. What is true here of the fiction of citizenship is equally true of the cases in which the plaintiff 'ficto se herede intendit'.[54] The aim is not to make Aulus Agerius constructively the heir of Lucius Titius but only, again, to attain a secure symmetry of consequence. The variation on this theme was contributed by the innovative Stoic praetor of 118 BC, P. Rutilius Rufus, later to be forced unjustly into exile after con-

[51] In a number of places Watson has inclined towards a much later date, the action being first mentioned by Neratius at the end of the first century AD and another Publicius being praetor in AD 93: A. Watson, *The Law of Property in the Later Roman Republic* (Oxford, 1968), pp. 105–6.

[52] G. 4. 37.

[53] D. 47. 2. 1. 3, Paul 39 *ad edictum*, followed by J. *Inst.*, 4. 1. 3.

[54] G. 4. 34.

demnation on a trumped-up charge.[55] His technique for achieving the effect now under discussion was to allow a change of names between the *intentio* and the *condemnatio* of the formula, so that the judge would be directed to inquire whether *X* owed money to *Y* but, if it appeared that he did, to condemn *X* to *Z*, the actual plaintiff in the case.[56] Even more obviously than the other, this technique does not ask the *iudex* to find or hold that *Z* is *Y*. Again what is aimed at is a symmetry of consequence: in the given facts the entitlements of *Y* ought to attach to *Z*. Graphic as it is to think of *Z* in *Y*'s shoes, even that metaphor of subrogation is unnecessary. The judge merely has two separate tasks. He has to find *Y*'s entitlements. And he has to enter a condemnation in favour of *Z*. A recent discovery adds a fascinating and relevant insight. A formula has been discovered in Spain, from 87 BC, which orders, not a *condemnatio*, but a declaration as to the truth of the *intentio*, essentially 'If it appears so and so, declare so and so to be the case.'[57] Such a formula could not use the Rutilian technique without transgressing the line between fiction and falsehood. 'If it appears that *X* owes to *Y*, declare that he owes to *Z*' would simply invite the judge to contradict himself. The new formula does indeed tell the court to assess the plaintiff's rights by reference to those of third parties. But it does so by an ordinary fiction, not by a Rutilian change of names. It does not cross the crucial line.

VI. CONCLUSION

Gaius condemned the kind of fiction which required a lawyer to assert that green was red, but he allowed that the law could resolve to treat green as though green were red. We have just seen that Roman lawyers, as legislators and as pleaders, found the latter technique useful and attractive. It was a neat and sure way of transferring known rules to new situations. It did not involve any intellectual dishonesty or covertness. On the contrary, the fiction declared itself openly in the formula or in the statute. Earlier we examined the action for money paid to illustrate the more dangerous kinds of fiction used and tolerated in the development of English law, which allowed the words of claims to be falsified and gave no notice of the falsification. For orderly minds this must have posed a special problem: how could the true rules be presented when in the end they had to be connected up to forms of action which misrepresented them? More specifically, could you, for instance, intelligibly affirm the recognition of an involuntary obligation independent of wrongdoing when the action which

[55] On Rutilius, see now R. Bauman, *Lawyers in Roman Republican Politics* (Munich, 1983), pp. 382–400. On his Stoicism, Cicero, *Brutus*, 113–14.
[56] G. 4. 34.
[57] *The Tabula Contrebiensis*, see (1983) 73 *JRS* 33, J. Richardson; (1984) 74 *JRS* 45, P. Birks, A. Rodger, and J. Richardson, esp., for the fiction, 52–4.

realized that obligation recited the defendant's request and promise?[58] Obviously, it was much easier to acquiesce in the notion of 'implied contract'.

It is well known that Bentham hated the common law's recourse to fictions: 'A fiction of law may be described as a wilful falsehood, having for its object the stealing legislative power by and for hands which could not, or durst not, openly claim it.' And again, 'What you have been doing by the fiction—could you, or could you not, have done it without the fiction? If not, your fiction is a wicked lie: if yes, a foolish one.' And a little later, 'Fiction of use to justice? Exactly as swindling to trade.'[59] But later Fry L. J., with his eye more on the plight of the individual than the constitutional proprieties, still said of the notional assignment which in his view underlay subrogation, 'This equity is based upon a fiction, which, like all legal fictions, has been invented with a view to the furtherance of justice.'[60] And more recently Lord Devlin, one of the greatest of the common law's jurist-judges, professed a preference for an undercover, benevolently dishonest approach to judicial law-making:

> It is facile to think that it is always better to throw off disguises. The need for disguise hampers activity and so restricts power. Paddling across the Rubicon by individuals in disguise who will be sent back if they proclaim themselves is very different from the bridging of the river by an army in uniform and with bands playing.[61]

From different viewpoints Bentham and Lord Devlin seem to be agreed on this, that there is no open, honest, legal creativity which does not usurp the function of the legislature. The rational Gaius would have inclined, more temperately, to Bentham's position. He would certainly have been in sympathy with this observation of Maine,

> Now among other disadvantages, legal fictions are the greatest of obstacles to symmetrical classification ... If English law is ever to assume an orderly distribution, it will be necessary to prune away the legal fictions which, in spite of some recent legislative improvements, are still abundant in it.[62]

Gaius, however, would not have accepted that the price of intellectual order was immobility.

When the action for money paid was fictionalized, why did it happen? No rule of law actually prevented counsel from devising an honest form of

[58] Thomas Wood, learned in both civil and common law, may be taken as a symbol of this tension. He evidently found it exceedingly difficult to carry the order of the *Institutes* into his treatment of the common law. Compare his *New Institute of the Imperial or Civil Law* (London, 1704) and *An Institute of the Laws of England* (London, 1720).

[59] J. Bentham, *The Theory of Fictions*, ed. C. K. Ogden (London, 1932), pp. 141ff., cf. intro. p. xviii.

[60] *Baroness Wenlock* v. *River Dee Co.* (1887) 19 QBD 155, 165.

[61] P. Devlin, *The Judge* (London, 1979), p. 12.

[62] H. S. Maine, *Ancient Law* (1861), ed. F. Pollock, 2nd edn. (London, 1930), p. 34.

action. But a new pattern of words would have encountered an instant demurrer. And the demurrer would have had to be met with novel, uncertain arguments. Experiments of that kind cannot be made at a client's expense. The opportunism of the adversarial process does not favour disinterested intellectual honesty. The common law, unlike Roman law, has traditionally put its law-making jurists into court, above, but not far enough above, the adversarial conflict. The dishonesties to which the law is prone are the consequence of thinking and uttering under that pressure. Fiction of the English kind is one response to a conviction that an acceptable principle could indeed be spelt out and would prove to be legitimately within interpretative reach, if only time and spare brain-power were available. Deeming serves to cover the intellectual deficiency. An alternative response, more honest but no better, is an avowedly unpredictable 'empiricism'.[63] Nowadays, such stratagems should be unnecessary, or necessary only in the short term. The role of the academic branch of the profession has been transformed. One of its main tasks is to make explicit the principles on which the courts are operating, and thus to safeguard the formal rationality of the law, something Gaius took for granted as his duty. There has to be a creative partnership between the universities and the courts.[64]

This change is undeniable. It can be seen as an evolutionary adaptation. Forensic and extra-forensic interpretation seemed to be equally viable, but in modern conditions reflective, extra-forensic jurists have turned out to be indispensable. This reality once perceived, the system has adapted by giving the extra-forensic jurists a monopoly in the formation of legal minds. Nothing less is entailed by the requirement that every lawyer must take a law degree. All this is very recent history. It is something which Tony Honoré's generation achieved, a responsibility which his successors inherit.

[63] e.g. *Orakpo* v. *Manson Investments Ltd.* [1978] AC 95, esp. Lord Diplock and Lord Salmon. The matter was subrogation; cf. n. 60 above.

[64] Sir Robert Goff, 'The Search for Principle'. Maccabaean Lecture in Jurisprudence for 1983, *Proc. Brit. Acad.*, 69 (1983) 169, esp. 187.

6

Natural Justice as Fairness

GERRY MAHER

IN a justly celebrated paper on social justice Tony Honoré provides an example of how jurisprudence should be done.[1] Honoré not only succeeds in making clear a concept which is both difficult and important but also provides a thorough examination of the general principles of justice which brings out the relationships (or lack of them) which each principle has with the idea of social justice. He argues that social justice should be taken to mean the requirement that all persons *considered simply as persons* have a claim to an equal share in all advantages which are commonly desired and which conduce to human well-being.[2] The argument is advanced that some principles of justice (e.g. the justice of transactions or rectificatory justice, and the justice of special relations) do not impinge upon the idea of social justice; whereas other principles of justice (e.g. certain forms of justice according to desert) do have connections with social justice.

One of the principles in this second category, to which Honoré devotes some attention, is justice of conformity to rule, a principle which generates the requirement that like cases be treated alike.[3] Honoré makes the point that this principle is not merely an empty or formal one but rather is a necessary (though not sufficient) aspect of social justice.[4] In his analysis Honoré provides sufficient detail for his immediate purposes of examining the links between social justice and commonly adduced principles of justice but nonetheless it is an interesting fact that what for lawyers at least is the embodiment of justice as conformity to rule, namely the idea of natural justice, merits mention only in a footnote and that does no more than concur in Hart's characterization of the rules of natural justice as being concerned with the impartial and objective application of rules.[5] At first

[1] 'Social Justice' (1962) 8 *McGill LJ* 78; revised version in R. S. Summers (ed.), *Essays in Legal Philosophy* (Oxford, 1970), pp. 61–94. References are to the latter version.

[2] Op. cit. pp. 62–3; cf. also p. 94. Emphasis added. Honoré makes the further important point that there is a limited set of factors justifying departures from the principle of social justice.

[3] 'Social Justice', p. 67.

[4] This is because the method of being treated according to rules which are properly applied is a demand which persons as persons are owed in dealings with the rest of society: 'Social Justice', p. 71.

[5] 'Social Justice', p. 66 n. 4, referring to H. L. A. Hart, *The Concept of Law* (Oxford, 1961), p. 156.

glance this lack of attention to the idea of natural justice is not surprising, for the rules of natural justice are often thought of as being technical legal matters relating only to the nuts and bolts of legal machinery, whereas central theoretical issues lie elsewhere. However, in this paper I wish to examine the theoretical basis of the notion of natural justice and I shall argue that the best justification of our present practices and rules in matters of natural justice uses the same ideas of claims made by persons as persons and of respecting persons as persons which Honoré places at the core of the concept of social justice. Certainly there is much of value in Honoré's argument that justice as conformity to rule (and its associated principle of natural justice) is one aspect of social justice in Honoré's sense; but at the same time it is a defect that Honoré appears to give natural justice so little attention, for it will be argued that there is a closer connection between social justice and natural justice than Honoré suggests. But it must be made clear at the outset that though Honoré may have been mistaken to play down the significance of the idea of natural justice, it is from the range of ideas discussed in depth in his own seminal paper that a clearer understanding of natural justice is to be derived.

I

There can be few judicial dicta which are well-established parts of common speech but it is a fairly safe bet to say that one of them is the remark of Lord Hewart 'that it is not merely of some importance but it is of fundamental importance that justice should not only be done, but should manifestly and undoubtedly be seen to be done.'[6] But if this remark is to be treated as more than a powerful rehetorical flourish, a question arises which calls for a direct answer: why, if justice is done, must it be seen to be done? It is hardly a proper answer to say (as some lawyers might) that this is what the rules of natural justice require, for the real question here is what is the justification of those very rules.

In any case the lawyer's reply is not really one that someone skilled in British law could properly give, for if one thing is clear from the writings of British lawyers on natural justice it is that recent developments in the area of natural justice have not always proceeded on a consistent basis. No doubt prior to the 1960s the law on natural justice could be stated with relative ease. There were two main points to be made: the first was that natural justice applied only to certain sorts of issue, namely those involving a judicial or quasi-judicial, but not an administrative, decision. Although this rule was clear enough, the distinction embodied in it was not. The second aspect of natural justice prior to the 1960s was that once the classi-

[6] *R* v. *Sussex Justices, ex parte McCarthy* [1924] 1 KB 256, 259.

fication as judicial (and quasi-judicial) or administrative was made, the content of natural justice to be applied to the issue was stated in two rules, namely those providing for the right to an unbiased judge and the right to a hearing.

Since the 1960s, however, especially since the House of Lords' decision in *Ridge* v. *Baldwin*,[7] there has been something of a flourishing of natural justice, at least in the sense of an increased judicial willingness to consider the applicability of natural justice to a wider range of issues. However, this growing judicial consideration of natural justice has not been without its critics and some writers have argued that developments since the 1960s have lacked any underlying rationale and may have widened the ambit of natural justice at the cost of weakening its strength.[8] One such development over the last twenty years has been the rejection of a rigid classification of issues as judicial and administrative, and the accompanying doctrine that the rules of natural justice apply only to the former. By 1971 in *Gaiman* v. *National Association for Mental Health*, Megarry J could lay down the proposition: 'as the authorities now stand, it may not be possible to do much more than say that the principles of natural justice will apply unless the circumstances are such as to indicate the contrary'.[9]

Another trend was the beginning of the view that natural justice coexisted with, or reflected, a wider principle of fairness in decision-making and that all judicial and administrative decision-makers had a duty to act fairly.[10] Although these developments have been welcomed by some commentators, they are not without difficulty. In the previous state of the law the range of natural justice was limited but at least that law was reasonably certain. However the more recent developments have proceeded very much on an *ad hoc* basis, with little attempt by the courts to lay down general and consistently applied principles to explain and justify the new natural justice. The view has been put that natural justice is now no more than the subjective discretion of judges and decisions relating to natural justice tend to reflect judicial sympathies with particular classes of litigant (such as that trade unionists are accorded natural justice in their dealing with their unions, whereas students are denied it in their dealings with educational institutions).[11]

[7] [1964] AC 40.

[8] See, e.g. D. H. Clark, 'Natural Justice: Substance and Shadow', (1975) *Public Law* 27; J. E. Alder, 'How Fundamental is Natural Justice?' in D. Lasok *et al.* (eds.), *Fundamental Duties* (Oxford, 1980), p. 68.

[9] [1971] Ch 317, 333.

[10] See D. J. Mullan, 'Fairness: The New Natural Justice', (1975) 25 *U. Toronto L.J.* 281; David Foulkes, *Administrative Law* (London, 5th ed., 1982), pp. 221–53; H. W. R. Wade, *Administrative Law* (Oxford, 5th edn., 1982), pp. 465 ff.

[11] For a characteristically blunt statement of this view, see J. A. G. Griffith, *The Politics of the Judiciary* (London, 2nd edn., 1981), ch. 7.

So not only does the present British law have no obviously clear principles, its more detailed rules are themselves subject to a degree of uncertainty. The time is then ripe for posing questions of justification of the idea of natural justice, and it is the issue of justification, not exposition of the law, which is the concern of this present paper. But it is hoped that what is said will not be dismissed as abstract theory, remote from the harsher realities of existing legal rules. Rather what is proposed is the enterprise of seeking to justify a concept, and this justification will at the same time provide a better understanding of some aspects of the law on natural justice and will also suggest arguments as to which elements in our still rather inconsistent law should be rejected as contrary to basic legal principle and which aspects retained and strengthened as embodying these underlying justificatory principles.

II

1 Accuracy of Determination

The first candidate for a principle which will provide both understanding and justification of the idea of natural justice is one which will be called instrumentalist and which argues that the rules of natural justice have their rationale in the ways in which they promote the efficiency and accuracy of fact-determination. An initial problem for this view is that the notions of fact and determination are themselves in need of explanation, but putting aside such problems we can suppose that a determination is a good one if it correctly discovers the facts relevant to a decision and applies the proper rule or other standard (such as a policy-based one) to those facts. On this basis, accordingly, the rules of natural justice are no more than a means to a particular end, and that end is the identification of the proper rule or standard (which includes rules based on policy) and the discovery of the appropriate facts. It is not exactly clear whether the characterization of natural justice adopted by both Hart and Honoré, that is as being concerned with ensuring that rules are impartially and objectively applied to a concrete situation, is based solely on this approach, but it is certainly consistent with it. In any case an argument based on this approach is clear enough and also has the advantage that some of the cases point to this feature as a component of natural justice. In *John* v. *Rees*, Megarry J noted:[12]

> As everybody who has anything to do with the law well knows, the path of the law is strewn with examples of open-and-shut cases which, somehow, were not; of unanswerable charges which, in the event, were completely answered; of inexplicable conduct which was fully explained; of fixed and unalterable determinations that, by discussion, suffered a change.

[12] [1970] Ch 345, 402.

Certainly for lawyers in the common-law tradition, for whom legal procedure is in essence adversary, truth is something which will out only after both sides to any dispute have had an equal crack at the whip. To infringe the rule of *audi alterem partem* is simply not to take seriously the law's own method for truth-finding.

There is no denying that the rules of natural justice, for the sort of reasons mentioned by Megarry J, do have some part to play in accurate and efficient determinations in disputes. But at the same time, it cannot be that this notion of accurate determination is the sole justification of all aspects of natural justice typically found in most common-law jurisdictions. The case from which Megarry J's dictum is drawn illustrates this very point, for that case is often cited as authority for the proposition that the courts will not accede to the argument that there is no need to apply the rules of natural justice where their application would have made no difference to the outcome of the decision. It is certainly true that this whole argument is one on which conflicting authorities exist, but it is also the case that commentators favour the view in cases such as *John* v. *Rees* as embodying the true position.[13]

Furthermore the other traditional rule of natural justice, the rule against bias, would in its accepted sense lack foundation on a purely instrumentalist theory. Take the classic case *Dimes* v. *Grand Junction Canal*[14] where the purportedly biased judge was no less a person than the Lord Chancellor of Great Britain, Lord Cottenham, who had dealt with a case concerning a company in which he was a shareholder. Lord Cottenham's decrees were set aside by the House of Lords which then proceeded to decide the case on its merits and ultimately arrive at exactly the same result. But despite this congruence in result, Lord Cottenham's previous decision was to no effect, not because his interest in the case led to the wrong decision but simply because he had an interest. In the House of Lords, Lord Campbell stated:[15]

No one can suppose that Lord Cottenham could be, in the remotest degree, influenced by the interest that he had in this concern; but, my Lords, it is of the last importance that the maxim, that no man is to be a judge in his own cause, should be held sacred. And that is not confined to a cause in which he is a party, but applies to a cause in which he has an interest.

[13] S. A. de Smith *Judicial Review of Administrative Action* (London, 4th edn. ed. J. M. Evans, 1980), pp. 243–45; H. W. R. Wade, *Administrative Law*, pp. 475–7; D. H. Clark, (1975) *Public Law* at 45–60. It should be noted, however, that some important recent decisions have accepted the argument that natural justice is not necessary if its application would make no difference to the outcome. See, e.g. *Cinnamond* v. *British Airways Authority* [1980] 1 WLR 582; *Cheal* v. *APEX* [1983] 2 AC 181.

[14] (1852) 3 HLC 759.

[15] At p. 793.

Lord Campbell also talked about the need not simply to avoid personal interest by decision-makers but also to avoid the appearance of such interest. Indeed later cases have tended to adopt the view that there is no need to show a real likelihood of bias but that it suffices to bring the rule *nemo iudex in sua causa* into play by showing only reasonable suspicion of bias.[16] To revert to the dictum of Lord Hewart in *McCarthy*, instrumentalism can only explain that justice ought to be done but cannot show why it must be seen to be done, and it is the second leg of the dictum to which natural justice is addressed.

2 *Indirect Instrumentalism*

A different response to the problem of justifying (and explaining) the rules of natural justice which retains features of instrumentalist argument and which seeks to account for the problems facing purely instrumentalist forms of justification can be labelled that of indirect instrumentalism. Consider, for instance, a passage from the judgment of Lord Denning MR in *Metropolitan Properties Co (F.G.C.) Ltd* v. *Lannon* on the issue of the 'test' or criteria which give rise to the application of the rule against bias:[17]

> There must be circumstances from which a reasonable man would think it likely or probable that the justice, or chairman, as the case may be, would, or did, favour one side unfairly at the expense of the other. The court will not inquire whether he did, in fact, favour one side unfairly. Suffice it that reasonable people might think he did. The reason is plain enough. Justice must be rooted in confidence: and confidence is destroyed when right-minded people go away thinking: 'The judge was biased'.

Indirect instrumentalism argues that, although the rules of natural justice do not always promote, and may even even hinder, accuracy of determination in the immediate case, they have a rationale related to fact-finding and rule-application functions in that they ensure that in the long run courts and tribunals will retain public confidence and thus their fact-finding and rule-application functions will continue to operate smoothly. This sort of reasoning has parallels with ethical theories known as rule-utilitarianism, but it should also be pointed out that it shares many of the defects to which critics of rule-utilitarianism have pointed.[18]

Rule-utilitarianism attempts to overcome some of the problems associated with direct or 'act-utilitarianism' by arguing that instead of doing an act which will maximize the desired outcome, we should do the act which conforms to a rule, whose observance will maximize the desired outcome.

[16] de Smith, *Judicial Review of Administrative Action*, pp. 262–4; Wade, *Administrative Law*, pp. 430–2.

[17] [1969] 1 QB 577, at p. 599.

[18] D. Lyons, *Forms and Limits of Utilitarianism* (Oxford, 1965), especially chs. 4 and 5; D. H. Hodgson, *Consequences of Utilitarianism* (Oxford, 1967), chs. 1–3.

For example, promising is a socially useful practice which ensures a degree of co-operation otherwise not obtainable in society. But act-utilitarianism finds it difficult to account for any particular promise giving rise to obligations where observing that promise would in the circumstances not maximize overall utility. Rule-utilitarianism argues that we can understand the reasons for the obligation to stand by promises made if we attend to the overall utility of the practice of promising and remind ourselves that this utility would be undermined if the general carrying-out of promissory duties were not undertaken, even in circumstances where in the particular case utility was not achieved. But critics have argued that rule-utilitarianism either collapses into act-utilitarianism or depends upon some non-utilitarian principle of justification. If a rule simply states 'always do A so that the desired outcome O will be maximized', then there is no difference between this formulation and the act-utilitarian approach of 'always do A' (because doing A will lead to O). If the argument is that doing A in circumstances C will not maximise O, then there is no need for any rule 'do A except in C as that will maximize O'—this rule again adds nothing to the act-utilitarian maxim 'do A except in C' (because such an act as specified will maximize O). At times defenders of rule-utilitarianism advance the argument that the point of following rules is that often we do not know for certain which act will maximize O and that in such circumstances we should follow the conventional rules of society.[19] In this approach the idea of rule is used to mean, not theoretical constructs or generalizations as mentioned in the examples above, but rather the accepted or conventional rules of practice whose non-observance might threaten (perhaps in the long run) achieving the desired outcome. Thus where we are unsure which act will maximize O, this argument tells us to follow the rule in that society most likely to maximize O. But taking rules to mean conventional rules of practice does not show that the purpose of the rule is to maximize O—it may well be but equally it may not be, for it could be the case that a particular rule serves to limit O because of some other, non-utilitarian, value (e.g. fairness).

Consider now the justification of the rules of natural justice as a species of rule-utilitarianism. If the desired outcome of the legal process is simply to maximize correctness of fact-finding and rule-application (the view which we are here calling instrumentalism) the question to be asked is how the rules of natural justice *as rules* achieve this outcome. Clearly in some instances they do not, for example those cases where the observance of the rules would have made no difference to the outcome of the decision. If we reject this part of the law the rules would not be in their present form but rather in the form that the rules of natural justice are to be followed where

[19] Cf. Hodgson, pp. 26–9.

so doing maximizes the desired outcome of sound fact-finding and correct rule-application. But this is no different from the direct form of instrumentalism which we examined above and adds nothing to it.

Perhaps a rule-utilitarian approach to natural justice appeals to the idea underlying the judgment of Lord Denning in the *Lannon* case, quoted earlier. Observing the rules of natural justice ensures that public confidence in courts and tribunals will be maintained and this will help to bring about (at least in the long run) correctness of fact-finding and rule-application. But why should public confidence in the correctness of an outcome in this sense of outcome be dependent on following the rules of natural justice? If it is because non-observance may lead to the wrong facts being found or the wrong rule being applied, the rules of natural justice are of the same sort as that noted in the preceding paragraph which said 'follow the rules of natural justice only when this helps to reach the correct outcome', which, it was argued, collapses into a direct form of instrumentalism. However if public confidence depends on some feeling that it is unfair or unjust not to let each party have a say or to have a judge who appears to favour one party over the other (even when it is known that he was not biased), then such a belief on the part of the public is not one that could be made to fit into a instrumentalist justification (either direct or indirect) of our existing rules of natural justice.

3 *Natural Justice as Fairness*

The difficulties arising from taking instrumentalism in either its direct or indirect form as providing a complete basis of justification for the rules of natural justice as they are found in most common-law jurisdictions lead to consideration of what for many lawyers is probably the best and most complete form of such justification: this is to be found in the idea of fairness. As we have already noted, fairness has recently been hailed as the 'new' natural justice and the courts and textbook-writers alike now talk of the duty 'to act fairly' where once they talked of the duty to observe the rules of natural justice. What is more, if a theoretical basis is needed for this conception of natural justice, there is an obvious source in John Rawls's celebrated *A Theory of Justice*, which sets out a detailed and elaborate statement of a theory of social justice, summed up in Rawls's own expression, 'justice as fairness'.[20]

Before we consider how the idea of fairness might help in justifying the rules of natural justice, we should also note here a potentially confusing factor, which has arisen in some of the more recent decisions, concerning the nature of the relationship between natural justice in its traditional sense and fairness. Some judges have taken the view that as the fairness doctrine

[20] John Rawls, *A Theory of Justice* (Oxford, 1972), pp. 11–17.

is not exactly the same as the traditional notion of natural justice, therefore it is something distinct from it and have held that by extension the duty to act fairly applies only in respect of decisions which do not call for the observance of the rules of natural justice.[21] But this sort of reasoning has been subjected to fierce criticism from commentators and in any case the decisions taking this view are the exception rather than the rule.[22] But what then *is* the relationship between fairness and natural justice? It makes more sense of the law in its present state to say that fairness is a principle which 'underlies' or 'explains' or 'justifies' the traditional rules of natural justice and that resort to basic legal principle was required especially in countries like Britain because of the sterile reasoning towards the traditional rules of natural justice which was manifested by the courts during the middle decades of the twentieth century.

But explaining the relationship of fairness and natural justice as one of basic principle to detailed rule does not end the matter—indeed it has already been noted that critics of the 'new' natural justice have argued that the courts have found it difficult to translate the broad principle of fairness into concrete particulars. If fairness does succeed in fully explaining and justifying the rules of natural justice, there is still work to be done in providing detail of what is involved in such a justification.

It is here that Rawls might be prayed in aid, for not only does Rawls put the idea of fairness at the core of his theory of justice but that theory itself uses the ideas of decisions and procedural justice. However there is one immediate difficulty in jumping straight into Rawls's discussion of the ways in which principles of social justice are arrived at by a very special sort of procedure, namely one made by parties unanimously agreeing on them in an 'original position' where they have certain imputed motivations and where they lack certain possibly biasing items of information about themselves. This is that Rawls explicitly and repeatedly states that the social contract he describes is purely hypothetical.[23] The device of the original position is no more than that, a device of argument which gives vivid illustration to Rawls's method of moral reasoning. It does not matter what parties anywhere have or have not actually agreed; what is important for Rawls is what people in the purely hypothetical conditions which he describes would have agreed and the principles agreed to themselves act as criteria for assessing the justice of actual societies and actual practices. But the problem of justifying natural justice is that of justifying actual modes of decision-making—the 'fairness' of substantive doctrines which would

[21] E.g. *Pearlberg* v. *Varty* [1972] 1 WLR 457; *Re Nicholson and Haldimand-Norfolk Police Commission* (1979) 88 DLR (3rd) 671 (Supreme Court of Canada).

[22] de Smith, *Judicial Review of Administrative Action*, pp. 238–40; Wade, *Administrative Law*, pp. 467–8.

[23] *A Theory of Justice*, pp. 12, 120, 167.

have been decided in purely hypothetical circumstances seems to have no role to play in explaining or justifying actual decision-processes. Further, it would be silly to imagine that the circumstances of the original position should be taken as setting the ideal for actual decision-processes, even for ones based on some principle of fairness. Requiring actual parties to actual decisions not to know who they are or what their interests are seems an almost irrational mode of making actual decisions.

We can sum up this point by saying that the problem in taking Rawls's theory of justice as fairness as the basis of a justification of natural justice is that given the place of fairness in the construction of the original position, Rawls has little to say about actual decision procedures. But this is not also to assert that Rawls says absolutely nothing about basic principles of decision procedures but rather that for his own direct purposes of expounding a theory of (substantive) justice as 'fairness', he is little concerned with the details of 'fairness' in procedure.[24] At the same time, however, he does at times discuss aspects of procedures and although the precise role of the idea of fairness as justifying procedure is left undeveloped, Rawls does give some hints as to the nature of a theory of legal processes, hints which will be used when we try in the next section to build up a theory of justification of natural justice.

Rawls argues that persons in the original position would decide upon certain principles of justice and much of his book is concerned with how these general principles are to be applied in more concrete stages, such as selecting which constitutional provisions best conform to the principles of justice, which pieces of legislation are required by them, and the mode of application of rules to particular cases which respects the principles of justice.[25] It is in this last context that Rawls discusses the rule of law and natural justice as one aspect of it. Rawls argues that the broad principle of justice as fairness would require application of rules on a regular and impartial basis. One element in securing this goal is by observing the rules of natural justice, which he characterizes as 'intended to preserve the integrity

[24] One important part of Rawls's book in this respect is the use which he makes of the distinction between 'perfect' procedural justice, 'imperfect' procedural justice, and 'pure' procedural justice. With perfect procedural justice there is an independent criterion for the correct outcome and a procedure for ensuring it; imperfect procedual justice arises where there is such a criterion in respect of the outcome but no procedure for ensuring it. Pure procedural justice obtains where there is no independent criterion for the correct outcome but this outcome is achieved simply by following the devised procedure: op. cit. pp. 85–6.

Rawls gives as an example of imperfect procedural justice the criminal trial, but he question-beggingly states that the correct outcome is determination of factual guilt; it may well be that legal trials (and *a fortiori* criminal trials) also embody aspects of pure procedural justice in that the correct outcome depends partly upon such an independently stated outcome but also on the specific forms of procedure. Such an argument could be used in explaining the central role of natural justice in litigation.

[25] Ibid., pp. 195–201.

of the judicial process.'[26] The general features of natural justice are described in the following passage:[27]

> The rule of law requires some form of due process: that is, a process reasonably designed to ascertain the truth, in ways consistent with the other ends of the legal system, as to whether a violation has taken place and under what circumstances. For example, judges must be independent and impartial, and no man may judge his own case. Trials must be fair and open, but not prejudiced by public clamor. The precepts of natural justice are to insure that the legal order will be impartially and regularly maintained.

This passage from Rawls is of interest for a number of reasons. In the first place, it is the nearest Rawls gets to a direct discussion of the implications of justice as fairness for the rules of natural justice. Secondly, he accepts that part of the justification of natural justice is instrumentalist in nature, that is, it helps to identify the proper rules and to discover the appropriate facts which are to be applied to a decision; but Rawls also notes that this instrumentalist aim must be carried out 'in ways consistent with the other ends of the legal system.' Unfortunately for our present purposes, Rawls does not go on to identify what those other ends are which constrain the instrumentalist goals of legal processes, nor does he show why they lead to rules such as those of natural justice. This is not to say that anyone who has mastered all Rawls's book could not go on to construct a theory of natural justice based on justice as fairness. The point is rather that we have not got much further on in searching for a full justification of the rules of natural justice. Merely to invoke the word 'fairness' is a poor substitute for providing a detailed theory and Rawls's own elaborate theory of justice is not a direct source for a theory of natural justice as fairness.

4 *Natural Justice and Respect for Persons*

In this final section I want to be less negative in approach and to offer some positive argument as to what should be included in any justification of natural justice. Although in the previous section it was argued that Rawls's own theory did not in terms answer the questions facing us, still it should not be thought that there is nothing of value in Rawls's work for this purpose. Indeed I shall use here some of Rawls's arguments but I shall not claim that this is a fruitful rendering of what Rawls would have written if he had examined in detail the idea of natural justice. My reason for doing this is not that I necessarily disagree with Rawls's general argument but that I want to move the discussion of natural justice away from the particular context in which Rawls places it, namely discussion of the importance of liberty.

[26] Ibid., p. 238.
[27] Ibid., p. 239.

Certainly what is of value in Rawls's approach to natural justice is that Rawls links the idea of natural justice to the concept of the rule of law. Rawls's own views on the nature of the rule of law and its more abstract statement in the idea of formal justice rely heavily on the arguments provided by Lon Fuller, the core of which is that law as a special means of subjecting human conduct to the governance of rules necessarily adopts a specific conception of moral personality, one which respects the autonomy of those subject to the legal order.[28]

We can apply this sort of reasoning to the idea of natural justice by formulating once again the question posed earlier on: what is wrong with the situation where justice has been done but has not been seen to be done? To arrive at an answer we should bear in mind that although much discussion of natural justice at the present time concerns the application of the rules to administrative and 'voluntary' decision-processes, this is because it is taken for granted that the rules clearly apply to the paradigm instance of decision-making in law, the judicial decision. Why then is there anything wrong with a court reaching the 'correct' outcome in terms of arriving at the right facts and applying the proper rule but in so doing infringing the precepts of natural justice? We have already seen that instrumentalism, whether in its direct or indirect form, cannot explain this additional requirement typically insisted upon by many legal systems. But an answer can be had if we adopt for the time being the perspective of the person against whom the 'correct' (in the sense just noted) determination has been made but who has been denied a meaningful hearing and who was faced with a possibly but not actually biased judge. Such a person might say, on a Rawlsian basis, that it was *unfair* for that determination to have been made against him but this would not do in itself for we need to explain why his complaint on the ground of fairness is a proper one and wherein lies the unfairness.

It is suggested that the basis of such a person's complaint lies in the general idea that his status as a rational, autonomous human has been denied by such a procedure. This has nothing to do with the fact that the 'objectively' wrong decision has been reached. *Ex hypothesi* this is not the case, though the converse situation does hold, for people do have a right that the correct facts be found and the correct rules applied to decisions affecting them and this right is denied when the objectively wrong decision has been reached. That is to say, it is part of procedural justice that justice in the sense of the correct outcome as measured by findings of fact and

[28] Lon L. Fuller, *The Morality of Law* (New Haven, revised edn., 1965), especially at pp. 204–24. For writings sympathetic to Fuller's views on this point, see P. P. Nicholson, 'The Internal Morality of Law: Fuller and his Critics' (1978) 84 *Ethics* 307; R. A. Duff, 'Legal Obligation and the Morality of Law', (1980) *Juridical Review* 61; John Finnis, *Natural Law and Natural Rights* (Oxford, 1980), pp. 270–6.

application of rules should be done. But in the circumstances under consideration the correctness of the outcome is not in issue. What is wrong with adopting a procedure which does not conform to the requirements of natural justice is that the person against whom the decision is made has suffered in that his status as a morally autonomous being has been denied and the reason why this is so is that it has not been shown why the particular decision should be proceeded with against *him*. Just as the rule of law insists that there should be general rules which function to provide reasons for the actions of people in society and thus respects their autonomy, as a corollary the demands of due process in general and natural justice in particular act to give reasons for the application of these general rules to particular persons. And just as the rule of law insists upon respecting the moral status of people generally, the rules of natural justice receive their justification in the way in which they particularize this general principle in the application of general rules to concrete cases.[29]

Consider in this light the force of the rule *audi alterem partem*. Although part of its rationale might be tied up in instrumentalist concerns, we still feel that this rule has force and should be insisted upon even when its observance would not affect the actual outcome. But once we concede that our procedures in applying rules should respect the moral status of the parties concerned, it becomes more evident why the rule has value. A decision, no matter how 'correct' in what it determines, which has some onerous or harmful effect on the interests of the person affected by it (e.g. refusal of a licence) presents itself to that person in quite different lights depending upon the degree to which the procedure which accompanied it either did or did not allow for that person to have some say. Although a person might accept that rules provide general reasons for acting, he will justifiably ask for further reasons why in a particular context a rule is to be applied against him. A mere decree or declaration to the effect that the outcome is such-and-such will provide no reasons of this individualized nature but will simply tell him of the general rule which is to be applied to him (and perhaps not even that). This reasoning has even greater force where the standard to be applied is not a rule as such but some policy at the discretion of the decision-maker; here too there is need for reasons explaining why the person has been 'singled out' by the decision. Providing the person affected by a decision with a fair hearing in the making of the decision not only ensures the objective correctness of the decision but also gives him reasons for appreciating why that decision is to be made against him.[30] The rationale of the rules of natural justice then lies in the fact that decisions which apply general rules and *a fortiori* those which apply

[29] See the similar reasoning in respect of the due-process provisions of the American Constitution of L. Tribe, *Constitutional Law* (New York, 1978), especially pp. 555–60.

[30] J. R. Lucas, *On Justice* (Oxford, 1980), p. 82.

discretionary standards prima facie affect the person against whom they are made by the very fact that he is singled out by the decision. This move from general rule to particular application accordingly calls for reasons to explain, especially to the person most directly affected, why such singling out has been adopted, even when the reason is that this is required by the application of general rules.

It was claimed earlier that instrumentalism failed as the basis of a justificatory theory of natural justice because it gave an incomplete account of the concept of natural justice and so failed to explain why some of the problems faced by lawyers and the courts concerning the application of the rules of natural justice are to be taken as problems. It was also argued that the idea of fairness lacked sufficient specificity to act as a means of justifying natural justice. The idea profferred here is that the best justification of natural justice lies in the moral requirement of respect for the autonomy of the party affected by a decision; this leads to using a procedure which gives him a role in it and can thus explain to him the basis on which the application of the rule or policy to him is justified. What advantages can be said to exist with this form of justification?

Take, for example, the traditional rule against bias. The fact that a decision-maker might appear to be biased, though he in fact was not, has some explanation in purely instrumentalist terms, but not a complete one. But a possibly though not actually biased judge can still operate a procedure which speaks to the party affected by the decision and which provides reasons to that person why a decision is made against his interest. But the broad principle of respect for persons brings out grounds for objecting to decisions by possibly biased judges. To the extent that anyone is a member of civil society he has exchanged his own right to judge for himself matters affecting him and has placed himself under a system of rules or laws. In giving up his right each person is entitled to demand that the right of judging one's own cause is given up by everyone else and is not transferred over to some other (interested) party. It is respect for the personality of all, who have each given up the right to judge their own cause, which generates the right to an unbiased judge in the application of rules or laws. This point can also be stated by considering the issue from the perspective of authority seeking to justify its actions by appeal to the law. Moral title to proceed on the basis of a decision calls for clear indication that there has been a proper application of the right rules to the particular case on the basis of correct determination of facts. No such moral title can be shown where the judge has some interest (even one *ex hypothesi* which did not affect his decision) in the outcome of a decision other than the impartial application of a general rule.

But it is also the case that taking the basis of natural justice as respect for moral autonomy has power to explain why aspects of the traditional rules have proved troublesome and also what the solutions to these problems may be. For example, it is a curious omission from the traditional rules of natural justice that there is no obligation on decision-makers to give reasons for their decisions.[31] Wade points out that there is no such requirement even on courts of law, still less on administrative bodies.[32] Yet although the rule as such is clear enough, it is also a noticeable fact that almost all courts and many tribunals do as a matter of practice give reasons for their decisions despite the lack of strict legal duty, and commentators have argued that there should be such a duty in many situations. But why this conformity in practice and why the arguments for a rule requiring the giving of reasons? It might well be that writers and courts alike in doing this are appealing to some unarticulated notion of respect for the individual in the application of rules to particular situations. Be that as it may, but if we do accept this general moral principle we can see why the requirement of giving reasons follows on from it. To some extent the giving of reasons is a requirement of the rule of law in that by giving reasons for his decision, the decision-maker indicates that his decision is in conformity with pre-existing rules or standards; it also allows for assessment of particular decisions as formally rational, for inasmuch as decisions affect different *individuals*, and on that basis at least are different in outcome, we need statements of the reasons for these decisions before we can say that like cases are being treated alike. (The other way of putting this is to say that giving reasons for each decision allows for assessment that the correct classifications of 'same' and 'different' have been made in the application of rules.)

But if we adopt the perspective of the person affected by the decision we get a further and perhaps stronger reason for requiring reasons for a decision to be given. Allowing that party to be involved in the deciding of the case, that is by providing him with a 'fair hearing', goes some of the way to explaining to him why he has been singled out for this sort of individualized treatment and also provides grounds for him to accept the decision as one he should respect and comply with. But no matter how detailed the procedure involved in arriving at a decision, it might still not convey sufficient reason for him to accept it as one which legitimately applies rules to *him* in this particular situation. But an express statement of the reasons for the decision will add to the set of reasons provided by the procedure involved in making the decision. It will act (in addition to those other provisions identified earlier) as a direct communication to the person affected

[31] See further J. W. Bridge, 'The Duty to Give Reasons for Decisions as an Aspect of Natural Justice', in D. Lasok *et al*, edd., *Fundamental Duties* (Oxford, 1980), p. 81; D. Foulkes, *Administrative Law*, pp. 254–60.

[32] *Administrative Law*, p. 486. It should be noted, however, that by section 12 of the Tribunals and Inquiries Act 1971 the various tribunals and authorities specified in Schedule 1 to the Act (which sets out a long list of such bodies) are required to give reasons for their decisions.

by the decision and give reasons to explain why the decision, although not in his immediate interests, is none the less one which he has reason to respect, if for no other reason that in the manner in which it was made his right as a morally autonomous person was respected.

As another illustration of the justificatory force of respect for persons as the basic principle behind the rules of natural justice, consider the vexed problem of the range of decisions to which the rules of natural justice are applicable. It was once the case that whereas established rights were to be protected by natural justice when under challenge, this was not the case as regards mere privileges. This particular distinction has proved to be largely untenable in practice and has been abandoned in the cases but only to reappear in a distinction between on the one hand established rights (including legitimate expectations) and on the other mere applications. A further point is that it is argued that it is politically undesirable that natural justice should be held to be applicable in areas where decisions are to be made on matters purely of policy. But once we accept that the basis of natural justice is respect for the moral personality of those involved in decisions which may adversely affect their interests, then such issues as the range of application of natural justice become resolvable. For then the crucial factor is that of the importance of the particular issue to be decided for the individual most directly affected by it and the extent to which the individual is singled out by the process which arrives at the decision in question. The feature of the importance of the issue perhaps explains the reluctance in the past to apply natural justice to decisions which were 'private' (i.e. non-state) in nature, for the underlying assumption was that public authority posed the greatest threat to the liberty and the general interests of the individual. The actions of voluntary associations were seen as based on the consent of their members and thus might not be thought to threaten the interests of their members. However it has become increasingly accepted to the point of orthodoxy that private as much as public associations can make decisions which seriously affect a person's interests (e.g. membership of a professional association or trade union). What is perhaps not so easily noted by the courts is the importance of state benefits (what Charles Reich called in the United States the 'new property') among the interests of individuals and the need accordingly to extend natural justice to all tribunals and institutions making decisions on this new property.[33]

Taking concern for individualized treatment of a person as the basis of natural justice also explains why the rules of natural justice do not apply to

[33] Charles Reich, 'The New Property', (1964) 73 *Yale LJ* 733. Reich appeals to the concept of property in this context mainly because of the provisions of the US Constitution in extending due process to issues of life, liberty and property. This particular conceptual device may not be necessary in legal systems such as those in the UK.

legislative decisions, for here the assumptions are that legislation is general rather than particular in effect and also that everyone in a democracy has an equal opportunity to participate in the political process which leads to the making of legislation. This reasoning must appear somewhat strained when applied to the actual circumstances of much of the legislative process at the present time. In *Bates* v. *Lord Hailsham of St Marylebone*,[34] it was held that natural justice did not apply to a decision of the Lord Chancellor to make secondary legislation concerning solicitors' fees where it was alleged there had been inadequate consultation with the solicitors' profession. But especially in matters of delegated legislation, there is a greater likelihood of individuals being singled out for special treatment and a correspondingly greater need for the application of natural justice in arriving at legislative decisions.[35]

Of course it is also possible to argue that even with the legislative process, current realities are far removed from the picture presented by theory. That may be so, but it is sufficient for our present purposes that a link has been shown to exist between theories of the legislative process which emphasize the importance of participation as a basis of legitimacy (such as Rawls's) and theories of the application of law which argue for non-instrumental values in natural justice. Indeed one fruitful way of seeing natural justice is as a form of participatory democracy at the level of rule-application rather than rule-making. It is not clear exactly how far one can press this analogy but it is not inconsistent with, and may be entailed by, the sort of argument which we have presented about justifying natural justice in terms of taking seriously the autonomy and moral personality of those against whom decisions are made.

III

What we have argued is that purely instrumentalist approaches to natural justice, which take the idea of natural justice as concerned with the correctness of outcomes of decisions, are deficient both in explaining the actual features of our law on natural justice and as providing reasons for certain parts of that law which at least intuitively we might wish to keep. Instead a better justification (and also explanation) of the concept of natural justice, it was suggested, is to be built round the idea of respecting persons as persons. It might be thought, however, that our presentation is incomplete,

[34] [1972] 1 WLR 1373.

[35] It should be noted that many Acts require consultation to be made in respect of subordinate legislation under them. However, there is a wide range of different circumstances necessary and/or sufficient to constitute such consultation. For an important illustration see the case of *Agricultural (etc.) Industry Training Board* v. *Aylesbury Mushrooms* [1972] 1 WLR 190.

for we have not provided arguments why any preference should be accorded to this general moral principle. Clearly that is a task which would need to be done if a full theory of natural justice were ever to be produced. But it is enough to say that the key component of the theory of natural justice as presented here is consonant with that which is at the core of the idea of social justice that calls for *what* can be claimed by all persons as persons. Our theory has attempted to show that persons considered as persons can legitimately make claims of *how* they are to be treated and thus suggests a deeper link than might be thought apparent between social justice and natural justice. If this is so, then we can take comfort from the fact that it enables us to rely on, as support for the idea of natural justice, the powerful arguments made by Tony Honoré in his analysis of social justice.[36]

[36] My thanks are due to Keith Ewing, Robin Fletcher, Neil MacCormick, and Tom Mullen, who gave me the benefit of their views on an earlier draft of this paper. Their comments guided me considerably in understanding both the law and theory of natural justice but responsibility for the final version of the paper is mine.

7

Speech Acts, Legal Institutions, and Real Laws

NEIL MACCORMICK AND ZENON BANKOWSKI

TONY HONORÉ'S contribution to the philosophy of law has been both profound and wide-ranging. Even apart from his huge contributions in legal history, legal dogmatics, and comparative law, his philosophical and jurisprudential work alone would have entitled him to a place in the front rank of contemporary jurists. To reflect on his philosophical work is at once to be reminded of the remarkable constellation of talents in post-war Oxford within which his own talent was developed. Some years ago in the *Festschrift* for H. L. A. Hart, he alluded in characteristically modest terms to all that:

> In the balmy days of the 1950s Hart was a central and I a peripheral figure in the movement called 'linguistic philosophy' which has since passed from fashion but from which lawyers can still learn much. We learned to pay precise attention to the way people speak and write. We repeated to ourselves and to anyone who would listen the salutary maxim that everything is what it is and not something else.[1]

That respect for things as they in their nature are is certainly a spirit which must inform any worthwhile philosophy of law, as it has informed Honoré's. Moreover, even while we recognize that linguistic analysis cannot be the be-all and end-all of any philosophy, we must still recognize it to be among the tasks which philosophers take on. In this paper, we wish to go back to consideration of one discovery of the Oxford philosophy of the 1950s, and to consider its implications for legal theory. Like Honoré, we think that 'lawyers can still learn much' from reflection on linguistic philosophy and its offshoot the philosophy of language. In particular, we shall try to show why the theory of 'speech acts' is of interest from a legal point of view. As our conclusions will show, the bearing which the theory of speech acts has on legal thought is, as one might almost have expected, of material relevance to the very questions which Honoré raised with such refreshing novelty in his paper on 'Real Laws' from which we have already quoted.

[1] See A. M. Honoré, 'Real Laws' in P. M. S. Hacker and J. Raz (eds.), *Law, Morality, and Society* (Oxford, 1977), pp. 99–118 at p. 117.

'Speech act' is a concept which in its terms reminds us that every saying is also a doing. Sometimes this is very obvious—when, for example, a jury foreman says 'Guilty', he thereby returns the jury's verdict; without the saying, there is no such doing. Speech acts are those very acts that we perform in and through the utterance of words. As our opening example shows, such acts are by no means foreign to lawyers' concerns. For what we call 'acts in the law' are acts often (indeed, usually) carried out by means of the utterance of words.

I. SPEECH ACTS AND ACTS IN THE LAW

Historically, the development by J. L. Austin of the theory of speech acts owed a certain amount to reflection on the nature of acts in the law. The theory emerged in a series of seminars conducted in Oxford in the post-war years by Austin, together with H. L. A. Hart. As Austin developed his ideas about 'performative utterances', about 'how to do things with words', Hart, on the basis of his pre-war practice as a private lawyer, showed the analogy between such acts and formal legal acts like the making of a will or the transfer of immovable property or the formation of a limited company. Hart also contributed the proposal (based on this analogy) that 'performative utterances' should be called 'operative utterances' on the parallel of what lawyers call the 'operative words' in a legal deed or instrument.[2]

If legal theory thus contributed to linguistic theory, an equally large converse contribution was made by Austinian linguistic philosophy to the development of Hart's philosophy of law. The contribution was, in effect, to Hart's theory of acts in the law.[3] Such acts, he argued, can take place only on the assumption that the actor is exercising a legal power—the power to make a unilateral promise, to enter a contract, to solemnize a marriage, to make a will, or even to enact a law. But such powers presuppose power-conferring rules; these rules stipulate what is required for the *valid* performance of an act of the kind in question, and stipulate which (classes of) persons may perform it. Hart's favourite illustration of this is actually the non-legal case of making a morally binding promise. His theory is that there have to be social rules stipulating what counts as a valid promise. These rules then necessarily connect on to another rule according to which there is a binding obligation to keep promises. Here there is both an acknowledged borrowing from and development of Austin's theory of performative utterances and also a prefiguring of the theory of John Rawls

[2] J. L. Austin, *Philosophical Papers* (Oxford, 1961), ch. 10, 'Performative Utterances'; *How to do Things with Words* (Oxford, 1962); H. L. A. Hart, *Essays in Jurisprudence and Philosophy* (Oxford, 1983), pp. 1-4; N. MacCormick, *H. L. A. Hart* (London, 1981), pp. 12-19.

[3] H. L. A. Hart, *The Concept of Law* (Oxford, 1961), ch. 5; cf. MacCormick, *Hart*, pp. 25-6, 92-120.

about 'constitutive' and 'regulative' rules, itself in turn further elaborated by John Searle in his theory of social institutions and speech acts.[4]

For Hart, of course, this distinction between rules conferring powers and rules imposing duties is fundamental to his whole analysis of the concept of law. The distinction between rules which confer powers to perform acts in the law and rules which impose obligations, including obligations arising from valid exercises of power, is a crucial one. It is a vital part of, though not the whole of, his theory of the distinction between primary rules (rules of obligation) and secondary rules (including power-conferring rules). It will be recalled that Hart's theory of law is explicitly a theory of law as 'the union of primary and secondary rules'.[5]

This theory of the structure of legal systems is not free from difficulties and problems, though it may be possible to reconstruct it in a way that both avoids internal incoherence and appears applicable to the explanation of real legal systems. This is not the proper occasion for pursuing these questions, however. Of greater present importance are some of the implications of this theory. Most striking is the radical incompatibility of such a theory with any thoroughgoing voluntarism as to the nature of laws, rules or norms.

The fundamental point already noted is that all valid acts in the law, all exercises of legal power, are held to presuppose some rule which is constitutive of the act as an act in the law, or (in the alternative) which confers the power exercised by doing the act in question. If this is correct, then it *necessarily* follows that not all rules can themselves be created by rule-creating acts, that is, by speech acts or acts of will aimed at creating rules. For an act can be a rule-creating act only if some rule confers rule-creating power. Thus, to avoid an unacceptable *regressus ad infinitum*, we must suppose that not all the rules which confer rule-creating power can themselves be created rules.

Furthermore, since an act is an act in the law only on condition that some regard or consideration *ought to be* or *must be* had to the new legal state of affairs which is created by its performance, the same conclusion applies in this case also. Normative rules cannot all be explicable in terms of performative utterances or of acts in the law. For it is clear that any performative utterance or act in the law presupposes some prior rule under which one ought to or must have regard to the new state of affairs it creates. So at least some normative rules must be envisaged as existing in logical priority to any performative utterance or speech act. Since normative rules are the most important species of the genus 'norm', it follows also that not all norms are explicable in terms of speech acts or acts in the law. The case

[4] Austin, op. cit.; J. Rawls, 'The Concepts of Rules', (1955) 64 *Philosophical Review* 3–32; J. Searle, *Speech Acts* (Cambridge, 1969), pp. 33–42.

[5] Hart, *Concept of Law*, chs 5–6.

is exactly the converse. Norms have to be explicable independently of speech acts, since the latter require the former for their explication.

This logically necessary presupposition of non-posited norms as prior to speech acts or acts in the law mirrors Hans Kelsen's theory of the basic norm as a norm which is presupposd but not posited in the juristic consciousness. Yet Kelsen's over-stress on the 'subjective meaning' of acts of will as determinant of their normative quality finally led him to the quite unsatisfactory and untenable conclusion that the basic norm is the meaning of a fictitious act of will.[6]

When we consider the parallelism of speech acts with acts in the law the error of Kelsen's theory as to the ultimate validation of acts in the law becomes obvious. For it is surely clear that *conventional* (*customary*) norms or rules are crucial to the possibility of speech both at the level of pragmatics and at the level of semantics. It is the custom and usage of speech-communities that enables us to make intelligible utterances to each other at all; it is the same custom and usage which makes some utterances intelligible as (e.g.) promises, and (perhaps) the same custom and usage which enables us to tell when someone has made a promise which *ought to be kept*. It seems obvious that the customary norms of language—linguistic conventions—lie behind our speech acts. So too in law. Behind formally promulgated law there is always some presupposition of custom, or at least of some non-positive reason for compliance with posited norms—that is, norms created by those legally regulated speech acts which are acts in the law. As against Kelsen, this lends credence to the Hartian theory of the 'rule of recognition' as the fundamental and customary rule of a legal system,[7] or to Friedrich Lachmayer's theory of 'präkonstitutionelles Gewohnheitsrecht'.[8] And on any view, we must not make the mistake of supposing that norms will prove ultimately explicable in terms of those speech-acts which are norm-creating acts.

The truth is that although there are indeed norm-creating speech acts, the norms which are created by such processes—e.g. legislation, commands, wills, company statutes—are all *derivative* norms. The speech acts themselves presuppose 'higher' norms. And not all these higher norms can have the status of derivative norms. Some of them must be non-derivative. Hence an adequate theory of norms is prior to any adequate account of speech acts or acts in the law.

This conclusion would seem to follow rigorously from the classical theory of speech acts of Austin and his successors such as John Searle. Yet the argument contains a mistake. The mistake is to suppose that all speech acts

[6] H. Kelsen, *The Pure Theory of Law* (Berkeley, 1967), ch. 1.

[7] Hart, *Concept*, ch. 6.

[8] F. Lachmayer, 'Präkonstitutionelles Gewohnheitsrecht', (1979) 99 *Juristische Blätter*, pp. 411–15.

are rule-defined or derivative from norms. As we shall show, however (in a manner driving in part from some of Paul Grice's work,[9] there are some speech acts which are not so derived. These include some cases of assertions, of promises and of orders. Speech acts of the kind in question we call 'informal acts'. We deal with them in the next section of the paper.

II. INFORMAL ACTS

As we have said, it is a mistake to suppose that all speech acts relate to norms or derive from norms in the same way as do those highly formalized acts, normally speech acts, which we call acts in the law. In this section of the paper we shall say a little about informal speech acts, in a way which will help us to draw the contrast with formal speech acts and acts in the law. What will be said here summarizes work previously published by one of us in three separate papers.[10]

Analytically the simplest kind of human act comprises some observable bodily movement coupled with some intention. It seems plausible to suppose that at least some speech acts involve the combination of the utterance of sound with an intention as to the meaning of the sound. An inarticulate warning cry may be uttered by one person to another. Noise is sent out with the intention to warn. This may be heard and understood as its utterer meant it, and may save its hearer from imminent danger. This is most likely to occur when the hearer understands that the noise was made with the intention of being recognized as intending to warn.

But no sort of speech is as simple as this case of inarticulate sound. Always involved in speech are complex linguistic conventions, at least at the semantic level. And the kinds of intentions one exhibits in speaking are just as complex as in the case of inarticulate warnings—intentions that one's hearer shall recognize one's speaking as being intended in some more or less determinate sense. When I assert something, I do not only disclose an intention that you should treat as true the proposition I have spoken to you. I intentionally disclose to you an intention that you take what I say as true and an intention that you should regard my saying it in that way as a reason for your so believing. Or when I make a promise, I do not merely disclose an intention to do a promised act. I also intentionally disclose to you an intention that you should take my utterance as one on which I intend you to rely. When I order you to do something, I do not only

[9] Cf. H. Paul Grice, 'Meaning', (1957) 68 *Philosophical Review*, 67; P. F. Strawson, 'Intention and Convention in Speech Acts', (1964) 73 *Philosophical Review* 439–60.

[10] N. MacCormick, 'Legal Obligation and the Imperative Fallacy', in A. W. B. Simpson (ed.), *Oxford Essays in Jurisprudence. Second Series* (Oxford, 1973), pp. 100–30; 'Voluntary Obligations and Normative Powers', *Aristotelian Society Supplementary Volume* 46 (1972), pp. 59–78; 'What is Wrong with Deceit', (1983) 10 *Sydney Law Review* 7–19.

disclose a wish that you do that thing. I intentionally disclose an intention that you should do that thing by way of obedience to me.

Even when these points are stated in this highly compressed form, one thing is clear. All such intentions, although they are complex, are quite independent of any presuppositions about normative rules or power-conferring rules. Provided I know how to utter an indicative proposition in a natural language, and provided I utter one to somebody else with the requisite intention, I assert that proposition to that person. Nor is there here any possibility of drawing distinctions between formally valid and formally invalid assertions. Either I succeed or I fail in asserting something; no question of validity arises. Likewise, I either succeed in conveying an intention to be relied on, or fail; I promise or fail to promise. I either succeed in issuing a call for your obedience, by giving clear indication of my intention to do so, or I fail. I either give you an order, or fail to. There is here no necessary invocation of any rule giving me competence to make a promise or authority to issue orders. In the simplest cases, intentionally induced reliance and intentionally induced obedience are fully sufficient.

Wherever it is possible to specify the nature of a speech act by reference only to the utterance of words (and thus under presupposition of the semantic conventions as to what the words mean) and to the complex intention disclosed by the utterance, here there is what may be called an *informal speech act*. Such acts do not usually involve the use of explicit performative formulae, it being normal to rely on simple sentences, such as:

'The train is running 20 minutes late.' (assertion)
'I will meet you in time to catch the 2 p.m. train.' (promise)
'Do not fail to catch the 2 p.m. train.' (order)

Nevertheless, since intention is essential to the nature of such a speech act, it can be helpful to declare the relevant intention openly:

'I assure you that the train is running 20 minutes late.'
'I promise to meet you in time to catch the 2 p.m. train.'
'I order you to make sure of catching the 2 p.m. train.'

In each of these three cases, there are normative considerations which are relevant to the act in question. As for assertions: save in exceptional cases, one ought not to deceive or to mislead one's fellow humans—deceit is wrongful and dishonourable and, in gross cases, wicked. As for promises: save in exceptional cases, one ought not to break one's promise—breach of promise is wrongful and dishonourable and, in gross cases, wicked. These normative considerations are *natural*, not purely conventional, although one would expect them also to be conventional in any human community. Even apart from conventions, there are reasons why deceit and breach of promise are wrong. But what makes deceit and breach of promise wrong is *not* what makes asserting or promising possible. Of course, if deceit and infidelity were usual, serious assertions and firm promises might grow to be impossible. But that is because no one would take them seriously. It does not show or imply that the idea of seriously intending one's utterance as an assertion or a promise must presuppose some 'normative power' emanating from or associated with the norms of truth-telling and promise-keeping. Likewise, in the case of ordering, there are natural reasons *against* one's issuing orders *except* in those particular cases where there is good reason for somebody else to obey—whether reasons of coercive power, family relationship, special emergency or whatever. In the simplest case, such reasons are not a matter of conventionally established normative *competence*, but simply reasons of prudence and of appropriateness.

In all three cases, the normative implications of assertion, of promising, and of ordering are such that it may be important to make absolutely clear the intention with which one makes a certain utterance. When this is important, the explicit performative formula is of value: 'I promise to catch the train.'; 'I assure you the train is late.' This is a conventional way of declaring one's intention in such a way that it cannot afterwards be denied—not in normal cases, anyway. So one can be held to one's assertions, or promises—or to one's orders.

In important cases, it can of course come about that no one is considered to have given an assurance, made a promise, or issued an order, unless he explicitly says so. For these cases nothing would count as an assurance or as a promise or as an order in the absence of a formal performative utterance.

Then for those purposes, a special procedure is required. Only if the proper formula is used has a relevant assurance, promise or order been given. Now we have a condition of validity: unless the special performative procedure is followed, no valid assurance, promise or order exists. So no special action would be appropriate against a wrongful falsehood or breach of promise, or the issuance of a wrongful order or wrongful disobedience to a rightful order. Without the valid act, no relevant wrong is in fact done.

In this way, in special contexts and for special purposes, certain acts which can also be conceived as purely informal acts would become formal acts. Moreover, further qualifications could be introduced: stipulations as to the qualifications persons must have, before they are deemed able to do the act in question; further stipulations as to the act itself and the procedural formalities called for; stipulations as to required circumstances, and as to defeating or vitiating circumstances. When one envisages matters at this stage, one can see that here now are formal requirements for the formal act. There ae rules about what to do and how to do it in order to give a formal assurance, or a solemn promise, or an official order. To do the act validly, one must comply. Here we have what may properly be considered a 'norm of competence', a 'power-conferring rule', and only where validity is achieved do the normative consequences envisaged for the special cases apply. That is why the special procedures and so forth matter.

Thus would it be possible for informal acts to become formalized; that is, to come to be defined in terms of compliance with special 'constitutive rules' or 'secondary rules' or 'power-conferring rules' or whatever is the preferred term. But since there *can* be (and are) some informal acts, it is clear that not all speech acts presuppose norms. On that ground, it might seem possible to give an account of norms which would show them as deriving in their simplest form from the simplest sort of informal speech act. As a matter of fact, this is almost exactly what proponents of the imperative theory of law such as Jeremy Bentham and the other John Austin tried to do in the eighteenth and nineteenth centuries.[11]

Yet this view is also false. It amounts to what one of us has called 'the imperative fallacy'—one can no more derive an 'ought' from an imperative ('shall') than from an indicative ('is').[12] As we saw at an earlier stage, what is crucial to the whole argument about the formalization of informal acts is the very fact that there are natural or natural-and-conventional normative reasons for having regard to the states of affairs created by performances of such acts. These reasons can no more be derived from informal than from formal acts. So although the classical theory is wrong in supposing that all speech acts have to be explained in terms of prior norms, it is not wrong in thinking that norms are not ultimately explicable in terms of speech acts.

III. INFORMAL AND FORMAL ACTS: AN ILLUSTRATION

It may still be doubted whether there is a real difference between informal and formal acts, such as that which we have advanced. Further to illustrate and clarify our theory, and in the hope of dispelling doubt, we shall give in this section a pair of contrasting examples: on the one hand, the act of saying that a particular person is guilty of a certain murder, and on the other hand, the act of returning a verdict of murder upon an accused person at the end of a criminal trial.

Notice the following points: I can *say* that Macbeth is guilty of a certain murder, without holding any sort of official position; I can *say* this using any particular form of words I please, and whenever I choose to say it; no particular context is called for; nor is any particular manner or procedure of utterance called for.

Of course, morally speaking, I should not say such a thing unless I have

[11] J. Bentham, *Of Laws in General* (edd. J. Burns and H. L. A. Hart, London, 1970), ch. 1; J. Austin, *Lectures on Jurisprudence* (ed. R. Campbell, London, 1885), chs 1, 2, 6.

[12] MacCormick, 'Legal Obligation and the Imperative Fallacy', above, n. 10.

strong evidence for it and unless, on the evidence, I genuinely believe it to be true. Legally, it will be most unwise for me to say it unless I have compelling evidence to back up what I say; for otherwise I shall be liable to pay extremely large damages to Macbeth. But apart from the possibility that what I say is the legal wrong of defamation, the law takes no further account of my saying it.

By contrast, the act of pronouncing the verdict 'guilty' at the end of a criminal trial for murder differs on all points. Only a person specially appointed to be a juror and then elected by his or her fellow-jurors to be the jury foreman is able to say that someone is guilty *with the effect of thereby giving a verdict*; the form of words used is specified by (at least) custom and usage; and the words are spoken in a standard dialogue between judge and jury foreman; the context must be that of a particular stage in a particular highly formal procedure, viz. a criminal trial; it must be said only of a specifically accused person after that person has had a fair trial and after the jury has been correctly charged by the judge as to the relevant law.

Of course, since here one says the same thing as in the informal case (and despite doubts sometimes expressed, one says just the same thing, 'Guilty',) it follows that morally one should not say it unless one has extremely strong evidence for it and, on the evidence, believes it to be true. But all the more so in this case. For this formally defined act is formally defined precisely because of the legal effect it has. To say 'Guilty' in these circumstances is to *convict* Macbeth. Thereafter he faces sentence for murder and the sentence is one which the judge is duty-bound to pass on whoever is convicted of murder. He must sentence to life imprisonment. All this is true because returning a verdict is what one of us has called a 'truth certifying procedure'.[13] What is said to be true by this procedure of the law is *taken as an established truth* for all the ulterior purposes of the law, unless and until it is quashed on appeal.

All the aspects of formalization of the *saying* of 'Guilty' (or 'Not guilty') follow from and depend on the normative setting of the criminal law. Since this is a procedure which is designed to have profoundly important legal effects, it is a carefully designed, legally-defined procedure. It is that kind of highly formal speech act which is, classically, an act in the law at one and the same time.

We hope that this contrast of examples serves to highlight the difference between informal and formal acts. It also helps as a reminder that acts in the law belong to the class of formal acts. We shall proceed in the final section to link these to the theory of legal institutions.

[13] Zenon Bankowski, 'The Value of Truth: Fact Scepticism Revisited', (1981) 1, *Legal Studies* 257–68.

IV. FORMAL ACTS AND LEGAL INSTITUTIONS

In the course of the preceding section, we have alluded to the fact that formalized speech acts require to be specified in terms of answers to questions such as the following:

(i) What qualification must a person have to be able to perform this act?
(ii) What is the nature of the act to be performed?
(iii) With what intention must it be peformed?
(iv) What special procedures must be observed in order to perform it validly?
(v) In what circumstances must it be performed in order to be done validly?
(vi) What are the vitiating circumstances whose presence will invalidate an otherwise valid act, or render it liable to subsequent challenge?

In any conditions in which speech acts have become formalized, there are likely to be rules, or at least conventions, enabling us to answer these questions; they set what J. L. Austin called the 'felicity conditions' for any speech act.[14] While it is easy for lawyers to recognize how these apply in the case of the law, that is, in the case of those speech acts which are also acts in the law, we should be aware that not only positive law (state law) allows of such formality. The rules of many games, the laws and rituals of many forms of organized religion, the practices of markets and Stock Exchanges, the rituals for naming ships, and doubtless many others are no less obvious cases.

In all cases, legal or non-legal, there is some standard result which is ordinarily intended, whatever ulterior aims the actor may have in view. That is, the actor intends to realize the standard effects of the act: that this person be ordained a priest, that the game (or the game, set, and match), be awarded to that player, that the ship be henceforward called the *France*, or whatever. Such normative consequences as these are intrinsic to the very act—just as much as, when a person makes a valid will at law, it is a direct and normally intended consequence that his heirs or executors are then obliged in law to distribute his estate in accordance with his instructions.

Just as, in the case of formal acts, there are rules or conventions which determine what counts as a valid and proper performance of the act, so there are rules or conventions which determine its direct normative consequences. And at least the standard intention of the actor is always to produce these very consequences, whatever be his ulterior reason for wishing to bring them about. This reflection is of particular significance in relation to positive law, where the very point of performing the act in the

[14] J. L. Austin, *How to do Things with Words*, pp. 14–15.

law is to bring about a significant change in the legal state of affairs—to bring into being some new legal consequences, such as those attending a valid contract or a valid will.

There are significant differences in law, of course, as between those acts which fall within the scope of public law and those which fall within the scope of private law. A key difference concerns the ulterior purpose for which it is deemed legitimate to act. Whenever it is deemed appropriate that a person act according to his or her own wishes directed at his or her own good or that of persons he or she chooses to favour, what is afoot is private acting. Whenever a person is required to act for the good of the community or a section of it identified without regard to personal friendship or relationship, the power of acting is a public power.

These differences are characteristically mirrored in the conditions for performance of an act. In the case of acts within the scope of private law, capacity to act depends upon such things as age, sex, marital condition, and the like, or upon an appointment made for private ends; it is a matter of *status* to determine who can do what. In the case of public acts, *competence* to perform them depends not only or necessarily on 'status' conditions, but rather upon appointment or election to some official position or office. A further difference is that public acts can and do normally have compulsory effect, regardless of the agreement or consent of persons affected. Private acts, by contrast, normally take effect only by agreement with parties affected, except in cases of special relationships, for example parent and child.

It is a common and helpful usage to say that formalized acts and the practices surrounding them amount to institutions, whether social and moral institutions such as promising, religious ones such as the sacraments, or legal ones such as contracts, wills, marriages, or the formation of limited companies, or in the public law sphere administrative decisions and judicial determinations of litigation. An adequate theory of formal speech acts as acts in the law is therefore a part of the theory of legal institutions. One of us has put forward a theory of legal institutions which is in fact the theoretical foundation for the approach taken in this paper.[15]

This theory states that every legal institution should be conceptualized in terms of a triad of interrelated rules. There have to be institutive rules stipulating what persons with what qualifications by what acts and with what intentions can, by following which procedures in which required circumstances and in the absence of what vitiating circumstances, create an instance of a given institution—for example make a contract, conclude a marriage, execute a will. There have to be consequential rules which

[15] MacCormick, 'Law as Institutional Fact', (1974) 90 *Law Quarterly Review* 102–29; N. MacCormick and Ota Weinberger, *Grundlagen des Institutionalistischen Rechtspositivismus* (Berlin, 1985), to be published in English as *An Institutional Theory of Law* (Dordrecht, 1986).

stipulate what are the legal results of a valid contract, or marriage, or will—these rules say who may, must or can do what sorts of things given the existence of a valid instance of the institution. Finally, there have to be terminative rules—concerning for example dissolution of contracts, divorce, or the winding-up of estates.

Such a theory makes various things clear. First, it shows us how to understand the existence of highly abstract legal entities. Secondly, it shows us how our legal concepts and thus our legal activities are structured. Institutive rules give us conditions of validity of institutions. As such, they guide our actions—what have we to be and to do in order to make a contract, and what defects must we avoid? What have we to be and to do in order to make an administrative decision, and what defects must we avoid? This guidance is of course only hypothetical—it is guidance on what to do if we *wish* to make a contract or an administrative decision. But we have reason to wish that only if we have reason to wish the relevant consequential rules to come into operation—so that we will owe each other enforceable contractual duties, or so that it will be lawful for the hospital to be built there. And these will be rational to wish if we have ulterior, non-legal motives for wanting these duties or that hospital to exist.

Also in providing criteria for validity of institutions, the institutive rules provide the possible grounds for challenging the effects of some purported contract or will or administrative decision. For example, in private law, we shall challenge the status or capacity of the contractor or testator—too young, perhaps, only a minor; or in public law we shall challenge the administrator's competence for the case—it is *ultra vires*, or he is disqualified by interest; or the wrong act was performed—the acceptance was not in the same terms as the offer, no 'decision' as such was made; or there were procedural defects either as to form (contract not in writing) or as to substance (failure to hear both sides); or defects in intention—(acting under a mistake in private law, or acting in absence of power, in public law; or the circumstances were wrong (the contract was about a non-existent entity); or some feature was lacking which is essential to the administrative authority's jurisdiction; or some vitiating fact was present (duress in contract, or some overriding provision of public law applying in this case).

Even to state matters in so brief an outline and with mere allusion to possible illustrations in private and public law is sufficient to exhibit the general analytical and explanatory power of the theory. The theory is one which draws on the classical modern theory of speech acts, but which does, in our opinion, go beyond it in helpful ways. In doing so, it helps to show the profound legal relevance of the theory of speech acts. Moreover, as a theory of the structure of legal activity it at least has the promise of yielding a new view of the overall structure of legal systems.

Why it should have that promise can best be stated in words of Honoré's.

The legal way of looking at life, he suggests, involves looking at things 'from a special point of vantage. To attain this point of vantage requires the transformation of the data of ordinary life into those of a special drama with its own personages, costumes, and conventions, not to mention the invention of new personages and relationships not found in the state of nature.'[16] Our thesis is that these transformation rules are to be found in what we have called 'institutive rules' of institutions, Honoré's own term for these is, however, 'existence laws' (a category which also includes our 'terminative rules'). And similar, perhaps, from our point of view are 'position-specifying rules'. What Honoré's terminology most happily indicates is the ontological implications of the process of legal transformation—certainly, we need a theory about existence broad enough to encompass the existence of entities and relations which exist only in and for the purposes of the law. This point has hitherto been seen clearly by Honoré and by Ota Weinberger, and perhaps by them only.[17]

To conclude, we believe that a concern with legal realities and with the reality of laws cannot be better signalized than through a hearty salutation to the author of 'Real Laws'. This all implies a concern with legal realities and thus with the ontology of law. Such a concern is no doubt apt to land one in deep water philosophically. It may also seem to remove one some way from the daily concerns of 'real lawyers'. But its unavoidable importance would be obvious to the author of 'Real Laws' and reflection upon it is therefore, perhaps, a proper tribute to him. Anyway, it would be difficult to doubt that any work in the spirit of 'Real Laws' could truly be irrelevant to the interests of any real lawyer.

[16] Honoré, 'Real Laws', p. 112.

[17] See Weinberger, 'The Norm as Thought and as Reality' and 'Facts and Fact-Descriptions' in MacCormick and Weinberger, *Institutional Theory*, chs 1 and 3.

8

Digest 23. 2. 6

ANDREW LEWIS

Denique Cinna scribit: eum qui absentem accepit uxorem deinde rediens a cena juxta Tiberim perisset ab uxore lugendum responsum est.

I. LITERARY CONTEXT

(*i*) *Ulpian*

THE text is from Ulpian's 35th book *ad Sabinum*, which is concerned, like the immediately preceding and following books, with the larger question of *dos*. The texts from the 35th book treat first the creation of marriage for the purpose of satisfying conditional promises of dowry[1] and secondly the consequences of termination of marriage,[2] a topic which is continued into book 36.[3] In Lenel's reconstruction[4] our text is immediately preceded by 35. 1. 15:

Cui fuerit sub hac condicione legatum 'si in familia nupsisset' videtur impleta condicio statim atque ducta est uxor quamvis nondum in cubiculum mariti venerit. nuptias enim non concubitus sed consensus facit.

Here Ulpian is dealing with a conditional legacy *si in familia nupsisset* which belongs in this context either because of the similarity of the legal issues raised, namely when is a woman married?, or, more simply, because it is the post-mortem equivalent of dowry from a living relative. The answer given is that a woman is married and the condition fulfilled as soon as the wife has been led in, although she has not yet entered her husband's bedroom. The *regula*, 'nuptias non concubitus sed consensus facit', recurs in 50. 17. 30. The only ground for questioning its authenticity seems to be its generalizing quality. Our text is then an extreme illustration of this proposition: it holds good even where the husband has not been seen by his wife and where he has not even entered the matrimonial home. The main concern of the text is not *dos* but the observation of mourning. For the example to work in Ulpian's context it must have been obvious without further

[1] e.g. D. 23. 3. 21. 'si nuptiae fuerint secutae'; 'si in familia nupsisset'.

[2] e.g. D. 24. 3. 2.

[3] e.g. D. 24. 3. 19.

[4] *Palingenesia Iuris Civilis* (Leipzig 1889, repr. 1960) vol. ii, vol. 1150.

demonstration that one who has to mourn has fulfilled the terms of the type of condition discussed, i.e. has been married.

According to our honorand's reconstruction of Ulpian's work programme this part of the Sabinian commentary was written during the year 216. It was excerpted by the junior member of the Sabinian Committee, the expert on the proprietary aspects of marriage (probably Dorotheus), during the second quarter of 531.[5]

(ii) Cinna

Cinna is amongst the least known of Roman jurists. According to the compilers' version of Pomponius' biographical history he was one of those who studied under Servius Sulpicius Rufus:

1. 2. 2. 44. Ab hoc plurimi profecerunt, fere hi libris conscripserunt: Alfenus Varus Gaius Aulus Ofilius Titus Caesius Aufidius Tucca Aufidius Namusa Flavius Priscus Gaius Ateius Pacuvius Labeo Antistius Labeonis Antistii pater Cinna Publicius Gellius ex his decem libros octo conscripserunt quorum omnes qui fuerunt libri digesti sunt ab Aufidio Namusa in centum quadraginta libros. ex his auditoribus plurimum auctoritatis habuit Alfenus Varus et Aulus Ofilius ex quibus Varus et consul fuit, Ofilius in equestri ordine perseveravit ...

With the exception of Labeo's father Pacuvius Labeo Antistius all the jurists named in the list are identified by praenomen and nomen or nomen and cognomen except Cinna.[6] The spare Gaius standing between the first two jurists must be deleted: it cannot be intended to refer to an eleventh jurist as the subsequent reference to 'eight of these ten' jurists makes clear. It is possible that the praenomen Gaius has been displaced and that it originally stood before Cinna. There are three known persons of the late Republic named Cinna. The most likely candidate for identification with the jurist is C. Helvius Cinna who was tribune of the plebs in 44 BC. He was killed by the mob in the aftermath of Julius Caesar's funeral in mistake for his namesake L. Cornelius Cinna, who was M. Brutus' colleague as praetor that year and suspected of complicity in the plot to assassinate Caesar.[7] Cornelius Cinna is himself a possibility as our judgment on the matter is little better than that of the Roman mob. The third is the poet Helvius Cinna, the *contubernalis*[8] of Catullus. Plutarch, indeed, appears to identify this Cinna with the tribune C. Helvius Cinna since he refers to the killing

[5] Tony Honoré, *Ulpian* (Oxford, 1982), p. 153; *Tribonian* (Duckworth, 1978), pp. 170, 258.

[6] Of the jurists mentioned by Pomponius in D. 1. 2. 2. 44 only Alfenus Varus, Aulus Ofilius and Pacuvius Antistius Labeo are familiar to us from other contexts. There is little doubt about the identification of the names of the others listed, however, with the exception of Publicius Gellius, whose praenomen is usually corrected to Publius. As his name is the last in the list this is the most economical explanation of the difficulty. Any other solution risks abandoning the reliability of the text altogether.

[7] Plutarch, *Caesar* lxviii. 3.

[8] Catullus, 10. 29: *meus sodalis Cinna est Gaius* and cf. 37. 1.

of the latter as of a *ποιητικὸς ἀνήρ*.[9] This in its turn provides Shakespeare with one of his more dramatic scenes,[10] for when attacked by the mob Cinna cries:

'I am Cinna the poet! I am Cinna the poet!', to which a voice replies:

'Kill him for his bad verses! Kill him for his bad verses!'

a qualitative judgment which a perusal of his remaining few fragments does little to refute.[11]

Only two texts of the jurist Cinna survive, our own 33. 2. 6 being the more important. The other is an indirect quotation made by Labeo or Javolenus and preserved in the latter's 2nd book of Labeo's posthumous works:

35. 1. 40. 1 Quidam ita legaverat: si Publius Cornelius impensam quam in fundum Seianum feci heredi meo dederit tum heres meus Publio Cornelio fundum Seianum dato. Cascellius aiebat etiam pretium fundi dari debere, Ofilius impensae verbo negat pretium significari sed eos dumtaxat sumptus quos in eum posteaquam emptus esset fecit. idem Cinna scribit adiecto eo quod non deductis fructibus impensarum ratio haberi debeat: et hoc magis verum puto.

There is a legacy in which Publius Cornelius is given the Seian estate if he reimburses the heir for the costs expended on the estate. A number of late first-century BC jurists offer their opinions. Cascellius, a follower of Quintus Mucius, thought that the legatee had to pay back the whole cost of the estate including the price which the testator had paid for it. Ofilius, a pupil with Cinna of Servius Sulpicius, reckoned that the word *impensa* excluded the notion of price so the legatee had only to pay the amount of subsequent expenditure on the upkeep of the estate. Cinna agreed, adding that in reckoning the cost there should be no deduction in respect of any profit which had accrued as a result of the exploitation of the estate: in other words, the costs should be gross and not net. It is the view of Ofilius as glossed by Cinna which is endorsed by Labeo and Javolenus. At first glance it might be thought that the later jurists are expressly referring to Cinna's opinion. But the better view must be that Cinna is only making express what is already contained in Ofilius' response. In the context Ofilius' *dumtaxat sumptus* seems only to contrast the expenditure subsequent to the purchase with Cascellius' opinion that the original price was included. The incautious might not conclude that all the subsequent expenditure was

[9] Plutarch, *Brutus* xx. 5: ἦν δέ τις Κίννας ποιητικὸς ἀνήρ. οὐδὲν τῆς αἰτίας μετέχων, ἀλλᾶ καὶ φίλος Καίσαρος γεγονώς. cf. Valerius Maximus ix. 9. 1. and Suetonius, *Div. Jul.* 85.

[10] W. Shakespeare, *Julius Caesar*, III. ii. 3. Shakespeare's literary source for this play was Sir Francis North's 1579 translation of Jacques Amyot's French version of Plutarch, published in 1559.

[11] For what remains of Cinna's verse see *Fragmenta Poetarum Latinorum*, ed. W. Morel (2nd edn., Leipzig, 1927, repr. Stuttgart, 1963), pp. 87–90.

claimable: hence Cinna's careful gloss. But *dumtaxat* need not be taken merely to exclude what is not properly an expense since the purchase but positively to include all such expenditure.[12] This view would of necessity exclude any set-off for an advantage gained from the exploitation of the estate. In this light Cinna appears as the careful if unoriginal fellow pupil of Servius Sulpicius, who spells out the implications of his more distinguished colleague, whose substantive opinion it is that is endorsed by the subsequent jurists.

Returning to our own text 23. 2. 6, I have already observed that the context is a discussion of the *tempus lugendi*, the period of mourning imposed upon a widow on the death of her husband. Even a wife who had never met her husband or been in the matrimonial house with him must undergo mourning.[13] According to Plutarch[14] in the early Republic the obligation to mourn lasted for ten months: during this period the widow was to refrain from remarriage under penalty of religious, if not also social, sanctions. Humbert has plausibly suggested from epigraphic evidence that it was customary to abstain for even longer periods if not permanently and that the supposed legislation of Numa, whatever its exact nature, was designed to limit rather than extend the practice. A remarriage during the *tempus lugendi* was not invalidated by the civil law but the Praetor's Edict gave effect to the ostracism which accompanied such a breach of *mos maiorum* by a provision in the edict *de cognitoribus*.[15]

II. ANALYSIS OF THE TEXT

(*a*) *absentem accepit uxorem*

The marriage has been effected between parties who were apart. The husband accepts the wife as a counterpart to her handing over—*collocare*, *tradere*, *dare* are all commonly used. The handing over will be effected typically by the bride's father as *paterfamilias*, though if she be *sui iuris* the language is not necessarily inappropriate. As has been argued by Corbett[16]

[12] For other legal contexts see especially D. 25. 4. 1. 10 (Ulpian 24 *ad ed.*): 'mittantur autem mulieres liberae dumtaxat quinque haeque simul omnes inspiciant' (from the edict *de inspiciendo ventre*). D. 26. 7. 12. 3 (Paul 38 *ad ed.*): 'cum tutor non rebus dumtaxat sed etiam moribus pupilli praeponatur ...'

[13] There are no certain clues to the context of Cinna's remarks. Servius Sulpicius Rufus wrote a book on *dos* referred to by Neratius (D. 12. 4. 8) and by Aulus Gellius (*Noct. Att.* 4. 3–4) and some would ascribe the responsibility for our text to Servius Sulpicius (W. Kunkel, *Herkunft und soziale Stellung der römischer Juristen*² (Graz, 1967), p. 35; F. Schulz, *History of Roman Legal Science* (Oxford, 1953), pp. 43, 48). But the question of mourning is not directly related to the recovery of *dos* except for the fact that the husband's death conditions both.

[14] *Numa*, 12; on the rule relating to remarriage, M. Humbert, *Le remariage à Rome* (Pubb. Inst. Dir. Rom. 44, Rome, 1972), pp. 113ff.

[15] Julian cites the text of the edict in D. 3. 2. 1 pr. and a similar version is preserved in *Frag. Vat.* 320 possibly from Paul *ad ed.*

[16] P. E. Corbett, *The Roman Law of Marriage* (Oxford, 1930), p. 55.

the *collocare/accipere* conjunction does not necessarily relate to the juridical analysis; in particular it does not follow from its use that the consent of the future wife was irrelevant. Rather it reflects the social reality of the younger wife who leaves her father's house, though not in free marriage his household, to live with her husband.

No ceremonial was of course required; hence the ease of arranging to marry whilst apart. For such ceremony as was thought socially and evidentially appropriate doubtless proxies might be used. No question of agency arises. The marriage itself is created by the consent of the parties. Since both (or all, supposing a *paterfamilias* to be involved—cf. Paul 23. 2. 2 'nisi consentiant omnes') must consent simultaneously the marriage can only be validly created if the one consents whilst the other is still consenting. Proof that the prior consent had been withdrawn before the latter was given must necessarily avoid the arrangement.[17] There is no discussion in the texts, perhaps reflecting the fact that proof is here as difficult as the law is straightforward.

If one be absent from another, then it must follow that the other is absent from him. Yet for the author of Paul's Sentences much turns on this:

P.S. 2. 19. 8 Vir absens uxorem ducere potest: femina absens nubere non potest.

The meaning of which would seem to be explained by Pomponius in his fourth (or fourteenth) book *ad Sabinum*:

23. 2. 5 Mulierem absenti per litteras eius vel per nuntium posse nubere placet si in domum eius deduceretur.

A woman can be married to an absent husband so long as she is led into his house.[18] The true significance of *deductio in domum* seems to be this: no act is required for the creation of a valid marriage, consent being both necessary and sufficient. However, when the parties are apart there needs to be certainty about the time from which the marriage is reckoned to take place and this is taken to be from the time the woman is introduced into her husband's house following her consent to the marriage.[19]

A *deductio* has taken place in the example in our text. *Rediens*, as will appear, should be taken in a local and not purely a temporal sense to indicate that the husband has to return from the place of feasting to his house where his wife is already installed. One immediate difficulty is that

[17] Similar problems are of course familiar from the law relating to simple contracts.

[18] Cf. Ulpian D. 23. 1. 4. 1 from the same 35th book cited and discussed below, n. 21.

[19] That *deductio* of itself is insufficient is shown by Scaevola in his 9th book *digestorum* (D. 24. 1. 66 pr.–1) where he gives two examples in which a gift was made after a woman had been introduced into the house but before the parties had agreed to marry or before the celebration of the usual ceremonials: not only is such a gift valid and not caught by the rules forbidding gifts between husband and wife but neither can it be reckoned as a part of the dowry.

the adjective indicating absence qualifies the wife and not the husband, who is the subject of the relative pronoun. Paul Faber indeed suggested *absens* for *absentem* in order to give the expected meaning that it is the husband who is absent from the house when the marriage takes place and the wife present, as the immediately preceding Digest passage of Pomponius (23. 2. 5) requires. Modern scholars have shared this opinion. Corbett in a footnote casually assumes that the emendation is to be made[20] whilst Capocci argued forcefully for it.[21] But the correction is of the crudest sort with no good reason other than a prejudice as to what should have been written to support it. There is no reason to believe that a copying scribe would have written the accusative in error for the nominative in view of the fact that the verb *accepit* occurs between *absentem* and *uxorem* and if, as urged by Capocci, he was influenced by the case of *eum* then his Latin must have been of the most elementary sort given the proximity of the pronoun in the nominative.

Those who urge this correction do so in order to square our text with those which require the woman to be *domi* and only the husband away from it. But this can be done with the text as it stands. *Absens* is not technical and is ambiguous: one who is absent is away from someone or somewhere. A *vir absens* is either away from his *uxor* or from his house and matrimonial home. In Pomponius' text, 23. 2. 5, the absence is local; it is spelt out that the wife must be led not into her own but into her husband's house as the matrimonial home. It is from his house that the husband is absent and hence apart from his wife who is there. But in our text the meaning is personal: the parties are apart, absent from each other. This can be as well expressed by referring to the wife as absent as it can by so referring to the man. The same meaning is apparent in the related Ulpian passage in 23. 1. 4. 1, also from the 35th book *ad Sabinum*: 'Denique constat et absenti absentem desponderi posse et hoc cottidie fieri'.[22] As our text stands in proximity to the Pomponius text there is a possibility of misunderstanding. But the original was written some considerable time before those using absence in a purely local sense.

[20] Faber's opinion stands in the apparatus of Mommsen's *editio major* (*Digesta Iustiniani* I, Berlin, 1870), 658; see P. Faber, *Semestrium lib II* (Geneva, 1660), 349.

[21] Corbett, op. cit., 93 n. 2. V. Capocci 'Il testo del responso di Cinna riferito da Ulpiano: D. 23. 2. 6', (1958) 24 SDHI 297–307. Capocci suggests restoring Faber's reading to the text of any future edition of the Digest and explaining the Florentine absentum as an error attracted by *uxorem*.

[22] *Denique* appears to be particularly Ulpianic. It is not discussed by Honoré in *Ulpian*, cit., but the *Concordance to the Digest Jurists* (T. Honoré and J. Menner, Oxford Microform) reveals that he used it 127 times in the Digest. Of these 16 are *denique si* and on 45 occasions *denique* is followed by a construction with *scribit*, *ait* or the like. Paul, by contrast, uses *denique* but 12 times, five of which are *denique si*: Papinian has it on 13 occasions of which two are with *si* and three are citations or similar.

(*b*) *deinde rediens a cena*

As I have already indicated, *deinde* here bears its literal maning 'from there'. The husband has been out feasting and returns thence to the matrimonial home where his wife is already installed. Such a dinner can only have been a celebration of the marriage. The possibility that this was an ordinary dinner engagement that the husband was unwilling to forgo even on his wedding-night can surely be set aside. Gentilis suggested that the party was at his father-in-law's. Presumably there was a celebratory drink or two.[23]

(*c*) *juxta Tiberim perisset*

The Tiber is rarely mentioned in juristic texts. In D. 1. 2. 2. 31. the *quinqueviri cis* and *ultis Tiberim* are discussed and in 39. 2. 9. 1 Trebatius reports a case which turns on the Tiber's flooding. Here it is merely, though significantly, a geographic location. The husband returns home beside the Tiber. Whilst thus engaged he died. What more likely than that he fell in, particularly if he were suffering in any way from the effects of over-indulging himself at the feast?[24]

CONCLUSIONS

The text is from Ulpian's discussion of *dos*. The context is the occurrence of marriage as an event upon which the giving of *dos* is conditioned. For Ulpian to have used this example it must have been clear that one who has to mourn has to have been married. For Cinna, of whom little is known save that he may be identified with the C. Helvius Cinna killed by the mob in 44 BC, the text concerns the *tempus lugendi*, and perhaps the original context was the Praetorian Edict *de cognitoribus* and a discussion of *infamia*. The only other opinion attributed to Cinna does not suggest originality.

The text shows that a marriage is held to have come into existence even though the parties have not met and even though the husband has not yet entered the matrimonial home. Despite earlier suggestions to the contrary, the text is good as it stands: the correction of *absentem* to *absens* is unnecessary since the meaning is that the parties are absent from each other and not from any particular place. *Deductio in domum* is perfectly compatible with the text.

[23] For Gentilis see R. Orestano, *La struttura giuridica del matrimonio romano* (Milan, 1951), 154 nn. 408 and 411. This portion of the text has not escaped the restorers' suggestions for improvement. One of the more entertaining is to read *Creta* for *cena* to explain the husband's proximity to the Tiber. We are to imagine his falling in whilst disembarking.

[24] A. Watson, 'Drunkenness in Roman Law' in W. G. Becher (ed.), *Sein und Werden im Recht* (Berlin, 1970), pp. 381–7 does not refer to our text and it is not one of his 'not more than six texts which relate in any way to intoxication, conduct influenced by alcohol, habitual drunkenness or heavy drinking' of which 'only two or three seem to concern acts done while drunk'. However, our text adds nothing to Watson's conclusion that drunkenness was neither a mitigating nor an aggravating circumstance in the law relating to civil liability or responsibility.

9

Ownership of Land in English Law

J. W. HARRIS

PROFESSOR HONORÉ'S seminal essay on ownership is famous among his many distinguished contributions to philosophy, jurisprudence, and legal academic studies.[1] It has been a constant point of reference for those seeking to grapple with this highly elusive concept. In it, he contends that the liberal conception of ownership is, in various degrees, taken for granted by all mature legal systems. English land law is, in his view, no exception: the terminology of 'ownership of land' may properly be employed to express the law's standard impact.

The conventional view amongst English lawyers, however, is that ownership of land is not a concept internal to our law.[2] In his daily technical work, this particular concept does not obviously cross the land lawyer's path. He conveys, or deduces title to, estates and lesser interests. As a student, he was obliged to wrestle with a menagerie of weird and wonderful specialist concepts; but speculations about the meaning of ownership did not trouble him. Could it be that, although English land law presupposes ownership, it does not actually employ it; that ownership of land is a socio-political, but not a legal, concept?

'English land law has made no contribution to the legal theory of ownership more striking, more brilliant and of more permanent value than the separation of the land from the estate in the land.... By distinguishing the land from the estate, English land law has shown conclusively that even within a society as individualistic and as legalistic as England in the nineteenth century, ownership is not a necessary legal concept. The problem of ownership remains, but it is not a legal problem: it is the concern of the politician, the economist, the sociologist, the moralist, the psychologist—of any and every specialist who can contribute his grain to the common heap. Ultimately the philosopher will try to unify this shifting mass into a coherent whole.'[3]

In these words, A. D. Hargreaves gives robust expression to a common view. We English get along fine without recognizing ownership of land as

[1] A. M. Honoré, 'Ownership', in A. G. Guest (ed.), *Oxford Essays in Jurisprudence* (Oxford, 1961). See also Honoré, 'Property, Title and Redistribution', in C. Wellman (ed.), *Equality and Freedom* (Wiesbaden, 1977).

[2] See, for example, B. Rudden, 'Notes Towards a Grammar of Property' [1980] Conv. 325.

[3] A. D. Hargreaves, 'Modern Real Property' (1956) 19 MLR 14, 17.

a distinct legal concept. Although the social, political, and economic contours of other systems may not differ radically from our own, our legal thought has been spared this particular facet of Romanism. Thanks to our conceptual heritage of estates and interests in land, we are able, as lawyers, to handle the problems of an evolving institution of private property in land without resort to this will-o'-the-wisp among concepts.

I propose to challenge this view. I shall argue that English land law does employ the concept of ownership of land, alongside all its more technical concepts. Since it is conceded on all sides that the concept is part of our political culture, this will require consideration of what it means for a concept to be a legal one. It will also involve some reflection on different senses of 'ownership of land'. First, however, I wish to look at the bare-bones structure of the institution of private property in land itself. With this in perspective, we can attend to the question of how English law, in the conventional view, manages the trick of operating a version of the institution without benefit of ownership.

When Jeremy Bentham attempted to lay the analytic foundations for a property code, he gave the following as the paradigm type of a rule of land law: 'Let no-one, Rusticus excepted', (so we will call the proprietor) 'and those whom he allows meddle with such or such a field.'[4] This may seem a surprising suggestion to any student of English land law. His materials appear far removed from any such rules—let us call them 'trespassory rules'. There are none in the 1925 property legislation, and much of the case-law is pre-occupied with identifying Rusticus and those whom he allows, rather than with the meddlers. The identification is made with the help of specialist entities—estates and interests. Surely the principles governing the deployment of these technical concepts are much more typical of land law than are trespassory rules.

For all that, there is a germ of truth in Bentham's proposal. There would be no legally protected interests in land if there were no trespassory rules, civil or criminal, according privileged enjoyment to some persons. Without such rules, one could have a public law relating to land consisting of rules prohibiting some kinds of land-use to all or to defined classes of persons—call them 'general use rules'. If there were only general use rules, there would be no private interests in land. Privileged individual use requires trespassory rules. To this extent property law presupposes the law of obligations. However, the institution of private property in land requires something further. It entails that some at least of the privileges vouchsafed by the trespassory rules must be transmissible by one person to another as part of his private wealth. Hence, wherever the institution prevails, systems of land law must evolve principles in accordance with which interests

[4] J. Bentham, *Of Laws in General*, ed. H. L. A. Hart (London, 1970), p. 177.

in land are created, terminated, and transmitted—call them 'transmission principles'.

Thus, in brief and crude terms, the institution of private property in land entails three kinds of legal provision: first, trespassory rules. Second, transmission principles (including formality rules, capacity rules, conceptual definitions and distinctions, and supervening doctrinal maxims of all kinds). Third, general use rules governing land-use by all or some members of the community.

General use rules are not analytically tied to the existence of the institution, since one could conceive of a society in which land-owners were free to do anything they liked, however heinous or anti-social, with and to their land. Historically, however, all instances of the institution have contained provisions of this sort. They limit the content of the privileges conferred by the trespassory rules.

The first two kinds of provision are analytically tied to the existence of the institution of private property in land. The institution would not exist, for example, in a nomadic community which enforced only general use rules. All members might be required to observe certain restraints in the use of watering-places, or in pitching dwellings. If, however, no trespassory rules existed (excluding all except a privileged 'possessor' from some part of the territory within the community's control), there would be land law, of a sort, but no private property in land.

Nor could the institution exist without transmission principles. Imagine a society in which the ideal of allocation of resources solely in accordance with present need was fully implemented. There might well be trespassory rules, but there could be no provisions allowing privileged possessors freely to transfer what they enjoy, for it could not be guaranteed that any such transfer would correlate with the present 'need' of the transferee.[5] Even if all that a flat-dweller has is a licence from the local party office to live in a state flat for so long as the party thinks fit, the nature of the licence presupposes that there are rules prohibiting other people from moving in. Private property exists only if such a licence, however described, is transmissible by its holder as something which is his.

Applying this analysis of the basic legal structure of the institution of private property in land to English law, we next ask whether the relevant provisions employ the concept of ownership of land. On a superficial reading, they do not. Our civil-law trespassory rules include those arising from the torts of trespass or nuisance, enforceable by damages or injunction. Most important is that rule which requires anyone who has taken possession of land as a trespasser to restore the land to whoever can show that he has a present right to possession by virtue of his title to a freehold or

[5] Cf. R. Nozick, *Anarchy, State and Utopia* (New York, 1974), pp. 160–4.

leasehold estate. This rule is enforceable in favour of the estate-owner by an order for specific restitution—what used to be called the remedy of ejectment—as of right. The court has no discretion to delay restitution.[6] The most important of our criminal law trespassory rules are now contained in Part II of the Criminal Law Act 1977. For example, section 7(1) makes it an offence for any person 'who is on any premises as a trespasser after having entered as such' to fail to leave on being required to do so by or on behalf either of a 'displaced residential occupier' or a 'protected intending occupier'.[7] These trespassory rules make no direct use of the concept of ownership of land. They protect those entitled to freehold or leasehold estates, and other licensed occupiers. Important instances of general use rules are comprised within the law of nuisance (which restricts landholder's enjoyment, as well as conferring privilege upon him), planning law, and public housing law. In such areas, frequent reference is made to owners of land. It is arguable, however, that such references can always be translated without change of meaning, into references to those entitled to occupy land by virtue of owning an estate or some other interest.

It is the transmission principles which bulk most large in English land law and conveyancing textbooks. They define estates and interests in land of all kinds, both legal and equitable. They stipulate the formalities required for the creation, transfer, devolution, and termination of such entities. And they comprise abstract, overarching doctrinal maxims delimiting the sorts of rights which can count as interests in land, as opposed to mere rights *in personam*. On the face of it, the concepts deployed within these principles are specialist technical ones, and do not include the concept of ownership. What may seem the most conclusive argument against ownership of land being a concept within English land law is that it plays no part in conveyancing or deduction of title. As the result of the tenurial origins of our conceptual structure, we convey or grant fees simple or leases. At no stage in our legal history has ownership of land, as such, been the subject-matter of transmission. When a vendor or anyone else is called on to prove his 'ownership', what he actually does is to invoke appropriate evidence that he is entitled to a freehold or leasehold estate.

If it could be shown that land-ownership is not employed within the three types of provision which structure the institution of private property in land, would that be enough to demonstrate that it is not a legal concept? We must distinguish two roles played by the collection of technical concepts

[6] *Department of the Environment* v. *James* [1972] 3 All ER 629; *McPhail* v. *Persons, Names Unknown* [1973] ch. 447.

[7] The category of 'protected intending occupier' includes an intending occupier who has just bought the freehold or a lease of at least 21 years (s. 7(2)), and a person licensed to enter by a local authority (s. 7(4)). Unlike the old law of forcible detainer, mere failure to leave, without any use or threat of force, is an offence.

which admittedly do form part of English land law, those concepts defined within the transmission principles. They may be used within the rules forming part of the present law, a momentary legal system. They may also be employed in those maxims which constitute land law doctrine, forming parts of non-momentary systems—'the common law' and 'equity'—in the light of which the law at any one time is interpreted and applied.[8] The present law on any particular issue may be clear because the rule in question uses a technical concept whose meaning, in context, is beyond dispute. Or there may be a 'hard case', where competing versions of the law are at least arguable. In a hard case, one of the accepted models of reasoning for settling the issue is the doctrine model.[9] The court may appeal to some contestable understanding of a concept as a reason for interpreting the rule one way rather than another. The familiar congeries of estates and interests features as part of such doctrinal reasoning.

Bentham believed that the deep structure of land law consisted of rules about what must, may, or must not be done in relation to land. He recognized, however, that surface information about legal provisions could not take this form. We might, for example, formulate one of Bentham's deep-structure trespassory rules as follows: 'If X is entitled to a freehold or leasehold estate in a parcel of land, and Y (who has no such title good against X, and no subsisting licence from X or his predecessors) is now occupying the land; Y must, on X's demand, forthwith restore possession to X'. This rule exists as part of the totality of legal rules governing use of land in England—that is, it is currently 'valid'.[10] It might be changed tomorrow were a tender-hearted parliament to ordain that squatters should be given some respite at the discretion of the court. At the time I write, however, this rule forms part of that momentary legal system which comprises that set of mutually consistent propositions, governing what must, must not, or may be done by law, which it is the court's duty, in accordance with the values of legality and constitutionality, to apply. The rule may be used to give clear legal answers to many issues that might arise in daily life. Yet no one could apply such a rule unless he were familiar with a whole set of concepts and distinctions concerning estates, titles, and so on. These latter form parts of historic (non-momentary) systems established by the tradition of English courts. They would be deployed even supposing parliament were to alter the law in favour of squatters.

Apart from being used within rules, these same concepts and distinctions constitute land law doctrine. A solution to some argued point of law may be reached by appeal to the essential nature of some concept, or to the

[8] I have discussed the differences between momentary and non-momentary systems in *Law and Legal Science* (Oxford, 1979), especially pp. 10–14, 41–3, 65–73, 97–102, 111–22.

[9] Ibid., ch 5.

[10] In one sense of 'valid'—cf. ibid., ch. 4.

necessary implications of some conceptual distinction. Thus, courts have held that a claim by one proprietor to a possessory use of his neighbour's land cannot exist as an easement because any easement (as distinct from an estate) by its nature involves user falling short of possession;[11] that a restrictive covenant must be appurtenant to dominant land because restrictive covenants resemble easements in many other respects and so should do so in this one;[12] that the right of a deserted wife to insist on continuing to occupy the matrimonial home as against her husband cannot rank as an interest in land capable of binding successors because it lacks the definiteness and durability which all interests in land must have;[13] that an option contained in a mortgage for the mortgagee to purchase the mortgaged property must be void because it is inconsistent with the nature of a mortgage transaction;[14] that a provision purporting to impose a total prohibition on alienation of a fee simple estate will be void as being inconsistent with the natural qualities of the estate;[15] and that a purported grant of a lease for an indefinite duration will be void, because it is of the essence of leases that they must be limited to endure for a fixed term or for a term capable of being rendered certain.[16]

Where does 'ownership of land' fit into all this? It might be answered 'nowhere', for one very simple reason. Unlike 'fee simple', 'term of years', and other concepts employed within land law rules and doctrine, 'ownership' is not a term of art. It has no technical meaning, no meaning for lawyers different from that it has for laymen.[17] This answer would be too simple. It cannot be a test for whether a concept is a legal one that the word which is used to represent it has a special legal meaning. Frequently legal rules make their application turn on concepts whose import is the same for lawyers and laymen alike. In the context of the criminal law, 'dishonesty' is a dispositive concept within many of the offences listed in the Theft Acts; yet it has been authoritatively laid down that the word has its ordinary meaning.[18] In labour law, legal consequences of various kinds follow only if a dismissal is 'unfair': but attempts to give 'unfair' a technical meaning have been resisted.[19] In land law, controversy has surrounded the meaning of the words 'actual occupation' in section 7(1) (g) of the Land Registration Act 1925, since the rights of persons who are in actual occupa-

[11] *Copeland* v. *Greenhalf* [1952] ch. 488.
[12] *London County Council* v. *Allen* [1914] 3 KB. 642.
[13] *National Provincial Bank Ltd.* v. *Ainsworth* [1965] AC 1175.
[14] *Samuel* v. *Jarrah Timber and Wood Paving Corporation Ltd.* [1904] AC 323.
[15] *Re Brown, District Bank Ltd.* v. *Brown* [1954] ch. 39.
[16] *Lace* v. *Chantler* [1944] KB 368.
[17] Cf. J. W. C. Turner: 'Some Reflections on Ownership in English Law' (1941) 19 *Can. Bar Rev.* 342.
[18] *R.* v. *Feeley* [1973] QB 530. *R.* v. *Ghosh* [1982] QB 1053.
[19] *Anandarajah* v. *Lord Chancellor's Department* [1984] ILR 131.

tion bind transferees. The House of Lords has now ordained that the words have their plain English meaning.[20] That decision cannot mean that 'actual occupation' has ceased to be a legal concept, any more than 'dishonesty' or 'unfairness' turned out to be non-legal once it was established that they were not terms of art. If the application of legal rules avowedly turns on the meaning of some term, judges and all other lawyers must treat it as part of the law. It is a legal concept, even if it is also a popular one.

If it could be shown that presently valid rules of English land law treat 'ownership of land' dispositively, it would accordingly follow that it is a legal concept. On one view—let us call it 'the strict positivist test'—this is the only criterion for a concept's being legal. Kelsen's pure theory of law incorporates this test: a concept is legal only if it figures in the conditions stipulated by a positive legal norm for the application of a sanction; everything else is merely ideological, extra-legal, material, even if it appears in legislative sources.[21] On another view—'the modified positivist test'—a concept is a legal one either if it is used dispositively within currently valid rules, or if it is employed within the tradition of a jurisdiction's courts as part of their doctrinal reasoning. From this perspective, law consists of both rules and doctrine. This is a view I have defended myself.[22] A third view—'the anti-positivist test'—would reject as misguided any attempt to distinguish legal from moral-political concepts: any moral notion underpinning a community's political institutions has a place within a fully articulated conception of its law. Such a conclusion follows, for example, from R. M. Dworkin's analysis of 'hard cases'.[23]

On the anti-positivist test, ownership is a concept of English land law if it is comprised within the background morality of our institutions. Undoubtedly, it is. A mass of legislation is premissed on the assumption that private house-ownership is a good thing; legislation governing leasehold enfranchisement, and public sector tenants' right to buy; legislation regulating building societies and other sources of financing home ownership; compensation provisions in compulsory purchase legislation. Revenue legislation subsidizes house-purchase by allowing mortgage interest to be set off against tax. It also subsidizes charitable trusts and institutions, and it has recently been decided that facilitating home-ownership amongst the elderly comes within the law of charity.[24] It is true that moral claims against owners, particularly by tenants and members of their families, are also

[20] *Williams and Glyn's Bank Ltd.* v. *Boland* [1981] AC 487.

[21] See, e.g., H. Kelsen, *General Theory of Law and State*, trans. A. Wedberg (Cambridge, Mass., 1945), p. 123. For the application of the strict positivist test to the concept of ownership, see Alf Ross: 'Tu-Tu' (1956–7) 70 *Harv. Law. Rev.* 812; and for criticism, Harris, *Legal Philosophies* (London, 1980), pp. 89–90.

[22] Harris, *Law and Legal Science*, especially pp. 10–14, 41–3, 65–73, 99–102, 111–22.

[23] R. M. Dworkin, *Taking Rights Seriously* (London, 1978), ch. 4.

[24] *Joseph Rowntree Memorial Trust Housing Ltd.* v. *A.-G.* [1983] 1 All ER 288.

recognized. Dworkin's super-judge, Hercules, would have to take these background rights into account in working out his conception of England land law. But the background right to own is one he could not ignore.

To satisfy the modified positivist test, it is not enough to establish the legal status of the concept of ownership of land to show that it is one of the ideological factors motivating legislation. It must be demonstrated that this particular relationship between an individual and land, his ownership of it, figures, within the tradition of our courts, as an acceptable ground for disposing of hard cases. Citation of it must constitute an appeal to 'law' in the sense of source-based doctrine, and not merely an invocation of extra-legal community or critical morality. Judges certainly do appeal to the latter, to what the man in the street would consider just, or to what their own intuitions tell them is just. In doing so, they are applying 'the utility model' of legal rationality.[25] They are weighting the consequences of rulings according to frankly ideological considerations. In applying the doctrine model, in contrast, they invoke as reasons for rulings the fact that 'our law' already embodies some principle, maxim, or concept. We have seen how the intrinsic nature of various land law concepts has been appealed to in just this way. Ownership of land will be a legal concept, according to the modified positivist test, if it, too, is similarly influential in hard cases.

I suggest that it is. Hard cases are of many kinds. Their uniting feature is not that the court found them difficult to dispose of, but that there was an arguable point of law so that a decision either way was open. A rare variety concerns situations in which there is no authority at all for or against a particular proposition, cases of 'first impression'.

In *Phipps* v. *Pears*, the question was raised for the first time as to whether there was known to the law any such easement as an easement to be protected from the weather. The defendant had pulled down a house which was built up against the plaintiff's house, and recognition of the easement would have meant that he was not legally at liberty to do this. Counsel on either side made contradictory assertions (for that is all they were) about whether or not recognizing such an easement would facilitate or impede worthwhile development of property. The court made no attempt to assess these competing assertions in consequentialist terms. The plaintiff's submission that such an easement should be admitted by analogy with the well-established easement of support was, in the Court of Appeal's view, clearly outweighed by the diminution in equally well recognized ownership privileges which such a novel ruling would entail. Lord Denning MR said:

> Every man is entitled to pull down his own house if he likes. If it exposes your house to the weather, that is your misfortune. It is no wrong on his part.[26]

[25] Cf. Harris, *Law and Legal Science*, ch. 5.
[26] [1965] 1 QB 76, 83.

Another sort of hard case is where there is a well-established rule which, on its face, appears to cover the present situation. Yet it has not hitherto been applied to these particular facts, and the arguable question is whether it ought to be modified by the admission of an exception. Again, land law doctrine may be invoked to settle the matter, including the concept of ownership of land.

In *Bradford Corporation* v. *Pickles*, the defendant sank a well on his own land to interfere with percolating water running to the plaintiff's waterworks. He did this in order to force the plaintiffs to buy his land at a high price. The House of Lords upheld the refusal of an injunction. It had already been laid down in an earlier decision of the House that interfering with percolating water was not an actionable nuisance. The plaintiffs argued that there should be an exception to this rule where the defendant was acting not to improve his own land but simply to damnify his neighbour. They invoked as warrant for introducing this exception the principle of the law of nuisance that conduct otherwise permitted to a land-owner is not so permitted if motivated by malice. The House regarded this argument as manifestly unsound. The privileges comprised within the concept of ownership of land obviously extended to economically self-seeking conduct. Lord Macnaghten said:

> [The corporation] say that under the circumstances the operation which Mr. Pickles threatens to carry out is something in excess of his rights as a landowner.... The position of the appellants is one which it is not very easy to understand.... They say that Mr. Pickles' action in the matter is malicious, and that because his motive is a bad one, he is not at liberty to do a thing which every landowner in the country may do with impunity if his motives are good.... Well, he has something to sell, or, at any rate, he has something which he can prevent other people enjoying unless he is paid for it.... He prefers his own interest to the public good. He may be churlish, selfish, and grasping. His conduct may seem shocking to a moral philosopher. But where is the malice?[27]

In a third species of hard case, an established rule may have been held to apply to the fact-situation in the past; yet it is contended that there has emerged a new principle which qualifies the rule. In the early 1970s, when the organized squatting movement was at its height, it was argued for the first time before English courts that there was an equitable discretion to adjourn an order for possession. The courts reaffirmed the rule that, as between a freeholder or leaseholder and a trespasser, the right to recover possession is absolute. The law had always protected land-ownership, and this principle was not to be weakened by consequentialist speculations about relative social justice. Lord Denning MR (who in other contexts had not been slow to adopt broad equitable principles) roundly rejected the suggested anti-ownership discretion.

[27] [1895] AC 587, 603–5.

[A squatter] may seek to justify or excuse his conduct. He may say that he was homeless and that this house or land was standing empty, doing nothing. But this plea is of no avail in law. As we said in *Southwark London Borough Council* v. *Williams* [1971] Ch. 734, 744: 'If homelessness were once admitted as a defence no one's house could be safe'.[28]

In instances such as these, 'ownership of land' plays a role in reasoning leading to a conclusion. This role cannot be supplanted by 'ownership of an estate'. It was not disputed that Mr Pears and Mr Pickles, or the plaintiffs in squatter cases, owned the legal estate. The question was what followed from that. What, by virtue of having the legal estate, were Pears and Pickles privileged to do in relation to the land, and what did the plaintiffs in the squatter cases have a right to claim? A legal estate is the right to possess land for a determinate or an indefinite period of time. Granted that one has that right, what rights, privileges, powers, and immunities relating to the land does one have? Keep out the world and live as a recluse; admit what visitors one wishes; create tenancies or subtenancies; grow mushrooms in the cellar; sing bawdy songs in the bath; paint the front door a luminous green; sunbathe in the nude—no one could list them all. Their open-endedness is and can only be captured by a conception whose imprecision makes it uncongenial to real property lawyers, though it plays as important a part in legal doctrine as does the traditional tally of technical terms. If one has the legal estate, one is empowered and privileged to do anything in relation to the land which the culture of the time, as represented and interpreted by the judiciary, accords to an 'owner' of land. This conception of ownership of land underlies the entire law of nuisance, with its vague maxim, *sic utere tuo ut alienum non laedas*. The subject-matter of 'tuum' is not the estate—one does not 'use' that—but the land itself.

Could one speak of 'possessing' rather than 'owning' the land? Indeed, one could. He who has the legal estate is privileged to do all that the culture accords to a 'possessor'. This, however, would be a terminological substitution without a conceptual change. The point is that ownership of the legal estate carries with it an ideologically loaded relationship to the land itself, entailing an open-ended set of exploitative privileges. Any one, or any given set, of these privileges may be docked from time to time either by general use rules or by private transactions; but these restrictions take place and have meaning only against the background of this person-land relationship. We might as well give it the name which English usage (lay and judicial) and political philosophy alike give it, and that is 'ownership'.

In England, we only ever convey or deduce title to a technical entity known as an estate. But the enjoyment-content of that entity, what it licen-

[28] *McPhail* v. *Persons, Names Unknown* [1973] ch. 447, 456.

ses to be done in relation to the land in which it inheres, is defined, with non-technical imprecision, by reference to the concept of ownership. Ownership is an incident of the legal estate. Is this true of every legal estate, including a tenancy for however short a period? The very imprecision of the ownership concept here in question makes it impossible to give a straightforward answer to this question. Apart from one special attribute, that of the liberty to commit waste (which I shall discuss later), land-ownership privileges incident to long leases are the same as those incident to the fee simple although, of course, the terms of the lease may cut them down. However, just as there comes a point at which a tenancy is so transitory that the lessee would not, in popular parlance, be spoken of as an 'owner', so too, at some such point, the ideology of ownership may run out as a relevant source of judicial reasoning.

The collection of maxims, principles, rules, classifications, and concepts to which appeal may be made in hard cases—our non-momentary 'land law'—is supposed, apart from statutory additions, to be attributable to one or other of two historic systems, the common law and equity. To which does the concept of ownership of land belong? I suggest, to both. Ownership of land is an incident of the legal estate. That explains the common claim that it was 'logical' of the draftsman of the Settled Land Act 1925 to vest the legal estate in settled land, not in settlement trustees, but in the tenant for life. This curious manœuvre was not required by the overall policy of the 1925 property legislation, which was to simplify conveyancing.[29] However, most ownership powers and privileges had been accorded to the tenant for life since the Settled Land Act 1882, and more were given him in 1925. 'Logic', in the shape of conceptual symmetry, suggested that, since land-ownership is the normal incident of the legal estate, he who had been vested with ownership of the land piecemeal should now receive its typical conceptual foundation.

The logic was not ineluctable. Equity, too, recognizes the concept of ownership of land. It is presupposed by its institution of 'trust'. Where the legal estate is held on trust, it is of the essence of what is traditionally termed the 'equitable estate'[30] that the beneficiary may insist that the trustee exercise all the rights incident to the legal estate, including ownership privileges over the land, not for his own benefit, but for the good of the beneficiary. This basic principle is now overlaid with a wealth of statutory and case-law detail, but it surfaces raw from time to time. One of the exceptional

[29] The two-document procedure (whereby one deed must vest the legal estate in someone, and a separate trust instrument must declare the trusts upon which the settled land is held), and the curtain principle (whereby a purchaser of the settled land is prohibited from examining the trust instrument), were designed to simplify conveyancing. Both reforms could, however, have been implemented with an undivided legal estate vested in the trustees.

[30] The 1925 property legislation prefers the expression 'equitable interest'.

circumstances in which a landlord may recover possession of a dwelling which is subject to a protected tenancy under the Rent Acts is where it is reasonably required by the landlord as a residence for himself. Landlords who are trustees are not normally able to take advantage of this exception, because such personal residence by them would necessarily involve exercising ownership privileges for their own benefit and hence amount to a breach of trust. It is otherwise if the reason for the trustees wishing to reside in the premises is that they will occupy them with infant beneficiaries in their guardianship, for then ownership privileges are being exercised for the benefit of the beneficiaries.[31]

There is enbalmed in juristic writing about the relations of common law and equity a famous controversy between Maitland and Hohfeld. Maitland maintained that equity supplements the common law, Hohfeld that it *pro tanto* replaces it.[32] The answer, I suggest, can be found in the distinction between momentary and non-momentary systems. 'The law' may be the legal situation as at a particular time, or it may comprise dynamic, timeless concepts. Given the former standpoint, Hohfeld is right. Is X (who is vested with the fee simple in Blackacre) legally free at time T to cut down the trees, or is he not? The common law says he may, because (as owner of the fee simple estate) he is privileged to act as 'owner' in relation to the land, and cutting down trees is one incident of ownership—assuming that he has not contracted it away, and that no tree preservation order or other general use rule has taken it from him. Equity says he is not free to cut down the trees because he is a trustee, and such 'waste' would not be in the interest of the beneficiary. It follows that, as to the relevant legal situation at time T, equity has repealed the common law. On the other hand, we cannot dispense with the separate concepts of legal estate, ownership of land, trust, and equitable estate in any generalized description of the law. For here 'the law' means that battery of concepts and principles which are called in aid in crystallizing the present law for any momentary fact-situation. We were only able to answer the question about the trees because we were equipped with these relatively timeless concepts. In that sense, Maitland is right, and equity fulfils and does not take away the common law.

On the modified positivist test, then, the case is made out. English land law does employ the concept of ownership of land as part of its historical doctrine, derived from common law and equity. The strict positivist test, however, denies legal status to a concept unless it is used dispositively

[31] *Patel* v. *Patel* [1982] 1 All ER 68 CA. Similarly, a lessee who holds a lease of a house as a bare trustee cannot claim to be occupying the house as his residence in right of his tenancy so as to be entitled to an extended lease under the Leasehold Reform Act 1967—*Duke of Westminster* v. *Oddy*, *The Times*, 27 March 1984 CA.

[32] F. W. Maitland, *Equity*, ed. J. Brunyate (Cambridge, 1936), especially lectures 9 and 12; W. N. Hohfeld: 'Relations Between Equity and Law' (1913) 11 *Mich. L. R.* 537.

within clear, presently valid rules. It will not be enough to show that 'ownership of land' played a part in the reasoning leading to the adoption of a rule. That would merely demonstrate that it is an aspect of what Kelsen called 'legal politics'. The rulings laid down in *Bradford Corporation* v. *Pickles* and *Phipps* v. *Pears* are that the person with title to a fee simple is permitted to intercept percolating water even if his motive is to do economic damage to his neighbour, or to pull down his house even if that will remove shelter from his neighbour's house. In formulating such rulings 'title' is used dispositively, but it appears that 'ownership' is not.

Title to land in English law is either based on prior possession, or is documentary in character. X need only show that, as between himself and Y with whom he is in dispute, he has the better title. This he will do, in unregistered land, by producing evidence that he or some predecessor of his was in possession before Y or his predecessors—provided that Y and/or his predecessors have not destroyed X's claim by being in 'adverse possession' for twelve years. The evidence about possession will usually consist of title-deeds, showing successive transfers of possession from some person at the root of title down to X; but may, exceptionally, consist of evidence about acts of physical use—evidence of the latter sort is always required where adverse possession is alleged. Title to registered land is made out if X is registered as proprietor at the Land Registry and can resist any claim to rectify the register made by Y. The Land Registration Act 1925 speaks of 'absolute title'. However, the substance of the law of limitation, with its concept of 'adverse possession', is specifically stated to apply 'in the same manner and to the same extent' as it applies to unregistered land;[33] and one of the grounds on which rectification may be sought is 'where a legal estate has been registered in the name of a person who if the land had not been registered would not have been the estate owner'.[34] Consequently, all the relativity of unregistered title is potentially incorporated within the registered land system.[35]

Thus for neither system is there any such thing as a genuine absolute title. The assertion that this is the case is sometimes all that is meant by denying that English law has the concept of ownership of land. This is

[33] Land Registration Act 1925, s. 75(1).

[34] Land Registration Act 1925, s. 82(1)(g).

[35] It is true, however, that Section 82(3) of the Land Registration Act 1925 (as amended by section 24 of the Administration of Justice Act 1977) provides a partial shield against rectification for a registered proprietor who is 'in possession'. A claimant for rectification who would have been entitled as of right to recover land had it been unregistered, on the ground that his title was derived from an earlier possession, may lose out where title is registered, on the ground that it is not 'unjust not to rectify the register' (s. 82 (3) (c))—*Epps.* v. *Esso Petroleum Co. Ltd* [1973] 2 All ER 465. The shield affords no protection, however, against one who has acquired title by twelve years' adverse possession, since such a person has acquired an overriding interest (s. 70 (1) (f)); and in such a case the ousted owner is not entitled to compensation—*Re Chowood's Registered Land* [1933] ch. 574.

true, for example, of a well-known debate between Holdsworth and Hargreaves. Holdsworth contended that certain cases witnessed the evolution of a defence of *jus tertii* to actions in ejectment, which presupposed a concept of absolute title and hence 'ownership'. Hargreaves rejoined that these were merely instances in which the plaintiff, although he had been in possession prior to the defendant, had not acquired seisin because of some defect in livery of seisin; and that prior seisin was still the basis of (relative) title.[36] The materials of the debate have long been obsolete. Transfer of possession by simple conveyance has been possible ever since the Real Property Act of 1845. I shall assume, in common with majority opinion, that (substituting prior 'possession' for prior 'seisin'), Hargreaves was correct; and that title to estates in land in England is, and has always been, relative.

Supposing, however, that ownership of land were itself dispositively employed in English law in the very process of establishing relative title. The concept would then constitute part of a complete formulation of all those trespassory rules which make title a condition, and ownership of land would be a legal concept even on the strict positivist test. I suggest that this dependence of title on ownership obtains in three contexts: first, in relation to what counts as a 'sham' conveyance; second, in elation to a squatter's title; and third, as part of the definition of 'adverse possession' for the purposes of the law of limitation.

Title-deeds are the normal means of proving that a vendor of unregistered land and his predecessors have been in possession since the root of the title, because any conveyance operates to pass possession.[37] Nothing will be transmitted, however, if a deed, although on its face a conveyance, is in reality a sham. There is no established formula for distinguishing the genuine from the sham, but in substance the test applied turns on whether the parties envisaged that the conveyee would act as owner in relation to the land. In *Ferris* v. *Weaven*,[38] for example, a husband purported to convey a house in consideration of a payment of £30 to a collaborator, merely so that the husband himself could dispose of it freed from his wife's residential rights. The device failed: the parties' true intention was that the husband should continue to act as owner, so the purported conveyance was a sham.[39] In *Miles* v. *Bull*, in contrast, a comparable manœuvre was successful. Completion was rushed through on the same day contracts were ex-

[36] W. S. Holdsworth, *History of English Law* (2nd edn., Oxford, 1937), vol. vii, pp. 57–81; A. D. Hargreaves: 'Terminology and Title in Ejectment' (1940) 56 LQR 376; Holdsworth, 'Terminology and Title in Ejectment—a Reply' (1940) 56 LQR 479.

[37] Law of Property Act 1925, s. 51 (1).

[38] [1952] 2 All ER 233.

[39] Or so the decision was interpreted in *National Provincial Bank Ltd.* v. *Ainsworth* [1965] AC 1175, 1223 (Lord Hodson), 1257, 1258 (Lord Wilberforce).

changed solely to frustrate any attempt by the wife to protect her rights by registration. Nevertheless, since the purchaser's wish to own the land was genuine, the conveyance was not a sham. Megarry J said:

If in *Ferris* v. *Weaven* the purchaser had sought to exercise acts of ownership, and the husband had ceased to do them, and there had been no common objective of enabling the husband (as distinct from the purchaser) to dispose of the property, it would, in my judgment, be very difficult to contend that the low price and the failure to pay it made the transaction a sham.[40]

Where a squatter takes possession of land, even for a period shorter than that required by limitation statutes, he acquires a title which is good against those who acquire later possession. Squatter 1 can recover the land from Squatter 2.[41] However, to obtain this title the squatter must have entered on the land, for no matter how short a time, in the character of owner of the land. The matter was thoroughly canvassed in the High Court of Australia in *Allen* v. *Roughley*. All the members of the court agreed that an equivocal entry by Squatter 1 would not enable him to maintain ejectment against Squatter 2. They characterized what further was required in different terms, but in substance their reasoning boiled down to sufficient acts of ownership by Squatter 1. In the words of Taylor J:

There is abundant authority for the proposition that evidence of acts of ownership in relation to land is received to make out a *prima facie* case of ownership ...'.[42]

Under the Limitation Act 1980, twelve years' adverse possession destroys the title of an earlier possessor. Two of the conditions which must be satisfied before possession counts as 'adverse' are relatively straightforward; first, an action must have accrued in favour of the person whose title is being barred; second, occupation must not be attributable to express or implied permission.[43] There is, however, a third condition characterized in many different ways in the authorities. What it amounts to is that the alleged adverse possessor must have performed unequivocal acts of ownership in relation to the land. It is a matter of degree, but in the end this condition for possession's being adverse is the same test as that which enables an earlier squatter to recover land from a later squatter. In both cases, the claimant must have been occupying the land openly and visibly as though he were owner of it. In the words of Lord

[40] [1969] 1 QB 258, 264.

[41] *Asher* v. *Whitlock* (1865) LR1 QB 1.

[42] (1955) 94 CLR 98, 144.

[43] Some authorities previously gave support to a rule that, where occupation was not inconsistent with the present or future enjoyment of the person entitled to the land, there was an implication of law that it was to be attributed to his permission. This rule was abrogated by s. 4 of the Limitation Amendment Act 1980.

Macnaghten delivering the judgment of the Privy Council in *Perry* v. *Clissold*:

> It cannot be disputed that a person in possession of land in the assumed character of owner and exercising peaceably the ordinary rights of ownership has a perfectly good title against all the world but the rightful owner. And if the rightful owner does not come forward and assert his title by process of law within the period prescribed by the provisions of the statute of limitations applicable to the case, his right is for ever extinguished, . . .[44]

On any test, then, ownership of land is a concept internal to English law. It is part of land law doctrine because it is employed, from time to time, in doctrinal reasoning in hard cases. It is part of the present law about what must, must not, or may be done in relation to land because many of the rules comprising this law have among their conditions that X is entitled to an estate, and, sometimes, whether or not X is so entitled turns on whether he, or some other, has acted as owner of the land. What, however, does it mean?

Professor Honoré lists the following standard incidents of the liberal conception of ownership:[45] rights to possess, use, and manage; rights to income, capital, and security; transmissibility and absence of term; prohibition of harmful use; liability to execution; residuarity. If a singular conception of ownership is to be looked for, these are certainly the kind of elements from which it would be constructed. The problem is that in disputes about its significance for English land law, different conceptions are presupposed. So that controversy may not be at cross-purposes, four differing, though related, senses of ownership must be distinguished.

OWNERSHIP AS ABSOLUTE TITLE

Sometimes, as in the controversy between Holdsworth and Hargreaves, the question of whether ownership of land is a legal concept is taken to be identical with the question whether English law, in any circumstances, recognizes absolute title. Even in the case of chattels, this was once an open question. On the one hand, statutes like the Sale of Goods Act and the Factors Act speak of 'the owner'. On the other hand, not only was relative title based on earlier possession sufficient to maintain the torts of detinue and conversion,[46] but it was arguable that there was no defence even if the defendant could point to some third party as the true owner. Now section 8 (1) of the Torts (Interference with Goods) Act 1977 has abolished any such *jus tertii* rule so that, in an action for wrongful interference with goods, proof of absolute title derived from a chattel's creator may be material. It is otherwise with land. As we have seen, title to unregistered land is always, in principle, possessory and hence relative; and such relativity is carried over,

[44] [1908] AC 73, 79. [45] See n. 1, above. [46] *Armory* v. *Delamirie* (1722) 1 Stra. 505.

with modifications, into the system of registered title. It follows that, if ownership means absolute title, English law does not recognize ownership of land.

TOTALITY OWNERSHIP

For many textbook writers, it is enough to establish that no one is ever owner of land to point out that, in English law, ownership of land is split and restricted. It is split by the doctrine of estates, which recognizes a temporal sequence of rights to possess; and it is restricted both by a host of use and security rights vested in someone other than the alleged owner and by rules of private and public law banning various kinds of exploitation of the land. In such discussions, what is presupposed is what may be called a totality conception of ownership. One begins with the idea that an 'owner' could do absolutely anything with or to his land, and demonstrates that no such totality of privileges is admitted. If that is what ownership means, it is not a conception internal to English law or to any other system of law.[47] Even if other systems do not provide for splitting of ownership in quite the way the doctrine of estates permits, there are, as mentioned earlier, always some general use rules bearing on occupiers of land. Recognizing this, Professor Honoré includes 'prohibition of harmful use' among the incidents of the liberal conception of ownership. Such a stipulation, however, makes it a misuse of terminology to say that 'ownership' has been restricted by the prohibition of some particular harmful use. I would suggest that the terminology of totality ownership is legitimate, provided its proper juristic significance is borne in mind. It is a concept employed, not within any system of law, but within legal science as a base-line for setting out and comparing the import of particular provisions. No system of law has ever countenanced the argument that a man is free to perpetrate treason and mayhem so long as he does it on his own land (or with his own chattels). But a legal historian may point out that ownership was successively restricted by the banning of man-traps, the introduction of the rule in *Rylands* v. *Fletcher*, and the enactment of planning law.

POSSESSORY OWNERSHIP

He who has a legal estate in land has the right to possess it, either for a time, or indefinitely. He has that right either now or, if the estate is reversionary, in the future. What he is or will be privileged to do in relation to the land by virtue of that right to possess is, as we have seen, determined by reference to a conception of ownership of land. It is so, as a matter of

[47] Cf. Max Weber, *Law in Economy and Society*, ed. M. Rheinstein (Cambridge, Mass., 1954), p. 221, and n. 77.

land law doctrine, when some 'hard case' arises; and, in some contexts, this conception of ownership of land is presupposed by rules about title. This conception may be called 'possessory ownership'. English law, on any test, recognizes ownership of land, in this sense, as an incident both of fee simple and leasehold estates—at any rate where the lease is not of so short a duration as to preclude a wide range of 'acts of ownership'. It is not a term of art. The law presupposes for it no meaning different from that which it bears in extra-legal usage—'He came to my house and behaved as if he owned the place!'

The possessory owner has a prima facie privilege to do anything in relation to his land which the dominant culture of his society accords to a landowner. The set of privileges entailed is not a total set, because everywhere some things are excluded. It is, however, an open-ended set, since its present content could never be exhaustively listed; and it is a fluctuating set, because cultural assumptions about what an owner may do vary. Its theoretical ambit was cut at a stroke in 1977 by a first-instance decision, in which it was held that we should no longer take literally the ancient maxim *Cujus est solum ejus est usque ad caelum et ad inferos*, and that trespass would not lie against overflying aircraft.

> The problem is to balance the rights of an owner to enjoy the use of his land against the rights of the general public to take advantage of all that science now offers in the use of air space. This balance is in my judgment best struck in our present society by restricting the rights of an owner to the air space above his land to such height as is necessary for the ordinary use and enjoyment of his land and the structures on it, and declaring that above that height he has no greater rights in the air space than any other member of the public.[48]

As with all other proprietary interests, the content of possessory ownership is circumscribed by a combination of trespassory and general use rules. Even within these limits, the privileges which it entails are prima facie only. The legal conclusion may always be that, although as owner X would have been free to do something, he or his predecessor in title had granted or contracted away this privilege, or his doctrinal claim to exercise it is outweighed by some other principle or policy of the law. Possessory ownership is elusive and incapable of precise definition. For all that, it is part of English land law.

EXPLOITATION OWNERSHIP

Where land is the subject of a long lease, the leaseholder is possessory owner now, and the freeholder will be possessory owner either at some far

[48] *Bernstein* v. *Skyviews and General Ltd.* [1977] 2 All ER 902, 907 *per* Griffiths J.

future date, or on earlier surrender or forfeiture of the lease. There is, however, an ill-defined sense in which the ordinary freeholder is more 'owner' than the long leaseholder. This is because it is presupposed that complete freedom of exploitation (including destructive exploitation) of the land is denied to the lessee—as it was denied, by the doctrine of waste, to the holders of lesser freehold estates than the fee simple. That ownership of land which is the peculiar incident of the fee simple estate is not totality ownership. Nevertheless, it comprises a fuller bundle of privileges than possessory ownership, since it includes deleterious use and denotes answerability to no one. We may call it 'exploitation ownership'.

Both the law and dominant culture allow the owner of a chattel, not merely to do what he likes with it, but also to destroy it. When Lady Churchill died, it was discovered that she had destroyed the portrait of her husband presented to Sir Winston by an admiring nation. The general public reaction was that, although this was very sad, it had been her property and so she was free to do what she thought fit. So too, as we have seen, the freeholder is prima facie free to pull down his own house, or to exploit his land in any way, without regard to his neighbours. Many more rules and principles of law impinge on exploitation ownership of land than is the case with chattels. Indeed, its economic significance is small. Nevertheless, it still has a widely diffused psychological importance. This is evident from the number of long leaseholders who are prepared to take advantage of the Leasehold Reform Act 1967, by purchasing the residual freehold reversion for a nominal sum; and also from the adverse reaction to the proposal of a section of the British Labour Party that freeholds should uniformly be replaced by long leases—a proposal which entailed only that possessory ownership of land should be substituted for exploitation ownership.[49] Despite the impact of restrictive general use rules, the self-regarding individualism of the developed common law retains its hold over the popular imagination. In Challis's words:

> [A fee simple] confers, and since the beginning of legal history it always has conferred, the lawful right to exercise over, upon, and in respect to, the land, every act of ownership which can enter into the imagination, including the right to commit unlimited waste; and, for all practical purposes of ownership, it differs from the absolute dominion of a chattel, in nothing except the physical indestructibility of its subject.[50]

[49] Brocklebank *et al.*, *The Case for Nationalising Land*, Campaign for Nationalising Land (London, 1973).

[50] H. W. Challis, *Law of Real Property*, 3rd edn., ed. Charles Sweet (London, 1911), p. 218. For support for the historical aspects of this claim, see Charles Donahue Jr, 'The Future of the Concept of Property Predicted from the Past' in Pennock and Chapman (edd.) *Property, Nomos XII*, NYUP, 1980.

10

The History of the Roman *Condictio* up to Justinian*

DETLEF LIEBS

CONSIDERING the many treatments of the Roman *condictio* published in the early fifties[1] it may seem superfluous to present an investigation of its history, all the more so since these publications were preceded by two comprehensive works in the mid-nineteenth century and two more in the early twentieth.[2] However, so far as they deal with the early history, those older works have been superseded since the Florentine fragment of Gaius was deciphered in 1933, though this has often not been appreciated. Moreover, in 1970–1 Raimondo Santoro made just a first beginning on the task

* This was the subject of my Legal History Seminar in the Summer semester of 1984. I owe thanks to all participants in the seminar for numerous suggestions but especially to Praxedis Möhring and Winfried Holtermüller for their commitment in helping both with the preparation and with the execution. I am greatly indebted to Peter Birks, who helped with the translation of a complex German text, and to Ranon Katzoff, who discussed with me the whole translation.

[1] Guido Donatuti, 'Le causae delle condictiones', (1951) 1 *Studi Parmensi* 33–169; John P. Dawson, *Unjust Enrichment—A Comparative Analysis* (Boston, 1951), pp. 42–63; Fritz Schwarz, 'Die Funktion des Irrtums bei Erfüllung gänzlich oder teilweise nicht geschuldeter Fideikommisse', (1951) 68 *SZ* 266–319; id., *Die Grundlage der condictio im klassischen römischen Recht* (Münster and Cologne, 1952); Johannes Georg Fuchs, *Iusta causa traditionis in der Romanistischen Wissenschaft* (Basel, 1952), pp. 163–253; Ulrich v. Lübtow, *Beiträge zur Lehre von der Condictio nach römischem und geltendem Recht* (Berlin, 1952), pp. 20–154; Hubert Niederländer, *Die Bereicherungshaftung im klassischen römischen Recht* (Weimar, 1953); Werner Flume, 'Der Wegfall der Bereicherung in der Entwicklung vom römischen zum geltenden Recht', *Festschrift H. Niedermeyer* (Göttingen, 1953), pp. 103–76; Gian Gualberto Archi, 'Variazioni in tema di indebiti solutio', *Studi in onore di V. Arangio-Ruiz* (Naples, 1953), vol. iii, pp. 335–89; Alvaro D'Ors, 'Observaciones sobre el *Edictum de rebus creditis*', (1953) 19 *SDHI* 134–201, summarized in German *RE Suppl.* 10 (1965) 1151–68 art. *creditum*; August Simonius, 'Zur Frage einer einheitlichen causa condictionis', *Festschrift Hans Lewald* (Basel, 1953), pp. 161–74; Erich-Hans Kaden, 'Das Schrifttum der Jahre 1950–1953 zur römischen Bereicherungslehre', (1954) 71 *SZ* 555–90; J. C. van Oven, 'La forêt sauvage de la condictio classique', (1954) 22 *T. v. R.* 267–307.

[2] Mid-19th c.: Albrecht Erxleben, *Die Condictiones sine causa*, 2 vols (Leipzig and Göttingen, 1850 and 1853): vol. i, *Die Condictio indebiti*, vol. ii, *Die Condictio causa data causa non secuta*; Moritz Voigt, *Ueber die condictiones ob causam und ueber causa und titulus im Allgemeinen* (Leipzig, 1862). Early 20th c.: Robert v. Mayr, *Die condictio des römischen Privatrechts* (Leipzig, 1900); J. v. Koschembahr-Lyskowski, *Die Condictio als Bereicherungsklage im klassischen römischen Recht*, 2 vols. (Weimar, 1903 and 1907). Also in that period H. H. Pflüger in a number of small articles, and, earlier, Friedrich Carl von Savigny, 'Die Condictionen', in *System des heutigen Römischen Rechts*, v (Berlin, 1841) pp. 503–642.

of marking out the history of the *condictio*'s development.[3] Questions had previously been directed, in a somewhat two-dimensional way, to the detail of its doctrine, its basic concept, and its form. That limited approach created puzzles and gave rise to questions which admit of no answer.[4] Escaping that non-historical method, an attempt had to be made to see how this legal institution grew from century to century, and to envisage not only regular incremental development but also dramatic leaps. Only in this way could it begin to be understood why, starting from the time of Proculus, efforts to establish for the *condictio* a systematizing scheme—whether by Julian, Pomponius, Paul, Ulpian, or Hermogenian—all succeeded only in limited parts of its territory but failed to conquer the whole field. In this present survey situations involving three or more parties are excluded, something which can the more easily be done in view of the fact that Tony Honoré, the originality and penetration of whose scholarship has been a great encouragement in this work, has already made it possible for us to survey the complex of the triangular relationships.[5]

I

The origin of the *condictio* is clear. Two statutes, probably *plebiscita* of the late third century BC, introduced a new procedure for reclaiming money debts and also for claiming specific quantities of other things. The procedure provided for such claims by the Twelve Tables (2.16) was the *legis actio per iudicis arbitrive postulationem*. Already in the fifth century BC that procedure allowed the debtor to defend himself in court, and similarly permitted the creditor to make his claim, neither having to pay down a *sacramentum* at the beginning nor risking a procedural penalty later.[6] The reform now brought two innovations, each of which was in tune with the other. The first gave us the name of the new procedure: in his suit against the debtor, the creditor could, at the first appearance before the praetor, only give notice (*condicere*)[7] for a judge to be assigned and hence for

[3] Raimondo Santoro, 'Studi sulla *condictio*', (1971) 32 *Annali del Sem. Giur. della Università di Palermo* 181–512.

[4] Thus Kaser—*Das römische Zivilprozeßrecht* (Munich, 1966), p. 81 (hereafter *RZ*) and *Das römische Privatrecht* vol. i (2nd edn. Munich, 1971), p. 593 (hereafter *RP*i)—still seeks something in common between *mutuum* and *furtum*. Gaius 4.20 is already unhistorical: *quare autem haec actio* (*legis actio per condictionem*) *desiderata sit, . . . valde quaeritur*.

[5] A. M. Honoré, '*Condictio* and Payment', (1958) 1 *Acta Juridica* 135–40.

[6] Gaius, 4.17a. This is overlooked by Kaser, *RZ*, pp. 81 f. and n. 15, and by Sturm, *Studi in onore di Cesare Sanfilippo* (Milan, 1983), vol. iii, 632 f. That claims arising out of stipulations before the XII Tables were not subject to immediate execution but had to be litigated by *legis actio sacramento in personam* is clear from Gaius 4.20. See also Horak, (1976) 93 *SZ* 267 f.

[7] Gaius, 4.17b and 18, on which Kaser, *RZ* 80; and, especially stimulating, Okko Behrends, *Der Zwölftafelprozeß* (Göttingen, 1974) pp. 97 ff; on which Horak, (1976) 93 *SZ* 277.

proceedings to begin in earnest thirty days thereafter. Thus, the debtor had a corresponding period in which to make up his mind whether to contest the debt and review the opportunities for a successful defence. On the other hand three passages from Plautus which speak of *abiurare* of a debt *in iure*[8] reveal that Gaius' short account overlooks a second innovation introduced at the time, namely the possibility of cutting short further proceedings by recourse to oaths. The plaintiff could demand that a defendant who had definitively denied that he owed should make his denial on oath. If the defendant took the oath demanded of him, he had to be absolved; if he declined, he had to be condemned. However, a third course of action was open to him. He could turn the challenge round and demand that the plaintiff should do the swearing, with corresponding consequences. This possibility of recourse to oaths was an advantage to the creditor in that through it he could escape the burden in time and trouble of having to prove his case. He could assess for himself the risk of perjury by his opponent, something which Plautus shows to have been not unknown to those involved in the law. As for the debtor, the recourse to oaths did not prejudice him at all. A further characteristic of the classical *condictio* is omitted by Gaius only in his treatment of the early history: the *sponsio* and *restipulatio tertiae partis*. As in interdictal procedure, in the *actio de pecunia constituta*, and in praetorian stipulations, this promissory penalty was introduced only later by the praetor as a matter of *ius honorarium*.[9] Only thereafter, it seems, did the *sacramentum*, originally exigible at the start of proceedings,[10] come to be suspended till judgment and payable only by the loser, as Gaius reports at 4.13 f.

A final special characteristic generally ascribed to the *condictio* from its very origin is its abstractness. That is to say, neither the spoken words of the *legis actio*, nor the later written formula, named the *causa debendi* but rather the mere fact of the debt, the *dare oportere*.[11] However, that peculiarity seems not to have been very remarkable originally, because there was only a single ground for making the claim: the *sponsio* or *stipulatio*. As for *mutuum*, I have sought to show elsewhere that it originally did not give rise to a claim in court, in that its actionability by *condictio* was not provided for by statute but was rather the result of an interpretative extension

[8] *Persa* 478; *Rudens* 13 f.; *Curculio* 496. For detailed rules, D. 12. 2. 34 pr., 4, 6, 7 (Ulpian, 26 *ad edictum*).

[9] Gaius, 4.165–9, 171 f.; Otto Lenel, *Das edictum perpetuum*, (3rd ed. Leipzig, 1927), §§280 ff. (hereafter *EP*). Different view: Kaser, *RZ* p. 81 and n. 15, as already in *Altrömisches Ius* (Göttingen, 1949), pp. 284 f., who, however, gives no weight to the importance which Gaius attaches to procedural penalties and, besides, overlooks the fact that the XII Tables freed claims under stipulations for the repayment of credit (stipulation then being the only source of such claims) from the burden of the *sacramentum*.

[10] Varro, *De lingua latina* 5.180.

[11] G. 4.176; Lenel, *EP* §95, on which Kaser, *RZ* p. 81, with speculation as to allegation of theft.

of *condictio*'s scope.[12] Ralph Michael Thilo has made similar conclusions likely with respect to the contract *litteris*, attractively explaining it as the product of legal development made in response to the upturn in the Roman economy after the Second Punic War.[13]

In the beginning, then, the only debts actionable by *condictio* were those created by stipulations for either *certa pecunia* or fungible *certae res*. Therefore too the classical *actio ex stipulatu* was principally confined to *incerta*.[14] The abstractness of the formula for the *condictio*, at first probably a mere result of the verbal economy typical of the Romans and without any ulterior significance, did, however, have the effect of enabling the action to be extended to other comparable causes of indebtedness.

II

The first addition, similar to stipulation in being appropriate for credit, will have been the *expensilatio*: a formal entry of a credit in the account-book of the creditor with the debtor's authority. Next would be the informal loan (*mutuum*). By 76 BC, when Cicero appeared for the actor Roscius in a *condictio* which was brought against him, that development had already been achieved.[15] In that period the *condictio* as framed to demand money must also have received the name *actio certae creditae pecuniae*.[16] Similarly, still during the Republic, the *condictio certae rei* was made available against thieves to owners of goods;[17] and still in that period, this was extended to possessors of land.[18]

The definitive replacement of the *legis actiones* by the formulary procedure under Augustus[19] maintained the *condictio* as a form of procedure, now the proper action for a claim recognized in substantive law or, more accurately, for a whole group of such claims. However, the giving of notice from which the action had taken its name now disappeared. It became superfluous once the praetor had provided, for all formulary claims, that

[12] Liebs, *Die Klagenkonkurrenz im römischen Recht* (Göttingen, 1972), pp. 98–100.

[13] *Der Codex accepti et expensi im römischen Recht—Ein Beitrag zur Lehre von der Litteralobligation* (Göttingen, 1980), pp. 276 ff. esp. 294 f.

[14] D. 12. 1. 24 (Ulpian, *lib. sing. pandectarum*), a text deeply suspect according to Emil Seckel, *Heumanns Handlexikon zu den Quellen des römischen Rechts* (9th edn. Jena, 1907) pp. 556 f. However, his reconstruction gives a text too banal to be plausible. To the point so far as it goes: Behrends, op. cit., n. 7 above, pp. 104 f. See also Honoré, *Ulpian* 117–120.

[15] Cicero, *pro Roscio comoedo* §§13, 14.

[16] Lenel, *EP* 234.

[17] According to Tryphoninus, D.13.1.20, the *veteres* already knew the *condictio* on the ground of theft. In view of the arguments of Santoro, op cit. 218 ff., I give up the doubt expressed in *Klagenkonkurrenz* p. 96 n. 43, whether by 'veteres' ought really to be understood the jurists of the Republican period, the meaning which it is indeed usually given.

[18] Ulpian, D. 13. 3. 2, taken with 12. 5. 6, drawing on Sabinus and the *veteres*. On this see Santoro, 190 ff.

[19] G. 4. 31, and on this see also Kaser, RZ pp. 25, 114–16.

the plaintiff should, at or before summons, give the defendant informal notice of the nature of his claim: *edere actionem*.[20] The formula of the *condictio* which had become ambiguous in that it now extended over a variety of *causae debendi*, could be focused upon a specified ground for liability by the inclusion of a *praescriptio*, as, for example, in the words *ea res agetur de sponsione illa et illa*.[21] In this way the plaintiff could limit the risk of the consumptive effect of *litis contestatio*.[22]

Only under the Empire do we have our first evidence of the admission of a new group of cases, which, however, did not all immediately acquire their own proper names. It appears that it was only at this time that the full potential of the open-ended nature of the formula was realized in the development of those cases which we in the civil law countries still call 'condictions' or claims arising from unjust enrichment. The chronological order in which they were recognized cannot be at all reliably deduced from the texts in which the classical jurists sought to achieve a systematic overview, since for their predominant purposes the thrust had to be to subsume the various kinds of cases under comprehensive categories.[23] Perhaps, however, the order of the *condictio* titles in the Digest between 12.1 and 13.3 does give some indication of the chronological sequence, in that they seem to follow the order of Ulpian's commentary on the Edict. This series gives the impression of being nearer the original order than does the order of the *Codex Justinianus* 4.1–10 (without the late 3 and 4). The *Codex* order seems to go back to Hermogenian, who paid special attention to the description and arrangement of the individual causes of action in unjust enrichment, at any rate more than Gregorius. Justinian's compilers took twice as many *condictio* constitutions from the *Codex Hermogenianus* as from the *Codex Gregorianus*, despite the former's being less than half the size of the latter.[24] Furthermore, in these constitutions and in his *Iuris Epitomae* Hermogenian for the most part distinguished the different species of *condictiones*, whereas previously not much value had been attached to the exercise of differentiating between distinct types.[25] Ulpian by contrast still seems to treat the *condictones* as not thoroughly differentiated, and he does not seem to have

[20] Lenel, *EP* §9. And see esp. Ulpian, D. 2. 12. 1.

[21] See esp. *Tabula Pompeiana* 7: J. G. Wolf, (1979) 45 *SDHI* 147 f. and his commentary, 148 ff.

[22] G. 4.130 ff., and on this Kaser, *RZ* pp. 196 f.

[23] This is especially true of the attempts at an integrated overview of the restitutionary possibilities of a *datio* (in German 'Leistung') of Pomponius, D.12.6.52, from his commentary on Quintus Mucius (around AD 140); of Paul, D. 12. 5. 1, from his commentary on Sabinus (under Marcus Aurelius?) and D. 12. 6. 65, from his commentary on Plautius (after Marcus Aurelius); and of Ulpian—not only for *dationes* but for all instances of unjust enrichment—in D. 12. 7. 1. 3, from his commentary on Sabinus (AD 216).

[24] Cf. Liebs, *Hermogenians iuris epitomae* (Göttingen, 1964), pp. 23 f.

[25] Loc. cit. 96 f. On Hermogenian's authorship of the private rescripts from AD 293 and 294 see Honoré, *Emperors and Lawyers* (London, 1981), pp. 119 ff., on which 100 *SZ* 505.

attempted to make proper headings for each type. However, though it is true that he did not develop any proper rubrics in his title on the *condictio* in books 26 and 27 of his commentary on the Edict, he does seem incidentally to have made a division in the treatment of the *condictio certae pecuniae*, the classical *actio certae creditae pecuniae*. There he not only distinguishes between *pecunia credita*[26] and *pecunia data aliis ex causis*[27] but, going further, creates three subspecies of the latter: *pecunia ob rem non inhonestam data*,[28] *pecunia data ob turpem causam*[29] and *pecunia indebita soluta*.[30] The *condictio* given *ex causa furtiva* he did not consider until he dealt, in book 27, with the so-called *condictio triticaria*, taking it as a species of *condictio certae rei*.[31] The order of causative events in unjust enrichment which is recoverable from Ulpian's book 26 is, then, more remote from the systematic scheme of the BGB and is, that suggests, likely to be nearer the original order than is Hermogenian's. Hermogenian puts the *condictio indebiti*, which is the principal case of the modern *condictio sine causa*, in the forefront (CJ 4.5), as do modern laws. In this he apparently followed Gaius, who introduced the *condictio* given for *indebitum solutum* into his *Institutes*, at 3.91, as the single example of a *condictio* based on unjust enrichment. Gaius brought it into the treatment of the real contract because of its structural similarity to *mutuum*. Again, in his *Res Cottidianae*, Gaius used the same *condictio indebiti* to represent all the unjust-enrichment *condictiones*, this time in the context of his treatment of those obligations which arise neither from contract nor from delict.[32] The *Institutes* of Justinian then devoted to this category its own special chapter, under the heading of quasi-contractual obligations.[33] For this reason we have long been dominated by the idea that the first and oldest claim in unjust enrichment was the *condictio indebiti*.[34] However, that does not really correspond with the perceptions of the classical jurists. For Ulpian, the case which struck him as having this central position was the restitutionary claim in respect of performances made *ob rem* with the subsequent failure of the consideration, *re* or *causa non secuta*. In just the same way Paul described the *indebitum datum* after the *datio ob rem*.[35] The demand to have the latter kind of payment back corresponds to the intentions of the parties manifested in an

[26] On this, Otto Lenel, *Palingenesia Iuris Civilis* (Leipzig, 1889, repr. Graz, 1960) vol. ii, Ulpian, 769–71. (Hereafter *Pal.*)

[27] *Pal.*, ii. Ulpian, 772–5, 778.

[28] Ibid., 772.

[29] Ibid., 773.

[30] Ibid., 774, 775 and 778; cf *EP* 234 n. 2.

[31] Ibid., 779–81.

[32] D. 44. 7. 5. 3.

[33] *Inst.* 3. 27. 6.

[34] Savigny, *System* v, pp. 109 f. and 521 ff.; so still Kaser, *RPI*, pp. 596 f.; Wunner, (1970) 9 *Romanitas* 460; and Sturm, *Studi Sanfilippo*, vol. iii, pp. 136 ff.

[35] D. 12. 6. 65 pr.

agreement at the time of the transfer. By contrast, one who had paid under a supposed liability could be told that he should bear the consequences of his own mistake, as indeed remained the case with mistaken expenditure on other people's property[36] and with transfers intended by way of reciprocation for something given or done by the transferee but made on the basis of mistake.[37]

None the less, a historical account of the recognized causes of action in unjust enrichment must at least attempt to fix as securely as possible the chronological order of their recognition. To that end, this study will first consider the *condictio* given *ex causa furtiva*, with its offshoots, especially the *condictio ex iniusta causa*; thereafter we will turn to the *condictio ob rem datorum re non secuta* together with *ob causam datorum causa non secuta*, *ob turpem causam* and *ob causam finitam*; then, in third place, the *condictio indebiti soluti*, together with its later generalization, the *condictio sine causa*. After that we shall consider the attempts, above all Ulpian's attempt, to arrive at a comprehensive rule to express the basis of all the *condictio* claims in unjust enrichment. Then, finally, we must address the so-called *condictio generalis* and the *condictio ex lege*.

III

As we have seen, in the case of theft and misappropriation the *veteres* already allowed the *condictio* to be brought for restitution of the stolen or misappropriated object. Ever since Savigny[38] it has repeatedly been stated that this was so because they construed theft as entailing a *datio* as in *mutuum* and thus made the extension by way of analogy. However, this seems wrong. More likely, it was based on an *a fortiori* argument: what a borrower has to bear, a thief must certainly bear. In contrast to the defendant in a *vindicatio*, the defendant in a *condictio* remained liable even when the object perished without his fault. It was, however, impossible to advance any reason why thieves and embezzlers should be subjected to a less stringent liability than borrowers; *odio furum receptum est* says Gaius (4.4) making a pointed reference to another related irregularity, namely that in the *condictio furtiva* the defendant did not have to convey the property in the *res* to the plaintiff, as in general, according to Gaius, the *condictio* did oblige him to do.[39] For Savigny and his followers informal loan for

[36] Julian, D. 12. 6. 33.

[37] Pomponius, D. 12. 6. 52; and Paul, D. 12. 6. 65. 2.

[38] Savigny, *System* v, pp. 110 and 551 ff., esp. 557 ff. See also Kaser, *RZ*, p. 81 and *RP* I, pp. 593 and 618; Sturm, *Studi Sanfilippo* vol. iii, 631 ff.; and, esp., D'Ors, op. cit. (n 1), and again (1974) 25 *Iura* 1 ff., while Santoro has broken this spell.

[39] G. 4. 4. See also Ulpian, D. 13. 3. 1. 1. and D. 7. 9. 12. Santoro, esp. pp. 213 ff. and 362 ff., has shown that this concept of rule and exception was created subsequently in the attempt to obtain dogmatic control over the ever-growing range of the *condictio*.

consumption (*mutuum*) was the case to which the *condictio* first applied,[40] an hypothesis which in the meantime has been shaken.[41]

One who drove an owner by force from his land could similarly be sued by *condictio* although he had not become owner of the land. This position too was also evidently reached by the *veteres*.[42] Since that event could not be called *furtum*, the plaintiff brought his *condictio* '*ex iniusta causa*'. If the person driven from the land was not the owner but rather possessor—whether *bona fide possessor*, *sequester*, usufructuary, mortgagee, or *precarium tenens*[43]—then, from the time of Celsus onwards, he could bring his *condictio* in respect of this mere possession,[44] something which Labeo had still declined to recognize.[45] Meanwhile, however, Aristo had conceded such a *condictio* in respect of possession to the pledge-creditor from whom a movable *res* had been stolen.[46] Aristo, followed in this by Paul, also gave to a husband from whom a wife had stolen, or to his heirs, the *condictio* against the wife *quia ex iniusta causa apud eam essent*.[47] To sue her in an action based explicitly on theft was not allowed.[48] Julian and Marcian came to similar conclusions.[49] And Ulpian gave the owner a *condictio* against his pledge-creditor with respect to fruits *ex iniusta causa percepti*.[50] A pledge-creditor who without the owner's consent used or sold the *res* delivered to him made himself liable for theft according to Gaius and Javolenus respectively.[51] For the case of sale the evidence is that Ulpian allowed the sale more generously to the pledge-creditor.[52] He seems also not to have defined every case of unauthorized taking of fruits as theft. However, with respect to the *condictio*, it seems that he thought it right to continue to grant it, though not as *condictio furtiva* but as *condictio ex iniusta causa*.

In another line of cases the classical jurists also allowed *condictiones* not based on a transfer by the plaintiff, that is to say, without requiring any

[40] Savigny, *System* v. pp. 109–11 and 511 ff., esp. 524 ff., 527 ff., and 532 ff. So too Kaser, *RZ*, p. 81 and *RP* 1, pp. 492 and 593.

[41] Liebs, *Klagenkonkurrenz*, pp. 96 ff., where, however, a wrong starting-point is taken in the assumption that the contract *litteris* is very old. Sturm, *Studi Sanfilippo*, vol. iii, pp. 630 f., also puts *stipulatio* and the contract *litteris* at the beginning, before *mutuum* and *furtum*.

[42] See *Pal.* ii, Ulpian, 2591b–2591e. Since the discussion of *condictio* here forms an excursus unlikely to have been extensive or various, it is very probable that there was originally a connection between D. 12. 5. 6 and D. 13. 3. 2. On all this see now the instructive treatment of Santoro, n. 3 above, 189 ff.

[43] Kaser, *RP* i. pp. 387 ff.

[44] Ulpian, D. 13. 3. 2.

[45] Ulpian, D. 47. 2. 25. 1.

[46] Ulpian, D. 13. 1. 12. 2.

[47] Paul, D. 25. 2. 6. 5.

[48] A. Wacke, *Actio rerum amotarum* (Cologne, 1963), pp. 107 ff.

[49] Julian through Paul, D. 13. 1. 19; and Marcian, D. 25. 2. 25. So too Pseudo-Ulpian, D. 25. 2. 24. On the author: Honoré, *Ulpian* 111–113; cf. now (1984) 56 *Gnomon* 446.

[50] D. 12. 1. 4. 1 '*et fructus . . . sunt*'.

[51] Gaius, D. 47. 2. 55 pr.; see also G. 2. 64; Javolenus, D. 47. 2. 74.

[52] D. 13. 7. 4.

datio. This is true even though they could not here refer to the *condictio* as arising *ex iniusta causa*. According to Africanus, Julian decided the following case.[53] A possessor, evidently believing in good faith that he is owner—he supposes himself to be the beneficiary of a legacy *per vindicationem*—sells the *res* before it perishes: and the particular circumstances are such that the risk passes to the buyer, and the latter can no longer sue the seller on the ground of eviction. The true legatee and owner can bring the *condictio* against the supposed owner for the whole sum received. The same holds good for Africanus,[54] in the case in which a slave who has been sold steals from the seller before delivery and then, after delivery, the buyer takes and uses the stolen property in good faith. The rationale for this is 'res mea [the seller's] ad te [the buyer] sine causa pervenerit'. And similarly in the case in which the slave steals from the old owner after delivery, to the extent that the *peculium* has thereby been enhanced.[55] According to Papinian a trespasser (*praedo*) who leased out another's land, ship, or slave was obliged by the *condictio* to give up the rent to the owner, and to this end he cited the maxim *praedoni fructus possunt condici*.[56] Paul always allows the *condictio* against a fraudulent depositee, even in circumstances where the elements of *furtum* are not all satisfied.[57] Ulpian equally makes the pledge-creditor liable in the same action when, despite discharge of his debt, he does not give back the pledge.[58] Ulpian deals similarly with the lessee who without authority continues to take fruits after the expiry of the lease[59] and with the landowner who comes upon the property of another which has been swept on to his land by a flood.[60]

By contrast Julian refused the *condictio* in the case in which one man built on another's land or in some other way made an expenditure on a *res* belonging to another, giving as the rationale 'quia nullum negotium inter nos contraheretur', while 'is, qui non debitam percuniam solverit, hoc ipso aliquid negotii gerit'.[61] There the matter ended. Within the field of the modern German *condictio* given other than after a transfer by the plaintiff,

[53] D. 12. 1. 23.

[54] D. 19. 1. 30 pr. at the end, from *si nummos* on. Already with the words *tamen in proposito* in the middle of the *principium* the text comes back to the initial case: sold but not yet delivered, the slave stole from his seller. This means that already here the text moves away from the opposite case: the theft occurs only after the delivery.

[55] Africanus, ibid.: 'si iam traditus furtum mihi fecisset, ... eatenus haberem [sc. condictionem] quatenus ex re furtiva auctum peculium fuisset'.

[56] D. 12. 6. 55. On this Santoro, art. cit. pp. 431 ff., is not satisfying.

[57] D. 16. 3. 13. 1.

[58] D. 12. 1. 4: '*res* ... potest'.

[59] Ibid.: 'nam et si ... condictio'.

[60] D. 12. 1. 4. 2: Kaser RP i, 595 n. 23, incorrectly takes this for a case of *alluvio* without considering D. 39. 2. 9. 1, also a text of Ulpian from his 53rd book *ad edictum* composed one year previously. On the chronology of Ulpian's works see Honoré, *Ulpian*, 129 ff.; outline summary, p. 187 f.

[61] D. 12. 6. 33.

that is when the claim is based on unjust enrichment by other means than by a performance made by the plaintiff (*Nichtleistungskondiktion*),[62] the Romans thus recognized to a remarkable extent those claims based on encroachment by the defendant (*Eingriffskondiktion*) including even cases of innocent encroachment; but in the same field, they refused the *condictio* for unauthorized expenditure (*Verwendungskondiktion*), which in German law is the second category of a recognized *Nichtleistungskondiktion*. Julian's argument relating to the presence or absence of a *negotium* between the parties only attaches at this point, and it was wrong to generalize it.[63] Furthermore, it was in particular cases also recognized that valid grounds for a *condictio* could be found in displacements of wealth which happened either through natural events or through the intervention of some third party for whose doings the defendant was not responsible, the third German category.

IV

In contrast to modern legal systems, in Rome the *condictio ob rem*, to use the abbreviated term, was very important. This is connected with the fact that there was a limited number of actionable contracts in Roman law, whereas today in principle every agreement is binding.[64] In the case of contracts which were in Roman law not binding, such as exchange or agreements for manumission in return for money, parties were left to voluntary performance, even when one person did his part, in particular the party who had promised money or delivery of a *res*. If the counter-performance was then forthcoming (the other giving up his *res* and so on) then, in the terms of para. 812 ch. 1 s. 2 BGB, the effect contemplated as the purpose of the transaction was brought about. In that case both parties had to be content. Contracts which, despite being unenforceable on the ground that they did not conform to a recognized contractual type, were nevertheless completely performed by both sides were given full effect, and to that extent the principle of freedom of contract did obtain. The only critical period was thus the time between performance by one side and the counter-performance by the other. If the counter-performance remained outstanding, it was only right and fair that one who changed his mind—as was his right—should give back whatever he had already received. The

[62] For a clear description: Hans-Georg Koppensteiner, *Ungerechtfertigte Bereicherung* (together with Ernst A. Kramer, Berlin, 1975), § 8, pp. 78 ff.

[63] This generalization is still in Kaser, RP 1. p. 594 f; Santoro, pp. 184 ff. and passim, is cautious. For the *condictio* arising from consumption, *accessio*, *commixtio*, or *confusio* effected by the enriched party, see A Wacke in (1976) 79 BIDR 49 ff., and, concisely, Ulrich Manthe, *Die libri ex Cassio* (Berlin, 1982), pp. 45–52.

[64] Brief review of the development in Liebs, *Römisches Recht* (2nd edn., 1982), pp. 193–223.

logical consequence was that the first performer was not bound either. That is, he did not need to wait to see whether the other party would perform but rather could bring his *condictio* so long as the counter-performance had not actually been made. In effect he therefore had a *locus paenitentiae*, a right of withdrawal.[65] Pomponius and Paul spoke here of *ob rem datum* and *res non secuta* and drew a contrast between that and *ob causam datum*.[66] By the last phrase they denoted a reciprocal performance in return for a kindness already done; and even on the case of a mistakenly supposed kindness this could not be recovered. Ulpian's usage was different. In book 26 of his commentary on the Edict, which he wrote in AD 213—the chronology has been determined by Tony Honoré—he did indeed still speak of *ob rem data* but he then referred to the sequel as *causa secuta*.[67] The same usage recurs in 214 in the *Disputationes*.[68] In AD 216 in book 43 *ad Sabinum*, where he was trying to reduce to one common denominator all the examples of the *condictio* in the field of unjust enrichment—an exercise to which we must return again later—Ulpian abandoned the language of Pomponius and Paul and spoke uniformly of *ob causam dare* or *promittere* and *causa non secuta*.[69] The jurists of Diocletian's time, Arcadius Charisius[70] and Hermogenian,[71] followed this usage, and the latter coined the phrase *condictio ob causam datorum* (*causa non secuta*). Out of that the compilers created the impressive staccato of *condictio causa data causa non secuta* in D.12.4. Under this head *ob causam datum* fell, already for Ulpian, not only a transfer made for a counter-performance as yet still outstanding but also, initially, a performance made to satisfy a condition, which later became unnecessary.[72] Paul still counted this as a special category and called it *dare propter condicionem*, from which he developed the notion of *agere per*

[65] This *ius paenitentiae* is indicated, without cause for suspicion, by Marcellus, D. 24. 1. 49 (7 *digestorum*). That text cannot be dealing with either *fiducia* or *mandatum*, for an obligation to make a certain testamentary disposition was contrary to *boni mores*. Thus there remains only the possibility of a *datio ob rem*. Hence it is rash to cast suspicion on the whole of D. 12.4.5, from Ulpian's *Disputationes*, even though the *ius paenitentiae* does appear to have been introduced *ex post* into D. 12. 4. 3. 2, 3. Probably some user of the *Disputationes* made the annotation in good faith. Kaser, *RP* II. pp. 423 n. 16, calls for reconsideration of the long-standing suspicions against the text.

[66] Pomponius, D. 12. 6. 52; Paul, D. 12. 6.65 pr., 2, 4; see also 12. 5. 1.

[67] D. 12. 4. 1 pr. So also presumably Plautius (or Paulus?) D. 12. 4. 9 pr.

[68] D. 12. 4. 6.

[69] D. 12. 6. 23. 3 towards *fin.*, 12. 7. 1. 12, 2. See also in Book 76 *ad edictum* of AD 217, D. 44. 4. 2. 3. So already Africanus, D. 12. 7. 4. For suspicions against these texts in Fritz Schwarz, *Die Grundlage* (cit n. 1) 117 f. and others, see now A. Wacke, (1972) 40 *T. v. R.* 238 ff.; and François Chaudet, *Condictio causa data causa non secuta* (Lausanne, 1973), pp. 89 ff.

[70] CJ 4. 6. 5. On the authorship, Liebs, (1983) 100 *SZ* 504.

[71] CJ 4. 6. 6; 9–10; and D. 12. 4. 2. The rubric from CJ 4. 6 is probably derived from him too, see above n. 24 and text thereto.

[72] D. 12. 4. 1. 1. I have attempted a survey of the whole spectrum of the Roman case-law in [1978] *Juristenzeitung* 608 f.

condictionem propter condicionem.[73] Ulpian was also the first to work out the case of *causa finita* as a distinct type, though in fact he did not allot it a separate section of his treatment. He mentions it in conjunction with the *condictio ob causam datorum causa non secuta.*[74]

In relation to this *condictio* no less than those considered earlier, we can look back as far as Servius, Labeo, and Sabinus.[75] These glimpses into the early history of the claim in unjust enrichment are especially informative. Here we can see that neither Labeo[76] nor Sabinus[77] insisted on the requirement that the enriched party must have become owner of the subject-matter. On the contrary, it was Proculus who first focused on this point.

Once the giving had been fulfilled—*res* or *causa secuta*—the recipient *ob rem* or *causam* only had to make restitution if his receipt offended good standards of social behaviour, that is, if his receipt had been *ob turpem causam*. In this case nothing turned on *res secuta* or *non secuta.*[78] In contrast to para. 817 s 1 BGB, the Romans did not run together the law on receipts contrary to statute and receipts contrary to *boni mores*. It was only Tribonian who took the step of modifying Hermogenian's category, which was perhaps already in the *Codex Gregorianus*, namely the *condictio ob turpem causam* as in CJ 4. 7, and widening it in D. 12. 5 to become *ob turpem vel iniustam causam*. However he was not able to add to this title (D. 12. 5) anything on this new type of *condictio* more than a general observation made by Ulpian in the context of the *condictio ex causa furtiva.*[79] Neither *turpitudo* nor even illegality in the agreement underlying the performance made the transfer itself—that is, the conveyance of ownership—ineffective. This is true even though in Roman law the applicable principle was the principle of 'causality' in relation to the conveyance, not the principle of 'independence' as in the BGB. Thus even conveyances in contravention of

[73] D. 12. 6. 65 pr., 3.

[74] 43 *ad Sabinum*, D. 12. 7. 1. 2 (*fin*); 76 *ad edictum*, D. 44. 4. 2. 3 (*fin.*). See already 32 *ad edictum*, D. 19. 1. 11. 6, and see immediately below in section V.

[75] Servius: through Neratius, 2 *membr.* D. 12. 4. 8. Labeo: through Pomponius, 22 *ad Sab.*, D. 12. 4. 15, from the chapter on *condictiones*; the beginning of the text, probably up to *oportuerit*, must come from Sabinus, on which Pomponius comments with 'Labeo ait' and so forth. On this, much to the point, Hans Julius Wolff, *Festgabe von Lübtow*, 1970, 537 ff, though in some respects still taking too narrow a view; and Álvaro D'Ors, in (1971) 22 *Iura* 138 ff. Compare the circumstances in D. 16. 3. 7 pr. Sabinus: further through Ulpian, 28 *ad edictum*, D. 19. 5. 17. 5; and 18 *ad Sabinum*, D. 7. 5. 5. 1: both of these were more properly *ob causam finitam*.

[76] D. 12. 4. 15; 46. 3. 19; and on these see Santoro, n. 3 above, 184 n. 4, 227 f., 477 ff.

[77] D. 12. 4. 15; D. 19. 5. 17. 5.

[78] Clear in Julian, D. 12. 5. 5; Paul, D. 12. 5. 1. 2, 9 pr.; and Diocletian/Hermogenian, CJ 4. 7. 4.

[79] D. 12. 5. 6, see above n. 42. On the other hand in D. 12. 5. 2 Ulpian classifies heinous breaches of statutory rules under *turpe acceptum*, as the original connection with D. 12. 5. 4 indicates.

criminal statutes were effective. These statutes were, as with most statutory prohibitions, *leges minus quam perfectae* if indeed not *imperfectae*; that is, a transaction which infringed them was not automatically void, as is provided by para. 134 BGB. It could indeed be that there was no sanction at all, and no provision for punishment.[80] Neither was an infringement of *boni mores* likely to render a causal conveyance void. It is important in Roman law to distinguish between three notions of *causa*. First, the minor *causa* which sufficed for conveyances, in relation to which putative *causa* was sufficient, as for example the intention to discharge a supposed liability.[81] The minor *causa* could survive illegality and breach of *boni mores*,[82] so that in this the Romans come very close to the consequences of the modern 'independence' principle. Then, the middle *causa* determined the right to retain, the immunity to a restitutionary claim. At this level a putative *causa* was insufficient. Illegality alone, however, did not render this middle *causa* null and void. That only happened when the transaction also offended decent standards of behaviour.[83] The major *causa*, finally, determined the question whether a promise was actionable. In classical law illegal promises were not automatically ineffective, i.e. not *ipso iure* void, but rather were often defeated by an *exceptio*, lacking special exceptions by the general *exceptio doli*.[84]

Thus, because of the merely 'imperfect' or 'less than perfect' statutory prohibitions, judgment as to infringement of *boni mores* was more important in Roman law than it is now, and, correspondingly, also the *condictio ob turpem causam*. Only after Theodosius II had in AD 439 abolished the categories of imperfect statutory prohibitions and turned every such statute into a *lex perfecta*[85] did Tribonian set about drawing appropriate inferences for the law relating to unjust enrichment. As a general rule, he brought statutory prohibitions to bear on the middle *causa* which determined the right of retention. He did this by allowing the claim based on unjust enrichment on account of *turpis causa* to be extended to another claim adjacent to it, namely the *condictio* on account of *iniusta causa*. More precisely, he extended the *condictio ob turpem causam* in the way which has been

[80] Kaser, *Über Verbotsgesetze und verbotswidrige Geschäfte im röm. Recht* (Vienna, 1977), esp. pp. 71 ff. Honsell, in the Roman section of his Habilitationsschrift, *Die Rückabwicklung sittenwidriger oder verbotener Geschäfte* (Munich, 1974), pp. 80 ff., did not take note of these connections.

[81] This has been shown in particular by Fuchs, loc cit. (n. 1 above). See further Neratius, D. 41. 10. 5. 1; and Africanus D. 41. 4. 11. Different Justinian, see Inst. 2. 6. 11.

[82] Kaser, *Verbotsgesetze*, pp. 74 f.

[83] Ibid., pp. 71 ff.

[84] Ibid., pp. 76 ff.

[85] Nov. Theod. 9 with concrete case; without that, again in CJ 1. 14. 5. On this, Paul Krüger, *Geschichte der Quellen* (2nd edn., Munich, 1912), 295 f.; and Kaser, cit. n. 80 above, 61 f. and 67 f.; and Voss, *Das Profil des Juristen* (Ebelsbach, 1980), pp. 244 ff., illuminatingly but failing to take Kaser into consideration.

described above.[86] The texts for the new category he naturally had to take chiefly from classical observations relating to *ob turpem causam condicere*. This, however, worked out easily enough because the classics, as we have said, did indeed characterize notable breaches of statutory provisions as *turpis*.

However, the right to bring a *condictio ob turpem causam* was denied to one whose performance had also involved him, on his side, in an infringement of good standards of behaviour. But this limitation on *ob turpem causam condicere* was not an afterthought, as might have been inferred from the final structure of this rule in the form of an exception. Rather, it was an inherent part of the cause of action by *condictio* based on *turpitudo* from the very beginning, since *ob turpem causam condicere* itself runs back just to Servius and then is seen again only in Proculus,[87] and the limitation appears quite shortly afterwards in Labeo and Sabinus.[88] That one person should be bound to return something to another on the ground that its receipt was immoral is only immediately obvious in the case in which the other, seeking the law's protection, is not himself open to the same objection. Legal redress never was developed for the sake of safeguarding shabby transactions. Some will perceive the law's refusal to intervene on such facts as abject inertia on the part of the legal order unable to achieve with the means at its disposal any improvement in a bad situation.[89] But that assessment proceeds from a premiss which supposes the existence of a comprehensive system of legal redress. Approaching the matter with that fundamental preconception, it is impossible to come to a proper appreciation of the range of causes of action in Rome in the early classical period. The situation throughout that period was basically that legal remedies were promised and provided only for special cases.

If, however, by way of logical development of the Justinianic generalization of the principal rule, one also extends the exclusionary rule to every illegality, as happened in post-Justinianic law and is codified in para. 817 s 2 BGB in connection with art. 2 EGBGB, the result is that a principle which was originally directed *inter alia* at the purpose of discouraging evil conduct becomes instead a vehicle enabling one man to exploit another to his own advantage without risk to himself.[90]

[86] Text after n. 78.

[87] Proculus through Julian, D. 12. 5. 5; and Servius through Alfenus, D. 12. 6. 36; see Alan Watson, *The Law of Obligations in the Later Roman Republic* (Oxford, 1965), pp 10 ff.

[88] Labeo and Sabinus, through Ulpian D. 12. 5. 4. 3 and pr. respectively.

[89] So Honsell, op cit. 90.

[90] For fuller exposition see Honsell, op. cit. 93 ff.

V

It is clear from Labeo on that an *indebitum solutum* could be recovered by *condictio*. However, at first the only case seems to have been the particularly obvious example of an unauthorized payment by or to a procurator.[91] Despite the *indebitum* and hence despite a defective *causa* the ownership in the thing passed to the recipient. This was not because of special rules for money, the object most often in question here, but rather because of the minimal requirements in relation to the *causa* for an effective conveyance and because of the great importance of *solutio* in Roman law even into the classical period. *Solutio* was not merely the discharge of a debt, as with us, but on account of the survival in the civil law of execution against the person, the release above all from this personal liability. This is the cause of what seems, according to modern perceptions, to be an unnecessary circuity: the fulfilment of a duty rather than the duty itself was conceived to be the legal basis of the transfer of ownership, and indeed equally a sufficient basis for *usucapio*. The duty was indeed the legal foundation of the cause on which the conveyance immediately rested; however its failure did not avoid the transfer but only rendered it reversible by *condictio*, whether the object was money or other goods. The passage of ownership to the recipient was certainly a characteristic circumstance leading to the *condictio indebiti* but it was not an indispensable prerequisite for a claim by that type of *condictio* at least not for Tryphoninus. He once allowed this *condictio* alongside a *vindicatio*,[92] albeit without expressly naming the latter. In fact in his case the *condictio* could also be explained *ex causa furtiva*. Hence his failure to attend to the issue of the passing of ownership would bear only on the classification, not on the actionability, of the plaintiff's *condictio*.

For a *condictio indebiti* to be actionable it was required that the transferor should not have known that in reality he owed nothing. He must have been labouring under a mistake.[93] That too will from early times have been an inherent requirement for an unhesitating grant of the *condictio*; in the absence of a mistake the matter will not have been immediately obvious. However, as *indebitum solutum* became more securely understood as a sufficient ground for a *condictio* it was inevitable that cases would come up in which, even where there was no sufficient error, nevertheless a *condictio* seemed well justified. One example was the case of bare mistakes of law made by children, women, soldiers, or peasants;[94] and another that in

[91] Paul, 3 *ad Sabinum*, D. 12. 6. 6. pr., 1.

[92] D. 16. 3. 31. 1 (*fin.*)

[93] Paul, 42 *ad edictum*, D. 50. 17. 53; Ulpian, 26 *ad edictum*, D. 12. 6. 1. 1; Caracalla, CJ 4. 5. 1; and, esp., Diocletian/Hermogenian, CJ 4. 5. 3–7 and 9; 1.18.10. See for modern law para 814 BGB.

[94] Paul, 3 *quaestionum* D. 22. 3. 25. 1; Gordian, CJ 4. 29. 9.

which some statutory prohibition which made the transfer *indebitum* created the need for a remedy by *condictio*, as was true, according to Ulpian, of the *lex Cincia.*[95] However, in this last case the position was reversed by Tribonian.[96] Again, the classics disputed the question whether a restitutionary claim was available to one who paid, not in the mistaken belief that he owed, but unsure whether he did owe. Here Tribonian's decision was that even the payer in doubt could recover his payment.[97]

Suppose that a launderer received something to be cleaned from another and had to pay damages because the thing was stolen from him. If the owner later recovered the thing, the cleaner could claim by *condictio* the amount of the damages which he had had to pay. This was held by Cassius, as well as by Sabinus and Labeo;[98] but the decision was reached without identifying a specific type of *condictio* or recognized ground for claiming. It was evidently made only in direct response to the actual facts. Ulpian here found a considerable difficulty. He observed that the *condictio indebiti* would not fit this situation because at the moment of the payment the damages were indeed due. However, the *condictio ob causam finitam* seems well suited to this case, so that the question arises why Ulpian did not mention that species at all. That type of *condictio* was, as has been said, introduced for the first time by Ulpian. But even he only made a beginning, and barely that. When Ulpian wrote this text in AD 215 he had previously only mentioned this distinct species of *condictio* in one single place, immediately before in the title on sale,[99] still with a direct link to the well-recognized *ob causam datum causa non secuta*, in which the possibility of *non sequi* was always present from the beginning. That was precisely what was lacking here. The same phenomenon presented itself several times in unexpected contexts. In AD 213 and 214 Ulpian had allowed two cases to slip by which would have fitted the new category very well.[100] Only in 216 and 217 did he formulate *ob causam finitam condicere* as an independent species.[101] The case of the launderer did indeed need to be integrated into the *condictio*; similarly in need of incorporation was the case of a promise

[95] Ulpian 26 *ad edictum*, *Frag. Vat.* 266.

[96] It was he who first introduced into D. 12. 6. 26. 3, in the text of Ulpian just mentioned in n. 95, a 'nisi sciens se tutum exceptione solvit', whereas Ulpian himself had said 'si ... exceptione tutus solverit'. Kaser, in *RP* 1, 603 f., smooths out this divergence unacceptably. But see now *Verbotsgesetze*, 22 ff, on Celsus, D. 39. 5. 21. 1, and Paul, D. 44. 4. 5. 5.

[97] CJ 4. 5. 11. The transferor may have been in doubt in the following cases: Ulpian, 16 *ad Sabinum*, D. 12. 6. 2 pr.; 3 *omn. trib.*, D. 49. 1. 11; and 76 *ad edictum*, D. 44. 5. 1. 10. See also Papinian, D. 12. 6. 55 'quod si ... solvendo'.

[98] In Ulpian 32 *ad edictum*, D. 12. 7. 2.

[99] 32 *ad edictum*, D. 19. 1. 11. 6. For the dates, see Honoré, *Ulpian*, 129 ff.

[100] 28 *ad edictum*, D. 19. 5. 17. 5; and 18 *ad Sabinum*, D. 7. 5. 5. 1.

[101] 43 *ad Sab.*, D. 12. 7. 1. 2 (*fin.*); 76 *ad edictum*, D. 44. 4. 2. 3 (*fin.*). Shortly before in AD 216 he had let pass a third example, or with our case from 215 a fourth: 34 *ad Sabinum*, D. 12. 1. 4. 1 *init.* See already Julian 23 *digestorum*, D. 37. 6. 3. 5; and Africanus, 8 *quaestionum*, D. 23. 3. 50 pr.

made under the mistaken impression of a liability and, in particular, the claim of a mistaken promisor to have the benefit of the promise surrendered to him by the promisee.[102] To achieve this, Ulpian generalized the old and narrow *condictio indebiti* to reach the *sine causa datum* and, in addition, *sine causa promissum*, still current in modern law. In para. 812 ch. 2 BGB *promissum* is expressly envisaged as a possible object of a transfer. To return to Roman law, the means by which such an asset, the *promissum*, could be transferred back was the release of the promisor, considered an *incertum*. The *condictio incerti* was conceived for such cases, certainly not later than Julian.[103] Ulpian, however, remained within the traditional analysis at least to the extent of continuing to see *indebitum solutum* as a category of case; and the generalization which he attempted was merely an enlargement of that category and was not a radical reorientation. Hermogenian[104] and Tribonian[105] also lead us down that path. So far as concerns Ulpian's special category of a *condictio ob causam finitam*, Hermogenian and Tribonian seem, however, to have rejected it as superfluous beside this enlarged *condictio sine causa*.[106]

Ulpian was not content to let the development stop with this breezy new construction around the still-extant old building. He sought to move forward to a general conception of the *condictio* arising from unjust enrichment. In contrast to the occasional experiments of Julian, who with his insistence on a *negotium* could only hope to limit *indebitum solutum*,[107] or of Africanus, who focused only on the *condictiones* based on a transfer by the plaintiff,[108] or again to the views of Pomponius and Paul, who tried to derive a scheme for all *repetere* claims through the analysis of the

[102] Ulpian, 43 *ad Sabinum*, D. 12. 7. 1 pr., 2; more concisely re-done a year later in 76 *ad edictum*, D. 44. 4. 2. 3.

[103] J. G. Wolf, *Causa Stipulationis* (Cologne, 1970) pp. 193 ff.; and A. Wacke, in (1972) 40 *T. v. R.* 259 f.

[104] The *Codex Hermogenianus* evidently had a title *De condictione indebiti*, which is CJ 4.5, whose constitutions 3–9 derive from the CH. It is more difficult to reconstruct the genesis of CJ 4.9, which contains exclusively Hermogenianic material though with an interesting chronological upset: CJ 4. 9. 1, which is also out of place in terms of its content, seems to have been moved up to the beginning of the title by Tribonian, with the aim of supporting the words *ex lege* in the rubric, which phrase also seems to derive from Tribonian: see below in section VI. The Hermogenianic rubric thus seems to have been *De condictione sine causa* (to which CJ 4. 9. 2 and 4 would fit) *vel ex iniusta causa* (to which would fit CJ 4. 9. 3).

[105] D. 12. 7 evidently has no classical precursor but was put together for the first time by Tribonian himself. Kaser seems still invariably to hold the entire category to be Justinianic, see *Verbotsgesetze*, 24 n. 15.

[106] For Tribonian that follows from its absence from the list of his *condictio* rubrics. For Hermogenian it can be inferred from the position of CJ 4. 9. 2 presumably already in his title *sine causa*, whereas for Ulpian a case of *causa finita*, cf. D. 19. 1. 11. 6.

[107] D. 12. 6. 33, as to which see above in section III.

[108] D. 12. 7. 4, from book 8, and therefore presumably taken from the chapter on the *condictio*.

requirements for a *datio*,[109] Ulpian wished to come to a general principle which would include all the *condictiones*, even those independent of a transfer (i.e. *Leistungskondiktionen* and *Nichtleistungskondiktionen* together). In his commentary on Sabinus, in the section on *condictiones*, he proposed this principle: 'constat id demum posse condici alicui, quod vel non ex iusta causa ad eum pervenit vel redit ad non iustam causam.'[110] This includes in its first part, as we can gather from the general *pervenit*, the examples of the *condictio* which are independent of a transfer, and focuses, as logically it must, on the receipt rather than the giving. The words *non ex iusta causa* are evidently meant to include more than *sine causa*, which never extended to displacements of wealth *ex iniusta causa*. This last expression in its turn was anyhow construed narrowly by Gaius,[111] Ulpian, and Hermogenian.[112] As has already been said, the classical jurists used the phrase to indicate displacements of wealth caused by *furtum*-like events without the effect of passing ownership;[113] or, put another way, roughly the quasi-delictual part of the spectrum of unjust enrichment as opposed to the quasi-contractual part, in which latter part the basis is always a transfer by the plaintiff and where the expression *sine causa* could be used as an appropriate generic term. However, Ulpian's comprehensive principle for all claims in unjust enrichment, the second part of which may indeed have been intended to reach even the *condictio* which lay for a credit when the time for repayment had arrived,[114] should be understood only as a maxim. It was not a new definitive statement of all the necessary elements, capable of being used as an immediate touchstone of liability. For immediate rules of liability on particular facts the old definitive figures remained, as before, indispensable.

VI

Ulpian, however, went even further, though it has often been somewhat hastily denied that this is truly his. He took seriously the abstract quality

[109] Pomponius, 27 *ad Quintum Mucium* (*De condictione*), D. 12.6.52, and Paul, 10 *ad Sabinum* (*De condictione*), D. 12. 5. 1, and 17 *ad Plautium* (*De condictione*) D. 12. 6. 65.

[110] D. 12. 7. 1. 3. *Pal.* ii, Ulpian 2898 §3, Lenel here is not satisfying, since he makes no serious attempt to reconstruct bk. 43 of Ulpian *ad Sabinum*, preferring essentially to present the fragments in the order in which he found them in the Digest.

[111] 11 *ad edictum provinciale*, D. 24. 1. 6, relating therefore to property-adjustment after divorce.

[112] See CJ 4. 9. 3 from the Hermogenianic title which closed the chapter on *condictiones*, 'De condictione sine causa vel ex iniusta causa'. Cf. above, n. 104.

[113] Kaser, *Verbotsgesetze*, p. 72 n 12, does not give quite the whole picture, in that in a case of bare *turpitudo* property did pass. Evidently Kaser's view is guided by the parallel created by Tribonian in the rubric of D. 12. 5.

[114] Not, however, other debts arising from stipulations or from contracts *litteris*.

of the *condictio* and began his explanation of the formula with these words:[115]

Actio certae creditae pecuniae competit ex omni causa, ex omni obligatione, ex qua cert*a pecunia* petitur, sive ex certo contractu petatur sive ex incerto. licet enim nobis ex omni contractu cert*am pecuniam pet*ere, dummodo praesens sit obligatio. ceterum si in diem sit vel sub condicione obligatio, ante diem vel condicionem non potero agere. competit haec actio etiam ex legati causa et ex lege Aquilia. sed et ex causa furtiva per hanc actionem condicitur. sed et si ex senatus consulto (sc. Trebelliano) agetur, competit haec actio, veluti si is cui fiduciaria hereditas restituta est agere volet. sive autem suo nomine quis obligatus sit sive alieno, per hanc actionem recte convenitur.

And a little later he says:[116]

Quoniam igitur ex omnibus contractibus cert*ae creditae pecuniae a*ctio competit sive re fuerit contractus factus sive verbis sive *litteris sive* coniunctim, referendae sunt nobis quaedam species, quae dignum habent tractatum, an haec actio ad petitionem eorum sufficiat.

There follow various complications in relation to contracts for credit.[117] The only other classical jurist in whom we find again such a very general statement is Marcian, who indeed develops the approach further. Marcian, as Honoré has discovered, is also especially close to Ulpian in his use of language.[118] In his account of criminal law, in the context of adultery and, in particular, of the claims for compensation maintainable by an owner whose slave had to be put to torture in the course of an adultery trial, he points out: 'quod ex his causis debetur, per condictionem, quae lege descendit, petitur.'[119] Every claim to a specific thing or quantity could be realized according to Marcian by the *condictio* so long only as the system recognized the particular claim in question. If that recognition was to be found in statute, then 'descendit condictio ex lege.' Gregorius and Hermogenian seem to have left this possibility out of consideration. But the idea remained alive. In the *Codex Theodosianus*, which sadly at this point survives only in fragments, the lost title which must have dealt with loans and *condictiones* was apparently followed by the existent *si certum petitur de chirographis* (2.27). In the latter title the actionability of written IOUs by *condictio* is assumed. Already Gaius had recognized this actionability, but only between peregrines.[120] Another title of the *Codex Theodosianus* dealt

[115] D. 12. 1. 9 pr.–2, in this case with Justinianic alterations which replace the classical *actio certae creditae pecuniae* with the *certi condictio*, Lenel, *EP*, 234.

[116] D. 12. 1. 9. 3, see *Pal.* ii, Ulpian, 768.

[117] D. 12. 1. 9. 4–9, 11, 13.

[118] Honoré, *Ulpian*, pp. 54, 80, 216.

[119] D. 48. 5. 29, from bk. 1 *De iudiciis publicis*, see *Pal.* i, Marcian, 187. On this matter: Ulpian, D. 48. 5. 28. 11–16.

[120] 3. 134, as to which Kaser, *RPI*, p. 545.

with the purchase of offices, a type of contract which Julian the Apostate could still say was unknown to the Roman statute book, but which Theodosius I recognized.[121] The title was called *Si certum petetur de suffragiis* (2.29). According to the conception of the editors of the Theodosian code, the action must have been the *condictio*. Tribonian took over this title in the corresponding place in the *Codex Justinianus* (4.3), but he created in addition a new category of *condictio*, the *condictio ex lege*. In four enactments from his time as *quaestor sacri palatii* he provided the *condictio ex lege* for newly regulated claims, three times as an optional alternative to a traditional action, as a back-up for the exceptional case in which the established action failed;[122] and once as an *actio popularis* with the function of reinforcing the main actions.[123] In the Digest he made an independent title for the *condictio ex lege* (13.2) though he felt able to assign to it only three lines of Paul, whose original provenance remains uncertain. Possibly they concerned not the *condictio* but rather the *actio legis Aquiliae*.[124] Finally, in the *Codex* Hermogenian's back-up category *De condictione sine causa vel ex iniusta causa* was enlarged to include the *condictio ex lege* and became an imprecise composite title, which now sounds incongruous: *De condictione ex lege et* (!) *sine causa vel* (!) *iniusta causa*. It was given by way of prefix a constitution of Diocletian, concerning *fenebris pecunia*[125] in which, since even the word *condictio* did not appear once, the new term *condictio ex lege* was necessarily also absent. Since *fenebris pecunia* would have been concluded by means of a *stipulatio* it would indeed have been enforceable by *actio certae creditae pecuniae* or *condictio certae pecuniae*. In the particular case the due date was advanced by reason of an overwhelming public interest, and in Diocletian's own time the technical means would have been either to accept premature exigibility or to refuse the *exceptio pacti* (sc. *dilationis*), both based on some emergency statute. At all events it is certain that Diocletian and Hermogenian would not have bothered to create for this case a special category of action.

A review of the whole story establishes that the Byzantines did not introduce any revolutionary changes into the law of the *condictiones*. The less one knows of them the more easily one thinks of them as monsters of whom anything might well be believed. If on the other hand we approach the matter soberly and assess what the jurists of Constantinople who were

[121] C.Th. 2. 29. 1. 2, as to which Liebs (1978) 95 *SZ* 174 ff.

[122] CJ 2. 55. 4. 4, from 30 Oct. 529; 3. 31. 12. 1c, from 1 Sept. 531; and 6. 30. 22. 6, from 27 Nov. 531. Tribonian was in office on the first occasion from Sept. 529 to Jan. 532; see Honoré, *Tribonian* (London, 1978), pp. viii, xiv, and 47 f.

[123] CJ 1. 3. 45. 6 *ad fin.*, from 18 Oct. 530. On this Murga, (1968) 15 *RIDA* 354 ff.

[124] D. 13. 2. 1 from bk. 2 of *ad Plautium*, see *Pal.* i, *Paul*, 1083; and T. Mayer-Maly (1965) 12 *RIDA* 445 f., where see 446 for Tribonian's concept.

[125] CJ 4. 9. 1; see above, n. 104.

responsible for the Theodosian and Justinianic codifications added to the law in the condition in which they found it, we are drawn to recognize that they developed the late and post-classical law as left by Ulpian and Hermogenian not only cautiously but also not without subtlety. This small example thus confirms the lesson which the scholar whom we now honour has repeatedly taught: Tribonian was indeed the legitimate successor to the classical Roman jurists.

11

L. Fufius—Another Undeserving Winner?

ALAN RODGER

THE legal mind which Tony Honoré admires is like his own: clear, well-ordered, and rational. Lawyers with such minds are critical and love the law only if it deserves to be loved. Honoré is, moreover, proud to be an academic lawyer, a member of a group whose mission it is, with the legislators (happily, practitioners are excused), to order the law and bring it up to scratch.[1] When dealing with ancient lawyers, he applies much the same approach. Ulpian is to be praised for his sense of proporion and moderation as well as for his sure instinct for the just solution,[2] whereas in the end, for all his devotion to legal scholarship, even Tribonian falls short of Honoré's exacting standards.[3] Those of us who fall even further short, however, find interest in aspects of the law which are less than clear and in decisions which are not wholly inspired by moderation. In presenting a case of this kind for Honoré's inspection, I merely cling to the hope that the co-author of *Causation in the Law*, that treasure-house of good stories, may at least enjoy rereading Cicero's tale.

The tale is told succinctly and concerns a litigation which occurred at about the beginning of the first century BC:

Cicero, *de oratore* 1. 39. 179. Quo quidem in genere familiaris noster M. Buculeius, homo neque meo iudicio stultus et suo valde sapiens et ab iuris studio non abhorrens, simili [in re] quodam modo nuper erravit: nam cum aedis L. Fufio venderet, in mancipio lumina, uti tum essent, ita recepit; Fufius autem, simul atque aedificari coeptum est in quadam parte urbis, quae modo ex illis aedibus conspici posset, egit statim cum Buculeio, quod, cuicumque particulae caeli officeretur, quamvis esset procul, mutari lumina putabat.

M. Buculeius owned a house which must have had servitude rights over neighbouring property to prevent certain neighbours building in such a way as to cut off light from the windows of his house. Buculeius sold the house to L. Fufius and, when conveying it by *mancipatio*, he gave an undertaking

[1] Tony Honoré, *The Quest for Security: Employees, Tenants, Wives* (London, 1982), p. 124.

[2] Honoré, *Ulpian* (Oxford, 1982), p. 242.

[3] Honoré, *Tribonian* (London, 1978), p. 256.

that the light to the windows would remain as it then was. When building was begun in a distant part of the city, this blocked a small part of the skyline. Fufius immediately sued Buculeius on the ground that the light to his windows was being altered by the building operations.[4]

Perhaps because the case is reported so briefly, it has been somewhat neglected by modern writers on the Roman law of sale.[5] This neglect may also be due to a feeling that the case turns too much on its own facts to be of more general interest. Griesinger[6] thinks that the action was brought as a joke and, more recently, Professor Watson[7] has felt that Cicero's text is more notable for its human interest than for what it tells us about servitudes of light. It is the purpose of this article to suggest that the action was certainly not a joke and that the text discloses points of some general interest to the legal historian.

I. THE DISPUTE AND THE PARTIES

The dispute concerned an undertaking given by Buculeius *in mancipio*, i.e. when actually conveying ownership of the house to Fufius. The undertaking was to the effect that the light to the house would remain as it then was. As will be seen in more detail in Part II, such an undertaking was treated as an assurance that the necessary servitudes existed in favour of the house. So Buculeius was saying that he was conveying a house which would continue to enjoy the same light and which had the servitudes necessary to secure this. Statements of this kind, declaring that a property has a particular quality or enjoys a particular advantage, could be made by sellers at various stages; for example, during negotiations leading up to the conclusion of the contract, or at the actual time of contracting, or at the time of the conveyance. Each situation would raise a different question as to whether the purchaser should have a remedy if the property turned out not to have the quality or advantage mentioned.[8] This text tells us something

[4] L. F. Griesinger, *De Servitute Luminum et Ne Luminibus officiatur* (Reutlingen, 1819), pp. 128 ff.; W. Rein, *Das Privatrecht und der Zivilprozeß der Römer* (Leipzig, 1858), pp. 322 ff.; M. Voigt, *Das jus naturale, aequum et bonum und jus gentium der Römer* (Leipzig, 1875), vol. iii, p. 306; H. J. Roby, *Roman Private Law in the Times of Cicero and of the Antonines* (Cambridge, 1902), vol. i, pp. 501 n. 1 and 534 ff.; E. Costa, *Cicerone giureconsulto* (2nd edn., Bologna, 1927), vol. ii, pp. 133 n. 4 and 134 n. 3; A. Watson, *The Law of Property in the Later Roman Republic* (Oxford, 1968), pp. 194 ff. The fullest and most important treatment is unquestionably that of Griesinger. The interpretation of Roby, which is unfortunately reflected in the *Oxford Latin Dictionary* (Oxford, 1968), s.v. *recipio* 15, proceeds on a mistranslation of *recepit*. While the translation given is possible for some texts, it is incorrect in the present passage.

[5] It is not found in the textbooks of Buckland or Kaser, nor yet in the monograph of Arangio-Ruiz. It is referred to in a footnote in A. Watson, *The Law of Obligations in the Later Roman Republic* (Oxford, 1965), p. 79 n. 2.

[6] *De Servitute*, p. 141.

[7] *Property*, p. 194.

[8] Cf. P. G. Stein, *Fault in the Formation of Contract in Roman Law and Scots Law* (Edinburgh and London, 1958), ch. 2.

about the position where such a declaration was made at the stage of conveyance, *mancipatio*.

Though the *de oratore* was not written until 55 BC, it purports to record an imaginary conversation in September 91 BC between two great orators and rivals, L. Licinius Crassus and M. Antonius. The story of Buculeius is supposed to be told by Crassus. So when he says that the events occurred 'recently', this means not long before 91 BC,[9] and any 'words of good-natured contempt',[10] while written by Cicero, are meant to be spoken by Crassus.[11] The text moreover gives us the law as it was at the beginning, rather than in the middle, of the first century BC.

Crassus' purpose in telling the story is to illustrate his theme[12] that it is important for orators to study and know the *ius civile*. Its real point must therefore be to show that victory was achieved by the orator who had a thorough grasp of the *ius civile*.

We know nothing more about M. Buculeius than we are told in this passage. L. Fufius,[13] on the other hand, was an orator who had made his name some years before in a celebrated prosecution of M'. Aquilius. Aquilius was eventually acquitted thanks to the influence of Marius and to a speech in his defence by Antonius, the other participant in this part of the *de oratore*. Elsewhere[14] Crassus is represented as having a low opinion of Fufius' style as an orator and plainly he was in the second rank. But one quality which Cicero at least ascribes to him is diligence.[15] Given, then, the avowed purpose of Crassus in telling the story, we can be certain that L. Fufius, the orator, overcame his opponent Buculeius by dint of his knowledge of the *ius civile*. Of course, in the text Crassus makes much of Buculeius being a man who did not shrink from the study of the civil law, and scholars have perhaps tended to concentrate on the fact that despite this study Buculeius made a mistake (*erravit*). The point of the story cannot, however, lie in Buculeius' work and his mistake, since that would suggest the futility of legal study, thereby undermining rather than supporting Crassus' thesis. Nor, so far as we know, would there be any apparent reference to an orator. Rather, Fufius the orator won, overcoming Buculeius, who was no slouch where legal matters were concerned, and he did so by some point of law which he took and argued successfully.

It is worth noting in passing that the story, when interpreted in this way, shows that Fufius was not only a party to the dispute, but he actually

[9] Griesinger, *De Servitute* tends to overlook this.

[10] Watson, *Property*, p. 194.

[11] J. Partsch, (1912) 33 *ZSS* 600, 603 Book Review, also loses sight of this when he describes Buculeius as Cicero's friend.

[12] 1. 36. 166 ff.

[13] See F. Münzer, *Pauly-Wissowa* 7.1 (Stuttgart, 1910), s.v. Fufius 5.

[14] *de oratore* 2. 22. 91 and 3. 13. 50.

[15] *Brutus* 62. 222; *de officiis* 2. 14. 50.

represented himself, argued his own case and achieved victory by his own efforts. In the United Kingdom today a lawyer who argued a case on his own behalf in court would generally be regarded as foolish. But Fufius was, of course, not a lawyer but an orator, and as such would doubtless be quite accustomed to speaking in cases where he was actively involved as a protagonist on one side of the dispute. Antonius, for instance, conducted his own defence when he was accused of incest.[16]

II. BUCULEIUS' UNDERTAKING AND ITS CONSEQUENCES

The declaration made by Buculeius related to the light to his house. As, for instance, Watson notes,[17] it corresponded to a type of undertaking which is mentioned elsewhere as being a standard clause (a *lex mancipi*) in a *mancipatio*. The effect of the clause was that the seller warranted that a certain servitude was due from a neighbour. The principal treatment of such clauses is in D. 8. 2. 17. 3, Ulpian 3 *ad Sabinum*:

> haec lex traditionis 'stillicidia uti nunc sunt, ut ita sint' hoc significat impositam vicinis necessitatem stillicidiorum excipiendorum, non illud, ut etiam emptor stillicidia suscipiat aedificiorum vicinorum: hoc igitur pollicetur venditor sibi quidem stillicidiorum servitutem deberi, se autem nulli debere.

The text came originally from a discussion of *mancipatio* in connection with sale, though the precise context cannot now be determined with certainty.[18] Ulpian[19] explains that a clause in the form *stillicidia uti nunc sunt ut ita sint* 'means' that neighbours are required to accept *stillicidia* and that 'therefore' the seller promises that a servitude of *stillicidia* is owed to him.

When Ulpian gives the meaning of the clause, he is not translating the Latin. Roman readers would not require a translation. Modern readers, however, require to remember what the Latin actually says: 'that the *stillicidia* may be as they are now'; the seller is declaring that the *stillicidia* will in future be the same as they are at the time of the *mancipatio* when the *lex mancipi* comes into operation. Ulpian's purpose is to explain the legal effect of such a clause. The wording is, after all, ambiguous:[20] it could mean

[16] Valerius Maximus 3. 79.

[17] *Property*, p. 194.

[18] O. Lenel, *Palingenesia Iuris Civilis* (Leipzig, 1889), vol. ii, col. 1123, which must be read with Lenel's comments in *Das Sabinussystem* (Strasburg, 1892), pp. 59 ff. Honoré would date book 29 of Ulpian's commentary *ad Sabinum* to AD 216: *Ulpian*, p. 153.

[19] It is, of course, quite possible that some at least of the text reflects the views of Sabinus as Schulz suggests: F. Schulz, *Sabinus-Fragmente in Ulpians Sabinus-Commentar* (Halle, 1906), p. 67.

[20] Cf. recently C. Krampe, 'Die ambiguitas-Regel: Interpretatio contra stipulatorem, venditorem, locatorem' (1983) 100 *ZSS* 185, 212 ff. with references.

either that the neighbouring land would continue to require to take *stillicidia* from the seller's land or that the seller's land would require to continue to take *stillicidia* from the neighbour. Ulpian resolves the ambiguity by explaining that the clause 'means' that the neighbouring land will continue to take *stillicidia* from the seller's land. It is only as a deduction (*igitur*) that we are told further that with this clause the seller promises that the servitude of *stillicidia* is due to the land.[21] So while a clause in this form does indeed amount to a promise that the land enjoys the appropriate servitude of stillicide, this is only because such a promise is implicit in the actual undertaking 'that the *stillicidia* may be as they are now'.

If we adopt this general approach and apply it to what Buculeius is recorded as having said, then his actual undertaking would have been '*lumina uti nunc sunt ut ita sint*', 'that the light to the windows may be as it now is'. This would be interpreted as 'meaning' that the neighbours had been put under the necessity of preserving the light to the seller's windows, and hence that the appropriate servitude(s) of light to achieve this were owed to Buculeius' house.

It was upon this undertaking that Fufius sued Buculeius when building began in a distant part of the city which could only just be glimpsed from the house bought by Fufius. His case must therefore have been that the construction of this building resulted in Buculeius being in breach of his undertaking that the *lumina* would remain as they were at the time of the *mancipatio*. The *iudex* decided in favour of Fufius.

To reach a decision on the case, the *iudex* required to decide whether, after the building operation, the light supply to the house bought by Fufius remained the same in terms of Buculeius' undertaking. The parties arguing the case and the *iudex* deciding it therefore needed to find a standard by which to assess whether any legally material change in the light had occurred. Fufius, whose contention succeeded, invoked a test which had been devised to decide whether a servient owner was in breach of a servitude *altius non tollendi*. Two texts are relevant.

In D. 8. 2. 16, Paul 2 *epitome Alfeni digestorum*, Paul reports the opinion of Alfenus who wrote not long after the time of the dispute between Fufius and Buculeius. According to Alfenus a servitude of light is a servitude 'that the sky may be seen'. He goes on to distinguish this type of servitude from a servitude of prospect on the ground that, while a view or prospect may come from below, light cannot come from a lower point. In other words

[21] Eisele, 'Beiträge zur Erkenntnis der Digesteninterpolationen' (1890) 11 *ZSS* 1, 17, rejects the part from *hoc igitur* to *nulli debere* as an explanatory addition, similar to a gloss. But contrary to what he says the first part of the sentence usefully expands on what goes before. One might wonder, however, whether there has been some compression in *se autem nulli debere* since a declaration implying that servitudes are due to a piece of land does not also imply that no servitudes are due by that piece of land.

for instance, one may look down towards a fine view of meadows or sea, but light must come from the sky, which will always be above.[22] The same theme of 'seeing the sky' recurs in D. 8. 2. 15 and 17, Ulpian 29 *ad Sabinum*, written almost three hundred years later. In these texts, which formed a unit in the original work,[23] Ulpian explains that a servitude of prospect gives the dominant owner greater protection than a servitude of light. None the less, he goes on, with a servitude of light 'whatever he does to block the light can be prevented if a servitude is due, and there can be *operis novi nuntiatio* if he merely does something which may have the effect of diminishing the supply of light'. Indeed, Ulpian concludes, planting a tree may be in breach of the servitude, 'for even a tree has the effect that less sky (*minus caeli*) can be seen'. So Ulpian stresses that a servitude of light prevents *anything* ('quodcumque') which may reduce the supply of light, the ultimate test being whether 'less sky' can be seen by the dominant owner.

When taken together, the texts from Paul's epitome of Alfenus and from Ulpian[24] indicate that an owner who had secured a servitude of light over other property could stop any building on the servient land which would have the effect of blocking his existing view of a portion of the sky. That was the standard by which any infringement was to be judged. Such a test may strike the modern reader as somewhat rough-and-ready or artificial, but it would be a practical and objective test. The judge need do nothing more than decide whether, before some particular building went up, the dominant owner would have been able to see a patch of sky which was now blotted out by the building. If so, the dominant owner could now see 'less sky' and so his servitude rights had been infringed. This straightforward approach eliminated the need to hear, far less to assess, inevitably conflicting evidence about whether the supply of light had been materially diminished—something which might be hard to determine without knocking down the disputed building.

In the *de oratore* passage, Fufius argues along the same lines.[25] He contends that the *lumina* are 'changed' for the purposes of the undertaking given by Buculeius whenever any small part of the skyline, even though far away, is blocked. That is to say, he argued that the light-supply to the windows was no longer the same as at the time of the *mancipatio* because a small piece of the skyline was now blocked out by the erection of a

[22] The interpretations of this text by O. Karlowa, *Römische Rechtsgeschichte* (Leipzig, 1901), vol. ii, p. 528 and Watson, *Property*, p. 194, while different, both seem unacceptable.

[23] Lenel, *Palingenesia*, vol. ii, Ulpian, fragment 2711.

[24] I note that in a well-known text, D. 8. 2. x, supposedly also from Ulpian book 29 *ad Sabinum*, but not to be found in standard editions of the Digest, the formulation 'quo minus caeli videri potest' occurs: see D. Daube, 'Interference with Light in Roman Law' (1943) 93 *The Law Journal* 180, 189.

[25] Cf. Griesinger, *De Servitute*, p. 131.

building. Hence, he submitted, Buculeius was in breach of his undertaking that the light supply would remain the same.

The *iudex* accepted Fufius' argument and so must have held that Buculeius was in breach of his undertaking because a small patch of sky could no longer be seen from the house. But if that criterion is applied, the scope of Buculeius' undertaking can be seen to be far-reaching indeed: he is undertaking that the skyline as viewed from his house will, so long as Fufius owns the house, remain the same and in particular that no part of it will be obscured by any building. Such an undertaking would mean that Buculeius was saying that all the owners of land where building could block the skyline were obliged not to build and block the skyline. This would in turn amount to Buculeius being held to have said that his house had the servitudes necessary to achieve this by preventing *all* the relevant landowners from building—a sweeping undertaking, indeed.

It might be objected that, since much of the land on which such buildings could be erected would lie a considerable way off, servitudes of light over them would not have been legally possible, and hence that the *iudex* could not have adopted an interpretation which implied that such servitudes could exist. Watson does not go quite so far, but more cautiously observes that the story does 'not allow us to conclude that such a theoretical right could have existed'.[26] There is no text which provides an answer on precisely this point, but it seems that servitudes over such distant land would have been legally possible. A priori there is perhaps no obvious objection to the existence of a servitude of light over some distant land if, as Ulpian indicates, servitudes of light were designed to stop *whatever* blocked light and if the test for infringement was whether less of the sky could be seen. Buildings at a considerable distance could cause that degree of inconvenience and on that basis an owner who wished and was able to do so should have been able to protect his property against even slight inconvenience by obtaining a servitude. The evidence in the Digest tends to support this approach. The servitude *altius non tollendi* was classified as urban, but urban servitudes could be found in connection with houses in the country.[27] The servitude of prospect in particular seems much at home in a country context. In D. 8. 2. 38, Paul 2 *quaestionum* we are told that a servitude of prospect cannot be created over your house if it is so far from mine that one cannot have a view from one to the other, or if a mountain cuts off the view. If these limiting factors were not present, then, we must infer, mere distance between the houses would not of itself prevent a valid servitude of prospect being created. In the same way, we may argue, mere distance between the *praedia* would not prevent a valid servitude of light being created, provided

[26] *Property*, p. 195.
[27] D. 8. 4. 1, Ulpian 2 *institutionum*.

only that building on the servient *praedium* could affect the light by blocking out a portion of the sky as seen from the dominant *praedium*. Another text of Paul, admittedly not in good order, suggests that a servitude *altius non tollendi* could be created even where the dominant and servient buildings were separated by a building in the ownership of a third party over which the dominant owner had not secured a servitude.[28] Fufius would not actually require to argue that point since, on his interpretation, Buculeius had undertaken that the house enjoyed a servitude *altius non tollendi* over every single plot of land where building could block out the skyline. So even if there were, say, twenty plots of land in different ownership between Buculeius' house and the land where the building actually took place, on Fufius' interpretation Buculeius had said that his house had a servitude *altius non tollendi* over every one of them. The question would be whether, if that had been so, a valid servitude could have been created over the twenty-first plot where building work had begun. As just explained, there are indeed good reasons for thinking that a valid servitude could have been created over that land.

If this is correct, then Buculeius' undertaking, even when interpreted as a declaration that the necessary servitudes existed, was legally quite capable of fulfilment. An owner in Buculeius' position could, in theory at least, approach the owners of all the land where building could block his view of the sky, and ask for a servitude *altius non tollendi* over their land. Of course, it may be pointed out that these owners would be unlikely to agree to submit to such a servitude. That is true. But in theory at least the necessary servitudes could be imposed and the mere fact that in practice it would be difficult to obtain them was of no relevance to the dispute between Buculeius and Fufius because Buculeius' declaration was not that he *would* obtain the necessary servitudes, but rather that the necessary servitudes *had* already been obtained. Provided only that the undertaking was legally possible, the difficulty or otherwise of fulfilling it was irrelevant: Buculeius had simply warranted that the desired state of affairs already existed.

In strict theory therefore Fufius' contention must have been this. After he became owner of the house, some building works in a distant part of the city blocked the view of the sky from his house. Buculeius had said that no such change in his light would occur. More particularly, Buculeius had warranted that the house enjoyed the servitudes necessary to prevent such building work. Such servitudes could have been created by Buculeius. In particular the house could have had a servitude over the distant land where the building which blocked the skyline had been erected. If the house had indeed had the necessary servitude over that plot of land, Fufius would have been able to stop the construction work. As it was, the requisite

[28] D. 8. 4. 7. 1, Paul 5 *ad Sabinum*. See A. Rodger, *Owners and Neighbours in Roman Law* (Oxford, 1972), p. 27 with references.

servitude did not in fact exist over the land and therefore the building work could not be stopped. In these circumstances there was a breach of the undertaking because (*a*) the sky was blocked by a building, (*b*) there was no servitude *altius non tollendi* over the land, and (*c*) if there had been a servitude *altius non tollendi*, Fufius could have stopped the building.

III. BUCULEIUS' MISTAKE

Fufius' action was based, of course, on the terms of the undertaking which Buculeius gave. Buculeius' predicament arose because he made a mistake (*erravit*)—he gave an undertaking which he should never have given. How did he come to make this mistake?

To trace the origin of his mistake we must assume, as all modern scholars rightly assume,[29] that in inserting this declaration Buculeius was not acting totally capriciously. Rather, he was aware that his house enjoyed a servitude of light over at least one neighbouring property. So when he made the declaration Buculeius meant to affirm that his house enjoyed this particular servitude of light over that property. Doubtless, as Griesinger says, an appropriate form of words to convey this limited meaning could have been devised. What Buculeius did, however, was to choose a formula which, instead of being confined in this way, could be interpreted as declaring that servitudes existed over lands far beyond the particular property which Buculeius had in mind.

We know from D. 8. 2. 23, Pomponius 33 *ad Sabinum* that the words *lumina quae nunc sunt ut ita sint* could be used by a seller, who was disposing of part of his land, to burden the land which he was selling with a servitude *altius non tollendi* in favour of the land to be retained. Some scholars have seen in this the source of Buculeius' mistake. According to them, he erroneously used this form of words, which was only apt to create a servitude over the purchaser's land, to give an undertaking to the purchaser about the existence of a servitude over someone else's land. While this explanation cannot be ruled out, it is unlikely. Such a mistake would be crass—not the kind of thing which someone like Buculeius, who was interested in law, would make.

A simpler explanation can be given. As we have seen from D. 8. 2. 17. 3, a clause *stillicidia uti nunc sunt, ut ita sint* was a sufficiently common *lex mancipi* to be commented on by Ulpian in his Sabinian commentary. It was used by sellers to declare that the property enjoyed the servitudes necessary to ensure that, for the future, the new owner would be able to drop rain-water from his house on to neighbouring land in the same way as the sellers did. It seems likely that a similar clause was used for *flumina*, the servitude

[29] For explanations see works cited in n. 4.

right to discharge surface-water on to neighbouring land. A similar formula could be used to give the purchaser an undertaking about the right of support over neighbouring property. In each case the seller's declaration would be interpreted as meaning that the land enjoyed the necesary servitudes. However by their very nature these servitude rights *could* exist only over immediately adjoining property. Rain-water could drop only on to the plots of land adjacent to the four sides of any building; surface-water could be discharged only on to the immediately adjoining *praedia*. What happened to the rain-water or to the surface-water once it reached that neighbouring land and, in particular, how it was drained from there on to the lands of remoter proprietors, was no concern of the original dominant proprietor. Providing he had the servitudes over the property on to which he dropped the rain-water or discharged the surface-water, that was enough. Likewise, an owner whose house required support would obtain it from his immediate neighbour, not from some owner with land a mile away. It follows that, say, the undertaking *stillicidia uti nunc sunt ut ita sint* would be fulfilled by an owner whose land had the necessary servitudes over immediately adjoining land. Provided that he had those servitudes, the purchaser would be able to continue to drop rain-water on to that land, and nothing which occurred on more remote plots of land could possibly interfere with this. The same goes for support: if there was a servitude *oneris ferendi* over the neighbouring property, the support would remain as it was and nothing occurring in the distance would affect it.

By contrast, as we have seen, even if he had a servitude or servitudes of light over the immediately adjacent land, a seller could still find himself in breach of a clause worded *lumina uti nunc sunt ut ita sint* since building operations carried out at many points far from the surrounding plots of land could cause a relevant change in the light. So Buculeius' mistake was to use the well-established form of words (...) *uti nunc sunt ut ita sint*, which could be used quite safely for such things as *stillicidia* and *flumina*, for *lumina*, for which it could not be used safely, but on the contrary only at the risk of imposing a far-reaching liability. Yet it is easy to understand how Buculeius might come to make this mistake. In drafting his conveyance, he would doubtless copy precedents and, if asked to give an undertaking about the light to the house, he would simply have adopted and adapted the form of words which he found used in a precedent for one of the other servitudes, say, *stillicidia*. What he did not appreciate was that this apparently straightforward adjustment to the standard clause produced wholly different and startling results. It is precisely the kind of mistake which a careful but inexperienced do-it-yourself conveyancer would be liable to make.

IV. FUFIUS' ACTION

Even so, Buculeius' blunder might have remained undetected and all might have been well if Fufius had not decided to exploit it. By doing so Fufius has attracted a considerable volume of criticism from modern scholars. For Wilkins Fufius' action 'goes to show that he was a shameless unprincipled fellow',[30] while Rein[31] and Voigt[32] talk of chicanery and deliberate misinterpretation, Voigt contrasting the guileless Buculeius with a rather scheming Fufius. It is not my purpose to go to the opposite extreme and to assert that Fufius' actions were motivated by the highest principles. Plainly they were not: Fufius saw his opportunity and seized it. But it is as well not to single him out for undue criticism on this account. Fufius was not the first person, nor was he the last, to capitalize on an opponent's mistake. Experience teaches that private individuals who litigate are rarely people of tender conscience: they frequently have a streak of determination bordering on ruthlessness. Fufius was doing no more than many others would have done in his position: he was standing on the rights which, he alleged, Buculeius had afforded him by giving the undertaking in these wide terms. Sergius Orata, whose case is mentioned in the preceding paragraph of the *de oratore*, would have been a kindred spirit.[33]

To make matters worse for his modern critics, Fufius not only brought the case: he won. That would not perhaps have been so interesting if the action which he brought and won had been a *stricti iuris* action. All the indications are, however, that the action was a *bonae fidei* action, an *actio ex empto*. We are not actually told specifically what kind of action Fufius raised, but only three possibilities suggest themselves: *actio auctoritatis*, *actio ex stipulatu*, or *actio ex empto*. For the reasons given by Partsch[34] the action cannot have been an *actio auctoritatis*. It might be suggested that it was an *actio ex stipulatu* on the basis of Buculeius having incorporated his undertaking into a stipulation. The difficulty is that we are told specifically that Buculeius gave his undertaking *in mancipio* and, while we hear elsewhere of undertakings given by way of stipulation at the time of purchase, we have no evidence for a practice of giving such stipulations at the moment of conveyance. Moreover, the terms of the declaration correspond, as we have seen, to the structure of a common *lex mancipi*, and again we have no reason to think that these *leges mancipi* were given effect by stipulation. The conclusion is that Fufius' action was an *actio ex empto*. As Partsch

30 *de oratore* 2 (Oxford, 1881), 246, note on 2. 22. 91.

31 *Privatrecht*, p. 322.

32 *Jus naturale*, vol. iii, p. 306.

33 Cf. A. Rodger, 'Concealing a Servitude', in P. G. Stein and A. D. E. Lewis (edd.), *Studies in Justinian's Institutes in Memory of J. A. C. Thomas* (London, 1983), pp. 134, 148.

34 (1912) 33 *ZSS* 603 ff.

points out,[35] this is confirmed by the way Crassus is made to stress the similarity of this case (*quo quidem in genere*) to the case of Gratidianus and Orata which precedes it and which undoubtedly involved an *actio ex empto*.[36]

One can indeed press the point a little further. The similarity between the cases is not confined to the fact that the action in each is an *actio ex empto* arising out of the events surrounding a *mancipatio*. There is some connection between the grounds of liability in the two cases. Gratidianus was successfully sued in an *actio ex empto* because at the stage of the *mancipatio* he deliberately refrained from mentioning a servitude which existed over his house. Similarly, Buculeius is successfully sued in an *actio ex empto* because at the stage of the *mancipatio* he in effect declared that certain servitudes existed in favour of his house. Since, as the case of Gratidianus shows, the jurists of this period were prepared to give an *actio ex empto* for something which was *not* said at the *mancipatio*, we can hardly be surprised to find that in an appropriate case they would give the same action in respect of something which *was* said at a similar stage in the transaction.

But even so we cannot safely conclude that the action in this case was an *actio ex empto* unless we face up to a fundamental point which was made by Beseler in his comments[37] on Partsch's review article. Beseler's point is that any breach of the undertaking by Buculeius would have caused so little damage, and fulfilment of the undertaking would have brought so little benefit, to Fufius that any action based on making good Fufius' damage or indeed on paying double an appropriate proportion of the price would have been an action for nothing. As the *condemnatio* in an *actio ex empto* would require to be for a sum of money and could not be for nothing, Fufius could not, Beseler argues, have won an *actio ex empto*. So Beseler concludes that the action must have been an *actio auctoritatis*—'Unless the praetor refused the idiotic action?'

For the reasons given in Part I, we can be quite certain not only that Fufius was given a formula by the praetor, but also that he went on to win his action. But Beseler's point that the damages in an *actio ex empto* would have been negligible is a crucial one and demands to be taken seriously.

If the action was an *actio ex empto*, then, since Fufius won, the *iudex* must have awarded a sum of damages. That much can be said with certainty. Beyond that, the text affords us no direct evidence of the approach adopted by the *iudex*, and it is well known that *iudices* must have enjoyed a considerable latitude in assessing damages.[38] So any suggestion about the

[35] Loc. cit.

[36] Cf. Rodger, *Thomas Studies*, esp. p. 144.

[37] G. Beseler, *Beiträge zur Kritik der römischen Rechtsquellen* (Tübingen, 1920), vol. iv, pp. 307 ff.

[38] Cf. Stein, *Fault*, pp. 22–3.

measure of damages adopted must be somewhat speculative. Even so, we may outline an approach which would not have led to Beseler's conclusion that no damages should be awarded and which is in accordance with the general view of the action advanced in this article.

Beseler concentrates on the result. He says that Fufius really lost nothing from the breach of the undertaking and would have gained nothing even if he could have stopped the distant building—what did it matter if a tiny patch of sky was blocked? If one views Fufius' case in this way, then, of course, Beseler is correct. But it is not the only way to look at the dispute. What the *iudex* may have been persuaded to do was not to look simply at those effects on Fufius, but rather to concentrate instead on what the action was about, viz. Buculeius' failure to fulfil his undertaking to Fufius. Buculeius undertook in effect to convey to Fufius a house enjoying all the servitudes necessary to prevent building operations over a wide area. Instead of doing so, he conveyed a house with at most one or two servitudes to prevent building on immediately adjoining land. So Fufius obtained a house which did not enjoy all the advantages which the seller had undertaken it would have. In such a case, it could well be argued, the seller who conveys the property without all the servitudes should pay the cost of obtaining the missing servitudes so that the purchaser may in effect have what he bargained for, namely, the house with those servitudes.

It is likely, however, that the measure of damages in Fufius' action would not have been so sweeping. The action was after all directed to one particular breach of the undertaking, Buculeius' failure to provide a servitude *altius non tollendi* over the distant plot of land where the building was erected. The damages would therefore be calculated by reference to the cost of providing a servitude *altius non tollendi* over that particular plot of land. Even on this approach the damages would not be negligible. Fufius could, for instance, lead evidence of the sum which the distant landowner would have demanded in return for the imposition of a servitude *altius non tollendi* over his land. Since we know that this distant landowner in fact wanted to put up a building on his property, we can readily surmise that he would have demanded a high price in return for subjecting his land to a servitude which in effect made it useless for the very purpose which he had in mind. His land was being sterilized, turned from building land into land on which an owner could either not build at all or could build only a low structure. In such a situation the sum demanded would presumably be so high, and the advantage to the owner of Buculeius' house so trivial, that no-one in Buculeius' position would ever have contemplated paying it. But that would, of course, be quite irrelevant to the calculation of damages in Fufius' action since this proceeds on the basis that Buculeius undertook that he *had* obtained these servitudes. So he would have to pay the cost of securing the servitude, even though no owner of the house acting sensibly would ever have paid that price to obtain the trivial benefit derived from it.

Yet, as we saw above, Buculeius' potential total liability was much greater. On the interpretation of the *iudex*, he had undertaken that servitudes had been imposed on *all* the plots of land where building could cover a patch of the sky as seen from the house. There would presumably be many, perhaps even dozens or more, such plots of land. So Buculeius was faced with the prospect of being sued by Fufius for a substantial sum of money every time someone built on one of these plots. Some scholars[39] indeed think that Cicero's account implies that Fufius had already brought more than one action. We do not need to decide. It is sufficient to notice that Fufius was in a position to bring the further actions if the circumstances arose.

The situation was a nightmare for Buculeius. The somewhat light-hearted approach taken by some modern scholars to the story is quite mistaken. Most inappropriate of all is the attitude of Griesinger.[40] He portrays Fufius as a man of humorous temperament, ready for a joke, who raised his action more to make a laughing-stock of Buculeius than to bring any financial reward to himself. There is, needless to say, nothing in Crassus' words which really justifies this approach, and nothing which we know of Fufius from elsewhere suggests that he was the kind of person to go to court for such an apparently recherché and light-hearted motive. On the contrary, he is depicted as a determined prosecutor and as one who, in a political context, 'rages'.[41] Such a man would surely have had easier ways of amusing himself than bringing an action which could be won only by careful legal argument. We are much more likely to be dealing with a cunning action brought by a determined man in order to exploit the horrendous slip which had delivered Buculeius into his hands.

V. THE DECISION OF THE *IUDEX*

The decision of the *iudex* was a disaster for Buculeius. Bekker,[42] for instance, clearly thinks that Buculeius ought to have won the action and that he lost only because the jurists of this period had still to work out the meaning and scope of *dolus*. Though Bekker does not spell out his argument, it would presumably be that Fufius must have known perfectly well that, when he gave his undertaking, Buculeius meant only to refer to a particular servitude or servitudes over adjoining property. So for Fufius to

[39] E.g. E. I. Bekker, *Die Aktionen des Römischen Privatrechts* (Berlin, 1871), p. 165 n. 19.

[40] *De Servitute*, pp. 141–2. In a complete muddle over dates, he even suggests that Cicero may have egged Fufius on!

[41] *de oratore* 2. 22. 91.

[42] *Aktionen*, p. 165.

turn round subsequently and bring an action based on giving the undertaking a much wider scope was dishonest, indeed fraudulent.

Let us concede at once that Fufius was probably well aware that the scope of Buculeius' undertaking was meant to be limited to adjacent property and that Fufius deliberately chose to interpret it more widely. Bekker's criticism of the decision in favour of Fufius then bears some resemblance to criticisms which could be levelled at the decision in favour of Orata mentioned in the immediately preceding paragraph.[43] Orata sued Gratidianus for failing to mention a servitude over a house which he was selling, even though Orata knew perfectly well that the servitude existed and was not deceived. Similarly Fufius sues Buculeius on the basis of what in effect is an undertaking that servitudes exist over many properties when Fufius knows perfectly well that only one or two servitudes exist and is not deceived. In one case the buyer knows that a particular servitude exists but sues because he is not told of it; in the other the buyer knows that many servitudes do not exist, but sues because he is told something which implies that they do. In each case the buyer is exploiting the predicament of the seller. Orata won his case. We can hardly be surprised that Fufius did also. But just as there is no reason to believe that the *iudex* in Orata's case reached his decision because of a lack of legal sophistication, so also we should not rush to the conclusion that the *iudex* in this case made his decision because he lacked a proper understanding of concepts such as fraud and good faith.

The *iudex* would not be concerned merely with whether Fufius' actions amounted to fraud in any narrow sense. What the *iudex* had to consider, rather, was whether, judging all the circumstances by reference to the standard of good faith, Fufius was entitled to succeed against Buculeius. In any such consideration of the case the cardinal point in Fufius' favour was the very words of the undertaking given by Buculeius. He had said that the position as to light would remain the same. The position had not remained the same. He had in effect undertaken that certain servitudes existed in favour of the land. They did not. On either interpretation of his undertaking, Buculeius had not fulfilled it. In a *stricti iuris* action, that would have been an end of the matter: Buculeius would have been held to the terms of his undertaking. The fact that Fufius' action was *bonae fidei* opened the door to wider considerations but, as we are frequently reminded, even by jurists of the high classical period,[44] the first requirement of good faith is that contracting parties should perform what they have agreed to perform. So there would be no question, at any period, of a *iudex* in a *bonae fidei* action ignoring or playing down the terms of the undertaking. On the contrary they would be important, the starting-point indeed, for considering what

[43] Cf. Rodger, *Thomas Studies*, pp. 144 ff.

[44] D. 19. 2. 21, Javolenus 11 *epistularum*; D. 19. 1. 11. 1, Ulpian 32 *ad edictum* (which Honoré would date to AD 215: *Ulpian*, p. 188).

the rights of the parties were and what *ex fide bona* Fufius was entitled to demand of Buculeius. In the dispute between Gratidianus and Orata, which also culminated in a *bonae fidei* sale action, the *iudex* rejected arguments based on equity (*aequitas*) and enforced the strict legal obligation of Gratidianus to make reference to the servitude at the *mancipatio*. The *iudex* in this case was being asked to make a not dissimilar relaxation in favour of the seller. His decision to hold Buculeius to the terms of his undertaking smacks of the same attitude, and this similarity of approach may be part of what Crassus refers to when he links the two stories (*quo quidem in genere . . . simili [in re] quodam modo . . .*).

Holding Buculeius to the terms of his undertaking, despite assertions that he meant something different as Fufius must have known, does not by any means necessarily indicate that the *iudex* does not understand the concepts of *dolus* or good faith. It may mean no more than that the *iudex* was persuaded to take the view that in this case the parties should be held to the objective interpretation of their agreement rather than to some interpretation based on considerations of what they actually intended. Questions as to the proper approach to interpretation were very much in the air at this period and, of course, Crassus himself, who tells the story of Buculeius, had appeared not long before in the *causa Curiana*, where just such matters were ventilated. The modern literature on this topic is enormous,[45] but the case of Buculeius, like that of Gratidianus, has not perhaps been given the attention which it deserves in discussions of the approach to interpretation. The matter cannot be investigated here, and one must be cautious in concluding that the decision reflects a general attitude or doctrine prevailing at the period rather than a response to the particular facts of the case. This is particularly so since there would be strong reasons for not giving effect in this case to the supposed actual intention of the parties. The *iudex* was not being asked to interpret a form of words which was entirely a creation of Buculeius. On the contrary Buculeius had chosen to use, or perhaps rather to misuse, a standard form of clause which must have occurred repeatedly in sales of land and houses. To depart from the normal meaning of such words and to interpret them differently by reference to the particular circumstances of the individual transaction would threaten to unsettle their meaning and to introduce the risk of uncertainty into the other transactions where they were used. One can easily see why a *iudex* could be persuaded that he should not yield to that temptation, and many modern courts of the highest authority in the Common Law world would approve of his approach. Moreover, since the whole case arose out of a mistake by Buculeius, the case for sticking to the received interpretation of the words is

[45] Cf. e.g. G. Gandolfi, *Studi sull'interpretazione degli atti negoziali in diritto romano* (Milan, 1966), esp. ch. 2 with references.

arguably even stronger. In effect, what Buculeius was doing was asking for the *iudex* to put a novel interpretation on the clause or somehow or other to relieve him from his obligation under it, not because of some hitherto undiscovered aspect of its interpretation which was now being uncovered for the first time, but simply because Buculeius had made a blunder in deliberately choosing to make the declaration in those particular terms. He was asking to be relieved of the consequences of his own mistake, a mistake for which, so far as we can tell, Fufius was in no sense to blame. To some legal minds at least such an argument has an unattractive ring, even, or perhaps especially, in an action where the rights of the parties are measured by reference to good faith, and we need not be surprised that the *iudex* rejected it.

Of course, the passage records nothing more than the decision of one particular *iudex*. Other *iudices* of the same period might have reached the opposite conclusion. It is quite possible that jurists of the classical period, far less of the Justinianic age, would have found in favour of Buculeius. Legal minds do after all change—not always for the better—and a difference of approach would seem not unlikely if those modern scholars are correct who believe that from shortly after the date of this dispute there was a general shift in the canons of interpretation and more attention was paid to the individual circumstances of a case. Ulpian, with that 'sure instinct for the just solution' which Honoré admires, might well have found a way to help Buculeius. I for one, however, should like to think that some at least of the classical jurists would have followed the *iudex* here—not only because his no-nonsense approach would ease the problems of any jurist called on to advise clients on the meaning of similar wording, but also because any practising lawyer must have a soft spot for the Fufii of this world who provide him with both the raw material of his trade and the means to earn his daily bread. For that reason alone they deserve to win—sometimes.

12

*Causam Mortis Praebere**

DIETER NÖRR

THERE are few Romanists in the world (and almost none in Great Britain) who have not written about the *lex Aquilia*, that well-known statute of uncertain date—though probably of the third century BC—on damage to property. I imagine that everyone who dares to offer a new contribution believes, with or without justification, that he has something original to say about it. The same is true in my case. I also think that I have found a new path toward understanding some aspects of the *lex*, although as yet I am not quite sure where it will lead. The subject is causation, and it is for two reasons especially appropriate that this should be considered in the present volume: first, problems of causality are a recurrent and indeed characteristic preoccupation of the legal mind; and secondly, there is no doubt that, in the great range of his scholarship, Tony Honoré is the acknowledged master of causation in the law. In this paper I am only to take the first steps, and it will be wrong for the reader to expect more than a fragile hypothesis and some shadowy impressions. My essential purpose is to introduce into the discussions some texts which, so far as I know, have been neglected.

I

In order to convey at least an impression of the present state of discussion about the *lex Aquilia* in relation to the subject-matter of this paper, it is necessary to begin with three famous texts, one from Gaius' Institutes and two from the Digest.

Gaius, 3. 210 gives, with some modifications which we can neglect, the text of the first chapter of the *lex Aquilia*. The third chapter, which is much more controversial, is irrelevant for present purposes.

Damni iniuriae actio constituitur per legem Aquiliam, cuius primo capite cautum est, ut si quis hominem alienum alienamve quadrupedem quae pecudum numero sit iniuria occiderit, quanti ea res in eo anno plurimi fuerit, tantum domino dare damnatur.

* The first draft of this article was prepared for a lecture given at Cambridge, Edinburgh, and Glasgow in November 1983, during my period as a visiting Fellow at All Souls College, Oxford. I should like to thank my British colleagues for stimulating discussions and Professor Birks and Dr Paulus for help with the translation. A monograph on *causa mortis* with full argument and citation of sources will probably be published in 1986.

For our purposes the essential term is *occidere* (kill). According to the usage of classical Latin *occidere* can be used for every kind of killing, no matter whether the connection between the act of the wrongdoer and the result (death) is direct (killing with a sword) or indirect (locking up a person and killing him by starvation). However, this must have been different at the time when the *lex Aquilia* was enacted, and in the period immediately thereafter as well, when it fell to be interpreted by the jurists or by others who applied the law. In that period *occidere* was a term which was limited to direct causation of the death. The chronology can be fixed at least roughly by using an indication which is given by Plautus in a play which was performed for the first time in 191 BC (*Pseudolus*, 349 ff.). Plautus there plays on the difference between the *gladius* and the *fames* that 'occiderit'. Hence, it was in this period at the latest that the broader meaning of *occidere* began to develop. But by then the narrow interpretation had already been established, and the consequence was: no *actio legis Aquiliae* in cases of indirect causation.

We do not know at what time and in what circumstances the need was first felt for a remedy in the case in which slaves or cattle within the wording of the *lex* were killed through indirect causation. The earliest documented evidence of how this need was met (though surely not the first case) is the following text, which can be traced back to Ofilius, a younger contemporary, and friend, of Caesar (D. 9. 2. 9. 3, Ulpian, 18 *ad edictum*):

Si servum meum equitantem concitato equo effeceris in flumen praecipitari atque ideo homo perierit, in factum esse dandam actionem Ofilius scribit; quemadmodum si servus meus ab alio in insidias deductus, ab alio esset occisus.

Here a slave was riding a horse; the culprit irritated the horse which then threw off the slave; the slave perished in a river into which he fell. Implicitly excluding the *actio directa legis Aquiliae*, Ofilius proposes an *actio in factum*. In brief, an action of that kind is one likely to have been framed on the pattern of the *actio legis Aquiliae* itself. In order to support this decision, Ofilius cites another case in which one person induces a slave into an ambush and another then kills him. Here the former is liable under the *actio in factum*, the latter to the *actio directa*. The decisive consideration seems to be evident in these cases: the person who irritated the horse or induced the slave into the ambush did not kill directly, with the consequence that the *actio directa* was therefore excluded.

Moving forward again some one and a half centuries we come to the third text. In this the distinguished jurist Celsus (*consul iterum*, AD 129) tries to formulate the principle which underlies the differentiation of the two types of action (D. 9. 2. 7. 6, Ulpian, 18 *ad edictum*):

Celsus autem multum interesse dicit, occiderit an mortis causam praestiterit, ut qui mortis causam praestitit, non Aquilia, sed in factum actione teneatur. Unde adfert eum qui venenum pro medicamento dedit et ait causam mortis praestitisse, quemadmodum eum qui furenti gladium porrexit: nam nec hunc lege Aquilia teneri, sed in factum.

The basis of the *actio directa* is thus *occidere*, while the basis of the *actio in factum* is *causam mortis praestare*, which obviously means 'indirect killing'. Celsus illustrates this by referring to two examples, one of which has the air of the schoolroom: the culprit hands over a poison to a slave pretending that it is medicine, the slave himself then takes it and dies; and in the other case, the culprit passes a sword to a slave who is in a bout of insanity—he is *furiosus*—and the slave then kills himself (or the slave of a third party?).

The concept of *mortis causam praestare* (*praebere*) is the focus of this paper. Before moving on to my texts, it may be useful to give some indication of Romanist reflections about this concept. So, for example, there are the different answers to the principal question, which is: why did interpretation of the word *occidere* limit its content to the case of direct killing, thus leaving a gap which could not be filled until—the date of this development is not easy for us to fix—the praetorian edict allowed the formulation of *actiones in factum*? Different kinds of answer can be found: in the original meaning of *occidere;* in the peculiarities of Roman legislative technique (and statutory interpretation); in the assertion that situations to which the *actio in factum* later applied were in their nature rare. Another line of explanation is not infrequently attempted: the Romans of the third century had no clear idea of indirect causality or no capacity to express that concept. If that were right we would have to conclude that the Romans, a warlike people, did not properly understand what they were doing when they killed enemies or criminals by starvation.

The focus of debate is sometimes the phrase *mortis causam praebere* itself. There are prominent scholars who, with irrefutable logic, demonstrate that a person who *occidit* does in every case also *mortis causam praebere*. The phrase is therefore said to be illogical, senseless, unworthy of the genius of the Roman jurists. However, the logic of this approach is defeated by its failure to appreciate that *mortis causam praebere* takes its meaning from the opposition between it and *occidere*. Furthermore, it is a logic which infringes the rules of ordinary linguistic usage, in which such phrases as 'cause death' are used instead of 'kill' precisely to stress indirect causality. Finally, however—and this is my provisional thesis—one can look for historical explanations of the phrase as well. The texts to which this paper now turns may serve to make this thesis plausible.

II

The first text comes from the ninth of Cicero's *Philippics*, in 43 BC. The background is the start of the civil wars after the death of Julius Caesar.

Servius Sulpicius Rufus, famous jurist, *vir consularis*, and at the same time an old and sick man, went, with L. Calpurnius Piso and L. Marcius Philippus, as *legatus* of the Senate to Marcus Antonius, who has laid siege to Mutina. The aim of the embassy was to deliver an ultimatum. Before arriving at Mutina Servius died.

The Senate debated the honours which should be conferred on the dead Servius. The *consularis* P. Servilius Isauricus pleaded for a public funeral (6. 14): ... *sepulcrum publicum decernendum Servio Sulpicio censuit*. On the other hand, he argued against the proposal to erect a statue of Servius. He based his case on a rule taken from the *mos maiorum* (1. 3): *hunc honorem statuae nemini tribuendum ... nisi ei qui ferro esset in legatione interfectus*. The honour of a statue should be conferred only on a person who was killed on an embassy *ferro*, 'by iron'. It was Cicero who, in the the ninth *Philippic*, pleaded for a statue, and succeeded.

Looking at Cicero's long argument, one point is of importance for us: his attempt to equate the non-violent death of Servius on the embassy with murder, that is, with a violent death. The *exempla maiorum*, and hence also the rule formulated by Isauricus, are apparently against his motion. To come to terms with that contrary authority, he therefore uses the well-known technique of looking for the *sententia* (the intention) which is behind the *verba* (the letter of the rule). He formulates the intention of the *maiores* as follows: ... *ut causam mortis censuerint, non genus quaerendum* (1. 3). Thus the decisive consideration should be the cause of death (embassy) rather than the manner of the death (*ferro*). And he maintains (3. 5) that Servius did not simply die by chance, *casu*, on the embassy but on the contrary that the embassy killed him: 'quis dubitat quin ei vitam abstulerit ipsa legatio?'

From a legal point of view this conclusion, that the embassy was responsible for the death of Servius, is not in itself of much interest. But, almost imperceptibly, Cicero shifts the argument from causation by the embassy to causation by Marcus Antonius. He replaces the verb *interficere*, and other less technical terms, by the more technical *occidere* (3. 7). Thus Antonius is made out to have killed (*occidit*) Servius just as murderers killed *legati* in the *exempla maiorum: ... Serv. Sulpicium occidit Antonius: is enim profecto mortem attulit, qui causa mortis fuit*.

Certainly, the equation of *occidere* and *causa mortis esse*, about one hundred and fifty years before Celsus, should set the student of the *lex Aquilia* thinking. He cannot evade the point by adverting to the different wording of the phrase: *causa mortis esse* with Cicero, *causam mortis praestare* (*praebere*) with the jurists. To be sure, one cannot entirely exclude the possibility that the different wordings indicate different origins. But leaving origins aside, in classical times the two versions mean the same. We have a proof in one of the *declamationes* (*controversiae*) under the name of Quintilian. These date, probably, from the second century AD but contain some ancient material. The *declamatio* 270 (R p. 101) starts, in the way that many of them do, with the following rule: *qui causa mortis fuerit, capite puniatur.* The point at issue is causality. In paraphrasing the rule, which uses the phrase *mortis causam esse*, the orator slips into the form familiar to the jurists: *causam (mortis) praestare* (p. 103, 14 ff.).

Still more important for us is another text, this time from the epoch of Augustus. It comes from the *Heroides* of Ovid, a work known for its rhetorical impact. In the seventh of the *Heroides*, Ovid feigns a letter from Dido. In this letter one central subject is the causation of suicide, a topic which was a favourite in rhetorical school exercises. Aeneas, who left (I do not know why) his sword with Dido when parting from her, would be the cause of Dido's suicide, as she now foretells. He would be her murderer. Dido then draws up an inscription for her tomb: 'Aeneas supplied the cause of death and the sword; with her own hand Dido cut herself down.' The poem ends with this inscription. The closing lines run thus (*Heroides*, 7. 181–96):

Si minus, est animus nobis effundere vitam;
  in me crudelis non potes esse diu.
adspicias utinam, quae sit scribentis imago!
  scribimus, et gremio Troicus ensis adest,
perque genas lacrimae strictum labuntur in ensem,
  qui iam pro lacrimis sanguine tinctus erit.
quam bene conveniunt fato tua munera nostro!
  instruis inpensa nostra sepulcra brevi.
Nec mea nunc primum feriuntur pectora telo;
  ille locus saevi vulnus amoris habet.
Anna soror, soror Anna, meae male conscia culpae,
  iam dabis in cineres ultima dona meos.
nec consumpta rogis inscribar Elissa Sychaei;
  hoc tantum in tumuli marmore carmen erit:
PRAEBUIT AENEAS ET CAUSAM MORTIS ET ENSEM;
  IPSA SUA DIDO CONCIDIT USA MANU.

It would be proper to celebrate this text. It is the first one which contains the phrase *causam mortis praebere*. The version which uses *praestare* (*causam mortis praestare*) seems to have been brought into use in the second century AD. The jurists use the two variants interchangeably. Furthermore, Ovid—in the final *sententia* of the letter, which clearly shows rhetorical skill—exploits both the abstract and the concrete meanings of *praebere* (*causam et ensem*). That indicates, I believe, that the phrase *causam mortis praebere* was already well established.

Wherever the concept came from, it was flourishing long before Celsus wrote his famous sentence, already cited above. Even if we assume that he introduced the concept into the field of the *lex Aquilia*, we have to ask what gave him the idea and what prompted him to use it. And as often with Celsus we could, perhaps, go back to his rhetorical education. So far as the chronology is concerned Quintilian could have been his teacher. However, for the moment the *lex Aquilia* and Celsus must be left aside, in order to carry the investigation more generally into the question of the origin of the expression *mortis causam praebere*.

III

In order to understand Ovid's use of the phrase we have had to allude to rhetorical technique. It is therefore not inconsistent to begin the search for the original context of the concept in the field of Roman rhetoric.

We have already quoted the rule which was the basis of some rhetorical *controversiae: qui causa mortis fuerit, capite puniatur*. In these *controversiae* the crucial point is causality. Some of the arguments in these speeches appear a little childish, at least to us. In his discussion of the topos of *definitio*, Quintilian makes use of the speech of Cicero which has already been quoted. He recommends the method adopted by Cicero: one should never begin the argument with the *definitio*; rather, the presentation should, as in the case of Cicero's equation of *interficere* and *mortis causam praestare*, lead into the *definitio* as the striking conclusion of the argument (*inst. or.* 7. 3. 17 f.). A little further on (7. 3. 31 f.) he describes a *controversia* on *mortis causa*. In our sources, this is the most ancient *controversia* of this type, though the origin of such *controversiae* on this theme must be earlier. We may use this one as an example.

The case is simple and artificial. Some young people have a banquet by the sea. By way of a joke they heap up a grave for an absent friend, with an inscription showing his name. They leave the place and the feigned grave. The father of that young man comes back from a journey, sees the grave, and kills himself. The young people are then prosecuted under the law: *qui causa mortis fuerit, capite puniatur*.

A preliminary observation is necessary: there is no controversy that 'indirect killing' is covered by the law. The point at issue is only the *definitio* of *causa mortis*. For us the issue would turn on fault or imputability; causality would at most play a secondary part. However, in the rhetorical discourse causality is essential. The prosecutor states the following definition of *causa mortis esse: per quem factum est ut quis periret*. That is, the person is the cause of death 'through whom it happens that somebody perishes'. The defendants oppose another definition: *qui fecit quid sciens per quod perire homini necesse esset*. That is, the person is the cause of death who knowingly did something whose necessary consequence was that a man would die. The prosecutor applies the theory of the *condicio sine qua non*. The defendants stress a distinction which in ordinary language we can call the difference between causes and conditions. To this end they use the argument of *reductio ad absurdum*: if one accepts the *definitio* of the prosecutor one must count as *causae mortis* prosecutors, judges, witnesses, friends who advised some act, and so on.

The basis of the rhetorical argument is the philosophical (especially Stoic) discussion of causality. It may be enough, by way of demonstrating this, to quote a short text from Cicero's *de fato* (16. 36):

Interesse autem aiunt, utrum eiusmodi quid sit, sine quo effici aliquid non possit, an eiusmodi, cum quo effici aliquid necesse (!) sit.

Here Cicero refers to the philosophical distinction between events of the kind without which some other event could not have happened, and events of the kind which necessitate the happening of the other event. An example of the first: Hecuba gave birth to Alexander (Paris), but she was not the *causa* of the ruin of the Trojans. An example of the second case: wounding causes death (*de fato* 15. 34).

It is not necessary to go into the details of the other *controversiae* on *mortis causa esse*. They are mostly fanciful variations on the same theme. For example: a father causes the death of his daughter's violator by abuse of the criminal process (*decl.* 270). Or again, there are suicide cases: for example, a father falls in incestuous love with his daughter and gives the girl to a friend under the condition that he shall never return her to him; then later he claims her back, and the friend refuses, whereupon the father kills himself (*decl.* 289). Ovid's letter in which Dido tells of her suicide could be cited as another example of this type.

Let us interrupt the story of the concept of *mortis causa* for a moment, in order to make some provisional remarks about the relation between the philosophico-rhetorical version and the juridical version of the idea. Both in the rhetorical and in the legal context *causa* is used as a term of indirect causation. At least one case used by the jurist Celsus could, as we have seen, easily have been the theme of a rhetorical *controversia:* the example in which the culprit gives a sword to an insane slave with the result that he kills himself (D. 9. 2. 7. 6). However, there is a difference in the application of the concept by orators and by lawyers. This difference lies in the degree of abstraction.

Simple as the orator's discussion of *causa* may appear, it is, in the last analysis, the philosophical concept of *causa* which they apply. The consequence is not only that the *declamationes* are susceptible of analysis in terms of such concepts as *causae proximae* and *remotae*, and of *causae principales* and *antecedentes*, but also that the artificial character of their themes may be partly explicable by the abstract nature of the concept of causation to be applied in the argument. As for the jurists, on the other hand, the cases which they produce are certainly not simply those of everyday life, but normally they are reasonably credible. The tendency of the juridical concept of *causa mortis* to become abstract is counterbalanced by the clear opposition between it and *occidere*. Hence *causae remotissimae* are excluded from serious discussion. Even if the jurists received the concept from rhetoric they adapted it to their use by cutting away its outgrowths.

IV

Resuming the inquiry into the origin of the concept, we may begin with a partial and provisional summary of what has been said so far: the concept of *mortis causa* is widespread in the rhetoric of the first century AD. Its use by Ovid, and by Cicero too, indicates a more remote origin. When we attempt to fix that origin more precisely the answer seems to be evident. Thus, in order to explain the rhetorical use, it was necessary to cite a philosophical text on causality; and, without doubt, Latin rhetoric and Latin rhetorical exercises do have their roots in the Greek school of rhetoric. Hence, a hypothesis of Greek influence on the concept of *mortis causa* seems obvious. However, the question of origin is, I believe, too complex to be resolved by this simple hypothesis.

It is necessary at the outset to distinguish as clearly as possible between two questions. The first has to do with the argument about indirect causality itself, treated with sophistication but often in an artificial and pedantic manner in philosophy and rhetoric. From the standpoint of *Geistesgeschichte* this could well be the more interesting of the two questions. On the other hand there is the wording of the rule actually formulated for the rhetorical exercises: *qui causa mortis fuerit, capite puniatur*. Inquiring into the origin of this form of words we come into contact with problems in the sphere of legislative technique.

As to the first of these questions, the argument about indirect causality itself, the answer is unequivocal: the discussion started at the latest in fifth-century Athens. Plutarch, in the *Life of Pericles* (36), tells of critical voices raised in Athens against Pericles' engagement in ridiculous debates, for example: if a man was killed in javelin-throwing, who was guilty, the javelin, the person who threw the javelin, the umpire? Again, in Antiphon's (or Pseudo-Antiphon's) orations it is especially notable that problems of indirect causality are widely discussed. To give some examples: the second tetralogy deals with Pericles' problem just mentioned and concludes with the statement that the careless victim of the javelin had killed himself. In the sixth oration the defendant is a *choregos*, a citizen charged with the training of the choir for a tragedy; he was accused of having killed a boy to whom somebody—not the defendant himself—had given a beverage for the purpose of improving the boy's voice.

The next stop should certainly be an analysis in detail of how the argument about indirect causality was formulated in these and other texts. However, in this paper it is only possible to do this in outline, so as to give a general impression. There was in principle no doubt that direct and indirect causality should be equated. This was a consequence of the Athenian law on homicide, which treated a person who intended the death of another (planning or preparing that death) in exactly the same way as the person who did the killing with his own hand. See, for example, Andocides, *de mysteriis*, 94: *τὸν βουλεύσαντα ἐν τῷ αὐτῷ ἐνέχεσθαι καὶ τὸν τῇ χειρι ἐργασάμενον*. It is obvious that when the law is formulated in this way the emphasis falls on intention (*bouleusis*), not on causation. This in turn has the consequence that the arguments of the Athenian orations normally differ from the arguments in the Latin *controversiae*. I know of only one exception, the speech of Demosthenes against Aristokrates (*or*. 23), which is unique in more than one respect.

Having made this somewhat free reference to the Athenian law on homicide we can turn to the second question: where should we look for the origin of the form of words: *mortis causa esse*? At this point it is possible to give only some suggestions which might provide an answer.

If we translate the rule *qui causa mortis fuerit* back into Greek, the form of words which we then have to look for is *aitios phonou einai* or *aitia thanatou einai*. I know of only one rule of Greek law, a very special and moreover very ancient rule, which uses the first variant in the sense of *mortis causa esse*. It is part of the famous law of Draco on homicide. Subject to some simplification, the context is as follows. The law lays down that one who kills (*ktenei*) a person unintentionally (*me ek pronoias*) should go into exile. It could become necessary to determine on a special procedure whether this killing was intentional or not. In order to draft this provision the law puts side by side both acting with one's own hand (*κτείνῃ*) and acting indirectly. The indirect case is rendered by the term already mentioned above, namely *bouleuein* (planning *vel sim.*). The person who killed, whether directly or indirectly, is *aitios phonou* answerable for homicide. I must stress the point at once that the meaning of this phrase here is not the same as that of *mortis causa* in the rhetorical *controversiae*; it includes cases of direct causation as well, indeed as the regular case. The terminology used in this part of the law dominates discussion of homicide in classical Athens.

It is different on the second occasion that Draco uses the form of words *aitios phonou*. The homicide law states that if the exiled killer is in his turn killed by anybody at his place of exile, the second killer is to be treated as though he had killed an Athenian citizen. In order to describe this second homicide, the draftsman uses the words *ktenei e aitios ei phonou* (kills or causes death). Through the opposition between *kteinein* and *aitios phonou einai* the law makes clear that the latter expression now indicates the case of bringing about the death by indirect causation.

Apart from the speech of Demosthenes which has already been mentioned, this usage of *aitios phonou* had no successors, for everywhere else the notion of indirect causality is expressed through words which take a subjective viewpoint, as *bouleusis, epibouleusis*, etc. The phrase *aitios phonou* by contrast is used of the person who is responsible for the death, no matter whether that death was caused directly or indirectly.

If one considers the gap in time between the use of *aitios phonou* in the sense of indirect causation in Draco (and Demosthenes) and the recurrence of *causa mortis* in Cicero and Quintilian, there is no evident continuity. On the other hand, our knowledge of the Greek law of homicide and of Greek rhetorical exercises on this topic is minimal, especially for the last three centuries BC. Therefore, we cannot exclude the possibility that there existed both rules on homicide and rhetorical exercises which employed the Draconic terms.

There is also another point. Up to this stage we have only considered the form *aitios phonou einai*. However, from Hermogenes of Tarsus (*c*. AD 160–225, e.g. *Peri heur*. 3. 10, pp. 154.9–158.18 Rabe), we find in the rhetorical exercises of the last centuries of Antiquity the *aitia thanatou einai* rule, which corresponds even more closely to the *causa mortis esse* rule of the Latin declamations. And a little earlier there appears the expression *aitian thanatou parechein*, which parallels the Latin *mortis causam praestare* (see esp. Luc. *Tyrannic*. 11). It is not impossible that an old Hellenistic tradition reappeared in the sources of the second century AD. On the other hand, there is some evidence that these sources point to a reception of the *aitia thanatou* clause from Roman rhetoric and Roman law; that is, that the borrowing may have been from Roman to Greek sources and not vice versa.

The conclusion is that we can neither affirm nor exclude the possibility that the *causa mortis* rule of the Latin *controversiae* had predecessors in Greek law and rhetoric. Precisely because we cannot affirm that there was a Greek root, we must allow ourselves to look for a specifically Roman stimulus for the appearance of that phrase. The obvious place to look first is the Roman law of homicide, more precisely the *lex Cornelia de sicariis et veneficis*. With that inquiry this paper will close, though once again a warning has to be given that at this stage only an outline of a provisional conclusion can be attempted.

V

The *lex Cornelia de sicariis et veneficis* is part of the extensive legislative work of L. Cornelius Sulla. The law is not, or at least not entirely, an original product of the eighties BC. We can trace some provisions directly back to earlier legislation, especially of C. Sempronius Gracchus. For other provisions we also have to assume predecessors in the second century BC. Marcianus, the classical jurist of the first half of the third century AD, gives a list, albeit not an exhaustive one, of the crimes which fell under the statute, e.g. murder, arson, dangerous preparatory acts (*cum telo ambulare occidendi furtive faciendi causa*), poisoning, and a series of crimes connected with criminal proceedings (false witness, bribery of a *iudex quaestionis*, etc.). This is in D. 48. 8. 1 pr.-1 (Marcianus, 14 *institutionum*):

Lege Cornelia de sicariis et veneficis tenetur, qui hominem occiderit: cuiusve dolo malo incendium factum erit: quive hominis occidendi furtive faciendi causa cum telo ambulaverit: quive cum magistratus esset publicove iudicio praeesset operam dedisset, quo quis falsum indicium profiteretur, ut quis innocens conveniretur condemnaretur. Praeterea tenetur, qui hominis necandi causa venenum confecerit dederit: quive falsum testimonium dolo malo dixerit, quo quis publico iudicio rei capitalis damnaretur: quive magistratus iudexve quaestionis ob capitalem causam pecuniam acceperit ut publica lege reus fieret.

The common basis of the crimes is a wilful act calculated to endanger the life of the victim. The crimes are capital crimes. Furthermore, the primary aim of the law, or more precisely of its predecessors, was probably not the protection of the individual but of the social order in general. We may safely start from the well-known thesis of Wolfgang Kunkel and John Cloud on the first chapter of the *lex*: that the first predecessor of the rule on *occidere* was not a general law on homicide but a law against gangs which haunted the city of Rome. To be sure, the *lex Cornelia* itself was a general law on homicide, but the special derivation left traces in its wording.

It seems that the best, albeit still by no means perfect, citation of the text of part of the first chapter of the *lex Cornelia* is a passage of Ulpian in the *Collatio* (1. 3. 1):

Capite primo legis Corneliae de sicariis cavetur, ut is praetor iudexve quaestionis, cui sorte obvenerit quaestio de sicariis quod in urbe Roma propiusve mille passus factum sit, uti quaerat cum iudicibus, qui ei ex lege sorte obvenerint de capite eius, qui cum telo ambulaverit hominis necandi furtive faciendi causa, hominemve occiderit, cuiusve id dolo malo factum erit. Et reliqua.

A free paraphrase of this serves to demonstrate that the law is drafted so as to bear primarily on the procedure: 'The first chapter of the *lex Cornelia* provides that the praetor etc. should together with judges etc. inquire *de capite* (concerning the life) of such persons as walked with a weapon with the aim of killing or stealing, or killed, or by evil intent brought it about that these things happened ...'. Other sources indicate that for *cum telo ambulare* there was *cum telo esse*, and for *necandi causa* there was *occidendi causa*. For the present theme it is important that the first chapter begins with the 'preparatory and endangering' crime (*cum telo esse occidendi ... causa*) and that only in the second place comes the actual crime which consists in the result of the preparation and which realizes the danger: *occidere*. The fact that the preparatory act is dealt with first may be explained by the original aim of the provision, as an instrument to deter the gangs which disturbed law and order. Then, the fact that the result, the *occidere*, is explicitly named in the law is attributable to the pedantic legislative technique of the epoch. Had this been omitted a gangster who killed could advance the technical argument that he was not going around *occidendi causa* but had simply killed. Considering some of the arguments used in Cicero's speeches (e.g. *pro Milone*) this suggestion is not too perverse. The later interpretation of the *lex* moved the *occidere*—that is, the completed as opposed to the preliminary crime—into the foreground. This is demonstrated in the text of Marcianus which has just been paraphrased.

If one looks into the other crimes contemplated by the *lex Cornelia* one gets the clear impression that all or most of them focus on the preparatory aspect of the offence, in the sense explained above in relation to *occidere*. Let us take the example of poisoning. Livy shows that in the second century BC there had been waves of poisoning and of fears of poisoning. This makes it plausible to venture the hypothesis that the crime of poisoning was in the beginning prosecuted, like the crime of homicide, because of the danger to society as a whole. And this may be true for the other crimes of the *lex Cornelia* as well. With regard to poisoning we can again start with Marcianus. This is D. 48. 8. 3 pr (Marcianus, 14 *institutionum*):

Eiusdem legis Corneliae de sicariis et veneficis capite quinto, qui venenum necandi hominis causa fecerit vel vendiderit vel habuerit, plectitur.

(By the fifth chapter of the same *lex Cornelia* a person is punished who, with the aim of killing, makes, sells, or keeps poison.)

From Cicero's *pro Cluentio* 148 we know that the words *emere* and *dare* also appeared. Apart from these words, what is notably missing in Marcianus' account is an expression covering the result of preparatory acts, *emere*, *facere*, and so on. In the time of Marcianus it had long ceased to be necessary to spell out separately the crime of achieving the consequence of the preliminary acts. However, from a comparison with the first chapter which distinguishes fastidiously between *cum telo esse occidendi causa* and *occidere*, we have to assume that the fifth chapter did also contain a similar complement to the words describing the preliminary crime. Thus, beside *facere*, *vendere*, etc., *venenum malum necandi causa* we should expect words expressing the result, the death of the victim. For this purpose the word *necare*, already present in *necandi causa*, suggests itself. Yet though *necare* was indeed from the outset much broader than *occidere*, it seems to be less than obvious that the lawgiver would find this an appropriate word to cover, for example, someone who sold poison to the actual killer. I believe that the phrase *mortis causam praebere* is much better fitted to this task. Therefore my proposal for the reconstruction of chapter five would be:

quicumque venenum malum hominis necandi causa fecit fecerit, vendidit vendiderit, emit emerit, habuit habuerit, dedit dederit, causamve mortis praebuit praebuerit...

This argument could be repeated for other crimes sanctioned by the *lex Cornelia*, for example false witness. The conclusion would be the same, namely, that we should expect some expression covering the completion of fatal purpose intended by the defendant; and everywhere the phrase *mortis causam praebere* suggests itself.

From a logical point of view, I believe, this hypothesis is plausible. In fact the reasoning has been based on a simple process of analogy. In the case of killing we have a first clause in the law which deals with the preliminary or preparatory stage and then a second clause which deals with the fatal result. In the case of poisoning (and in other cases) the sources as they come down to us give only the provision dealing with the first stage, the preparatory crime. Here too we have to expect some reference to the completed purpose. The textual gap is closed with *mortis causam praebere*.

Good logical arguments are, however, often not good historical arguments. It is therefore helpful to have at least one textual support for our hypothesis. In *Pauli Sententiae* 5. 23. 1–2 we find a modernized extract from the *lex Cornelia:*

Lex Cornelia poenam deportationis infligit ei qui hominem occiderit eiusve rei causa furtive faciendi cum telo fuerit, et qui venenum hominis necandi causa habuerit vendiderit, falsum testimonium dixerit, quo quis periret, mortisve causam praestiterit. Quae omnia facinora in honestiores poena capitis vindicare placuit, humiliores vero in crucem tolluntur aut bestiis obiciuntur. Homicida est qui aliquo genere teli hominem occidit mortisve causam praestitit.

This text speaks of killing (including the preliminary acts), poisoning, false witness. The penalties as described have been adjusted to the system of late law. At the end we find the by this time self-evident equation of *occidere* with *mortis causam praestare*. On the other hand, the text still preserves the differentiation between *occidere* and *occidendi causa furtive faciendi causa cum telo esso*, the plurality of terms describing the preliminaries to poisoning (*habuerit*, *vendiderit*, *paraverit*), and, above all, the original wording *cum telo esse* instead of the more vulgar *cum telo ambulare* of Ulpian and Marcianus. Of course, the *Pauli Sententiae* are a problematic source for classical law, but, especially in the field of penal law, the text includes genuine ancient material. This is, I believe, true of our fragment too.

In the middle of this text there is the clause *mortisve causam praestiterit* (instead of a probably original *praebuerit*). In the present context the meaning of this is obscure. It can be related to the crime of false witness on its own or to both poisoning and false witness. Futhermore, it can be understood as indicating an independent crime of killing by indirect means, and it is this sense that would probably have occurred to the fourth-century reader. But if we combine this clause with the second section of the fragment, containing the equation of *occidere* with *causam mortis praestare*, it is plausible that the corresponding clause in the first section originally had its own proper reference. If our earlier 'logical' argument was correct, the original meaning of the clause in PS 5. 23. 1 becomes evident: the *causam mortis praestare* complemented the crimes of preparing or planning death by production or procurement of poison, or by false witness in a capital trial, in exactly the same way as the *occidere* of the first chapter complemented the preliminary crime *cum telo esse occidendi causa*.

Before leaving the *lex Cornelia* I want to stress a point which is important for the understanding of *causam mortis praebere* in this context. The way in which it is used in the *lex Cornelia* has virtually nothing to do with an abstract concept of causality. Rather, it denotes the concrete result of specific conduct on the part of the defendant. This can be explained by contrasting two different questions. Thus, under this statute, the general question simply does not arise, namely: how ought one to explain the connection between the conduct of the defendant and the consequence of that conduct? Rather, the question which arises should be formulated as follows: did the defendant buy poison with the intention of killing the victim, and did he succeed? In order to develop the clause into an abstract concept of causation, another impulse was necessary; and that came probably from Greek philosophy and Latin rhetoric.

VI

To sum up: it is short-sighted to begin the history of *causam mortis praebere* with the famous words of Celsus. The concept goes far back in the past of Roman law and Roman civilization. A double approach—from rhetoric and from law—is necessary. As to rhetoric the clause emerges at the latest in the time of Cicero and Ovid. It flourishes in the school of rhetoric and there absorbs some fragments of philosophical discussion on causality; it is characterized by a tendency to abstraction and to scholastic abuse. There is uncertainty about Greek precedents. Except for Draco's law on homicide and the speech of Demosthenes which we mentioned, we find the Greek equivalent only in texts from the second century AD onwards. As a provisional hypothesis we might affirm that the rule of *causa mortis* has a Roman background, while many of the arguments used in discussion can be traced to a Greek origin. The second line of approach starts from the *lex Cornelia* (or its predecessors). Here the discussion is about the legislative technique and practice of Roman draftsmen, not about an abstract concept of causality.

If one proposes two approaches to one concept, one is obliged to reflect on connections between the two. This issue depends, obviously, on the unsolved problem of Greek predecessors. I might just mention one sequence of development. Perhaps the notion of *causa mortis* grew up from Roman legislation, was then adopted by rhetoric and influenced by philosophy; then, having developed from both of these some theoretical abstraction, it was given back to the law, in a condition a good deal changed from the original.

This paper began with the *lex Aquilia*, and should end with it. In keeping with the experimental nature of the study, I should like to end with some questions. First, is it reasonably credible that the concept of *causa mortis* was introduced into the Aquilian field by Celsus? These considerations justify us in wondering whether it may not actually go back much further. The concept itself, as we have seen, is much older than Celsus. Next, Labeo, whose special interest in problems of causality is well known, uses the phrase *causam praebere* (not *mortis causam praebere*) in the context of *locatio conductio* (D. 19. 2. 11. 4, Ulpian 32 *ad edictum*). Finally, the developing *actio in factum* supposes a pleading which must have been based on some such concept.

The second question, which owes something to suggestions made by Professor Selb, is closely connected with the first. If we try to reconstruct the formula of the *actio in factum ad exemplum legis Aquiliae*, so far as it was concerned with the problem of indirect causation, what precise words ought we to employ? I think the expression *mortis causam praestare* would fit very well. However, we cannot be certain whether it was indeed used for this purpose too.

The third question comes back again to the meaning of the expression. If we contrast its sense in the *lex Cornelia* with its use in the Aquilian field, we notice that it became more abstract. Having deprived Celsus of most of his claim to originality perhaps we should concede to him the doubtful honour of having introduced the more abstract sense of the expression into the discussion of causality under the *lex Aquilia*.

And the last question: the history of the clause is, doubtless, a clear example of the—active and passive—contacts of Roman law with ancient culture in general; but was its reception into the argumentation on the *lex Aquilia* really such an important step in legal thinking as modern discussion sometimes suggests?

13

Obligations, Sanctions, and Obedience*

NICOLA LACEY

TONY HONORÉ's contributions to the literature of legal theory have been a source of illumination and inspiration to many scholars, so often identifying and tackling, as they do, problems apparently ignored by more conventional positivist or natural law theorists. Of no article is this more true than of his 'Groups, Laws, and Obedience',[1] an essay which touches upon such wide-ranging issues as the nature of legal theory, the analysis and place of rules and sanctions within such a theory, and the primacy to a proper understanding of the nature of law of the emergence of shared group commitments, followed by that of an intricate system of interlocking norms and, later, rules.

In this essay I shall attempt to follow the direction of Tony Honoré's thoughts in 'Groups, Laws, and Obedience' in examining the question of the nature of legal obligation. It seems to me that a particular view of the nature of legal obligation is implicit in Honoré's article; but my main focus will be on the light thrown by his comments on the place of sanctions in motivating obedience, and their analytic or contingent connection with the existence of legal obligation. My ultimate aim is to draw some conclusions from these observations as to their implications for the justification of the imposition of punishment by legal authorities. This seems to be a particularly apt subject to consider in view of the comments made at the start of 'Groups, Laws and Obedience' about the inevitability of the legal theorist being committed, legal theory being a form of practical reason. The article then goes on to deal with what is said to be essentially a question of *descriptive* legal theory, and the reader is allowed to speculate about the particular commitments of the writer and their bearing on the subject-matter of the article. The difficulty of preserving a clear distinction between descriptive and normative theory—indeed the very question of whether a purely descriptive account is possible—has dogged studies of the issue of legal obligation perhaps above any other. How can there be a wholly descriptive account of the normativity of law? Do all such accounts merely represent crude sanction or probabilistic theories? In this essay I shall try

* I should like to thank Joseph Raz for his helpful comments on an earlier draft of this article.

[1] *Oxford Essays in Jurisprudence*, 2nd ser., ed. A. W. B. Simpson (Oxford, 1973), p. 1.

to keep this fundamental issue in the forefront of my discussion of the place of sanctions in the legal system.

LEGAL OBLIGATION AND THE NORMATIVITY OF LAW

At first sight, the expression 'legal obligation' is highly ambiguous, and the strategy of most theorists, in an effort to keep separate descriptive and prescriptive questions, has, naturally enough, been one of dividing in the hope of conquering. The clearest division which has been made is that between the legal obligation having to do with our duty to obey the law, which I shall refer to as political obligation, and legal obligation in the sense of what is meant by a law's being *binding*, which I shall refer to as the question of legal obligation. The former is generally treated as a question of moral or political philosophy, thus being 'banished to another discipline' at least by extreme positivist writers. The latter, on the other hand, can be taken as a question of analytical jurisprudence; in describing the content of a legal system, we use the language of duties and obligations rather freely, but apparently without meaning to make any final moral judgment about whether the laws we speak of as generating obligations ought to be obeyed. This second question is thus closely linked to that of legal validity; but not all valid laws directly generate obligations, at least for the private citizen. Some, for example, confer powers—probably a less problematic concept for analysis in purely social fact terms. But even power-conferring laws are ultimately supported in the structure of legal norms by rules which impose obligations on legal officials to recognize and enforce the powers. Thus, in the end, the question of the nature of legal obligation must bear a central place in any legal theory, and we return to the puzzle of how it is that we can talk in these frankly normative terms without taking a particular, committed position on the wider question of political obligation. Nor is this a difficulty peculiar to positivist theory: perhaps the most sophisticated exponent of the 'divide and conquer' strategy is in fact the natural lawyer, John Finnis,[2] who has distinguished four types of obligation relevant to legal theory: empirical liability to be subjected to a sanction in the event of non-compliance; legal obligation in the intra-systematic sense (or, in our terms, validity), where the premiss that conformity to law is socially necessary operates as a framework principle insulated from the rest of practical reasoning; legal obligation in the moral sense, or the moral obligation which some writers argue to be presumptively entailed by a valid duty-imposing rule; and fully fledged, independent moral obligation. We shall bear in mind this useful framework in considering the apparent contradiction with which we are confronted.

[2] *Natural Law and Natural Rights* (Oxford, 1980), pp. 354 ff.

OF WHAT RELEVANCE IS THE THREAT OR IMPOSITION OF SANCTIONS BY A LEGALLY CONSTITUTED AUTHORITY TO THE QUESTION OF LEGAL OBLIGATION?

One traditional but now discredited set of answers to the puzzle of legal obligation was that the meaning of the claim that a particular legal rule generated an obligation was either that a sanction was likely or certain to follow on from its breach (the predictive account) or that another legal rule should have prescribed that a sanction be imposed on breach (the sanction-rule account). The development of these views has been traced by Peter Hacker, in his article 'Sanction Theories of Duty',[3] through the works of Bentham and Mill and even into the 'normative' account given by H. L. A. Hart in *The Concept of Law*.[4] Hart, of course, expressly dissociates himself from the sanction theories, emphasizing the intelligibility and conceptual possibility of legal rules *not* backed up by sanctions, and distinguishing between the ideas of being *obliged* and being *obligated* by means of his famous analysis of the internal aspect of rules. Nevertheless, when he addresses the issue of identifying which laws do actually generate obligations, Hart (who discusses the question only relatively briefly) appears to say that legally *obligatory* laws are those which are backed up by serious pressure and which are most crucial to the maintenance of social life, sometimes even demanding behaviour running against strong natural inclinations[5]—which appears in itself to be a modified form of sanction theory. It is certainly true, as Hacker argues, that there is another strand in Hart's account, and that it is one inimical to the sharp description/prescription divide. I shall, however, temporarily set this matter aside in order to concentrate specifically on the relevance of sanctions.

Another writer who has recently given some consideration to the place of sanctions in the analysis of legal obligation is Tom Campbell, who approaches the question as part of a rather different enterprise. In his book, *The Left and Rights*,[6] Campbell seeks to establish that there would be a place for legal rights even in a Utopian Socialist society. In order to do this, he sets himself the task of answering the Marxist objection that all laws are inherently coercive. He therefore has to produce an analysis of legal obligation (correlative to his interest-protecting conception of legal rights) which is not sanction-based. Campbell does very persuasively despatch some of the most famous sanction theories, essentially relying on the Hartian argument that the content of any particular legal rule is quite intelligible without any references to a reinforcing sanction. For example, it seems perfectly sensible to say that the legislation making the wearing of

[3] *Oxford Essays*, p. 131.
[4] Oxford, 1961, pp. 79–88.
[5] *The Concept of Law*, pp. 84–5.
[6] London, 1983, ch. 4.

seatbelts compulsory which was passed in New Zealand some years ago generated a legal obligation even before the deferred sanction provisions came into effect. Nor does it seem to be the case that our recognition of the legal obligation of the judge to apply and enforce both duty-imposing and power-conferring legal rules depends in the slightest degree upon the existence of sanctions threatened or applied on failure to do so. What we seem to be left with once we have dismissed sanctions as the explanation of the apparent propriety of the use of the concept of obligation in legal discourse is the idea that the law *itself* claims obedience, *claims* to create an obligation to obey, independently *both* of any threat of sanction *and* of any separate or parallel moral argument.[7]

Tony Honoré's views, as expressed in 'Groups, Laws, and Obedience', would certainly endorse the idea that sanctions are *not* conceptually integral to laws: indeed he emphasizes that in some societies none of his 'remedial' norms would have to be punitive. Instead (or, of course, additionally) they could simply supplement the already existing rationality-, morality-, or tradition-based reasons for obedience by offering rewards, attempting to induce conciliation, and so on.[8] But he certainly oversteps the *traditional* positivist view in his early comment that it is fundamental to the idea of law that it is concerned with *obedience* in the sense that the very (apparently descriptive) statement 'X is a law' betrays a special posture with respect to whether or not it should be obeyed and how disobedience is to be justified. Thus for Honoré, as for Hart and Campbell, the place of sanctions in reinforcing legal rules is a factual question, contingent upon the nature of the group subject to the laws, the content of the laws, and so on. But Honoré's claims about the need for law to motivate obedience seem to be analytic claims relating to the function of law as a form of social regulation. Again, this is an issue to which we shall return after considering some further possible solutions to the puzzle of the nature of legal obligation.

NORMATIVE LANGUAGE AND THE ADOPTION OF POINTS OF VIEW

Two more sophisticated attempts to explicate the concept of legal obligation may now be considered: each purports to stand firmly on the positivist side of the alleged line, and each satisfies more nearly than the others we have already considered Hacker's injunction that any such explanation should focus on the nature of legal rules themselves as guiding standards of conduct and the reasons or motivations which they (analytically or typically) generate.

[7] Cf. Hart's view expressed in *Essays on Bentham* (Oxford, 1982), p. 160.

[8] 'Groups, Laws and Obedience', p. 10.

First of all, let us consider Hart's account of the internal aspect of rules, which purports to explain the difference between merely being obliged (as one would be by the gunman's threat) and having an obligation under a rule. The internal attitude which some citizens and all officials adopt towards the rules means that they treat them as a guide to or reason for their own behaviour and as a justification for the critical reactions they express when others breach the rules. This agent-centred analysis, based on a particular kind of acceptance or adoption of rules by those subject to the legal system of which those rules form a part and where at least the officials of the system share this internal attitude, shows, at least from the agent's point of view, why laws generate obligations. On the other hand, the account does *not* purport to tell us when or why the legal obligations ought, in the full-blooded moral sense, to be met.

Closely linked to this analysis is that offered by Joseph Raz, which relies on the viewpoints from which normative statements about what should be done according to the law are made[9] and which has been acknowledged by Hart as a 'valuable supplementation' of his own account.[10] In addition to Hart's fully external and internal viewpoints, Raz adds a third: a detached viewpoint (said to be implicit in the work of Kelsen, who, indeed caused the whole idea of the special, restricted, legal sense of 'ought' to become a familiar idea in jurisprudence) which nevertheless generates normative statements, albeit not ones adopted by the speaker herself. For example, the carnivore who advises her (morally) vegetarian friend that she ought not to eat a particular dish because it contains meat acknowledges in her statement her friend's committed, internal viewpoint with respect to vegetarian norms, but the speaker does not adopt that viewpoint herself, nor does she in any way endorse the standard she tells her friend she ought to maintain. In this case, again, what is being offered is an account of legal obligation from a particular point of view: from this stance a legal order can be understood as generating obligations independently of the question of the moral worth of the rules in question. In contrast to Hart's view, however, the explanation of the use of normative language depends solely on reference to an individual commitment, and not also on a background of other committed attitudes within a society. It can thus be applied to a wider set of situations than can Hart's social-rule analysis, so avoiding some of the criticisms put forward by Dworkin in his article 'The Model of Rules 2'.[11]

In the legal context, for Raz, it is the fact of the courts' adopting the belief, sincerely or as a pretence, that laws are valid reasons for action which is necessary to the existence of a legal system and thus to that of

9 *Practical Reason and Norms* (London, 1975), pp. 170–7.

10 *Essays*, pp. 154–5.

11 *Taking Rights Seriously* (London, 1977), ch. 3.

legal obligations.[12] On this view, statements of legal obligation or what ought to be done according to law state what one has reason to do *from the legal point of view:* they tell us what we should do *if* legal norms are valid norms, but assume rather than state the conditional. This concept of normative legal discourse as based on the assumption of the law's providing reasons for action is a clear departure from the perhaps more straightforward Hartian theory and has in fact drawn some criticism from Hart himself.[13]

One set of criticisms of these types of account suggests that they do not place themselves as firmly in the positivist camp as (most of) their proponents claim. Both MacCormick[14] and Finnis,[15] commenting on Hart's account of the internal aspect of rules, have argued that ultimately the legal theorist must examine the *reasons* for the agent's adoption of that attitude. As such, they draw the boundaries of descriptive jurisprudence more widely than does Hart. Is this, then, ultimately an argument about the proper scope of jurisprudence (or, perhaps, about the limits of competence of writers on the subject)? It certainly does raise the question of the basis on which we should choose to draw those boundaries. Several reasons for drawing the lines in the wider way advocated by MacCormick and Finnis can be suggested, although in my own view none of them ultimately destroys the fundamental arguments of Hart or Raz. Let us examine the reasons suggested. First of all, it is argued that a legal order will only be stable if a hard core of the population (and especially the officials) do in fact adopt the internal attitude for *moral* reasons. In times of crisis (such as revolutionary situations, or the emergence of a system from a pre-legal state), systems unsupported by such a core of moral approval and endorsement will quite simply fail to survive or emerge. Now this may very well be true as a factual generalization (although perhaps examples such as South Africa tend to put this in doubt) but it does not affect Hart's essentially conceptual argument; nor does it establish a conceptual link between law and morality, at least in any objective sense. It may be that a small number

[12] *Practical Reason and Norms*, p. 171.

[13] *Essays on Bentham*, pp. 157–61: Hart objects to Raz's analysis of legal obligation in terms of reasons for action, and prefers to proceed on the basis of a non-cognitive theory of duty in which statements asserting that an individual has a duty refer to actions due from him 'in the sense that they may be properly demanded or extracted from him according to legal rules or principles ...' (p. 160). This corresponds to the idea of the law's *claiming* obedience for itself, discussed below (p. 226), a characteristic of law which, of course, will be of no *practical* significance if there are no agents who adopt the legal point of view themselves. It seems to me, however, that a difficulty remains in that the force of the word 'properly' in the passage quoted must either be a moral one or one simply referring to the accurate interpretation of the content of the law; yet the normative nature of statements about that content is just what the account itself is meant to explain.

[14] *Legal Reasoning and Legal Theory* (Oxford, 1978), pp. 285–92.

[15] *Natural Law and Natural Rights*, pp. 11–18.

of officials will be able to maintain a legal order by use of their monopoly of force even where their moral enthusiasm for the system is not shared by the populace. It is equally true that we can imagine systems maintained solely in and by the self-interest of a dominant upper class, unbuttressed by any moral beliefs whatsoever.

Secondly, it has been argued that (perhaps as a matter of consistency?) Hart should not have omitted (at least in the absence of some justifying argument) to use the central case technique, used to such good effect in constructing the rest of his legal theory, when it comes to the internal attitude. The point seems to be that the burden is on Hart to explain why the technique of selecting a focal meaning of an internal attitude should *not* be used here, plus a positive assertion that it should be so used because of the practical significance of differences between various types of internal attitude. Certainly, as Hart explicitly allows, there is a whole range of viewpoints which could count as fully internal (as well as the enormous number of possible external attitudes). Such views might be based on moral approval or concern for the community, tradition, fear, self-interest, and so on. And if a central case selection is to be made, Finnis and MacCormick certainly make out a good case for regarding volitional commitment (MacCormick's weaker version) or disinterested interest in others and moral concern (Finnis's stronger one) as the paradigm upon which the other types are parasitic. For this does indeed appear to be the fullest form of acceptance, adoption, commitment, that we can imagine. But what is the significance of this? Does it once again reduce to the factual claim considered above? Perhaps three additional points need to be made here. First, even if we allow the propriety of the use of the central case technique as MacCormick and Finnis suggest, this only establishes a weak connection between law and morality. For presumably the link itself would *necessarily* exist only in central case legal systems. Secondly, the idea of an implicit reference to the moral element in the explanation of legal obligation in even non-paradigm cases is, I think at least in Finnis's case, tied up with the idea that legal validity or intra-systemic obligation presupposes as a framework principle presumptively moral obligation: when we use normative language intra-systemically, we are assuming through our discourse that legal obligations are prima facie moral obligations. This is not a view endorsed by Hart, nor, I would argue, is it an accurate representation of the basis on which intra-systemic legal discourse proceeds, as reflection on the diversity of possible and actual internal attitudes illustrates. Finally, in the case of Raz's account, it is clear that the central-case technique could not be applied to his separate, third type of viewpoint. Of course, MacCormick and Finnis might wish to argue that we should apply the technique to the fully internal attitude to which detached statements refer, and on which they depend for their sense. If so, arguments recited above will apply.

What does emerge, however, from the Hart and Raz accounts is the conclusion that the explanation of purely legal obligations *does* depend on what we might variously call commitment, adoption, acceptance, or something like it. This commitment must be given by some of the agents subject to the legal system—most obviously the officials: but it is reflected in the normative language quite properly and commonly used by others who, though detached themselves, are acknowledging by the use of the language of obligations and so on the commitment of others. Apart from *factual* doubts about stability, it is not clear why, at least for the restricted purposes of analytical jurisprudence, we should wish to enquire into the reasons for the adoption, acceptance, or commitment of others, although analysis of the concept of and justifying arguments for legal authority will clearly be both part of jurisprudence and political philosophy and integral to a rounded understanding of the nature of law. Nevertheless, all that really matters for this *limited* enquiry is the fact that certain individuals have taken a decision or adopted an attitude which puts them in a special relationship with the rules of a particular legal order: this means that those rules generate reasons for action for them, independently of their moral status or the threat of sanction, by the very reason of their pedigree plus the agent's adoptive attitude.

This discussion has, however, left one important ambiguity unresolved: can a person who does not adopt an internal or committed attitude be said to have legal obligations? Does someone who refuses to acknowledge or accept the rule of recognition of a system have obligations under it? Clearly, for both Hart and Raz, at least one person (and more, for Hart) must have such an attitude (or have had it, in the case of discourse concerning archaic systems, or be assumed to have it, if the discourse is hypothetical) in order for normative discourse to have a proper footing. It would be an extraordinary feature of this type of account if indeed it restricted the existence of legal obligations to those with internal attitudes, in view of the fact that the normative language which we are seeking to explain is used generally—for example, by a lawyer advising a non-law-abiding client. What we need to bear in mind, I think, is that what is in issue is, as Raz puts it, the 'legal point of view': the point of view taken up by the person with an internal attitude is an attitude implicitly contained within *the law itself*. As Tony Honoré puts it, the law 'claims allegiance': it purports to generate reasons for action. Naturally the types of reasons for action which it does generate will *in fact* differ for different citizens; but the viewpoint theory depends only on the *assumption* that laws are valid norms; no further enquiry need be undertaken with respect to the types of reason for action involved. Thus we do have an account of why normative language is used *irrespective* of the attitudes or commitments of the particular agents in question, which itself, however, depends on the existence of attitudes held by some agents corresponding to the stance taken up by the law itself.

EXCURSUS ON THE LIMITS OF ANALYTICAL JURISPRUDENCE

The defence of this kind of view is really tied up with the defence of a particular conception of the nature and limits of jurisprudence itself, and since I anticipate that many readers will object to the conclusions I have drawn in the last paragraph by reason of the narrow view of jurisprudence which is assumed, perhaps I should break the flow of the argument to say a few words in defence if this methodology. Taken as a statement at large, it is clearly ludicrous to suggest that the question of why people adopt internal attitudes is of no interest. It is clearly a question of enormous fascination and importance for historians, sociologists, anthropologists, psychologists, legal theorists, and indeed anyone who is concerned with reflecting on the nature and function of law as a form of social organization. But to affirm this is not to admit that all interesting questions which can be raised with respect to the nature and function of law can be dealt with within the confines of one discipline or one mode of thought. The question of why people obey the law seems primarily to be one of sociology or psychology; that of why people ought to obey the law, one of moral and political philosophy; the question of what is meant by the claim that an individual has a legal obligation when that claim is *not* meant to imply a moral one also is, I would argue, a discrete question of analytical jurisprudence. I do not think that this necessarily means that the analytical jurist is not influenced in her task by certain cultural and other factors, and I am thus not claiming that the analysis of legal obligation would be a universal one, cutting across cultural, geographical, or historical borders. My argument is merely that within any one society and culture there will be an acknowledged conceptual distinction between various different theoretical tasks which bear on the understanding of law, and that one legitimate and illuminating such task is analytical jurisprudence. To reach a rounded understanding of the nature and functions of law, one has to draw on many disciplines; blurring the boundaries between them will lead to confusion rather than breadth. The enterprise of those of us who do find it ludicrous that more legal theorists do not enquire into questions such as why people adopt an internal attitude to the law ought to be to encourage each other to extend our study and research into fields such as political philosophy, sociology, and so on, rather than to pretend that jurisprudence encompasses them.

HONORÉ'S VIEW OF OBLIGATION

Moving back to the main argument, the conclusions which I have drawn seem to be in line with two positions put forward by Tony Honoré in 'Groups, Laws and Obedience'. On the one hand, he argued that the *origins* of the shared commitments and understandings of the group were unimportant; what mattered was their present existence, and not their source, whether that was to be found in agreement, force, custom, or some other factor. This, I would argue, equates with the Hartian view of the lack of need further to analyse or differentiate the internal attitude: in each case, the present commitment to the norms of the system as guides to and reasons for conduct is the distinctive feature of a legal order. On the other hand, as we have already mentioned, Honoré argued that legal theory involves *commitment* and that the very statement 'X is a law' strikes a special position as to whether or not it should be obeyed. This points up the serious ambiguity of the word 'commitment': it suggests a full, moral attitude—but it can also be used, as I have been using it, to mean something closer to 'adoption', which, as I have argued, does not necessarily have any moral flavour. However, linguistic ambiguities aside, on the commitment/adoption theory of legal obligation we can reconcile this second statement of Honoré's with the essentially descriptive nature of his article. For both committed *and* detached statements of the law, using normative langauge, *do* strike a posture on the issue of obedience, in that they acknowledge the law's own claim to allegiance and the added reason provided by the agents' own adoptive decisions. Honoré's reference to the implicit position taken on how disobedience should be justified can also be reconciled with this moderate interpretation so long as we bear in mind that *from the point of view of the agent with the internal attitude* the existence of the law provides a reason for action, although, of course, the way in which this reason bears upon other reasons (such as moral ones) which the agent may have is a separate, very complex question which cannot be resolved here.

My interpretation is also in keeping with the other views expressed in 'Groups, Laws and Obedience'. For example, the restricted idea of making a commitment is parallel to Honoré's idea that membership of a group necessarily involves a sacrifice of freedom; in just the same way, adoption of an internal attitude towards the norms of a legal system, thus taking laws to generate legal obligations on oneself, involves a limiting of one's freedom to decide for oneself what one ought to do in a wide range of situations: there is a surrendering of autonomy to legal authority. The limited sense of commitment which I have tried to describe is also reflected in Honoré's assertion that the idea of a group is constituted by a lack of professed rejection rather than express or, perhaps, wholeheartedly moral acceptance: the origins of and reasons for the acceptance are unimportant from the point of view of exploring and developing the nature of a group as a tool for analysing and understanding the nature of law.

Before returning finally to the question of the relationship of sanctions to legal obligations, it will be as well to consider the question of the relationship of legal obligation, in the sense outlined above, and political obligation—the moral obligation on individuals to obey the law. Does our 'committed' view of legal obligation in turn commit us to the view that legal obligation entails at least prima facie political obligation, or can the two be kept separate, as positivists would wish? A moment's reflection shows that the question of political obligation can only be concluded by an enquiry into the *content* of identified legal obligations and of the *reasons* for agents' adoption of internal attitudes to legal rules, which we dismissed as irrelevant to the question of legal obligation in the strict sense. Many types of reason have been put forward as grounding a prima facie obligation to obey the law: agreement, acceptance of benefits resulting in a corresponding obligation to accept the burdens of a legal system, consistency with objectively moral principles, and so on. With a possible exception in the case of a very crude version of natural law theory in which only laws consistent with, and indeed derived from, objective moral principles count as laws at all (a thoroughly discredited view, even in the eyes of most natural lawyers),[16] my own view is that none of these suffices to establish general prima facie political obligation.[17] But what is important here is that we can understand the idea of the agent's adoption of legal obligations without having to enquire into either the moral worth of the substance of the law or the *moral* assessment made by the agent herself of the content of the legal obligations. Raz's legal point of view, for example, depends only on the *assumption*, rather than the acceptance, of the idea that laws generate reasons for action; nor is it the case that such reasons would always be moral ones. It may be true as a generalization of the facts in present-day developed countries that agents subject to their legal systems do regard their legal obligations as a species of at least presumptively moral obligations, but it would not affect our analysis if in fact they regarded the question of obedience to legal norms as a mere matter of prudence or convention. And despite the apparent credibility of the factual generalization referred to above the existence of many morally neutral or arbitrary laws reinforces the advantages of our non-committal analysis. Once questions of legal obligation have been determined, other questions remain for the agent to answer, concerning how she should weigh the legal reasons for action with, for example, moral ones. From a practical point of view, as Kelsen's theory assumes, there are strong reasons for the agent to work out

[16] Ibid., pp. 363–6.

[17] On the basis of the forceful argument made out by M. B. E. Smith, 'Is there a Prima Facie Obligation to Obey the Law?' (1973) 82 *Yale LJ* 950.

for herself a system of priorities such that her obligations make up a 'non-contradictory normative field of meaning'.[18] But to assert a prima facie obligation to obey the law seems to be either to make a trivial claim or to underestimate the importance and frequency of conflicts, arising for all agents who go through this reflective process, between moral and legal obligations; and this is simply to miss out an important dimension of moral life within complex political society.

SANCTIONS AND EFFECTIVENESS

Let us now move away from the strict question of analytical jurisprudence to our original, wider question of the views expressed by Tony Honoré in 'Groups, Laws and Obedience' on the place of sanctions in legal systems. As we have already noted, he identifies as one of the main functions of law the task of motivating obedience to itself.[19] Clearly, if legal orders are to achieve their primary task of regulating the behaviour of and relationships between members of a group (again, the assertion could be taken as analytic, factual, or both) constituted by shared understandings (which themselves become embodied in the law, for example in constitutional norms), it must have mechanisms by which it can reinforce already existing and perceived motives and reasons to obey, in the cases of citizens both with internal and with external attitudes. Some disobedience may be tolerated or even valuable, perhaps in the Durkheimian sense of providing instances for punishment which may in turn reinforce social solidarity by strengthening collective moral commitments to the content of the law, but widespread disobedience would lead to dissolution of the group. Of course, if the shared commitments themselves have become seriously eroded over time it may well be that even a sophisticated set of interlocking remedial norms may not be sufficient to maintain the group. Honoré makes it quite clear that these remedial norms need not be punitive, but allows that, as a matter of fact, sanctions may be necessary at some stage in the interlocking sets of norms in many kinds of society.

One can, I think, draw an interesting analogy between this view of sanctions and their relationship with legal obligation and the Kelsenian view of the relationship between effectiveness and validity.[20] For Kelsen, the effectiveness of system was a necessary but not a sufficinet condition of the validity of the norms of that system; if the system as a whole was not by and large effective, legal obligations (in our terms, not Kelsen's) would not be generated by it. Similarly, for Tony Honoré, general effectiveness of

[18] See J. W. Harris, *Law and Legal Science* (Oxford, 1979), pp. 34–43, 81–4.

[19] A view also expressed in 'Real Laws', in Hacker and Raz (edd), *Law, Morality, and Society* (Oxford, 1977), p. 104.

[20] *General Theory of Law and State* (Cambridge, Mass., 1945), pp. 41–2, 118–22.

common understandings and prescriptions is a necessary condition for the existence of the group and thus for laws to be created by it: hence the practical need for methods of enforcement. Of course, in Kelsen's legal theory, the other necessary conditions sufficing to ensure validity are not ultimately clearly enumerated, but within his framework, which distinguishes between the factual concept of effectiveness and the normative one of validity, I think we can accommodate our two notions: legal sanction and legal obligation. As a matter of *fact*, it seems likely that sanctions will be necessary, at least in legal orders governing large and heterogeneous populations, in order to preserve and guarantee the general effectiveness of the system as a whole. But this does not entail that individually valid (and effective!) legal obligations cannot exist without being backed up by the threat of sanctions. Sanctions are thus to be seen as a matter of lending credibility and effectiveness to the system as a whole, rather than as guarantees of obedience towards or sources of obligations arising from individual laws.

Thus Honoré's approach has the great merit of putting sanctions in perspective: they are simply one technique among others (such as offers of rewards or conciliation) employed by legal orders to motivate obedience, which exist alongside extra-legal motivations deriving from the reasons for adopting the shared understandings in the first place—which may or may not have been moral ones. It is interesting at this juncture to note that in a sense Honoré equates sanction-stipulating (remedial) norms and constitutional norms as serving at least one purpose in common: that of reinforcing motivation to obey. Thus any individual derivative norm is reinforced both by remedial (possibly punitive) norms and by the genetic norm from which it derives—the authority enjoyed by the source of the law reinforces the reason to obey. This may, although contingently, be because, just as the sanction gives most people a prudential reason to obey, the constitutional genetic norms give many citizens some form of moral motivation, highlighting as they do the ultimate, for instance, democratic pedigree of the norm in question. Thus an apparently morally neutral norm may be seen in a different light when the subject reflects that it has emanated from a democratically elected legislature, or a much-respected ruler; the fundamental reasons for adoption of the internal attitude may play an important role here in actually motivating obedience; and this, I would argue, is where Finnis's arguments, referred to above, really have their place. Equally, one particular norm may be seen in a very different light by two citizens equally bound from the point of view of the law itself: one may be motivated to obey by the process of reflection just described, whereas the next may be motivated largely or exclusively by prudential reasons connected directly or indirectly with the existence of sanctions. Indeed, one can see how this structural feature of legal systems as a matter of fact increases their stability because, as Tony Honoré points out, it allows derivative norms to be challenged (morally) without necessarily (morally) challenging the genetic norms from which they get their validity. But none of this affects the analytical question of the existence of legal obligation. For it is the internal attitude itself, and not its origins, nor simply the sanctions which may be threatened on breaches of legal duty, which constitutes and explains the concept of legal obligation itself.

EFFECTIVENESS AND THE JUSTIFICATION OF PUNISHMENT

I shall now finally turn to what may seem to be a rather different question from those I have so far been considering: how may the imposition of sanctions by a legal authority be justified? Clearly we are now moving away from the realms of analytical jurisprudence and indeed of sociological speculations about law. But the relationship between this normative question and the analytical one of legal obligation is nevertheless important. If, for example, we had concluded that there was a necessary analytic connection between the concept of legal obligation and that of sanction, this would have led to the conclusion that any possible justification of the existence or adoption of a legal system or a set of laws would include or entail a justification of punishment: thus the primary question would be whether we can justify having a legal order along with the punishments and/or threats of punishment which that entails, rather than treating the two normative questions separately.

But in fact more or less this position holds true even on the view we have reached about the relationship between legal obligations and sanctions. For even on the basis of a contingent relationship, the justification for the existence and maintenance of an actual, effective legal system will involve us in justifying the sanctions which guarantee and maintain the effectiveness which we have described as a necessary condition for validity. The justification of punishment is thus sought through arguments about the necessity of punishment if we are to enjoy the benefits of a legal order, and the primary question then becomes whether those benefits outweigh the costs, including those of punishment, which having such a system involves. The contingent relationship need not always hold, and indeed we can not only find intelligible but also espouse as an ideal the sort of legal order of unsanctioned co-ordinating standards envisaged by Tom Campbell. But in the world as we know it, one who is convinced as to the justifiability of legal systems necessarily faces the moral dilemma of punishment.

The salient features of retributive/consequentialist debate on punishment are well known and do not need to be repeated here. What I want to do is merely to poont out the close relationship between our conclusions on the relationship of sanctions to legal orders and legal obligation and one familiar set of theories of punishment. For the effectiveness/validity distinction, or the idea of sanctions as backing systems as opposed to individual rules, bears a close resemblance to the mixed or rule-utilitarian theories of punishment espoused by writers such as Hart[21] and Rawls.[22] Rawls, for example, argues that the ultimate justification for having *institutions* of punishment is the good effects which they can achieve, notably in deterring breaches of the law, preventing resort to self-help, maintaining respect for the legal order, and so on. But in order to overcome the stock criticisms of such thoroughgoing utilitarian arguments for punishment such as their justifying victimizations in certain cases, Rawls argues that at the individual level what justifies punishment is quite simply the fact of a rule of law having been broken. This along with the existence of the sanction-stipulating norm which is thus brought into operation explains and justifies individual acts of punishment.

It is my own view that these arguments do not really overcome the objections to utilitarian accounts, and I think that this can be demonstrated quite well in the light of the foregoing discussion of sanctions and legal obligation. Our own conclusions have certainly led us towards some form of consequence-oriented, forward-looking justification of punishment. The reason for the existence of sanctions has been said to be to provide a motive for obeying the law, and the reason for wanting to motivate, or being justified in motivating, obedience to the law is most obviously the good effects in terms of efficiency, smooth co-ordination, social protection, and general quality of life to which the existence of a stable legal system can contribute. Thus far we are in line with the Rawls analysis. But is it not strange then to change tack at the individual level? Would we not expect the general justifying arguments for punishment to dictate when we should apply punishment in individual cases? The problem for the rule-utilitarian here is that she must either keep hold of her utilitarianism at the cost of occasional, utility-directed breaches of the rules, or she must stick to the rules whilst acknowledging values other than the original utilitarian goals—perhaps most conveniently referred to as values of fairness or equality.[23]

Our descriptive, non-sanction-based account of legal obligation shows that the mere fact that legal rules themselves may dictate sanctions in certain cases of breach in no way contributes to the moral justification of those sanctions in the large sense—yet Rawls's argument seems to be perilously close to asserting just this. How could the argument 'because she broke a rule' ever constitute a sufficient moral argument for punishment?

[21] 'Prolegomenon to the Principles of Punishment', in *Punishment and Responsibility* (Oxford, 1968), ch. 1.

[22] 'Two Concepts of Rules' (1955), 64 *Philosophical Review* 3–52.

[23] For a fuller critique of rule-utilitarianianism in the context of punishment, see T. Honderich, *Punishment, the Supposed Justifications* (London, 1969), ch. 3 : 6.

It certainly furnishes the beginnings of an argument, most obviously in terms of the effects of the breach, such as harms to the victim, and social costs in terms of resentment, and so on, but the argument is not fleshed out by Rawls, and of course if it were it would defeat the initial object of the exercise. For this was to find some limiting principle to overcome the difficulties of utilitarianism—and the argument which I have begun to sketch is essentially a utilitarian argument. This is not in any way meant to deny the reality of the problem which Rawls and Hart were addressing; it is merely to suggest that the answer lies in the slightly different direction of a tying-together of the two strands of the argument at a deeper, normative level, in pursuit of a sophisticated consequentialist theory which incorporates a distributive principle, absence of which in utilitarianism gives rise to the problem of victimization, among many others.

CONCLUSION

In conclusion, Tony Honoré's article 'Groups, Laws and Obedience' puts forward a picture of law as a system for the reinforcement of group pressure by means of the adoption of rules of various interlocking kinds. Implicit in his arguments is a view of legal obligation, as a matter of analytical jurisprudence, and also a view of the contingent relationship between such obligations and sanctions, as a matter of descriptive sociology. This contingent relationship makes the justification of punishment dependent upon at least part of a general political philosophy which would provide a justification for the maintenance of a legal system. This mode of analysis emphasizes the truth that no theory of punishment can ignore the problem of justifying punishment in an unjust society: if the laws themselves are unjust, the connection we have identified renders the idea of an independent justification of punishment a nonsense. This conclusion would be too obvious to merit explicit statement were it not for the fact that so many writers have attempted to produce justifications of punishment which deal with that issue in isolation from its context in moral and political philosophy. Our discussion has ranged, as do most of Tony Honoré's, over factual, analytical, and normative issues. I cannot aspire to match the quality of his arguments, but hope that I have at least followed his encouraging and inspiring example both in favouring eclecticism and in avoiding confusion of the borderlines between these differing species of question.

14

Law and Punishment: the Western and the Traditional Chinese 'Legal Mind'

G. D. MacCormack

The aims of this paper, offered to a scholar distinguished for the breadth and richness of his work, are (i) to explore at a general level the way in which the Western legal mind regards the relationship between law and punishment, this in turn involving consideration of the relationship between coercion, sanction and punishment, and (ii) more specifically to compare the approach of the Western legal mind to these matters with that of the traditional Chinese legal mind. Still too little is known in the West about the conception of law that prevailed in China for three thousand years from the beginning of the Chou dynasty around 1100 BC to the end of the Ch'ing in 1911.[1] From a number of points of view Chinese thinking provides an interesting contrast to Western.

I consider first some of the ways in which the relationship between law and punishment has been regarded in Western juristic thinking, with a glance also at a possible difference between the 'legal' and the 'lay' perspective. To avoid confusion it is necessary to distinguish between coercion, sanction, and punishment and to consider each of these notions in its relation to law. They have in common the element that all involve either the actual application of force, the infliction of something unpleasant on an individual irrespective of his will, or at least the threat that force will be applied; but equally there are important differences, especially between punishment on the one hand and sanction and coercion on the other.

The relationship between law and coercion can be understood in different ways and from different perspectives. At the most neutral level, that is, without commitment to some particular view of the nature of law or its function, one may say that law and coercion are related in the sense that the law provides a means for compelling people to behave in the manner required by the legislator. As a statement of fact this merely expresses the existence of rules of law which establish that under certain conditions

[1] Of course, not all Chinese thinkers viewed law in exactly the same way throughout this period; nevertheless, as a result in the main of the predominance of the Confucian ethic and the line of thought on which it drew, a remarkable consistency of approach can be detected.

people are to perform or abstain from performing certain acts and establish penalties to be imposed in the event of a failure to obey. More specifically one would have to distinguish between the rules which establish penalties and so indirectly exercise pressure on individuals by inducing them to conform through fear of the penalty, the rules which provide the mechanisms for the application of the penalty where an individual has infringed a rule, and the actual application of force to the individual. Hence from this point of view one is merely drawing attention to the existence of legal rules which provide for the imposition of penalties; one is making no assertion as to the proportion of such rules to the whole body of the law.[2]

As against this neutral appraisal one has to consider the conceptions of law and coercion that are in fact held by people. Here one is likely to find a difference according to whether the viewpoint is that of a legally-trained or even educated person or not. One who is neither educated nor trained in law may well associate law with a crude element of coercion represented by the police and the courts, that is, with the notion of being told what to do under threat of something unpleasant happening if one disobeys. Legally trained or educated persons, on the other hand, are likely to have a more accurate knowledge of law and a better appreciation of the variety of legal rules, in particular of the difference between rules which carry sanctions and those which do not. Even so one may find among jurists very significant differences in the way law is deemed to be related to coercion. A positivist, for example, sees law more in terms of coercion than a natural-lawyer. Some positivists go so far as to make coercion an identifying characteristic of law. Thus Austin built the notion of a 'threat of evil' into his definition of a legal rule and for Kelsen every primary norm stipulated a sanction. Hart on the other hand took a less extreme position and rescued positivism from its exaggerated commitment to coercion by insisting upon the distinction between, first, a rule and its sanction and, second, between rules which prescribed behaviour and those which conferred powers.[3]

Rather than view law and coercion in terms of the content of the rules, that is, of the extent to which legal rules establish a means of coercion, one may instead focus upon the aspect of function and ask in what way law can be considered to have a coercive function. In raising this question one

[2] A more precise view of coercion is taken by Neil MacCormick in his essay 'Coercion and the Law', which appears as ch. 12 of *Legal Right and Social Democracy. Essays in Legal and Political Philosophy* (Oxford, 1982). His point is that the essence of coercion being deprivation of real choice, the mere existence of legal rules which establish penalties is not itself coercive (as distinct from the actual application of the penalties against the will of the offender). Analysis of law in terms of coercion differs according to whether one takes a 'practical' or a 'logical' perspective (p. 244). As will be apparent, it is the former perspective that is taken in this paper.

[3] See also the important study by A. M. Honoré, 'Real Laws' in P. M. S. Hacker and J. Raz (edd.). *Law, Morality and Society. Essays in Honour of H. L. A. Hart*, (Oxford, 1977), p. 5.

has to reflect upon the meaning of the word 'function'. Does it mean the purpose which those who make the law have in mind (legislative intent) or the purpose which members of the society assign to law (social understanding)? Or does it have no reference to anyone's actual intent or understanding but express the role which law and coercion have as a means of holding society together? Thus, depending on the perspective taken, one may find various answers to the question: 'does law have a coercive function?' Possible affirmative replies are that the legislators intend to ensure good order within society through the enactment of rules of behaviour carrying penalties for those who do not conform, that members of society understand the purpose of law to be the forcible prescription of behaviour, or that the society in question is held together (or able to function) because of the existence of rules which establish penalties for deviant behaviour.

A final, perhaps the most significant, issue concerns the relationship between law and coercion in the sense of the ability possessed by certain persons or bodies within a society to compel the rest through the use of force to obey the instructions which they issue. Is law to be identified with the order of those who happen at any time to command the monopoly of force within society? Undoubtedly there does seem to be a close connection between law and the monopoly of force within a society (leaving aside the problem of law in 'primitive' societies where no individual or group holds such a monopoly). In a modern society it is inconceivable that the legislature, the body primarily responsible for the making of new laws, should not either itself control the use of force or have the backing of the executive body which does.

Understandably legal theorists have been reluctant to accept the conclusion that ultimately (whatever the disguises) law is in fact the command of those within society with the ability to enforce it. While natural-lawyers are able to discount the physically coercive aspect of legal rules and construct a theory of law and the obligation to obey law on the basis of the moral content of the rules, positivists are in greater trouble. Since they cannot adduce the moral content of the rules as a criterion of law, in order to show that people are under an obligation to obey the law as distinct from being merely obliged, they have to construct a formal criterion for the identification of law. Hence one has Austin's habit of obedience, Kelsen's *Grundnorm*, and Hart's rule of recognition. In so far as these criteria presuppose (in their different ways) that members of a society 'accept' that certain persons may make rules for the whole society, one may say that the distinction between 'acceptance' freely arrived at and that which itself is induced by pressure becomes difficult to detect. In other words if those who acquire a monopoly of force within society (the 'gunmen') maintain that monopoly for a long period of time people continuously subjected to pressure will come to 'accept' that the 'gunmen' may make rules for the society.

The relationship between law and sanction obviously raises to some extent the same issues as that between law and coercion since the provision of sanctions is the most effective means available to the law for the exertion of pressure. Nevertheless the inquiry takes a different form according to whether one focuses upon the general element of coercion or the more specific element of sanction. What one is concerned with is not the general question of the way the law as such exercises coercion but the particular relationship between individual rules of law and sanctions. In considering this relationship the first question which suggests itself is: what exactly is a sanction? In answering this question one has to distinguish between a whole range of possibly adverse consequences that may follow upon breach of a rule from a penalty explicitly provided by the rule and intended to ensure compliance. By 'intended' is meant that those framing the rule attached a penalty with the object of seeing that the behaviour prescribed by the rule was followed. It is only a penalty of this kind that properly and strictly can be treated as the sanction of the rule. A sanction provides for the infliction of an unpleasant consequence upon a person who breaks the rule. The nature of the consequence may vary. It may be deprivation of a licence, a fine, imprisonment, or death. What these unpleasant consequences have in common is the fact that they are all intended to ensure compliance with the rule to which they are attached. In this sense they can be regarded as penalties. It will be argued below that some in addition to being penalties are also punishments.

The next issue to be raised is the relationship between a rule of law and its sanction. To what extent are these logically separable notions? In view of the strong association already mentioned, held to obtain between law and coercion, it would not be surprising to find that many people think of rules of law as being rules which provide for the imposition of penalties. What demonstrates the strength of this association is the fact that some legal theorists (notably Austin and Kelsen) also hold that no rule can be a proper rule of law unless it stipulates a sanction. The approach that treats provision of a sanction as a necessary part of a legal rule is reflected on the one hand in the widespread reluctance to regard international law or 'primitive' law as proper law and on the other in the forcing of all rules of law into a mould of the type 'if behaviour *X* occurs penalty *Y* is to be imposed'. Both these conclusions can be maintained only at the cost of an over-rigid and distorted understanding of rules of law.

It is more in accord with reality to accept that there is no necessary connection between rules of law and sanction. This proposition may be restated in two different and less general forms. First, there may be rules of law which lack sanctions. Such a class may even include rules which require people to behave in certain ways. Most rules of this kind will, it is true, have sanctions. But exceptions occur. A well-known example from Roman antiquity is the *lex Cincia* of 204 BC which prohibited the making of gifts above a certain amount but provided no penalty for infringement of the prohibition. On the other hand rules which establish the conditions under which transactions may be completed and determine what counts, for example, as a valid will, contract, or conveyance characteristically lack sanctions.[4] Failure to observe them may attract an undesirable consequence in that the purported transaction is void. But on the definition given above nullity does not constitute a sanction because it is not a penalty attached to a rule with the aim of securing its compliance. A rule or set of rules may establish the conditions for the validity of a particular transaction and expressly provide that if these conditions are not met the transaction is to be void. Such a formulation makes it look as though nullity is being attached as a penalty to secure compliance with the rules, but in fact this is not the case. To say that failure to observe the rule entails a nullity is merely to state negatively that compliance is necessary for a valid transaction[5].

The second, more specific form of the proposition is that even where a rule does provide for a sanction there is no necessary connection between rule and sanction in the sense that the former logically embraces the latter. A rule prescribing behaviour and stipulating for the imposition of a sanction in the event of non-compliance may be analysed as a single composite rule or as two distinct rules, the one prescribing the behaviour and the other providing for the sanction.[6] The rule which prescribes behaviour is perfectly capable of standing alone without the addition of that providing for a sanction. The fact that the two rules are normally found together or as a single composite rule shows not that the sanction is a necessary element of the behaviour prescribing rule but that the latter is not likely to be effective without the former.

Where a sanction is provided for the failure to observe behaviour prescribed by a rule the formal relation between rule and sanction may vary. The sanction may be provided by the behaviour prescribing rule itself. For example one may have wording of the following kind: persons are to do (or refrain from doing) *X;* if they disobey, *Y* penalty is to be applied. Alternatively the rule prescribing the behaviour may not in so many words establish the sanction. It may state merely that particular behaviour is to constitute an offence of a certain kind. In order to find the sanction one

[4] It is not impossible that there should be sanctions in such cases. A rule might conceivably require persons to make wills or contracts and provide a sanction for non-compliance.

[5] On nullity see H. L. A. Hart, *The Concept of Law* (Oxford, 1961), pp. 33 f.

[6] I have somewhat over-simplified the position. See Honoré, 'Real Laws', pp. 117 f., and in general the subtle categorization of legal rules which he suggests. He points out that rules which in form directly prescribe behaviour are in fact rare.

has to look at another rule or set of rules which stipulate the sanction for the kind of offence in question.

The relationship between law and punishment touches upon that between law and coercion or sanction. The fact that the law established punishments for offences can be seen as related to or even identified with the notion of law as a system of coercion. Equally, punishment in a loose sense can be seen as the equivalent of sanction. Although such identification or equivalence can be asserted the very broad sense it assigns to the notion of punishment leads in the end to confusion rather than to clarity. The reason is that some important issues are likely to be obscured if one takes punishment as vaguely meaning the same as coercion or sanction. It is significant that discussions of law as a coercion system or as to whether there can be law or rules of law without sanctions do not normally use the language of punishment. There is no assumption that the terms 'coercion', 'sanction', and 'punishment' can be used interchangeably. In other words punishment is best taken as having a narrower sphere of reference than coercion or sanction.

Punishment entails the infliction of a pain upon a person who has commited an offence. It thus constitutes coercion in two senses. On the one hand, viewed prospectively, it furnishes a 'threat of evil' which is intended to deter people from committing prohibited acts. On the other hand, viewed retrospectively, it is the actual application of unpleasant measures to a person (irrespective of his consent) on the ground that he has already committed a prohibited act. Punishment may also constitute a sanction in the sense that one of the reasons for which it is imposed is simply the wish of the legislator to ensure that a rule is kept.

Although punishment has a coercive aspect and, when established by a rule, can be said to function as a sanction to ensure the keeping of the rule, neither the notion of coercion nor that of sanction provides an adequate explanation for the nature of punishment. Neither notion seems to strike at the essence of punishment. Does the reason lie in the connection between punishment and offence? While one may be coerced into doing something or may be subjected to a sanction even though one has committed no offence, it would be odd to be punished unless one had committed an offence. One can speak of a person being punished although he has done nothing wrong but such a statement is advanced as a criticism carrying the implication that he should not have been punished.

This explanation is not in itself satisfactory because if one is speaking of coercion or sanction in a legal context one is implying that the commission of a legal offence is a necessary condition for the application of coercion or the imposition of a sanction. The very fact that a rule of law has been broken constitutes a legal offence. Hence the distinction between coercion and sanction on the one hand and punishment on the other can be maintained only if one postulates a division of offences into two classes, one entailing sanctions and the other punishments (which might also constitute sanctions). The criterion by which one identifies the offences belonging to each division is their nature. If the offence consists merely in the breach of the rule, that is, if one cannot say that there is any wrong other than the failure to comply with a rule established by the legislator, it falls within the division of mere penalties or sanctions. If the offence constitutes something more than this, that is, if it would be regarded by members of the society as a wrong independently of its character as breach of a legal rule then it falls into the division of punishments. Examples of the former would be many of the rules governing the driving of cars on the road or the payment of taxes and their breach. Examples of the latter would be the punishments imposed for killing, rape, or theft. It is this division which is enshrined in the old distinction between *mala in se* and *mala prohibita*.[7]

A corollary of the argument is that the language of punishment may serve as an indicator of the importance attached by the framer or upholder of a rule to the behaviour which it prescribes. Stress on the punishment that will be inflicted if the rule is broken implies the seriousness with which the offence is regarded. The word 'punishment' more effectively conveys this sense of seriousness than the word 'sanction' or 'penalty'.

Other issues raised by the relationship between law and punishment can only be touched upon in the barest outline. These concern the nature of the behaviour which should be punished and the question of the just punishment for a particular offence. The first of these issues has led to protracted discussions on the extent to which commonly accepted morality should be enforced by the criminal law. An interesting aspect of the discussion has been the prominence of the argument that maintenance of a society's moral standards is necessary for its existence and hence is the proper concern of the law. The assumption which appears to underlie this argument is that the state (the central authority) is responsible for good order within society and that the infliction of punishment for offences against morality is an exercise of this responsibility. The state should punish breaches of sexual mores just as it should killings or thefts. Either kind of deviant behaviour constitutes a threat to good order within society.[8] The second issue touches upon the proper role of punishment. Ought it to be apportioned on a retributive as well as (or instead of) a deterrent basis? That is, should the degree of wickedness of an act be reflected in the amount of punishment accorded? To what extent should the existence of a guilty intention (*mens*

[7] See in particular the remarks of Lord Devlin in *The Enforcement of Morals* (Oxford, 1965), 30 ff. and cf. also the discussion in G. H. Gordon, *The Criminal law of Scotland* (2nd edn. Edinburgh, 1978), pp. 17 ff.

[8] I am not pronouncing a judgment on the merits of the argument.

rea) be taken into account in determining the application of a punishment or of its amount?

Much of the discussion on the topics which I have mentioned has been conducted on an abstract and theoretical plane. Writers have been interested in systematizing, attaining a correct classification of heterogeneous data, and in identifying the elements common to them. Obvious examples have been the attempts to characterize the essence of law, to distinguish between varieties of legal rules, and to analyse the relationship between law and sanction. Investigation of punishment may also take this form, involving attempts to classify the various justifications for, or functions of, punishing. At the same time not all writing on legal theory has remained unrelated to practical questions. Some has been directly inspired by specific deficiencies in the law or has been presented as an argument for legal reform. Well-known examples are the debates on law and morality in the context of the enforcement of morality by the criminal law and the appropriateness of punishment in the context of the proper way to treat offenders.

The Chinese material—at least that which has been accessible to me—presents a marked contrast in outlook. It shows little concern with issues in the abstract unconnected with practical results. Not all Chinese writing on law necessarily had a practical result but it was produced with the object of influencing events. Chinese writers were interested not in law as such but in law as an instrument of government. Their principal theme was the right way to govern the people; their emphasis lay on the role of the ruler and the use which he should make of law. Consequently analysis of law and legal notions of a kind familiar in the West is not found in Chinese writing of the Imperial age. This belongs more to the genre of politics or history than of law itself.

What is called traditional Chinese law covers a period from the beginning of the Western Chou dynasty around 1100 BC to the fall of the last Imperial dynasty, the Ch'ing, in 1911. Throughout this period law was very closely associated with coercion, sanction, and punishment. This association was made not only in the minds of the masses of the people but also in those of the scholars and officials comprising the ruling class. There was of course much variation in detail and emphasis but certain general themes recur throughout this enormous span of time. These themes were given their classic formulation during the turbulent period of Chinese history known as the Warring States (463–222 BC). China was divided into a number of rival states whose rulers were struggling either to avoid subjugation themselves or to subjugate others. Consequently rulers were seeking the best means to make their states powerful and heeded the debates of scholars and statesmen on the relevance of law for this purpose.

The outcome of the debate was the crystallization of two divergent attitudes to law associated respectively with what came to be called the Confucianist and Legalist schools of thought.[9] The former drew on long-standing thinking, the roots of which go back at least to the early Chou dynasty, whereas the latter represented a more radical approach which broke decisively with previous orthodoxy.[10] Both Confucianists and Legalists conceived law primarily (although not exclusively) in terms of one specific mode of coercion, namely, as consisting of a set of rules prescribing behaviour and imposing punishments for failure to behave in the prescribed way and rewards for conformity. They differed in the role they assigned to law in the government of the state. The Confucianists assigned to it a place that might be subordinate to, and certainly could rank no higher than, that taken by moral persuasion and good example on the part of the ruler. Ideally on their view resort should be had to law (that is, to measures of coercion) only where moral guidance had not succeeded in inducing people to behave in the right way. On the other hand the Legalists assigned primacy to law as an instrument of government. In their view the best way for a ruler to make his state powerful was to concentrate his people's efforts on agriculture and war. This could be done effectively only by the impartial and consistent application of a set of rules directed at securing the desired behaviour through the provision of punishments and rewards.

The debate on the place of law in government had immensely important consequences since the state which most thoroughly put into practice Legalist doctrine was the one ultimately to triumph over the others and secure the unification of the empire under the Ch'in dynasty (221–206 BC). However this rather harsh and brutal regime barely survived the death of its founder. The collapse of the Ch'in and the rise of the Han in its stead led to a revulsion against Legalist doctrines and a return to Confucianism as the most favoured political philosophy, a position which lasted until the present century. Nevertheless Legalism was not suddenly deprived of all influence. Apart from its continuing effect in the practice of government and the formulation of the dynastic law-codes it seems to have influenced Confucian thinkers in their description of the proper relation between law and moral guidance.[11]

Both Confucianism and Legalism were, with respect to their treatment

[9] General accounts may be found in J. Needham, *Science and Civilisation in China*, vol. II (Cambridge, 1956), chs. 9, 12 and 18; Fung Yu-lan, *A History of Chinese Philosophy* (tr. D. Bodde) vol. I, 2nd edn. (Princeton, 1952), chs. 4, 6, 12–14, 16; T'ung-Tsu Ch'ü, *Law and Society in Traditional China* (Paris, 1961), ch. 6; Kung-chuan Hsiao, *A History of Chinese Political Thought* (tr. F.W. Mote) I (Princeton, 1979), chs. 2, 3, 6–8. Further literature is cited in the succeeding notes. I am not taking account here of other schools of thought such as the Taoist, which have a marginal reference to law, nor of writers or books which offer amalgams of the thought of the two main schools.

[10] See, however, R.T. Ames, *The Art of Rulership. A Study in Ancient Chinese Political Thought* (Hawaii, 1983) for the view that the differences between the two schools have been exaggerated in some modern, influential accounts.

[11] See on Hsün Tzu below.

of law, political philosophies. They were concerned with the role of law in the government of the state. Neither doctrine showed interest in the nature of legal rules as such or in the relationship between law and sanction. One does not find in Chinese writings the kind of analysis familiar to Western readers from the works of Austin, Kelsen, or Hart. Thus there is no explicit discussion either by Confucianists or Legalists of the relationship between law and punishment, and no discussion of the question whether law is to be identified with a set of rules emanating from the ruler, each of which established a punishment. Although Confucianists and Legalists thought of law purely as a coercive system and laid great stress upon the aspect of punishment, it would be a mistake to think that adherents of either school identified law with rules imposing punishments. Incidental remarks on law show they accept that the ruler might enact rules, counting as laws, which did not stipulate a punishment.[12]

A special feature of Legalist doctrine in this connection merits a separate comment. This is the reliance upon rewards as an alternative to punishment. Legalists habitually spoke of law as comprising rules which imposed punishments or offered rewards. It is possible to construe rewards in this theory as sanctions because they are attached to rules as a means of getting people to observe the behaviour which is prescribed. But there is still some difficulty in identifying rewards as operating coercively. They are not measures which can be said to deprive those to whom they are directed of real freedom of choice. Rather, they provide inducements for complying with the behaviour prescribed by the rule. The Legalists themselves do not discuss these problems of classification.[13]

The association between law and punishment stressed in the political philosophies of Confucianism and Legalism was manifested at the practical level in the great dynastic codes. These were purely penal in character in that they consisted of rules imposing punishments for prohibited behaviour, or rules defining who was to be exempt from punishment, or the conditions under which a lesser degree of punishment might be imposed, and so on. Dynasties also promulgated comprehensive sets of rules on administrative matters, particularly on the duties of officials entrusted with the administration of the central government and the provinces. Apart from penal and administrative law, rulers did not concern themselves with areas that a Western lawyer would regard as equally falling within the sphere of law. Thus, with some important exceptions, the state did not regulate matters of contract, succession, or entitlement to property. Significantly, the exceptions were made part of the penal code. For example, it was provided that a debtor who failed to pay his debt in time might, at the instance of the

[12] Illustrations are given below.

[13] On reward as sanction, see MacCormick, *Coercion and the Law*, p. 244 ff.

creditor, be subjected to a beating.[14] Consequently for the mass of people the law administered by state courts was entirely a matter of offences and punishments. A legal theorist, if such there had been, would have found it relatively easy to fit the codified law into the Austinian model of commands addressed by political superiors to inferiors backed by a threat of evil.

After these general remarks, one may pass to some illustrations of Confucianist and Legalist thought. In considering Confucianist thought, one can return to the beginnings of recorded opinion on law and punishment. This is because Confucius himself and his successors largely built on attitudes evidenced throughout Chinese history. Two early and instructive sources for such attitudes are the *Shu ching* and the *Tso chuan*. The *Shu* is a collection of documents purporting to emanate from the archives of the earliest dynasties. Some are now held to be forgeries, but among those generally regarded as authentic is the *K'ang kao*, a lengthy statement on the proper use of law and punishment by the first ruler of the Chou dynasty.[15] The *Tso* as a whole was put together in the Warring States period and one cannot be sure of the extent to which views held at that time were attributed to earlier historical figures.[16]

It is not possible here to go into all the problems of interpretation raised by these early sources. Basically, if taken more or less at face value, they show a remarkable uniformity of aristocratic and official thought on the role of law and punishment stretching over a period of around eight hundred years from the early Chou to the Warring States. The main features of this thought may be summed up as follows:

(i) The notion of law in the sense of rules enacted by the ruler is consistently linked with the notion of punishment, that is, rules of law are consistently presented as rules imposing punishments. However, one should add two qualifications to this statement. At least for the earliest thought there is evidence of a belief in a 'higher law', that is, of norms of behaviour enjoined by Heaven. Further, although there is explicit discussion of the point, it does not seem that a necessary connection was assumed to exist between a rule of law and a punishment. Some rules conceivably might be

[14] Cf. further my 'The T'ang Code', (1983) 18 *Irish Jurist* (n. 5.) 132–50.

[15] There are three main translations of the *Shu* into Western languages; those of J. Legge, *The Shoo-King* (The Chinese Classics III repr. Taipei, n.d.), S. Couvreur, *Chou Kong* (repr. Taipei, 1971), and B. Karlgren, 'The Book of Documents', *Bulletin of the Museum for Far Eastern Antiquities* 11 (1950), 1. Karlgren's translation is that most frequently cited by modern scholars. On the question of authenticity, see H. G. Creel, *The Origins of Statecraft in China* (Chicago, 1970), vol. i, pp. 447 ff.

[16] There are two translations into Western languages: those of J. Legge, *The Ch'un Ts'ew with the Tso Chuen* (The Chinese Classics V), and S. Couvreur, *La Chronique de la principauté de Lou* (3 vols., Paris, 1951). On the question of its compilation see Creel, *Origins of Statecraft*, p. 475.

enacted by a ruler that counted as law even though they did not impose punishments.[17]

(ii) Law in the sense of rules imposing punishments is only one of the methods which a good ruler should use in guiding the behaviour of his people. He himself and his ministers should set an example of virtuous conduct and attempt by precept and persuasion to inculcate right behaviour. Only in the case of the irredeemably wicked should resort be had to law (punishment). The prime function of punishment is thus seen as deterrence[18] although, as will be seen, retributive thinking enters into the calculation of the punishment appropriate in particular cases. The passages in the *Tso*[19] which discuss the attitudes of a good ruler generally rank moral guidance and law as of equal importance and do not represent the latter as an inferior form of control.[20]

(iii) One finds constant injunctions on the ruler to exercise mercy and justice in the infliction of punishments. They should be moderate and proportioned to the gravity of the offence; in particular, intentional offences should be punished more severely than inadvertent offences. Pardons should be granted where possible, that is, the full severity of the punishment prescribed for an offence should be mitigated. Punishment should be applied only in accordance with the law, not at the whim of the ruler. High status should not warrant entire exemption from punishment.[21] Persons who committed the same offence should receive the same punishment.[22]

In writings of the Confucian philosophers the attention paid to law varies. Both Confucius himself (551–479 BC) and his chief follower Mencius (372–289 BC) say a great deal about virtue and moral guidance but very little about law. In the case of Mencius this absence of interest in law may be due in part to his conviction of the essential goodness of human nature. His nature being good, man should be amenable to moral instruction. On

[17] See '*K'ang kao*' (Karlgren, cited above, n. 15, pp. 39 f.) and from the *Tso* cf. the laws cited at Legge, *Ch'um Ts'ew*, p. 616 (Couvreur, *Chronique* III, p. 129) with that cited at Legge, 656 (Couvreur III, p. 249).

[18] Legge, pp. 33, 317, 395, 577 (Couvreur I, pp. 60, 403; ii, p. 126; iii, p. 13).

[19] Cf. Legge, pp. 211, 317, 395 (Couvreur i, p. 403; ii, p. 126).

[20] However, there are two well-known passages—(Legge, pp. 609 f, 732; Couvreur iii, pp. 116 ff., 455 f.)—whose genuineness has in fact been doubted (H. G. Creel, 'Legal Institutions and Procedures during the Chou dynasty', in J. A. Cohen, R. R. Edwards, and F. C. Chen (edd.), *Essays on China's Legal Tradition* (Princeton, 1980), pp. 35 ff,, and cf. also his *Origins of Statecraft*, 162 n. 8)—in which a more extreme position appears to be taken and the casting of laws on bronze tripods by the states of Ch'eng and Ch'in is represented as a retrograde step. The exact interpretation of these passages is disputed. Cf. Ames, *Art of Rulership*, pp. 118 f.

[21] Confucian thinking did differentiate punishment according to status: cf. Ch'u, *Law and Society*, pp. 172 ff. But the *Tso* records a case of punishment applied to a relative of a ruler and held by the latter to be just (Legge, p. 420; Couvreur, vol. II, pp. 194 f.).

[22] See '*K'ang kao*' and from the *Tso:* Legge, pp. 108, 213, 428, 440, 541, 646 (Couvreur, vol. I, pp. 177, 410 f.; vol. II, pp. 215, 241, 505; III, pp. 248 f.).

the other hand the Confucian thinker who gave the most attention to law believed that human nature was essentially bad. This was Hsün Tzu (306–212 BC), who also appears to have been considerably influenced by Legalist thought.[23] Hsün Tzu is interested not in the analysis of law as such but in its political role in society. He clearly recognizes the necessity of law along with moral guidance on the part of the ruler and argues for a synthesis of the two techniques of government. A good ruler makes and applies law in accordance with moral principles. This is the point of Hsün Tzu's insistence that the ruler should not literally apply the law but should 'deliberate', that is, look into the real nature of the case and make a proper use of analogy and precedent.[24]

From a political perspective Hsün Tzu still conceives law predominantly as a set of rules imposing punishments, though it does not seem that he went as far as holding that rule would not count as law unless it imposed a punishment.[25] Law is a necessary part of government because it is necessary to deter people from wrongdoing through the threat of punishment.[26] By wrongdoing Hsün Tzu means the failure to observe the important Confucian values. Hence he looks upon law as the ultimate means for the enforcement of basic Confucian morality. One can detect, too, a retributive tinge in some of his remarks on punishment. There is an implication that the wicked deserve punishment, and some insistence upon the fact that the amount of punishment should be proportioned to the seriousness of the offence.[27]

Legalist writing on law is best represented by the book attributed to Lord Shang and the works of Han Fei Tzu. Lord Shang was chief minister of the state of Ch'in (which ultimately founded the Ch'in Empire) in the early fourth century BC. He was remarkable in his own time and in after ages for the harshness with which he applied in practice the main tenets of Legalist philosophy. These are stated in the book which bears his name and, even if there is little of this work that Lord Shang himself composed, much in it accords with his thought.[28] Han Fei Tzu was a scholar of the succeeding

[23] He was in fact a pupil of the great Legalist writer Han Fei Tzu. There are translations of Hsün Tzu's writings by H. H. Dubs (*The Works of Hsüntze*, repr. Taipei, 1973) and B. Watson (*Hzün Tzu, Basic Writings*, New York, 1963). There is also a translation of his chapter on Kingly Government by Y. P. Mei, (1970) 8 *Tsing Hua Journal of Chinese Studies* 36.

[24] Cf. the versions of the relevant passage by Dubs (p. 123), Watson (p. 35), and Mei (p. 62). Cf. also Ames, *Art of Rulership*, p. 123 and the passage translated by Ch'u, *Law and Society*, p. 257.

[25] Cf. for example the list of rules given to illustrate the king's law (Watson, p. 43; Dubs, pp. 132 f.).

[26] Dubs, p. 142; Watson, p. 49 and Dubs, p. 194.

[27] Dubs, pp. 194 f. Cf. also the remarks of the same author in *Hsüntze, The Moulder of Ancient Confucianism* (repr. Taipei, 1966), pp. 265 f.

[28] For Lord Shang and his *Book*, see J. J. L. Duyvendak (tr.), *The Book of Lord Shang* (London, 1928).

century—he died in 233 BC—who belonged to the princely house of the state of Han. Without political influence, he achieved the most thorough and mature theoretical statement of the Legalist position.[29]

Both Lord Shang and Han Fei Tzu advocate a form of government in which moral guidance or virtuous conduct on the part of the ruler plays no part. Indeed so far from being held beneficial these qualities are represented as a positive source of harm for the conduct of government. The reason for so decisive a repudiation of the orthodox Confucian perspective lies in the Legalist objective. This was at all costs to secure and strengthen the power of the state and its ruler, an objective that necessitated a channelling of the energies of the people into the pursuit of agriculture and war. People, the Legalists considered, would not voluntarily engage in such hard and dangerous activities. They needed to be induced by means of punishments and rewards. Hence the Legalists advocated as the centre-piece of government a system of laws establishing punishments and rewards to be applied universally and impartially by the ruler.

The version of Legalism found in the *Book of Lord Shang* is cruder than that propounded by Han Fei Tzu. Lord Shang more or less uses the terms for 'law' and 'punishment' interchangeably and, although he contemplates also the use of rewards, it is clear that he places the greater faith in punishments. He argues that even the lightest offence should be heavily punished on the ground that if punishments are made severe enough the ruler will in the end be able to dispense with punishment altogether.[30] From this it appears that the sole object of punishment for Lord Shang was to deter people from acting in ways contrary to the interests of the state and the ruler. However the *Book* holds that law should not be merely a statement of the ruler's wishes with regard to punishments and rewards. It recognizes that the system of rewards and punishments can only work effectively if it is applied impartially and rigorously by the ruler once it has been established, and not changed at random to suit his whim.[31] This statement of the position represents more a desideratum of good government than a rule of constitutional law. If a ruler chooses to act in an arbitrary fashion and disregard the laws established by himself or his predecessors he may be acting foolishly and may in the end lose his position, but he cannot be said to be acting unlawfully.

Han Fei Tzu's treatment is somewhat more sophisticated than Lord Shang's but the same basic themes recur. Law is conceived as a system of rewards and punishments designed to promote conduct beneficial to the state. At the same time some of his definitions appear to allow for the fact

[29] His works are translated in W. K. Liao, *Han Fei Tzu. Works from the Chinese*, vol. I (London, 1939), vol. II (London, 1959).

[30] Duyvendak, *Book of Lord Shang*, pp. 203 f.

[31] Duyvendak, op. cit., p. 317.

that a rule of law is not exclusively a rule which imposes a punishment or provides a reward.[32] The fact that punishments should be definite and heavy is stressed.[33] Their deterrent function is seen as the most important although Han Fei Tzu seems to admit that those who do not obey the laws themselves deserve to be punished.[34] Even more than Lord Shang he stresses the need for the ruler to abide by the law, neither distorting its provisions nor at random changing them.[35]

With the fall of the Ch'in empire Legalism as a political ideology lost the battle to Confucianism. Orthodox official thought again stressed the importance of moral guidance on the part of the ruler. In fact, however, Legalist doctrine was to some extent applied in the practice of the Confucian administrators of the Han and later empires. Not that these administrators advocated a set of punishments and rewards in order to promote agriculture and war, but they did increasingly use the penal codes to control areas of behaviour deemed suitable for state intervention, including some treated as important by Confucian moral theory.[36] With successive dynasties the penal codes became more elaborate and comprehensive.

If, on the basis of this admittedly highly summary account of the traditional Chinese 'legal mind', one compares it with the Western 'legal mind' (that aspect outlined in the first part of this paper) what conclusions can be stated? In the first place the traditional Chinese view of law was dominated, rather more so than the Western, by a political perspective. Interest was directed not to the nature of law as such but to the use which the ruler should make of law. Attention was thus focused on the role of law *vis-à-vis* that of moral guidance in the government of the state. This contrast naturally led to emphasis being placed on the coercive aspect of law. The people might either be induced voluntarily to follow the right behaviour or be compelled through the threat of punishment so to do. Given the theme which occupied Chinese political discussion for centuries, namely the relationship between ruler and people and their respective rights and duties, law as distinct from moral guidance could by and large be seen only as rules prescribing the people's behaviour established by the ruler and made effective not through persuasion or teaching but through the threat of punishment. Despite the occurrence of rewards in Legalist thought it was clearly punishment which thinkers of both schools saw as the cornerstone or hallmark of law.

[32] Cf. Liao, *Han Fei Tzu*, vol. I, p. 166 ('The ruler makes laws so as to establish the standard of right'), vol. II, p. 188 (the latter passage also translated in W. T. Chan, *A Source Book in Chinese Philosophy* (Princeton, 1963), p. 256 and Hsiao, *Chinese Political Thought*, p. 397).

[33] Liao, vol. I, pp. 282 f., vol. II, pp. 242 f.

[34] Liao, vol. II, p. 243.

[35] Liao, vol. I, pp. 135, 138, 140.

[36] Cf. K. Bunger, 'Die Rechtsidee in der chinesischen Geschichte', (1953) 3 *Saeculum* 204 f.

Another factor responsible for the emphasis on coercion and punishment in traditional Chinese thinking about law was the conceptions held of the task of the ruler. For Legalists the ruler should primarily be concerned with strengthening the position of his state *vis-à-vis* other states through the promotion of agriculture and war. Achievement of this task necessitated rigorous application of a policy of coercion towards his subjects, a policy implemented through the law. Confucianists, although not directed in so single-minded a fashion to the strengthening of the power of the state, still held a somewhat restricted conception of the ruler's task. Apart from defence of the state against foreign enemies he was responsible for the maintenance of good order within it, and in particular for the suppression of murderers, thieves, and bandits generally. Furthermore it was conceived proper for him to make enforceable through the provision of punishments certain aspects of Confucian morality such as the rules governing marriage and mourning for the death of relatives. In other words, both Legalists and Confucianists held that the ruler should rejoin or prohibit certain forms of behaviour and should use punishments or rewards in order to achieve this. They did not regard the ruler as having a direct interest in, or responsibility for, matters of contract, succession, and property. Where for some reason he intervenes in these areas he does so by making certain behaviour enforceable through the threat of punishment.

There is no analysis of punishment of the kind familiar from Western writing, though a considerable amount of information is given on the correct way to use punishment and on the conditions under which it should be imposed. No distinction between punishments and other penalties appears to have been drawn. As one would expect the Confucianist and Legalist perspectives are very different. Legalists push to the extreme the deterrent and coercive aspects of punishment. They consider it advisable to impose a severe punishment even for a trifling offence on the ground that an effectively applied regime of severe punishment will eventually produce a situation in which recourse to punishment ceases to be necessary. People will have been successfully coerced into following the prescribed behaviour and deviance will no longer occur. Although Legalists reject the view that the amount of punishment should be proportional to the gravity of the offence, as also the view that intention is a relevant factor in determining the degree of punishment, they do admit, indeed stress, one aspect of justice in punishment. This is the fact that punishments should be consistently and impartially applied. However the reason for their insistence is not an abstract concern for justice but the need to produce an effective system of deterrence and coercion. Unless the ruler is seen to punish consistently and impartially in accordance with the law the people will not be effectively driven to engage in the appropriate behaviour.

Confucianists also emphasize the coercive and deterrent function of punishment. Although they prefer moral guidance and persuasion as an instrument of government they accept that punishment is the only means by which the really depraved can be induced to refrain from wrongdoing. However, in contrast to the Legalists, they themselves and the current of thinking upon which they drew paid attention to the equity of punishment in the individual case. Less serious offences should not receive the same punishment as the more serious, and, in particular, inadvertent offences should be punished less heavily than intentional. One can see here an element of retributive thinking added to the general conception of deterrence. Both the Legalist and the Confucian approaches can, of course, find their echoes in Western treatments of punishment.

Concentration upon law's political role meant that analysis of the nature of law itself was neglected. Scholars were not interested in studying the varieties of legal rules, nor in analysing abstractly the relationship between a rule and its sanction or the nature or proper function of punishment. The codes themselves were not regarded as objects of serious study by a number of the educated Confucian élite,[37] apart from the knowledge of them which one necessarily had to have as judge or administrator. Possibly if Legalism had survived as a respectable political philosophy its adherents would have undertaken studies of this kind, but with the Confucian triumph not even a beginning seems to have been made.[38] There is rich material even within the confines of the penal codes for an investigation of the types of legal rule, the manner of formulation employed, and the ways in which the sanction related to the rule. Furthermore, the sharp contrast between the rules emanating from the central authority (whether codified or not, or penal in character or not) and the host of national or local customary rules governing the undertaking of commercial transactions, dispositions of property, and the like provides fascinating scope for general studies of the nature of law in Imperial China. But such investigations remain to be done and their results would not be ones which the traditional Chinese scholarly élite would have found familiar.[39]

[37] Cf. the remarks of P. Pelliot, 'Notes de bibliographie chinoise, ii, Le droit chinois', (1909) 9 *Bulletin de l'École Française d'Extrême-Orient* 123.

[38] One has to allow for the possibility that works now lost contained theoretical and analytical legal studies.

[39] I should like to thank Professor Neil MacCormick for generous help with the preparation of this paper.

15

The Formation of the Scottish Legal Mind in the Eighteenth Century: Themes of Humanism and Enlightenment in the Admission of Advocates*

JOHN W. CAIRNS

On 25 January 1854 the Faculty of Advocates established a committee to consider and report on 'The Qualification of Intrants'. When presented, the committee's report, dated 11 July 1854, noted that intrants had to satisfy three requirements for admission as an advocate. The first was to show a knowledge of Latin as a test of general scholarship. This was examined by requiring the intrant to read aloud a passage of the Digest *ad aperturam libri*. The committee commented that this 'ensures but slight acquaintance with the Latin language'. Next, there were examinations in Civil Law and Scots Law, but—stated the committee—these had 'degenerated into nearly a formal proceeding' and could be passed 'by persons whose study of the subjects of Civil and of Scotch jurisprudence has not been great'. The committee reserved its greatest scorn for the third qualification: the preparation of a Latin thesis upon a title of the Digest. The committee said of this thesis that, 'written as it is, in very many cases, by others than the person whose name it bears, it is no test of the scholarship of its professed author, and tends somewhat to throw ridicule upon the whole of the Faculty examinations.'[1] Such criticisms were not new. In 1818 the Professor of Logic and Rhetoric in the University of Glasgow, George Jardine, in an influential work on educational method and theory, had stated that the Faculty's examinations rendered 'the study of the law altogether nugatory'.[2] In 1826 in evidence before a Royal Commission investigating the Scottish

* Much of this paper derives from study of the records of the Faculty of Advocates, and I am most grateful for the courtesy of permission to examine and to cite them. I have benefited much from the comments of Peter Birks, John MacLean, and Hector MacQueen, on an earlier draft.

[1] J. Lorimer, *The Universities of Scotland Past, Present, and Possible: With an Appendix of Documents Relating to the Higher Instruction* (Edinburgh, 1854), appendix A, pp. 1–2.

[2] G. Jardine, *Outlines of Philosophical Education, Illustrated by the Method of Teaching the Logic Class in the University of Glasgow* (2nd edn., Glasgow, 1825), p. 462.

universities, Thomas Thomson, a member of the Faculty, Deputy Clerk Register, and a noted scholar, had said the examinations were 'too slight to afford anything like a test of actual advancement',[3] and the Whig advocate and one of the founders of the *Edinburgh Review*, Francis Jeffrey, had merely commented that the Faculty's examination was a 'farce'.[4]

While in 1854 the Faculty's committee thought that for two centuries there had been a general continuity in desired admission requirements,[5] it seems, on the contrary, that in the course of the eighteenth century a crucial change took place, whereby the Faculty's views on the necessary qualifications of an advocate markedly shifted from a Humanist-inspired overwhelming, stress on examination in Civil Law as valuable and sufficient in itself, to a rationalist and Enlightenment emphasis both on proof of polite learning (in the sense of polished and civilized knowledge) and on examinations in Civil and Scots Laws, now viewed as prerequisites for practice. It is impossible to fix any precise date for this change in attitude, not only because elements and themes from Humanism and Enlightenment could be present together, but also because many of the Enlightenment emphases grew out of Humanism, even if they came to take on a new meaning in the changing circumstances of Scottish life. Despite there being obvious difficulty in relating specific events to major cultural movements—which are not, in any case, monolithic—to approach the changing views on the admission of advocates from the perspectives of Humanism and Enlightenment does provide a basic and useful interpretative framework for understanding them.[6] It may be added that many of the proposals put forward in the eighteenth century were only to be fully worked out in the very different context of nineteenth-century professionalism,[7] and this paper, therefore, will not deal with the finally effective reforms (although events

[3] *Report of the Royal Commission of Inquiry into the Universities of Scotland, Minutes of Evidence vol. I. University of Edinburgh*, 1837 PP XXXV, p. 405.

[4] Ibid., p. 394.

[5] Lorimer, appendix A, pp. 19–20.

[6] Obviously the picture to be presented here lacks an appropriate sociological dimension. The following works usefully point to ways forward in this respect; J. S. Shaw, *The Management of Scottish Society 1707–1764* (Edinburgh, 1983), pp. 18–40: N. T. Phillipson, 'Lawyers, Landowners, and the Civic Leadership of Post-Union Scotland', in D. N. MacCormick (ed.), *Lawyers in their Social Setting* (Edinburgh, 1976), pp. 171–94, and 'The Social Structure of the Faculty of Advocates in Scotland 1660–1840', in A. Harding (ed.) *Law Making and Law Makers in British History* (Royal Historical Society, 22, London, 1980), pp. 146–56; A. Murdoch, '*The People Above*': *Politics and Administration in Mid-Eighteenth Century Scotland* (Edinburgh, 1980), pp. 52–62, and 'The Advocates, the Law and the Nation in Early Modern Scotland', in W. Prest (ed.), *Lawyers in Early Modern Europe and America* (London, 1981), pp. 147–63; and P. S. Lachs, 'Scottish Legal Education in the Nineteenth Century', in E. W. Ives and A. H. Manchester (edd.), *Law, Litigants and the Legal Profession* (Royal Historical Society, 36, London, 1983), pp. 155–61. R. Cocks, *Foundations of the Modern Bar* (London, 1983) indicates the kind of work that could be done.

[7] See, e.g., Lorimer, appendix A, pp. 48–58 and, more generally, M. S. Larson, *The Rise of Professionalism: A Sociological Analysis* (Berkeley, 1977).

after 1800 and before 1700 will be discussed to some extent, as not to do so would be arbitrary and artificial).[8]

Changes in admission requirements could initially seem a rather narrow topic; but not only do they relate to wider intellectual issues in early modern Scotland, they are also an important part of the history of the formation of the legal mind, even if the conclusions here may tend to the tentative.

I

The qualifications for admission as an advocate at the start of the eighteenth century were set out by Spottiswoode and Forbes.[9] There were two modes of entry. The first was by trial on Civil Law. Such an intrant, after petitioning the Lords of Session for admission, was referred by them to the Dean of the Faculty of Advocates for both a private and a public examination in Latin on Civil Law. After succeeding in such examinations, the intrant read a lesson on Civil Law to the Lords and was thereafter admitted. This procedure was first clearly established by an Act of Sederunt of 1664,[10] solicited from the Lords of Session by the Faculty[11] and confirmed by the Lords in 1688.[12] The private examination took place before a number of elected examiners, and the public examination, on a specific title of the Civil Law, before the entire Faculty. From 1669 the examiners were always appointed at the Faculty's anniversary meeting in January.[13] On 17 December 1692 the Faculty considered further proposals on the public trial and decided that in future intrants should print and publish theses and corollaries to be impugned by any member of the Faculty. The Lords were to be informed of this, and a number of advocates were to consider and report on the topic to the first meeting of the Faculty in January 1693. The Dean was to draw up the necessary act.[14] On 3 January 1693 the Faculty accordingly agreed on an act whereby, after the private

[8] Lord Macmillan, *A Man of Law's Tale* (London, 1952), pp. 25–33, gives the details of admission in the late 19c.

[9] J. Spottiswoode, *The Form of Process Before the Lords of Council and Session* (2nd edn., Edinburgh, 1718), pp. xliii–xlvi; W. Forbes, *A Journal of the Session Containing the Decisions of the Lords of Council and Session* (Edinburgh, 1714), p. viii. Spottiswoode held a private 'college' of laws in Edinburgh at the start of the 18c. Forbes was the first appointee to the Glasgow chair in law.

[10] R. K. Hannay, *The College of Justice: Essays on the Institution and Development of the Court of Session* (Edinburgh, 1933), p. 153.

[11] *The Minute Book of the Faculty of Advocates, 1661–1712 and 1712–1750*, ed. J. M. Pinkerton (2 vols., Stair Society, 29 and 32, Edinburgh 1976 and 1980), vol. i, pp. 8–9 (2 and 9 July 1664 and 7 Nov. 1664).

[12] *The Acts of Sederunt of the Lords of Council and Session, from the 15th of January 1553, to the 11th of July 1790* (Edinburgh, 1790), p. 181 (6 July 1688).

[13] *Minute Book*, vol. i, p. 19 n. 6.

[14] Ibid., vol. i, p. 119.

examination, the Dean was to assign to intrants a title of Civil Law for such printed theses and corollaries, which were to be defended in Latin in the public examination. The Dean and the private examiners were to oversee the writing of the theses and any member of Faculty could impugn them, though the Dean was specially to appoint for this task six or seven members of Faculty who were to be unknown to the intrant.[15] On 19 November 1698 the Faculty decided that the function of censuring and revising intrants' theses before printing, to ensure no error or incongruity of style and matter, was to be given solely to the Curators of the Library, the Clerk, and the Library Keeper.[16] The Faculty introduced further changes on 22 March 1707, when it determined to replace the nomination of six or seven public examiners by the Dean with an election at its anniversary meeting. Public examiners were authorized to examine candidates generally on their assigned titles.[17] The lesson before the Lords was an early requirement.[18] From 1680, if not before, the practice was for the Dean to assign a law from the title on which an intrant had been publicly examined as the subject of this lesson.[19] This practice continued after the introduction of the printed theses.

The second mode of entry was by trial on Scots Law and applied to candidates who were admitted 'extraordinarily' upon a bill. Originally candidates who entered by bill were not examined at all; but on the prompting of the Faculty[20] the Lords issued an Act of Sederunt on 6 July 1688 which required that in future any admitted on a bill should be examined by the Lords on their knowledge of Scots or Municipal Law.[21] On 25 June 1692 the Lords issued a new Act by which such intrants on a bill were to be remitted to the Dean and Faculty for trial on Scots Law.[22] Initially there was only a public examination on Scots Law, and the *Minutes* give no clear indication of how it was carried out;[23] but on 15 January 1696 the Faculty decided that in future there would be both a private and a public examination for intrants on Scots Law. Two or more advocates were accordingly to be added to the private examiners. The Dean was to assign one or more titles of Scots Law to the intrant for the public examination, which was to be conducted exactly like the public examination in Civil Law, except that

[15] Ibid., vol. i, p. 121. On 6 Jan. 1694 (ibid., vol. i, p. 130) the Faculty decided that intrants should have notice of who these public examiners would be.

[16] *Minute Book*, vol. i, p. 190.

[17] Ibid., vol. i, p. 268. See also ibid., vol. i, p. 207 (1 Feb. 1700), where first is determined the extent of the permitted questioning.

[18] Hannay, pp. 142–3. Hannay suggests that some public lessons related to instruction; I am inclined to doubt this.

[19] *Minute Book*, vol. i, p. 51 (11 Dec. 1680) and see n. 2 thereon.

[20] Ibid., vol. i, p. 85 (5 June 1688).

[21] *Acts of Sederunt*, p. 181.

[22] Ibid., p. 200.

[23] *Minute Book*, vol. i, pp. 115–16 (2 July 1692) and 117 (8 and 23 July 1692).

no theses were to be printed.[24] Such intrants did not read a lesson before the Lords.

These two modes of entry found some precedent in earlier practices for admission, and their regularization in the late seventeenth century undoubtedly was part of the advocates' search for greater corporate status, noted for that period by Hannay.[25] With some adjustments and fine tuning,[26] this system remained in operation until 1750. It may be added that initially the titles for theses appear to have been allocated randomly to intrants from the whole *Corpus Iuris Civilis*; but from 1717 the titles, with only few exceptions, were given out in sequence for theses. The sequence started with the Institutes, and after its titles were exhausted, moved on to the Digest. While the Faculty's minutes do not explain this change in distributing titles, it shows an efficient and logical method which avoided duplication. According to Professor Honoré's own interesting arguments, the compilers of these very titles would have been sympathetic to such an economical and direct approach.

Both Spottiswoode and Forbes stated that to enter by trial on Civil Law was more honourable.[27] This provides a key to understanding the procedures established in the late seventeenth century. Entry by bill was tainted with suspicions of judicial favouritism. Thus an Act of Sederunt of 24 November 1691 forbade admission by bill of close relatives of judges;[28] this was repeated in the Act of 1692 already referred to.[29] Those who entered by bill need not have undertaken the lengthy and expensive study of Civil Law, usually abroad, which was considered likely to ensure that the intrant's 'breeding' was 'more liberall and worthy'.[30] The Act of 1688 accordingly required the Lords of Session to be well informed of the 'integrity and honest deportment'[31] of intrants by bill, and that of 1692 required the Lords to be 'well informed of the person's integrity, good-breeding, honest deportment and fitness for exerceing the office of ane advocate'.[32] No such requirements of fitness were made of intrants by examination on Civil Law.

It seems rather curious that ordinary intrants were not tested on Scots Law at all. The Act of 1692 does talk of 'the ordinar tryall' as being 'both

[24] Ibid., vol. i, pp. 164–5.

[25] Hannay, pp. 135–64.

[26] e.g., *Minute Book*, vol. i, pp. 185, 190, 207, 209 and 268. It has not seemed worthwhile to pursue the minutiae of development.

[27] Spottiswoode, p. xlv: 'The *Admission* by a *Trial* on the civil Law is looked to be the most honourable, and makes the *Intrant* to be more respected, than those who pass upon *Scots* Law.' Forbes, p. viii.

[28] *Acts of Sederunt*, p. 195.

[29] Ibid., p. 200.

[30] J. Lauder, Lord Fountainhall, *Historical Notices of Scottish Affairs, Selected from the Manuscripts of Sir John Lauder* (2 vols., Bannatyne Club, Edinburgh, 1848), vol. ii, p. 464.

[31] *Acts of Sederunt*, p. 181.

[32] Ibid., p. 200.

in our law and the civill law';[33] but there is no evidence that there was in fact an examination on Scots Law for such intrants, and Spottiswoode is quite definite on the point.[34] In practice, no doubt many, if not all, ordinary intrants would have studied Scots Law from books and attended the courts and the consultations of advocates, and a number seem to have spent time in the chambers of writers to the Signet;[35] but the lack of any examination of them on Scots Law is none the less striking, especially when, given the trial on Scots Law of intrants by bill, it must have been conceivable—and indeed possible—to examine all intrants on it. Examination on Civil Law alone must have had a value quite outwith any consideration that learning in Civil Law was a prerequisite for a knowledge of Scots Law adequate for practice, for otherwise all intrants should have undergone such examination. The explanation must be sought elsewhere.

I would suggest that the advocates' stress on education in Civil Law is related to the Humanist culture of late seventeenth-century Scotland, and the advocates' vision of their place within that culture as a *universitas* of learned men. It was a culture much concerned with questions of honour, precedency and status. Scottish Humanism has been studied mainly from the perspective of literature:[36] the role of law in it has been little attended to.[37] It is associated with figures such as Pitcairne, Sibbald, Mackenzie of Rosehaugh and, in the eighteenth century, Ruddiman.[38] I do not wish here to discuss Humanism generally, or even its Scottish variant; but it may be

[33] Ibid.

[34] Spottiswoode, pp. xliii–xliv. Perhaps the Act was alluding to the practice of intrants having studied the 'practick' before admission, and so narrating in their petitions for admission. Hannay, pp. 143–7.

[35] See, e.g., *Journal of the Hon. John Erskine of Carnock*, ed. W. MacLeod, (Scottish History Society, 14, Edinburgh, 1893), pp. xix–xx, and Lord Kames, reported in *Private Papers of James Boswell from Malahide Castle*, ed. G. Scott and F. A. Pottle (18 vols., privately printed, New York, 1928–34), vol. xv, p. 269.

[36] e.g., D. Duncan, *Thomas Ruddiman, A Study in Scottish Scholarship of the Early Eighteenth Century* (Edinburgh, 1965); J. MacQueen, *Progress and Poetry* (Edinburgh, 1982), pp. 1–41; and F. W. Freeman, *Robert Fergusson and the Scots Humanist Compromise* (Edinburgh, 1984).

[37] With honourable exceptions: see H. Ouston, 'York in Edinburgh: James VII and the Patronage of Learning in Scotland, 1679–1688', in J. Dwyer, R. A. Mason and A. Murdoch (edd.), *New Perspectives on the Politics and Culture of Early Modern Scotland* (Edinburgh, 1982), pp. 133–55 at 144–9, and A. J. MacLean, 'Mackenzie and Scottish Criminal Law', unpublished paper read to the Scottish Legal History Group, Edinburgh, 13 Oct. 1984. I am much indebted to the insights of Mr MacLean's paper in particular.

[38] Archibald Pitcairne and Sir Robert Sibbald were prominent physicians and Episcopalians (Sibbald briefly became a Roman Catholic). Sibbald was instrumental in the foundation of the Royal College of Physicians in Edinburgh. Pitcairne wrote Latin poetry (including an elegy on Sir George Mackenzie). See, e.g., Ouston, and Duncan, *passim*. Sir George Mackenzie of Rosehaugh is too well known to require introduction. A. Lang, *Sir George Mackenzie* (London, 1909) is unfortunately out of date. A new biography of this major figure is much wanted. For Thomas Ruddiman, see Duncan's biography (n. 36, above). Ruddiman was a noted literary scholar and Latinist; he eventually took charge of the Advocates' Library.

said that its focus on an attempt to gain a proper understanding of the ancient world through philological and historical analysis, in order to apply knowledge thereby gained to the contemporary world, contained a paradox for legal studies. Philological analysis of Civil Law revealed its historical origin and its contingency as the law of a specific people and time;[39] yet Humanism also stressed the continued applicability of Civil Law as a system of universal law, and it remained, with Canon Law, the sole object of legal study in European universities until towards the end of the seventeenth century.[40] Gennaro, in his significantly entitled *Respublica Jurisconsultorum* (1731), said of Roman Law that: 'unlike the laws of other peoples, it is not restricted by the limits of need and mere nature. Only the Romans are discovered to have invented so many ways of giving justice to everyone.'[41] In 1689 Sir George Mackenzie, that epitome of Scottish Humanism, in his oration on the inauguration of the Advocates' Library stated that: 'Of books on Roman Law, pride of place must be given to the text itself and its various editions, since on it both our calling and our library are based. It is a divine achievement, which we owe more to Heaven than to Rome, vouchsafed to us on earth to be a pattern to legislators and an arbiter among the races of men.'[42] Scots lawyers, drawing on the other aspect of legal Humanism, had, however, no difficulty in distinguishing clearly between Scots and Civil Law,[43] and in a very well-known passage Mackenzie commented: 'I love equally ill to hear Civil Law spoke to in the terms of a Stile Book or accidental Latin (as is most ordinary) as to hear the genuin

[39] As ever, the work of Alan Watson has been most enlightening and stimulating in developing this line of thought on the significance of Humanism, and I am considerably indebted to it: A. Watson, *The Making of the Civil Law* (Cambridge, Mass., 1981), pp. 72–7. See also J. G. A. Pocock, *The Ancient Constitution and the Feudal Law* (Cambridge, 1957), pp. 1–29, 70–123; J. H. Franklin, *Jean Bodin and the Sixteenth-Century Revolution in the Methodology of Law and History* (New York, 1963), pp. 18–58; D. R. Kelley, *Foundations of Modern Historical Scholarship: Language, Law, and History in the French Renaissance* (New York, 1970). The work of Hotman was especially important in this respect: Watson, *Making of the Civil Law*, pp. 73–6; Kelley, *François Hotman: A Revolutionary's Ordeal* (Princeton, 1973), pp. 183–97.

[40] See C. Chêne. *L'Enseignement du Droit Français en Pays de Droit Ecrit (1679–1793)* (Geneva, 1982), pp. 1–7; J. W. Cairns, 'Institutional Writings in Scotland Reconsidered', in A. Kiralfy and H. L. MacQueen (edd.), *New Perspectives in Scottish Legal History*, (London, 1984), pp. 76–117, and 'Blackstone, an English Institutist: Legal Literature and the Rise of the Nation State', (1984) 4 *Oxford Journal of Legal Studies*, 318–60 for the general background.

[41] G. Gennaro, *La République des Jurisconsultes*, tr. Dinouart (Paris, 1768), p. 14. This was the only edition available to me. I decided to translate Dinouart's translation, though aware of the possibility of adding a different layer of meaning to Gennaro's words, as it did not seem particularly useful to quote him in French.

[42] G. Mackenzie, *Oratio Inauguralis* (Edinburgh, 1689), trans. J. H. Loudun, (1946) 2 *Transactions of the Edinburgh Bibliographical Society*, 273–84 at 278.

[43] J. Dalrymple, Viscount Stair, *Institutions of the Law of Scotland* (Edinburgh, 1981), pp. 80, 85–9 (1.1.12, 16), and Mackenzie, *Institutions of the Law of Scotland* (Edinburgh, 1688), 1.1, *passim*.

words of our Municipal Law forced to express the phrases of the Civil Law and Doctors.'[44]

Examination on and learning in Civil Law allowed the advocates to consider themselves members of a pan-European legal culture, a *Respublica Jurisconsultorum*. The trials of intrants in Civil Law closely corresponded to the examinations and laureation procedures of contemporary European universities. The Act of Faculty regulating public trial by printed theses stated that this mode of examination was 'observed amongst other nationes' and that it would 'add to the honor of the society ... if the said publict tryall shall proceid in the same way and method as is practised abroad'.[45] Experience of the universities of the Netherlands must have influenced the Faculty here. The foundation of the Advocates' Library and the attempts to establish a professor of law in Edinburgh[46] were other aspects of the advocates' conception of themselves as a learned body equivalent to a university. Since the advocates hoped that the foundation of one or two chairs of law would obviate the necessity of study abroad, and might even attract foreign students, and since they considered the possibility of acquiring professors from abroad, it may be inferred that the chair or chairs were to be, at the very least, mainly and substantially devoted to Civil Law.[47] One bred in Civil Law was considered necessarily well bred or educated, as Civil Law studies were thought to encompass the totality of knowledge and ensure in themselves a complete liberal education. The *Gloss* of the thirteenth century had argued that it was unnecessary for lawyers to study theology because theology was included in the Civil Law. This attitude survived Humanism, and Kelley comments that, 'the study of law, more than any other field, represented an encyclopedia, a total *Weltanschauung*' for jurists.[48] The Faculty adopted this view when on 24 December 1695, in its proposals for erecting a chair or chairs of law, it commented that: 'The professione of the laws carys necessarly with it all the belles Letres and the knowledge of ancient and modern history'.[49] Examination of intrants in Civil Law was not related to the main requirements of practice at the Scots bar, which was then largely devoted to the property concerns of the landed

[44] Mackenzie, 'What Eloquence is fit for the Bar', *Pleadings in Some Remarkable Cases* (Edinburgh, 1673), p. 17.

[45] *Minute Book*, vol. i, p. 121 (3 Jan. 1693).

[46] Hannay, pp. 135–64.

[47] *Minute Book*, vol. i, pp. 65–6 (12 Jan. 1684), and 159–60 (24 Dec. 1695). That there were to be two chairs could suggest that one might be devoted to Municipal Law, and there is some circumstantial evidence to support this. On the other hand, it could be that one professor was to teach the Institutes and the other the Pandects (later there were to be separate courses on these in Edinburgh and Glasgow). It is impossible to be certain; but what is quite definite is that Civil Law teaching was what concerned the Faculty.

[48] Kelley, *The Beginning of Ideology: Consciousness and Society in the French Reformation* (Cambridge, 1981), p. 186.

[49] *Minute Book*, vol. i, p. 160.

classes, areas of practice where the law was not particularly, if at all, Roman in origin.[50] This said, it cannot be denied that areas of Scots Law had been Romanized by 1700, nor that Civil Law at the start of the eighteenth century could still play, and apparently was to play, a creative role in Scots Law.[51] In this context, the advocates' stress on Civil Law could be seen as linked to practice at the bar. While the emphasis on examination in Civil Law is plausibly to be connected with the continuing reception and influence of Roman Law in Scots Law, it is quite clear that the reason for examining most intrants only on Civil Law was not a practical one. The advocates' trials on Civil Law certainly promoted advantageously 'the advancement of the knowledge of the comon [i.e. Civil] law' among the Faculty;[52] but the advantage did not derive from the fact that Civil Law was potentially a usable source for Scots Law. Had this been so, all advocates should have been tried on Civil Law, and, indeed, *a fortiori* on Scots Law; the advantage rather was that study of Civil Law guaranteed the advocates' profession as a liberal art and ensured that the Faculty was an honourable society. On the other hand, admission by trial on Scots Law was positively discouraged by the requirement to pay twice the fees exacted from intrants in Civil Law;[53] and Fountainhall noted a number of intrants and advocates admitted by bill who claimed they would rather resign their gowns than pay the high fees.[54] The evidence put forward by Shaw indicates that advocates entered overwhelmingly by trial on Civil Law: of the 295 who were admitted between 1707 and 1750, 260 were tried on Civil Law, while the trials of the remainder are unknown[55] (which does not necessarily mean they were tried on Scots Law).

Though the regulations for admission did not change until 1750, the Humanism that gave meaning to trial exclusively on Civil Law lost ground in the early years of the eighteenth century.[56] Though it is inexpedient here to enter into an account of the origins and nature of the Scottish

[50] Consider the oft-quoted description by W. Eccles, *An Historical Account of the Rights and Privileges of the Royal College of Physicians and of the Incorporation of Surgeons in Edinburgh* (Edinburgh, 1707), p. 14, of the Court of Session as 'the Land-Mercat Club'. See also Phillipson, 'Lawyers, Landowners, and the Civic Leadership of Post-Union Scotland', pp. 176–7.

[51] Though the detail of the reception of Roman Law in Scotland still needs further study, rather more than excellent beginnings are made in Watson, *Legal Transplants: An Approach to Comparative Law* (Edinburgh, 1974), pp. 36–56, and 'The Rise of Modern Scots Law', *La formazione storica del diritto moderno in Europa* (Atti del Terzi Congresso Internazionale della Società Italiana di Storia del Diritto, 3 vols., Florence, 1977), vol. iii, pp. 1167–76. Also very useful is P. Stein, 'The Influence of Roman Law on the Law of Scotland', (1963) 8 *Juridical Review* (NS) 205–45.

[52] *Minute Book*, vol. i, p. 121 (3 Jan. 1693).

[53] Spottiswoode, p. xlv.

[54] Fountainhall, vol. ii, pp. 787 and 805.

[55] Shaw, p. 27.

[56] Duncan, p. 147.

Enlightenment,[57] it may be said that its roots obviously lie in the seventeenth century and beyond, there being a certain continuity of development from Humanism to Enlightenment in Scotland, and that it is connected with the political, cultural, and material changes Scottish society had undergone and was undergoing.[58] It is impossible to sum up in a few words a movement as complex as the Scottish Enlightenment; but certain themes stand out. There was a desire to explain scientifically the material and social world. Economic progress and agricultural improvement were of vital concern. History was made a discipline of major importance. While the Scottish universities had in the seventeenth century mainly been institutions for the education of the clergy, there was now a broadening of curricula to emphasize subjects which promoted polite learning and civic virtue.[59] At the same time, and plausibly linked with these strands in the Enlightenment, changes in Scots Law and legal culture were under way. Chairs teaching Scots Law and Civil Law were established in Glasgow and Edinburgh.[60] The origins of feudalism in Scotland and the significance of the *Regiam Majestatem* were debated and disputed.[61] Scots Law had been reduced to an intelligible system in the writings of Stair and Mackenzie.[62] Even before

[57] I do not intend to suggest that Scotland earlier was 'unenlightened': G. Donaldson, 'Stair's Scotland: the Intellectual Inheritance', (1981) 26 *Juridical Review* (NS) 128–45.

[58] Out of a growing but varied literature I have found useful: J. Clive, 'The Social Background of the Scottish Renaissance', in N. T. Phillipson and R. Mitchison (edd.), *Scotland in the Age of Improvement* (Edinburgh, 1970), pp. 225–44; Phillipson, 'Towards a Definition of the Scottish Enlightenment', in P. Fritz and D. Williams (edd.), *City and Society in the 18th Century* (Toronto, 1973), pp. 125–47, and 'Culture and Society in the 18th Century Province: The Case of Edinburgh and the Scottish Enlightenment', in L. Stone (ed.), *The University in Society* (2 vols., London, 1975), vol. ii, pp. 407–48; MacQueen, pp. 1–41; and the essays in R. H. Campbell and A. S. Skinner (edd.), *Origins and Nature of the Scottish Enlightement* (Edinburgh, 1982).

[59] R. G. Cant, 'The Scottish Universities and Scottish Society in the Eighteenth Century', (1967) 57 *Studies on Voltaire and the Eighteenth Century*, 1953–66, and 'Origins of the Enlightenment in Scotland: the Universities', in *Origins and Nature of the Scottish Enlightenment*, pp. 42–64; P. Jones, 'The Polite Academy and the Presbyterians, 1720–1770', in *Politics and Culture of Early Modern Scotland*, pp. 156–78 and 'The Scottish Professoriate and the Polite Academy, 1720–46', in I. Hont and M. Ignatieff (edd.), *Wealth and Virtue: the Shaping of Political Economy in the Scottish Enlightenment* (Cambridge, 1983), pp. 89–117. Instructive in this respect are the emphases on certain courses and their content in 'A Short Account of the University of Edinburgh, the Present Professors in it, and the Several Parts of Learning Taught by Them', (Aug. 1741) 3 *The Scots Magazine*, 371–4: see Jones, 'The Scottish Professoriate', p. 97.

[60] J. Coutts, *A History of the University of Glasgow* (Glasgow, 1909), pp. 193–4, and A. Grant, *The Story of the University of Edinburgh during its First Three Hundred Years* (2 vols., London, 1884), vol. i, pp. 283–90.

[61] See, e.g., H. Home, Lord Kames, *Essays upon Several Subjects Concerning British Antiquities* (Edinburgh, 1747), pp. 1–25; A. MacDouall, Lord Bankton, *An Institute of the Law of Scotland in Civil Rights* (3 vols., Edinburgh, 1751–53), vol. i, pp. 13–19, 29–32, 38–9, and D. Dalrymple, Lord Hailes, *Annals of Scotland* (3 vols., 3rd edn., Edinburgh, 1819), vol. iii, pp. 275–326. These debates deserve further study.

[62] Stair, *Institutions* (Edinburgh, 1681) and Mackenzie, *Institutions* (Edinburgh, 1684). See n. 43 above for current editions.

Montesquieu formulated such ideas in a coherent, theoretical way,[63] Scots considered their law to be particularly suited and adapted to the 'genius' of the Scottish people.[64] Furthermore, after 1750 or thereabouts, the practice of Scots going abroad, particularly to the Netherlands, to study law came generally to an end.[65] Though many of the general themes of the Enlightenment would only become explicit in the second half of the eighteenth century, together with the renewed stress already mentioned on the specifically Scottish aspects of Scottish legal culture, they must have tended in the long run to undermine the near-exclusive reliance on examination in Civil Law as the necessary requirement for admission as an advocate.

Given this background, it is hardly surprising that the examination of intrants came under scrutiny. As early as 1724, the Dean, Lord Advocate Robert Dundas of Arniston, proposed to the Faculty that all intrants should be examined in both Civil and Scots Law, though this proposal, while agreed in principle by the Faculty and the Lords of Session, ultimately came to nothing.[66] Dundas's proposal was based on the rational ground of 'preventing Persons entring into the Society not endowed with a sufficient Stock of Knowledge'.[67] In 1728 the Faculty considered inviting university students of Civil Law to take part in the impugning and disputing of theses to render 'the publick Examinations of Intrants more solemn'.[68] There is further evidence of dissatisfaction with the current procedures. Reflecting in 1778, Lord Kames considered that his education in law prior to his admission in 1723 had been dull and inappropriate. He had spent time in a writer's chamber and had also attended the lectures of Professor Craig on Civil Law.[69] The Faculty's examinations only required 'common mechanical preparation', which Kames neglected in pursuit of more interesting legal studies: a neglect which he told James Boswell nearly caused him to stumble at his trials.[70] Though Kames spoke with the benefit of hindsight, his comments are instructive, not only in demonstrating his attitude in 1723, but also in revealing the views held on the earlier entrance procedures and requirements by such a significant Enlightenment figure in the last quarter of the eighteenth century.

[63] C. de Montesquieu, *The Spirit of the Laws* (trans. T. Nugent, 2 vols., London, 1823), vol. i, p. 6. See Cairns, 'Institutional Writings', pp. 105–6 and 'Blackstone, an English Institutist', pp. 323–4.

[64] See, e.g., A Bayne, *Institutions of the Criminal Law of Scotland* (Edinburgh, 1730), pp. 5–6. This attitude among institutists precedes Montesquieu's famous formulation.

[65] Phillipson, 'Lawyers, Landowners, and the Civic Leadership of Post-Union Scotland', p. 194, appendix.

[66] Cairns, 'Institutional Writings', pp. 95–7.

[67] *Minute Book*, vol. ii, p. 74 (15 Feb. 1724).

[68] Ibid., vol. ii, p. 110 (2 Jan. 1728).

[69] Boswell, *Private Papers*, vol. xv, pp. 269 and 270.

[70] Ibid., vol. xv, p. 271. Kames was distracted from his preparation by deeper study of the Civil Law, including apparently the perennially popular search for interpolations.

II

In 1748 Robert Dundas of Arniston was appointed Lord President. On receiving the congratulations of the Faculty on his promotion to head the bench, he took the opportunity in returning his thanks to set out what he considered to be the educational prerequisites for admission as an advocate. He stated that 'there was no science or part of polite and useful Learning for the knowledge of which some in the Faculty were not distinguished' and he hoped that the Faculty would continue not only to be learned in Civil and Scots Law but also to maintain its reputation for the other branches of learning which were requisite for 'the Character of Gentlemen' and necessary even for the practice of an advocate's profession. He accordingly recommended the advocates to advise prospective members:

> that over and above being careful to learn thoroughly the principles of the Roman Law and the Laws of Nature and Nations they should take pains to acquire the other Sciences and accomplishments becoming the Character of Gentlemen, particularly not to neglect Academical learning, before they should apply themselves to study the municipal Laws of their Country, in order to the practice thereof. That it was more natural, yea necessary, that the Law should be the last part, not the beginning of their Studies.[71]

Lord President Dundas's remarks likely reflected the views of many members of the Faculty, and they set the tone for over fifty years' debate on the proper qualifications of an advocate. The debate focused on the relative significance of Scots and Roman Law, the importance of polite learning (Ramsay stated that Dundas while 'no polite scholar ... was far from despising polite literature'),[72] and the character of advocates as gentlemen. Dundas's views could be interpreted as a continuation and renewal of the Humanist stress of the late seventeenth century; but this seems unlikely, or only partly correct. The changing curricula of the Scottish universities would have meant that preparatory studies in 'Academical learning' would not be of a Humanist cast. Dundas, as Dean, had also been the main proposer of reform in 1724. In this respect it is notable that Dundas succeeded Duncan Forbes of Culloden, and Ramsay of Ochtertyre remarked that Forbes died 'when a new tide of opinions and manners was setting in strong'.[73]

The first move came in 1749, when it was again proposed that all intrants be examined in Scots Law as well as Civil Law. As in 1724, the grounds were rational: 'it was of the highest importance to the publick Interest of the Nation and the honour of the Faculty that the Members thereof should

[71] *Minute Book*, vol. ii, p. 225 (3 Nov. 1748).

[72] J. Ramsay, *Scotland and Scotsmen in the Eighteenth Century from the MSS. of John Ramsay, Esq. of Ochtertyre*, ed. A. Allardyce, (2 vols., Edinburgh, 1888), vol. i, p. 69.

[73] Ibid., vol. i, p. 65.

be sufficiently qualifyed for their Office' so that intrants 'should be exactly examined'. The abolition of heritable jurisdictions by the Heritable Jurisdictions (Scotland) Act 1746 (20 Geo. II. c. 43) was considered to make this reform more pressing because advocates would now be appointed to the shrieval bench.[74] This proposal was carried out, and from 1750 intrants were first to be examined privately on Civil Law, and then, after a year's elapse, to be examined privately on Scots Law. After this, the intrant was to be examined publicly by defending his printed theses on a title of the Civil Law.[75] The year's gap between the private examinations on Civil Law and Scots Law was likely intended to allow the intrant to attend university classes on Scots Law, which were normally taken after those on Civil Law.[76] Though not mentioned in the advocates' proposals, the Act of Sederunt issued by the Lords on 28 February 1750 to give effect to them also stated: 'That, in order to his public examination, the candidate shall, and may annex to his theses, such positions from the law of Scotland, in the native idiom to the subject of dispute, upon the trial, as he shall think proper ...'.[77] The spirit behind these new provisions, with their stress on the necessity of 'the regular and speedy dispatch of business' and 'the full administration, and free course of justice',[78] was radically different from that which supported the late seventeenth-century trials, with their Humanist emphasis on Civil Law.

The new admission procedures made no provision for requiring students to attend certain classes or to be qualified in polite literature and learning. In the 1750s and 1760s the Faculty tried in a number of resolutions to compel prospective intrants to attend the classes in the University of Edinburgh on Universal History, Greek and Roman Antiquities, and the Law of Nature and Nations, because 'it concerns the honour of the Faculty that their members should be versant in every part of polite literature'.[79] Given the views of the Faculty in 1695 on the benefits of establishing law chairs in Scotland, these resolutions could be seen as demonstrating a continuing Humanism; and no doubt to some extent they do. On the other hand, the new intellectual background in Scotland would give these courses a content infused with Enlightenment ideas.[80] The number of resolutions passed by the Faculty suggests that there was difficulty in enforcing them, and the

[74] *Minute Book*, vol. ii, pp. 231–2 (3 Jan. 1749).

[75] Ibid., vol. ii, pp. 239–40, 241 and 241–2. For further details of regulations, see National Library of Scotland, *FR* 2, 'Minutes of the Faculty of Advocates 1751–1783', pp. 4 and 11.

[76] Later practice shows this to have been so.

[77] *Acts of Sederunt*, pp. 450–1.

[78] Ibid.

[79] *FR* 2, pp. 84 (30 Nov. 1756), 127 (8 Jan. 1760), 147 (5 Jan. 1762), 156 (24 Nov. 1762) and 259 (19 Nov. 1768). The chair of Universal History was under the patronage of the Faculty; encouraging students would improve the earnings of the appointee.

[80] See the syllabi in the (1741) 3 *Scots Magazine* 371 and 372–3.

Faculty required the private examiners to ask intrants questions relating to these courses.

The Faculty's examinations in Civil Law were conducted in Latin, and in this period anxiety began to be expressed about the sufficiency of intrants' knowledge of the language. On 5 March 1768 the Dean and Faculty deplored Professor Millar's innovation of lecturing in English rather than Latin to the Civil Law class in Glasgow, and the Dean was requested to approach the Rector of the University of Glasgow to ask him to order Millar to end this practice.[81] On 17 January 1777, on the motion of Andrew Crosbie, the Faculty appointed a committee to consider what he had described as a great decline in knowledge of Latin among intrants and to suggest remedies.[82] Though continued on 20 December 1777, the committee does not seem to have reported; and on that date Alexander Wight, *praeses* of the last set of Civil Law examiners, stated that neither he nor his colleagues had any reason to complain of the standards of candidates' Latin.[83] Whether there had been a decline in intrants' knowledge of Latin cannot now be known, apart from, perhaps, by a study of their theses. Certainly Boswell's theses of 1766[84] were notoriously found by Johnson to contain errors. Johnson concluded his criticisms by stating: 'Ruddiman is dead.'[85] This was an apt remark on two levels. Ruddiman was a noted Latinist, and one of his tasks as Keeper of the Library and Clerk Depute of the Faculty had been to revise and censure theses.[86] At a deeper level, Johnson's remark highlights the fact that the Faculty's lingering commitment to the Humanist ideals that created the custom of printing and defending Latin theses was contradicted by the new circumstances and learning of Scotland in the later eighteenth century, whereby Civil law was to be seen as just one element in the polite learning required of intrants, rather than as the totality of polite learning. Linked with this must have been a reassessment of the general role of Civil Law in an advocate's education. The attempted reform in 1724 and the effective one of 1750 conceived of trial on Scots Law as a test of knowledge for practice: what then was the purpose of the private and public examinations in Civil Law when assessed by the same, rather than Humanist, criteria? In 1780 Kames remarked to Boswell that no one now read the commentators on Civil Law, to which Boswell responded: 'The study of

[81] *FR* 2, pp. 255–6.

[82] Ibid., p. 414.

[83] Ibid., pp. 432–3.

[84] Boswell, *Disputatio Juridica, Ad Tit. X. Lib. XXXIII. Pand. De Supellectile Legata* (Edinburgh, 1766). See F. A. Pottle, *The Literary Career of James Boswell, Esq.* (Oxford, 1929), pp. 24–6.

[85] Boswell, *Life of Johnson Together with Boswell's Journal of a Tour to the Hebrides and Johnson's Diary of a Journey into North Wales*, ed. G. B. Hill, rev. L. F. Powell, (6 vols., Oxford, 1934–50), vol. ii, p. 21.

[86] See text at n. 16, above.

Civil law is much gone out.' Kames explained that whereas Civil Law had originally been used to help settle points of Scots Law, 'a Man would be laughed at were he to quote civil law now that they are settled'.[87] The Humanism which had promoted exclusive trial on Civil Law also ultimately promoted study of local and national laws: and the new intellectual stress on Scots Law, together with the growing rationalist emphasis in trials, seems to have put at issue the purpose of the study of Civil Law for advocates, when it was no longer considered the sole means of ensuring the Faculty's status as a body of learned men, and when, judged by the new rationalist criteria, its usefulness in Scots Law was thought to have declined.

Further proposals for reform were provoked in the 1780s by a minor crisis faced by the Faculty when in 1781 John Wright petitioned for admission.[88] Wright had started life as a shoemaker in Greenock,[89] and at the time of his petition was a private teacher of law and mathematics. In the Faculty's minutes, opposition to Wright's admission was stated to be on account of his advanced age,[90] and the fear that he did not intend to practise law. Boswell reported in his *Journal*, however, that Wright's petition was opposed because he was 'of low origin and gaining his livelihood as a teacher of law and Mathematicks'.[91] After what the minutes suggest may have been a heated debate, the Faculty decided not to interfere, and Wright was in due course admitted.

The Wright affair, and the embarrassment it must have brought to the Faculty, presumably caused reflection on what Lord President Dundas had called the character of the advocates as gentlemen, and in 1785 the Faculty appointed a committee to consider and draft resolutions on the proper qualifications of intrants.[92] The committee laid its draft before the Faculty on 2 July 1785.[93] On 18 July the Faculty debated, amended, and approved the draft regulations.[94] These were: first, that an intrant would not be

[87] Boswell, *Private Papers*, vol. xv, pp. 290–1.

[88] *FR* 2, pp. 489–91 (8 Dec. 1781).

[89] F. J. Grant, *The Faculty of Advocates in Scotland 1532–1943 with Genealogical Notes* (Scottish Record Society, 76, Edinburgh, 1944), p. 222.

[90] Grant does not give a date of birth.

[91] Boswell, *Private Papers*, vol. xv, p. 48.

[92] National Library of Scotland, *FR* 3, 'Minute Book of the Faculty of Advocates 1783–98', pp. 25 and 26 (26 Feb. and 5 Mar. 1785).

[93] *FR* 3, p. 30.

[94] Ibid., p. 31. National Library of Scotland, *FR* 339[r] (Miscellaneous Papers of the Faculty of Advocates) Box IV contains two versions of this report, entitled 'Report of the Comittee appointed to prepare Regulations, respecting the Course of Studies, necessary to be followed, and the other Qualifications, which ought to be required, in those who wish to become Members of the Faculty'. One is obviously an earlier draft, because of the amendments made to it and its lack of certain passages found in the other. Whether the later version is that approved by the Faculty and the changes in it those made by the Faculty, or the final draft presented to the Faculty, cannot be known. The contents of the report were not entered in the minutes.

admitted to trials until he furnished proof of seven years' attendance at a university, three of them in law; secondly, that such an intrant had to be under twenty-seven years of age;[95] and thirdly, that the Faculty at its anniversary meeting would appoint seven members to form a committee to determine whether an intrant should be sent for trial on law. This third proposal provided a mechanism whereby the Faculty could reject petitioners for admission on grounds other than failure to pass their trials: in the debate over Wright's admission the Faculty had decided that it had not power under its regulations to reject him—it had to examine any petitioner remitted to it by the Lords of Session.[96] The requirement as to age was obviously aimed at someone in Wright's position. The provision on university education, first, would promote the polite learning and academic education called for by Lord President Dundas in 1748 and encouraged by the Faculty's resolutions in the 1750s and 1760s, and secondly, when combined with that on age, would also operate as a bar to intrants from less wealthy classes. The premises on which the regulations were based are instructive. The committee considered that the 'enlightened understanding' and 'liberal sentiments' appropriate for practice at the bar had to be acquired 'by an early course of well directed study, and an early admission' to the Faculty. While the educational provision was important, it was vital that it be undertaken young, so that the 'habits of life' of the advocate be suited to his office: indeed the 'most material of all qualifications' could not be acquired by academic education alone. The committee considered that the Faculty had always sought that its members should not only pursue legal studies but also have 'a knowledge of the learned languages and philosophy, in a word that liberal education' which was the mark of 'the scholar and the gentleman'. The honour of the Faculty as a whole was seen as linked to the character and repute of each member. The proposals requiring four years' education in arts are very significant. They demonstrate a complete rupture with the old Humanist ideals and stress on Civil Law, in that by the 1780s the four-year arts curricula of the Scottish universities, especially Edinburgh and Glasgow, reflected Enlightenment ideals in their stress on philosophy, science, *belles-lettres*, and polite learning generally.[97] Though the Faculty committee considered that general scholarship had always been demanded of intrants, while once that demand had been met by education in Civil Law, now the new learning of the Enlightenment was to be required. The proposal of three years' study of law derived presumably from the practice of devoting two years to Civil Law (a course on the Institutes followed by one on the Digest) and a further year to Scots Law. Despite the Faculty

[95] In the earlier draft, twenty-five years: in the later draft 'twenty-seven' is written over an erasure.

[96] *FR* 2, pp. 490–1 (8 Dec. 1781).

[97] See references in n. 59, above.

agreeing on these regulations, they either do not seem to have been presented to the court for approval, or were not approved:[98] the reason is unknown.

It is unjust and misleading to judge the Faculty by modern standards, as the concern for 'politeness' reflected the ideals of the Scottish Enlightenment; and Ramsay of Ochtertyre clearly thought that Lord President Craigie, for example, had been too learned in law and too lacking in the 'elegancies of life', so that his story was one to 'teach Ministers of State never to place a man at the head of a supreme court of justice who is deficient in point of breeding'.[99] One who was 'underbred' and lacking in 'manners' was unfitted for the bar and bench. Concern with the character of intrants was found in the late seventeenth century; but the Humanist learning of intrants on Civil Law was taken to be a guarantee of their integrity, liberality and good breeding. By the time of Wright's petition for admission, Civil Law alone was obviously no longer thought to guarantee suitability, perhaps because it had not yet gained a clear new role in the admission of advocates, and because the development of the Scots Law Faculties opened the possibility of Civilian learning to broader strata of Scots society.

Towards the end of 1787, reform in admission requirements was again mooted.[100] The new proposals, which were unanimously agreed, were for intrants to present to the Dean certificates 'of their having had a regular and proper education' which the Dean would lay before the Faculty, who would then vote by ballot whether or not to remit the candidate to the examiners.[101] What exactly the certificates were to cover is not specified; but the testimony of Thomas Thomson indicates that, following the new Enlightenment emphases, they were 'evidence of attendance upon the Philosophy classes' and 'certificates of attendance upon the Civil and Scotch Law'.[102] This new procedure was first used on 12 February 1788, and continued into the 1790s.[103]

[98] *FR* 3, p. 31 (18 July 1785) indicates a clear intention to send the regulations to the Lords for approval.

[99] Ramsay, vol. i, p. 116. See also his remarks at pp. 380, 386, 390–1 and 392, where he seems to have linked deficiencies in Braxfield to his background and education, and pp. 418–19, where Macintosh is described as having been considered 'an underbred, forward, pragmatical man, who was not likely to do honour to the Faculty. And he was no *belles-lettres* man or philosopher, which was in those days the best recommendation to the *tonish* men.'

[100] *FR* 3, p. 62 (1 Dec. 1787).

[101] Ibid., p. 63 (10 Dec. 1787).

[102] 1837 PP XXXV, p. 405. It is likely, however, that certificates relating to attendance in Scots Law were not immediately required, as a number of candidates had their remits to the examiners postponed until they finished their Civil Law classes, while Civil Law was generally attended before Scots Law. See *FR* 3, pp. 100–1 (17 Jan. 1789) and 190–1 (17 Dec. 1791). Perhaps such certificates had to be produced to the examiners in Scots Law.

[103] *FR* 3, pp. 75–6. When exactly the practice ended is unclear. A report considered by the Faculty on 27 Nov. 1813 (National Library of Scotland, *FR* 4, 'Faculty Minutes 1799–1813', pp. 442–50) implies that it ended in 1791; but in that year only the balloting ended (see

On 2 August 1788 the writing of theses and the public examination came under consideration. The motion put forward noted that many members were dissatisfied with the existing examination. The basis of the examination on specific titles and the nature of the disputes and impugning were both questioned. It was thus suggested that 'discourses' or 'essays' be prescribed rather than theses, and that the examination should take 'a simpler and more natural form' than the impugning and defence of an advocate's theses, corollaries, and *annexa* in 'syllogistical disputes'.[104] (It should be remembered that the theses were not dissertations but generally consisted of a *proemium* briefly discussing the law in the title, then a series of theses extracted from it, followed by a number of corollaries or *annexa*.) This motion obviously expresses dissatisfaction with what was seen as an antiquated procedure smacking of a despised scholasticism. Though Civil Law itself as the object of the public examination does not seem to have been attacked, this move suggests that its position in the established procedures was not sacrosanct, and the attempt to revitalize the examination possibly reflects attitudes such as those of Kames and Boswell in 1780, and hints at a re-evaluation of the place of Civil Law in the trials of intrants. (It is notable that the Act of Sederunt of 1750 had already permitted intrants to append propositions of Scots Law to their theses; whether any had ever done so is unknown, and certainly no theses that I have seen contain such propositions.) The recent debate on the qualifications to be required of intrants, and the realization that the orderly assigning in sequence of titles of the Digest for theses was nearing the last title of the last book[105] may well have prompted this consideration of the public examination in 1788. Though the Faculty named a committee to consider the matter, it apparently did not report, perhaps because a new crisis over admissions occurred in 1790, again provoking a general review of policy.

As with the proposals of 1785, the review resulted from a petition for admission from a man the Faculty considered unsuitable. When in February 1790 Robert Forsyth renewed his petition for admission, he was a law student in Edinburgh University, and held a licence to preach from the Church of Scotland.[106] The Faculty was occupied with Forsyth's case until

below). *FR* 3, pp. 190–1, after the ending of balloting, and the evidence of Thomas Thomson (admitted 10 Dec. 1793) indicate that the practice continued thereafter. The problem is that the stopping of balloting ended the reporting of presentation of certificates in the minutes, apart from in exceptional circumstances. Perhaps the practice died out at the time of the 1795 proposals for reform (see below).

[104] *FR* 3, pp. 87–8.

[105] On 31 May 1796 (ibid., p. 309) the minutes note that the books of the Digest are exhausted for theses. Given the rate of entry to the Faculty, it must have been obvious in 1788 that the time for reconsideration was not far off.

[106] *FR* 3, pp. 133–4 (13 Feb. 1790) and 135 (20 Feb. 1790).

June 1791, when he was finally remitted to the examiners.[107] In the Faculty's minutes opposition focuses on Forsyth's position as a probationer of the Church (that is, one who, though licensed to preach, is not yet an ordained minister).[108] Forsyth was the son of a shoemaker,[109] and Cockburn stated that 'the real ground' of opposition was that of 'not being of high origin'.[110] The Faculty's investigation extended to Dewar Masterton Gibson, the son of a writing-master, who had allegedly married the daughter of Sir John Gibson of Pentland while she had been a pupil on the writing-academy in which Gibson himself taught.[111]

In the course of these investigations, on 4 December 1790 the Faculty again considered 'what steps should be taken for placing on a proper footing the important business of the admission of intrants', and the Dean and his Council were to confer with the court on the topic and report.[112] On 21 February 1791 the Faculty resolved not to consider any further petitions for admission until 1 May 1791, in the hope of by then having new regulations authorized by the court.[113] Regulations were in fact not laid before Faculty until 21 May 1791.[114] These regulations were not enforced, nor do the minutes disclose any detailed discussion of them. The proposals were entirely concerned with providing a mode of regulating the fitness of the character of intrants and a method of rejecting unfit, though academically qualified, candidates. All that the Faculty did at that time was to abolish the system of balloting on intrants, so that now candidates would automatically be remitted for examination unless objection were made to them, in which case an open vote would be taken.[115]

On 11 July 1794 the question of regulations on admission was reopened, and once more a committee was set up to report.[116] The report was finally

[107] Ibid., p. 182.

[108] Ibid., pp. 135 (20 Feb. 1790), 137–8 (6 Mar. 1790), 150–1 (4 Dec. 1790), 161–2 (5 Feb. 1791), 171 (3 June 1791), 173–6 (11 June 1791), and 177–82 (14 June 1791). After Forsyth had renounced his licence, the debate turned on the use he had made of it, and if he had truly informed the Dean about such use.

[109] Grant, *Faculty of Advocates*, p. 75.

[110] H. Cockburn, *Journal of Henry Cockburn being a Continuation of the Memorials of his Time* (2 vols., Edinburgh, 1874), vol. ii, p. 153. Cockburn stated that opposition was also based on Forsyth being a Whig. Given that the conflict of Tories with Whigs in the 1790s is an obsession of Cockburn's, and that Whigs were regularly admitted to the Faculty, Forsyth's low origin is a more convincing cause of opposition; indeed Cockburn himself stated, ibid.: 'The Faculty of Advocates ... was then a highly aristocratic body, and used to curl up its birse at every plebeian who tried to enter ...'

[111] Grant, *Faculty of Advocates*, p. 80; *FR*3, pp. 162 (5 Feb. 1791) and 188–9 (14 Nov. 1791).

[112] *FR 3*, p. 150.

[113] Ibid., pp. 163–4.

[114] Ibid., pp. 165–8. On 14 May 1791 the minutes (ibid., p. 165) noted that on Saturday next they would consider the petitions then lodged with the *Clericus Intrantium* by candidates in Civil Law.

[115] *FR 3*, p. 168.

[116] Ibid., pp. 263–4.

presented on 13 January 1795.[117] Much of the report again was devoted to providing a mechanism for preventing the admission of candidates considered unsuitable for personal reasons. Before a candidate petitioned the Lords for admission he was to present to the Dean certificates testifying to 'his having received a regular University education previous to his having studied the Civil Law two years in a University'. (That certificates of studying Scots Law were not demanded presumably reflected the already noted practice of attending university courses in it in the year between the Civil Law trial and the Scots Law trial.)[118] If the Dean was satisfied with these, he was to remit the candidate to a special committee which was to satisfy itself of the candidate's 'integrity, good breeding, and honest deportment': a test adopted from the Act of Sederunt of 25 June 1692. Appeal procedures were provided for dissatisfied candidates. The last proposal in the report replaced the printed theses and formal public disputation with the preparation and reading of a Latin dissertation on 'some title or point of the Roman Law' to be assigned to the intrant by the Dean, and on which any member of Faculty could ask questions. The intrant was no longer to read a public lesson in Latin before the Lords.[119] The Faculty debated the report on 9 February 1795, and agreed to it by a vote of thirty-seven to eight.[120] The resolutions were presented to the court; but the Dean reported to the Faculty on 4 March 1795 and again on 1 June 1795 that there was no sign that the Lords would soon come to any decision, and on 1 June candidates whose remit to the examiners had been delayed, presumably pending an Act of Sederunt, were finally remitted because of their complaints and because the funds of the Faculty were 'in danger of suffering' (entrance fees were payable on examination).[121] Though these proposals were allowed to fall, the requirement of a general university education, the substitution of a dissertation for theses, and the abolition of the reading of a public lesson before the Lords all point to a growing rationalist emphasis in the qualifications to be required of intrants. (The

[117] Ibid., p. 274. The committee had been asked on 11 July 1794 (ibid., pp. 263–4) to report in November next. There is a gap in the MS of *FR 3* between 13 Nov. 1794 and 13 Dec. 1794 and half of p. 226 and all of pp. 267–8 are blank. Some minutes have obviously been omitted (presumably the spaces were left for copying the minutes into the minute-book). Though it cannot definitely be known that the omitted minutes dealt with proposals on the qualifications of intrants, it is quite likely that they did, as the minute dated 13 Nov. 1794, the last before the blank space, noted, after some discussion on the topic, a decision to delay dealing with it until the next Monday, with circular cards being sent to members to request them to attend.

[118] Though it may fairly be pointed out that the timing of the trials would not always work out so neatly. The intrant might well have started attending lectures on Scots Law before his private trial on Civil Law.

[119] *FR 3*, pp. 274–8.

[120] Ibid., p. 279.

[121] Ibid., pp. 280 and 282.

sequence of assigning titles of the Digest for theses was now almost at the end of the last book.)[122]

In 1812 the Lords intimated to the Dean that they wished to end the practice of intrants reading a lesson before admission.[123] This stimulated the Faculty to a further review of its admission procedures.[124] While the committee appointed to consider the matter appears to have required prompting to produce its report,[125] when the report appeared in November 1813 it had some novel features.[126] Five years' university attendance was to be required, two of which were to be devoted to Civil Law, and a third, in a Scots University, to Scots Law. Attendance was to be established by certificates. The certificate of attendance in Scots Law was to be presented to the *praeses* of the Scots Law examiners; the other certificates were to be presented to the Dean. This reflected the practice already alluded to. The conduct of the Faculty's own private examinations was to be made stricter, and the practice of informing the candidate of the titles on which he would be questioned was to end. A majority on the committee wanted the public defence of theses to be abolished; of that majority, one wanted nothing put in its place, though the others considered that it should be replaced with either a Latin discourse on Civil Law or an English discourse on Scots Law, at the option of the candidate. The committee opposed specific regulations to determine the personal suitability of candidates: intrants instead were to intimate in advance their intention to apply for admission to allow competent objections to be brought forward. The committee finally reported that since the Faculty's regulations did not require the lesson before the Lords, it was for the Court to determine whether or not to preserve it. These proposals indicate how far the Faculty had moved from the Humanism which informed the original admission procedures: in this respect the proposal to substitute not only a dissertation on Civil Law but also the possibility of an English dissertation on Scots Law for the Latin theses on Civil Law is particularly striking. A series of motions was put on these proposals, and those which were carried were to approve in principle the regulations on university attendance and not to innovate as regards the other procedures and examinations (though no indulgence was to be given to candidates). The Faculty also unanimously resolved that it was neither expedient nor consistent with the Faculty's privileges to dispense with the traditional forms by which a candidate was received by the whole Court of

[122] See n. 105 above. In May 1796 the Faculty authorized the Dean to settle the subject of theses with intrants until it could consider the matter more fully. It did not do so, perhaps in expectation of ultimate reform: *FR 3*, p. 309.

[123] *FR* 4, p. 397 (20 June 1812).

[124] Ibid., pp. 398–9 (1 July 1812).

[125] Ibid., p. 436 (1 June 1813).

[126] Ibid., pp. 442–50 (27 Nov. 1813).

Session.[127] Between 1814 and 1817, the Faculty received more reports and discussed further these matters, eventually agreeing to dispense with the requirement of university attendance for a literary and philosophical education, though candidates were to produce evidence of a regular and proper education.[128] These agreed regulations were not acted on.[129] Spurred on by the existence of the Royal Commission then investigating the Scottish universities, in 1828 the Faculty produced further proposals; but these were allowed to drop,[130] so that the regulations of 1750 continued to remain in force.

III

The view of the Faculty committee in 1854 that 'for nearly two centuries there has been a nearly uniform and consistent course of regulation' on the qualifications demanded of intrants[131] is thus misleading, because although there had always been a stress on a general education, where once study of Civil Law alone had been thought sufficient to satisfy this, in the course of the eighteenth century the polite learning of the Enlightenment came to be required. Further, while at the end of the seventeenth and beginning of the eighteenth centuries the examinations for admission in Civil Law were not concerned to test knowledge useful for practice but were designed to uphold the Humanist learning that gave intellectual status to the Faculty, during the eighteenth century the trials came to be seen as a means of testing knowledge for practice in a rational way, and so in 1750 examination in Scots Law was introduced. The 1750 reform preserved the existing private and public examinations in Civil Law, with the addition that intrants could annex to their theses propositions of Scots Law, though there is no evidence of this having become an established practice. The same rationalist emphasis also resulted in criticisms of the lack of rigour of the private examinations. Between his admission in 1723 and his appointment to the bench in 1752, Kames had served a number of times as either a private

[127] Ibid., pp. 451–3.

[128] Lorimer, appendix A, pp. 12–17; and see *FR* 339r, Box IV, (printed) 'Report of Committee, Relative to the Admission of Advocates' (1817).

[129] In 1826 Professor Irving explained to the Royal Commission that after the court had approved Faculty regulations requiring general university education and university education in law, the Faculty changed its mind and required only attendance at law classes. This seems to refer to these developments from 1813–17. Iriving further explained that the then Dean considered that the Faculty had placed itself in such a contradictory position that he refused to present the new regulations to the court: 1837 PP XXXV, pp. 180–1. The matter obviously requires further research; but given this paper's focus on the 18th c., it has not seemed necessary to pursue the topic, though I hope to do so elsewhere.

[130] Lorimer, appendix A, pp. 17–19.

[131] Ibid., appendix A, p. 19.

examiner or a public examiner.[132] He complained 'that a number of ignorant young Men were now admitted Advocates, so that they really could not tell intelligibly at the bar what they wanted'. He claimed when an examiner to have 'had a hand in remitting several upon their trials', and said that 'the Examinators should fairly tell young Men who want to come to the bar to get a livelihood whether they are qualified or not, for that is the meaning of the trial'.[133] Obviously not all the examiners adopted Kames's robust attitude; and furthermore the practice of informing the candidates in advance of the topics on which they would be tested in the private examinations was also subject to criticism.[134] When a private examiner in Civil Law, Henry Brougham thought the procedures so ridiculous that as a joke he always prescribed D. 25.4 as the title on which he would examine intrants.[135] The various attempts to require intrants to produce certificates of attendance at law classes were clearly intended to remedy this by ensuring that intrants had a broad knowledge of law. There was likewise a desire to modernize and make more rigorous the conduct of the private examinations, and in 1813 the Faculty decided not to give any indulgence to candidates, though it had originally been proposed to end the practice of indicating to intrants the topics of their examination. The public examination in Civil Law was considered particularly antiquated: hence the proposals to substitute for the printing and defence of theses a Latin dissertation on Civil Law, and eventually the alternative possibility of an English dissertation on Scots Law. The same spirit of rationalization influenced the Faculty's desire to require the polite learning stressed by Enlightenment thought, as such studies, together with scientific knowledge, helped to

[132] As private examiner: *Minute Book*, vol. ii, pp. 84 (5 Jan. 1724), 115 (7 Jan. 1729), 151 (7 Jan. 1735), 162 (4 Jan. 1737), 180 (6 Jan. 1741), 209 (6 Jan. 1747), and 239 (2 Jan. 1750). As public examiner: ibid., vol. ii, pp. 104 (3 Jan. 1727), 120 (6 Jan. 1730), 133 (4 Jan. 1732), 188 (4 Jan. 1743), 200 (8 Jan. 1745), and 203 (5 June 1746). Shortly before his elevation to the bench, Kames became an examiner in the new Scots Law trial: *FR* 2, p. 12.

[133] Bowell, *Private Papers*, vol. xv, p. 275. True to his age, Kames 'allways excepted heirs to estates whose Fathers made them enter Advocate'. Remitting candidates on their trials must refer to Kames's duties as a private examiner, as the minute-book for the relevant periods does not contain an instance of failure at the public examination. The only instance I have noticed of failure at the public examination is that of Gilbert Elliot of Minto on 10 Dec. 1687 (*Minute Book*, vol. i, p. 82), who eventually passed on 14 July 1688 (vol. i, p. 85). This was before the introduction of theses. There may be more, as I have not searched specially for them. Certainly, failure at the public examination obviously was virtually unknown. Since Elliot became a baronet in 1700 and a Senator of the College of Justice in 1705, his initial failure obviously did him no harm. Kames's attitude is interesting, since he confessed to almost failing his own trials (see text at n. 70 above).

[134] Jardine, pp. 462–3.

[135] See J. Browne, *Remarks on the Study of the Civil Law; occasioned by Mr Brougham's Late Attack on the Scottish Bar* (Edinburgh, 1827), p. 18. D. 25.4 is entitled: *De Inspiciendo Ventre Custodiendoque Partu.* For a fascinating glimpse of the law of this title in operation, see J. F. Gardner, 'A Family and an Inheritance: the Problems of the Widow Petronilla', (Nov. 1984) 9 *Liverpool Classical Monthly* 132–3.

ensure not only that a suitable type of person was admitted, but also that the intrant was properly equipped for practice. In 1807 Tytler wrote:

This profession, more than any other, requires an enlarged acquaintance, not only with human nature, in the knowledge of the passions and affections of the mind, (a knowledge not to be gained but by the study of philosophy); but it demands an extensive information of the various arts and sciences which constitute the occupations of mankind, and of course give origin to a very great proportion of those legal questions which occupy the courts of justice.[136]

The requirement of polite and practical learning to be demonstrated by certificates of university attendance is a constant theme in the proposals of 1785, 1787, 1795, and 1813.

The substitution of a modern rationalism for the Humanism which had underpinned the original Civil Law trials would seem likely to have been reinforced by the contemporary view that the practical utility of Civil Law had greatly declined in the course of the eighteenth century. The views of Kames in 1780 have already been referred to.[137] Professor Irving supported this in 1826 when he said:

Those branches of the Civil Law which have been admitted as of authority with us, after they have entered into the works of our Institutional writers, and are confirmed by judgments and decisions of the courts, become part of the Scotch Law, and are studied in the class of Scotch Law, so that the student has less occasion to resort to the Civil Law than originally.[138]

Professor Cheape spoke in similar terms in his inaugural lecture of 1827.[139] The purpose of the Civil Law examinations seems to have been rationalized as now deriving from Scots Law's historical debt to Roman Law; and Professor Cheape, after stating that the influence of the Civil Law 'has been superseded in many instances by the very precedents which have been founded on it', asserted that knowledge of it was needed to understand Scots Law and Scots cases.[140] This obviously lessened the importance of the Civil Law trials, as they no longer had value in themselves, but only insofar as they aided an understanding of Scots Law. It also explains the attempts to reform the public examination. Such attitudes in the long run must have led to the neglect of Civil Law noted by Boswell and Kames as early as 1780, and by the early nineteenth century observers considered that knowledge of Civil Law had considerably declined. Irving, for example,

[136] A. Fraser Tytler, Lord Woodhouselee, *Memoirs of the Life and Writings of the Honourable Henry Home of Kames* (2 vols., Edinburgh, 1807), vol. i, p. 16.

[137] See text at n. 87 above.

[138] 1837 PP XXXV, p. 183.

[139] D. Cheape, *An Introductory Lecture on the Civil Law, Delivered in the University of Edinburgh, on Tuesday, 13th November 1827* (Edinburgh, 1827), pp. 30–1.

[140] Ibid., pp. 30–1 and 33.

thought that many passed advocate 'very ill instructed upon the subject of Civil Law', and he reported that by the end of his lecture-course in Edinburgh the numbers attending had generally dropped to one-half, while not only was attendance at any examinations he held 'very bad', but also the answers given.[141] Professor Cheape considered that Civil Law was 'one of those sciences which have been more praised than studied'.[142] In the 1820s Brougham provoked a series of newspaper articles by attacking in the House of Commons the appointment of a Scots advocate to the South African bench by claiming that the Scots bar was generally ignorant of Civil Law.[143]

By the 1820s the traditional style of Civil Law teaching then prevalent in Scotland was being rendered obsolete by the new historical scholarship in Germany, and the creative reception of Roman Law in Scotland was clearly thought to be over; none the less, these utilitarian doubts of the practical usefulness of study of Civil Law, and the opinion (whether correct or not) that knowledge of Civil Law among the bar was slight, jointly demonstrate the extent to which the advocates' new rationalist stress in admission procedures—whereby examinations were seen as related to the requirements of professional practice—had replaced their former Humanism, which had considered the trials on Civil Law as a means of upholding and affirming the Faculty's claim to be a *universitas* of learned men.

[141] 1837 PP XXXV, pp. 183 and 184.

[142] Cheape, p. 2.

[143] Browne, n. 135 above, contains these articles from the *Caledonian Mercury* and *Carlisle Journal*.

16

Legal Tradition, with particular reference to Roman Law

W. M. GORDON

TONY HONORÉ says of Ulpian,[1] 'His importance lies in the part he played in the transmission of the Roman legal heritage'. His interest in Ulpian and that legal heritage may justify the dedication to him of these few remarks on legal tradition, although one of his own claims to honour must be that he is a pioneer who is not content merely to follow tradition.

It was until recently a commonplace that one of the notable features of Roman law was the strong element of tradition, especially among the jurists who to a large extent created that law. That view was stated with characteristic assurance by Fritz Schulz, who in his *Principles of Roman Law* devoted his sixth chapter to 'Tradition'.[2] The jurists have therefore been described as traditionalists. Grosso may be regarded as typical both in accepting Schulz's views and in linking the jurists' sense of tradition with the creation of Roman law, which he describes as 'the greatest monument of legal wisdom' (*il più grande monumento di sapienza giuridica*).[3] More recently, the question of the jurists' sense of tradition has been re-examined with equally characteristic subtlety by Dieter Nörr. In the light of this re-examination it is no longer possible to use the term 'traditionalists' of the jurists with the same assurance as before, if indeed it is possible to continue to use the term at all. He would discard a sense of tradition from the 'principles' of Roman law, without denying that there were traditional elements in the law; a tendency to follow tradition was simply one of various tendencies operating and the place of tradition among these tendencies needs to be more carefully considered.[4]

[1] *Ulpian* (Oxford, 1982), p. 247.

[2] (Oxford, 1936, repr. 1956), pp. 83 ff. This work is a revised and enlarged version of his *Prinzipien des römischen Rechts* (Berlin, 1934) translated by Marguerite Wolff. In the original the chapter on Tradition is at pp. 57 ff.

[3] '*Meditazioni sulle tendenze e sulle concezioni dei Romani*' in *Festschrift für Fritz Schulz* (2 vols., Weimar, 1951), vol. ii, pp. 172 ff.

[4] '*Zum Traditionalismus der römischen Juristen*' in *Festschrift für Werner Flume* (2 vols. Cologne, 1978) vol. i, pp. 153 ff.: 'Der Begriff des "Traditionalismus" hat für das römische Recht keinen generellen Erklärungswert. Er ist ein "Prinzip" des römischen Rechts nur dann, wenn

In fairness to Schultz it might be said that tradition is only one of the principles which he identifies in Roman law, but quite apart from the possibility that these other principles, such as isolation, abstraction, and simplicity, might not survive equally close scrutiny it seems reasonable to enquire why there should be a divergence apparently so great. One reason is no doubt to be found in differing attitudes towards the jurists. While Schulz discards as too strong Savigny's description of the Roman jurists as 'fungible personalities' and admits differences between the individual jurists, he has no truck with the idea of individual scientific personalities.[5]

> None of the Roman jurists taught anything fundamentally different from his forerunners and successors, nor was there any more fundamental difference between the teachings of the schools of Sabinus and Proculus than there is in Oxford and Cambridge ... in the small, conservative group of Roman jurists bound by the fixed tradition of their handicraft the emergence of the individual would ... have appeared revolutionary and therefore blameworthy.[6]

In contrast the modern tendency is to seek to identify and highlight the scientific personalities of the Roman jurists. *Ulpian* is only one of many recent studies, however different it may be in its methods from others, and all those who have adopted this approach are attempting afresh what Schulz regarded as the hopeless task essayed by nineteenth-century individualists of making individuals of their 'dearly loved Roman masters'.[7] In this changing climate of opinion it is less easy to believe in the force of tradition among the jurists as Schulz envisages it or at least to believe in the importance of tradition as a constant determining factor in the development of the law. Nörr does in fact discuss the application of the notion of 'traditionalists' to jurists such as Labeo, Pomponius, and C. Cassius Longinus, part of whose speech in the Senate against remission of the penalties of the *SC Silanianum* in a particular case of murder of a master by one of his slaves is referred to by Schulz as evidence of juristic conservatism.[8] In so

man den normalen Sprachgebrauch verläßt. Eher handelt es sich bei ihm um eine nicht einmal besonders charakteristische Tendenz, die sich mit anderen Tendenzen kreuzt, sich überlagert, von ihnen unterlaufen wird, je nach Situation vor-oder zurucktritt.' See also his article '*I giuristi romani: tradizionalismo o progresso?*' (1981) 84 BIDR 9 ff.

[5] *Principles*, p. 107.

[6] Ibid., pp. 107–8.

[7] See for example the contributions in *Aufstieg und Niedergang der römischen Welt* II, '*Prinzipat*), vol. 15 (*Recht*) (Berlin–New York, 1976) which include one by Nörr on Pomponius (pp. 497 ff.).

[8] 'Traditionalismus', pp. 163 ff. The speech is quoted, or re-created, by Tacitus, *Annals* 14. 43. The *SC* required the questioning and execution of all the slaves in the household when their master was violently murdered, unless they had actively sought to prevent the crime. See D. 29. 5 on the *SC* and Nörr's discussion of the speech, 'C. Cassius Longinus: Der Jurist als Rhetor' in *Althistorische Studien. Festschrift für Hermann Bengtson* (*Historia* Einzelschriften, Heft 40, Wiesbaden, 1983). pp. 187 ff.

doing he brings out some of the difficulties and uncertainties involved. Labeo, for example, is described by his contemporary Capito as conservative and by the later Pomponius as an innovator—specifically in contrast to Capito, who, he says (D. 1. 2. 2. 47) adhered to the doctrines which had been handed down to him.[9] But this difference in viewpoint does not seem to be the whole story.

One other factor is the precise meaning of 'traditionalist' in the context of the discussion and this in turn involves at least two separate or separable points. The first of these is whether adherence to tradition necessarily implies total opposition to change and a belief that the older law is invariably or almost invariably better. In quoting C. Cassius Longinus as a typical representative of the Roman jurists and, more generally, of those responsible for the establishment of the law, Schulz would seem to suggest that this is his conception of a traditionalist. Cassius, says, or is made to say, that in every situation the former legal provisions were better and more correct and any change was for the worse ('super omnibus negotiis melius atque rectius olim provisum et quae converterentur in deterius mutari'). Nörr says in the third part of his article that if the Roman jurists had been traditionalists one would have expected to find at least some indications of regret at the replacement of older institutions by new imperial law, if not criticism of the new law, and one would have expected a more respectful attitude towards the *veteres* and a greater stress on *mos maiorum* in the discussion of customary law. This would seem to imply that adherence to tradition involves or at least might be expected to involve a rigid conservatism, which would in turn be difficult to reconcile with the acknowledged evolution of Roman law over the centuries in response to changing circumstances.

That Schulz did not in fact mean to go so far is suggested by his reference to Ihering's *Geist des römischen Rechts*.[10] In the passages to which Schulz refers Ihering refers to a combination of conservative and progressive attitudes which lead to a slow but sure development of the law. He thereby indicates that for him a sense of tradition does not inhibit progress but rather ensures a sound, because gradual, development. It should also be made clear that Nörr himself does not suggest that 'Traditionalismus' necessarily leads to opposition to all change, merely that one would expect more reluctance to admit change than appears from our sources if the jurists' sense of tradition had been as strong as is sometimes suggested. If then the

[9] Schulz of course regarded the section on the history of Roman law in Pomponius' *Enchiridion*, of which D. 1. 2. 2. 47 is an excerpt, as a corrupt abridgement—*History of Roman Legal Science* (Oxford, 1946, repr. with additions 1953), pp. 134, 168–71.

[10] R. von Ihering, *Geist des römischen Rechts auf den verschiedenen Stufen seiner Entwicklung*, 4 vols. (editions by Ihering himself between 1852 and 1891). Schulz refers to the fourth edition (Leipzig, 1878), vol. i, pp. 69 ff. and 334 ff. The references were checked in the second edition (1866).

sense of tradition is to be stressed as an important feature of Roman law it must be clear in what sense tradition is used. It is one thing to cling to tradition at all costs and another to try to fit change into the existing system and make only minimal changes in order to avoid what is seen as possibly harmful breach of continuity. That the term 'traditionalist' can be and is used in different senses is brought out by Nörr's own opening remark that 'Traditionalismus' or 'Konservatismus' or 'Traditionsbewußtsein' is ascribed almost without question to Roman legal science. Grosso, in fact, in the article already referred to, combines '*tradizionalismo*' with '*conservatorismo*' in a way which might imply that they were different qualities, although he does not discuss exactly what he means by either. He apparently regards both terms as self-explanatory in the context of what he has to say. One of the merits of Nörr's treatment is to bring out the complexity of the phenomenon supposedly referred to by what may seem a simple and obvious descriptive term.

This leads to the second of the points referred to above regarding the precise meaning of 'traditionalist'. It does seem that part of the reason for a divergence of view on the place of tradition in Roman law is that it is not always clear whether the reference to tradition is purely descriptive or whether it involves a value judgment. If one looks at the examples which are used to show that Roman law did rely on or adhere to tradition, examples such as the retention of the *ius civile* side by side with the *ius honorarium*, the use of the formal *mancipatio* and *in iure cessio* as modes of transfer of property along with the informal *traditio*, which was, practically speaking, as effective, the retention of the oral *stipulatio* and the failure to develop a written form of contract with the same general scope of application, it is clear that these examples can be considered in two ways. One is to regard the list as recording the fact that Roman law tended to develop by the addition of new law to old rather than by the replacement of old law by new.[11] The other is to regard the examples as proving the existence of a particular characteristic or combination of characteristics which is viewed either with approval or at least with very guarded disapproval. Particularly where the attitude is one of approval there will be a tendency to fasten on and emphasize the examples of supposed adherence to tradition as evidencing a general characteristic or principle of the law.

It seems very probable that Schulz's view of the place of tradition in Roman law was influenced by his approval in general of the Roman approach to legal development. It is true that he is critical of the failure of Roman law to develop in certain directions, for example its failure to recognize agency in the full sense, and he ascribes this failure to the effect

[11] F. Wieacker, *Vom römischen Recht*, (2nd edn. Stuttgart, 1961), p. 14: '... unter allen Umständen der Anbau dem Umbau, der Umbau dem Neubau vorgezogen wird'.

of tradition but his remark (at p. 84) that 'Never did the Romans attempt to interrupt the even flow of legal development by radical changes. Restless experiments, eager reforms, and reconstruction were not to their taste' reveal a general approval of their gradualist approach. The same approach is shown by his description as 'very apt' of the similar remarks of Ihering, who was even more openly in favour of the Roman approach to the development of a legal system. Grosso also clearly thinks highly of the Roman 'tradizionalismo e conservatorismo' described by Schulz and sees it as one of the roots of the greatness of the Roman system. From such a point of view it is inherently probable that certain characteristics and features of Roman legal development will be explained as resting on a sense of tradition rather than, say, mere inertia or a blindness to the possibilities of change for the better.

In fact admiration of the Roman achievement appears to have had a distorting effect on the assessment of the force of tradition in two main ways. In the first place tradition is given the credit for what could not have been changed in any case or what could not have been changed except with considerable difficulty. In the second place it is assumed that the slowness or absence of change is due to the force of tradition when other factors are at least equally relevant and perhaps of even greater significance. That Roman law did develop in the main by a slow process of evolution is true but it is by no means clear that this was a matter of deliberate policy. It could very reasonably be argued that it was because there was for long no machinery which could readily provide for rapid change. Comitial legislation or legislation by *plebiscitum* was cumbersome and the requirement that a proposal put to the relevant assembly be either accepted or rejected but not amended made this form of legislation less than ideal. The praetorian edict could no doubt in theory make rapid and radical changes, even if indirectly by creating new remedies, but as each praetor's edict lasted only for a year and need not be accepted by his successor the theoretical possibilities were in practice limited; the radical changes which were in fact made in the civil law from this point of view had to be made over a period of time. It is arguable that the law made by the jurists by its nature depended on gradual settlement of rules. Grosso in fact suggests that it was not a peculiar characteristic of the Roman jurists to be 'traditionalist'; the legal mind is essentially inclined to follow tradition.[12] Nörr raises the question how far the jurists on their own could have abolished institutions which

[12] Op. cit. n. 3 at p. 172: 'Il giurista, nella stessa *forma mentis* che implica il prospettare i rapporti della vita sociale *sub specie juris*, è essenzialmente tradizionalista e già in varii scritti ho cercato di cogliere e sottolineare questo aspetto della mentalità dei giuristi'. He refers to three articles: 'Il valore della tradizione; (1945) 43.1 *Riv. dir. comm.* pp. 32 ff.; 'Il tradizionalismo dei giuristi' *Rassegna* n. 13: '*Labeone e Capitone. Tradizionalismo e conformismo dei giuristi*', (1947) 1 *Quaderni di Roma* 335 ff.

were no longer in keeping with the times, even assuming that there was the will to abolish them.[13] The answer to this question must be that no doubt by a concerted effort they could have seen to it that the law was changed but it is hard to see how this would in fact be done except over a period of time, if the jurists relied on their own authority. The wider question raised by Grosso will be considered below. Returning to the question of vehicles of rapid change, the only Roman source left is, for practical purposes, imperial activity in its various forms, including the use of *senatusconsulta*. But in the case of imperial activity the authority of the emperors to make changes in the law took time to establish itself. There is then a plausible argument for the view that if Roman law changed slowly, and if slow change is a good thing for a legal system, it was largely by good fortune and not by a deliberate option for slow change based on tradition that Roman law developed as it did.

Where Roman law changed slowly or not at all it may also be a mistake to assume that tradition was the retarding factor. Schulz, for example, says (at p. 95) that, 'The *mancipatio* as a form for transferring ownership really became superfluous with the recognition of bonitary ownership [by the praetor]; nevertheless it was preserved until well into post-classical times.' Nörr rightly points out that on the one hand we do not know whether in fact the ancient and rather cumbersome form was actually used or whether documents alleging a *mancipatio* were drawn up and not challenged, so that in effect *mancipatio* became a simpler written formality (the evidence which we have for *stipulatio* suggests that this is quite a strong possibility, and the post-classical emphasis on actual delivery in the case of gifts is perhaps an indirect indication to the same effect); on the other hand it is possible that it was found useful to have a *mancipatio* in the case of gifts, for which special formalities are not unusual even in modern law.[14] To these considerations it might be added that *traditio* was not a wholly satisfactory substitute for *mancipatio* even if the praetor protected the recipient of a *res mancipi* virtually as if he were the the full *dominus* of the *res*, and made him what is called a bonitary owner. In particular we are told by Gaius that it was usual to mancipate land without going on to the land itself.[15] This meant that although possession would not pass, ownership could be transferred without the need for delivery of the land, and there are clear advantages in having such a possibility. *Mancipatio*, by virtue of the *actio auctoritatis* also carried with it automatic liability in the case of eviction of the acquirer by a third party. In due course it did become possible to make a *traditio* without going to the land, by using a *constitutum possessorium*

[13] 'Traditionalismus', pp. 178 ff.

[14] Op. cit., pp. 178, and 180–1.

[15] J. 1. 121; see also Nörr, op. cit., p. 180 n. 128 on the value of formality in the case of sales of land.

under which the transferee obtained ownership by means of an arrangement which left the transferor holding the land under a title such as usufruct; in turn the title retained might be fictitious.[16] But it is not clear how far this development had proceeded in the clasical law; the evidence for retention of fictitious usufructs is certainly late. The place of the *actio auctoritatis* could be taken by a stipulation for a similar twofold liability. However, it can be seen that there was no obvious practical reason for the jurists to rush to abolish *mancipatio* even if it was no longer essential to use *mancipatio* in order to give the benefits of ownership to the recipient of a *res mancipi*. There was indeed a good deal to be said for retaining it.

In the case of *stipulatio* Nörr points out that the jurists seem to have been quite willing to assist in the practical limitation or even elimination of the need for an oral stipulation where the making of an alleged stipulation was documented. For present purposes it is unnecessary to discuss how far they were prepared to go, but it must be said that it would in any case have been surprising if an attempt had been made to abolish stipulation. It was, after all, a very simple form of contract which required nothing more than an exchange of question and answer by the obligee and obligor. Why should the jurists have sought to introduce a requirement of writing in place of this formality? The only logical step would have been to provide an additional written contract rather than a replacement. It has been argued elsewhere that the failure of Roman law to develop agency in contract is not as surprising or open to criticism as might at first sight appear, when account is taken of all the relationships between agent, principal, and third parties. There are certainly some advantages in having direct agency in contract but the advantages are not overwhelming, especially in a slave-society in which slaves could be and were used extensively in business transactions, could acquire for their masters and could to an important extent bind them by virtue of the *actiones adiecticiae qualitatis*.[17] It is all too easy to say that Roman law should have taken a particular course, looking at it with hindsight, and to say that if it did not it was because of adherence to tradition. In some cases at least there were good reasons why development stopped short of what might seem to modern eyes the obvious next step. These reasons must be considered along with the force of tradition or inertia in assessing what lay behind a particular course of development or a particular cessation of development.

One might equally raise objection to others of Schulz's indications of the Romans' attachment to tradition, such as the statements that the Roman

[16] See the author's *Studies in the Transfer of Property by Traditio* (Aberdeen, 1970), chs. IV–V.

[17] See the author's article 'Agency and Roman Law' in *Studi in onore di Cesare Sanfilippo*, 5 vols. (Milan, 1982–84) vol. iii. pp. 341 ff.

was not easily impressed by foreign legal institutions and that there was a disinclination to abolish any valid law (pp. 84–85). An explanation of the former which is at least as plausible as attachment to tradition is chauvinism, to which legal imperialists such as the Romans are prone. While much of Roman law in the shape of institutions of the *ius gentium* was open to foreigners it was open as Roman law and on the assumption that a foreigner in a Roman court must accept the application of Roman law to his transactions. In a sense it could be said that the existence of the *ius gentium* testifies to the readiness of the Romans to abandon their own traditions in the form of the *ius civile* applicable only to Roman citizens, but to do so on their own terms so far as non-Romans were concerned. This would be one aspect of the adaptation of Roman law to new conditions which makes it impossible to say that adherence to tradition meant for the Romans a refusal to depart from tradition in any circumstances, or a belief that the old ways were always better.

So far as disinclination to abolish valid law is concerned this may be regarded as good sense rather than an unwillingness to abandon the old in favour of the new. There can never be an assurance that new law will be an improvement on the old law in every respect. Unless it is essential for some particular purpose to remove old law there is a good deal to be said for allowing new provisions to supplement rather than replace the old until experience has shown that the old can be discarded without loss. This consideration would apply quite apart from any other considerations such as technical considerations of competence to abolish the old law or questions of political prudence which might argue against an open attempt to repeal older provisions. As Schulz gives no examples of what he has in mind more specific comment may be unnecessary, but so far as political considerations are concerned his view of Augustus' restoration of the *libera res publica* would seem to confuse attachment to legal tradition precisely with political prudence. No doubt it is true in a sense that Augustus in legal terms restored the Republican constitution but it is surely applying hindsight to suggest that there was any political possibility of introducing a new constitution to mark what was, or was to become, the new monarchy. In legal terms it was a shrewd use of the law and precedent to give legitimacy to a new situation and, again, an indication of willingness to depart from tradition at least as much as an indication of desire to adhere to it. The failure to amalgamate civil and praetorian law also involves questions of constitutional importance. The relationship of civil and praetorian law is a reflection of the constitutional standing of the praetor and it would have required radical change to effect an amalgamation. In terms of practical politics only imperial intervention could achieve the amalgamation, quite apart from the technical problems involved. The difficulty of amalgamating common law and equity in England should be a warning against an assumption that there was an active desire to retain a separation simply because it was traditional.

It is now time to return to the question raised by the remarks of Grosso on the 'tradizionalismo' of the jurist. If what he says is correct it would follow that a sense of tradition was not something peculiar to Roman law for the very reason that a sense of tradition will be found in any legal system which owes its development to 'jurists', a term used in the sense of lawyers whose opinions or judgments are an important formal source of law. In other words, to say that a sense of tradition is to be found in Roman law would be to say no more than that Roman law was created by the Roman jurists, although Grosso would apparently also say that this fact accounts largely if not wholly for the merits of Roman law as a legal system. Now it is probably true that Roman law was in fact the creation of the Roman jurists not only in the sense that the opinions of the jurists were a formal source of law but in the sense that their advice lay behind changes in the law made by other agencies such as the magistrates and, later, the emperor. Tony Honoré has sought to identify more closely the connection of particular jurists with particular imperial acts,[18] but, that apart, their influence on imperial administration and development of the law is well established and indeed was institutionalized from the time of Hadrian by the inclusion of leading jurists in the imperial *consilium*. This would help to explain the absence of any considerable volume of criticism from the jurists of the new law made under imperial aegis. It remains to be considered whether it is true that adherence to tradition and the gradualist approach of Roman law to change and reform is a reflection of the fact that it was so largely jurists' law and whether that gradualist approach is a signal merit of the Roman system.

The argument that jurists' law must be founded on tradition and so is incapable of sudden shifts of direction is apparently based on two main arguments, that jurists or lawyers tend to look to the past for guidance on what the law should be and that their authority is based on adherence to tradition. Neither argument is entirely secure. It is doubtful whether it is a specific characteristic of lawyers to look to the past for guidance, unless in the sense that any person who has to make or apply rules, or more specifically to make rules in the course of applying them, will tend to look at what has been done in the past on the basis that what has been done is known and if it has been accepted in the past it may well be accepted in the future. But in the case of a body of law-makers each of whom has an authority to influence the development of the law but who are operating independently in the sense that they do not meet formally to decide what the law should be, as the Roman jurists operated when giving *responsa*

[18] *Emperors and Lawyers* (London, 1981).

or writing, it is at least equally important to have regard to the present, in the sense of what is being done concurrently by others. Advice which is to be influential in settling the law, or even in settling a particular dispute if the advice is not binding on the decision-maker, must be likely to gain acceptance from others who have a share in settling the law. Following existing practices may be more likely to gain the necessary approval but this depends on the attitude of the others concerned. If they are open to new ideas, new ideas can flow into the law, whether or not they fit into existing traditions.

A similar point may be made with regard to treating adherence to tradition as a source of authority. It is true that the Roman jurists came to enjoy their authoritative position not by any specific act of recognition but by the exercise of their function—the somewhat enigmatic *ius respondendi ex auctoritate principis* given by Augustus and later emperors apparently as a mark of favour may have influenced but did not create the authority which a jurist enjoyed, and of course juristic opinion had been creating law long before Augustus intervened. The existence of a tradition then helped to support the influence of the jurists as a body, but there does not seem to be an essential connection between the source of juristic authority and the operation of juristic influence in the development of the law. In so far as the Romans, or certain leading Romans, in the Republic stressed the value of Roman tradition and the *mos maiorum*, a jurist who supported that tradition would find readier acceptance than one who sought to discard it, but this is an accidental circumstance. The important thing is that the jurist does have authority and, particularly if there is no formal grant of authority, adherence to tradition, or too close adherence to tradition, may weaken his authority if values change. This can be seen in modern challenges to the authority of the British or English judiciary by assertions that the views of members of the judiciary are influenced or determined by outmoded traditions, in particular the traditions of the class to which the judges are said to belong[19] For present purposes it is not important to decide whether these challenges are successful or whether there is even a conscious desire in every case to weaken the authority of the judiciary. Studies of the judiciary may be carried out with the utmost scientific impartiality, and may quite rightly expose sources of influence not hitherto taken into account in assessing the way in which the law operates, but demystification does in fact weaken authority and there is no doubt that in some cases the object of demystification is to do so. The relevance of this to tradition is that it is not adherence to tradition as such which creates the authority. The authority rather depends on acceptance, and adherence to tradition will not

[19] See, for example, J. A. G. Griffith, *The Politics of the Judiciary* (Manchester and London, 1977; 2nd edn, 1981; 3rd edn, 1985), with particular reference to their political views.

necessarily help in gaining acceptance or in retaining the confidence of those who have accepted the authority in question. Retention of authority may require recognition of the need to respond to changing circumstances by departing from tradition.

The argument that it is a merit in a legal system to develop by slow degrees is an old one. Stair, writing in the seventeenth century and arguing the merits of Scots law, says[20]

> Yet surely they are most happy whose laws are nearest to equity and most declaratory of it, and least altering of the effects thereof, except in cases eminently profitable, like unto these now pointed at. Yea, and the nations are more happy, whose laws have entered by long custom, wrung out from their debates upon particular cases, until it comes to the consistence of a fixed and known custom. For thereby the conveniences and inconveniences thereof through a tract of time are experimentally seen; so that which is found in some cases convenient, if in other cases afterwards it be found inconvenient, it proves abortive in the womb of time, before it attain the maturity of a law. But in statutes the lawgiver must at once balance the conveniences and inconveniences; wherein he may and often doth fall short: and there do arise *casus incogitati*, wherein the statute is out, and then recourse must be had to equity. But these are the best laws, which are approbatory or correctory of experienced customs. And in a customary law, though the people run some hazard at first of their judges' arbitrement; when that law is come to a full consistence, they have by much the advantage in this, that what custom hath changed, that is thrown away and obliterate without memory or mention of it: but in statutory written law, the vestiges of all the alterations remain and ordinarily increase to such a mass, that they cease to be evidences and securities to the people, and become labyrinths, wherein they are fair to lose their rights, if not themselves; at least they must have an implicit faith in these, who cannot comprehend them without making it the work of their whole life.

It requires only a brief acquaintance with the tax laws or employment laws of modern Britain to induce anyone to agree that Stair has a fair point to make with regard to the possible weaknesses of legislation as a source of law, although the tax laws and employment laws may not be regarded as typical. On the other hand one might suspect, even if one did not know from the context, that Stair was indulging in special pleading for the making of law by judges or jurists as preferable to comprehensive legislation. If nothing else, he assumes that there will be opportunity for experiment and that it is possible to achieve a settlement of interests in society which will give general satisfaction.

[20] James Dalrymple, 1st Viscount Stair, *Institutions of the Law of Scotland*, sixth edn. by D. M. Walker (Edinburgh, 1981) I. 1, 15. The sixth edition, published as part of the commemoration of the tercentenary of the first edition of Stair's work, is based on the second edition, the last by Stair himself. Stair's remarks find an echo in Ihering, but no connection is suggested.

There is an element of truth in the contention that a gradual growth of a legal system, largely directed by legal experts, is a good type of development in that the result should be a harmonious system well adapted to the society in which it operates, and well understood by those whose conduct it is meant to regulate. Roman law as created by the Roman jurists and English law as created by the judiciary are often cited as examples of such systems. Their relative perfection, because no human system is wholly perfect, is as often ascribed to their unbroken tradition of largely self-sufficient development. What tends to be forgotten is that this perception of these systems has not invariably been shared by those who have lived under them at all times in their history and that both were and perhaps have had to be rescued from becoming the labyrinths which Stair feared by legislative intervention. The Humanists of the sixteenth century deplored the loss of so much of the work of the Roman jurists by the actions of Justinian and Tribonian. It is true that there was a loss of which we are in part made aware by the survival of pre-Justinian material, for example, in the Vatican Fragments. That there was also a significant loss is clear, but it is worth considering that the loss may be considered a greater one by legal historians than by those who had to apply the law, and that if Roman law had not been reduced to the *Corpus Iuris* it would almost certainly have been lost altogether. Where loss is concerned it is clear that the juristic writings were at greater risk than the imperial legislation. These writings had apparently presented an insuperable challenge to Theodosius' compilers. With the function of reducing the juristic writings to the more manageable form of the Digest may be compared the consolidating legislation of the nineteenth century, such as the Sale of Goods Act, which temporarily reduced English case-law to more manageable order. Whether either system was made accessible to those expected to live under it even by legislative intervention is more than doubtful;[21] whether either gave or gives as much satisfaction as the praise bestowed upon them would suggest is an open question. So long as there are conflicts of interests no legal system can give universal satisfaction and where non-lawyers are concerned the way in which a case is dealt with may be more important than the actual content of the rules applied, in giving rise to a feeling or opinion that the law is in a satisfactory state. Where law is made by legal experts there is a constant danger of losing

[21] It may be a delusion to suppose that the law can be made directly accessible to all those affected by it. The simplicity of the French *Code civil* is deceptive. The attempt of the Prussian *ALR* to spell out the law in detail and reserve all questions of interpretation to the legislative commission which produced the code did not succeed. The corollary is that expertise should be readily available to those who require it through some form of legal aid. The efforts of bodies such as the Law Commissions set up by the Law Commissions Act 1965 (c. 22) can of course effect improvements but it would be unwise to suppose that in performing their statutory duty *inter alia* to simplify the law (s. 3) they will be able to remove the need for legal expertise.

touch with those who lack the same legal expertise, at least so far as the way in which the law is expressed is concerned, even if the result is regarded as acceptable. Where law is made by expert opinion it may well achieve an even more labyrinthine form of expression than legislation if too much attention is paid to what has been done in the past and, indeed, if too much attention must be given to what is being done by others in the present.[22] Despite Stair's preference for a gradually-settled law, in practice too little is 'thrown away and obliterate without memory or mention of it', as witness not only modern case-law but the writings of the Roman jurists and the literature of the *ius commune*. In the result too much effort may be expended in establishing what the law is or is supposed to be at the risk of losing sight of the issue of what is the just resolution of a particular conflict, not only according to what seemed good in the past but according to present-day views.

The truth of the matter seems to be that no legal system can survive on tradition alone and in particular circumstances a strong sense of tradition or a firm adherence to tradition may be a weakness rather than a strength. Clearly the past cannot always offer guidance on how to act in new situations—although to those with a knowledge of history supposedly new situations are often not as new as is supposed by those who are unaware of the extent of past human experience, whether in the field of law or otherwise. The stability and continuity offered by adherence to tradition must be balanced by willingness to fit the new into the context of tradition. In this process juristic or judge-made law has the disadvantage that it cannot so easily make sudden changes of direction as can legislation, although the House of Lords has shown by its declaration on precedent that sudden changes can be made in what are thought to be immutable rules. Co-operation may be needed between the legislature and the jurists or judges who guide the application of the law. In this way changes can be made as required, but are made in harmony with existing rules and tradition plays its proper role as an element, but not the dominating element, in the system. If there is constant change in the law it becomes increasingly difficult to see the law as a coherent system and indeed to maintain it as a coherent system. Time is needed to assimilate all the implications of a change which may be more far-reaching than appears or has been foreseen; Stair's warning of the fallibility of the legislator is a theme easily illustrated. But a steadfast refusal to change when change is necessary is equally the death of a legal system. Whether Roman law achieved the right balance it is impossible to say, as there can be no final judgment on such a matter, but its history does show the necessity of both tradition and change in a healthy legal system.

[22] It is interesting to compare discussions of the way to handle case-law with discussion of the handling of their authorities by writers of the *ius commune*—see on the latter L. Lombardi, *Saggio sul diritto giurisprudenziale* (Milan, 1967), ch. II.

17

The Tasks of Historical Jurisprudence

PETER STEIN

THE labelling of any area of study may be crucially important to the way in which it is regarded and the respect in which it is held. This may be exemplified by considering the efforts that are made to have certain disciplines that straddle the borderline between the arts and the sciences classified as 'sciences'. For subjects such as psychology, archaeology, or geography, the level of financial support that they receive may depend to a large extent on whether or not they are accepted as 'sciences'. To create the right impression, the staff are encouraged to wear white coats, the places they work in are designated laboratories, and their studies are cast in the form of scientific papers. In Britain and in the English-speaking world generally law is not treated as a science, but in Germany, for example, law is a *Wissenschaft* and the Max-Planck-Stiftung, which encourages research in the *Wissenschaften*, maintains six separate research institutes in the field of law.

Labelling is also important *within* the area of legal studies themselves, where the acceptance of a particular form of enquiry as respectable may depend on the attribution of an appropriate title. Labelling can work to the disadvantage of a subject, if it cannot free itself from the disfavour which a certain line of enquiry has attracted. Something of this kind has happened in the case of historical jurisprudence.

It is a commonplace that, as a recent work on American jurisprudence[1] expresses it, there have been three great traditions in Western legal theory, analytical positivism, natural-law philosophy, and historical jurisprudence. The first two are alive and well, but the third attracts little current attention. In fact we are told that 'historical jurisprudence never did gain much of a foothold in America,'[2] and in 1973 a survey of the teaching of jurisprudence in British universities concluded that 'historical jurisprudence seems to be presently in decline as a taught discipline in this country.'[3] This finding was confirmed in a similar survey in 1984, whose authors commented that 'the

[1] R. S. Summers, *Instrumentalism and American Legal Theory* (Ithaca, 1982), pp. 11–12, 19.

[2] Ibid., p. 35.

[3] R. B. M. Cotterell and J. C. Woodliffe, 'The Teaching of Jurisprudence in British Universities, (1974), 13 *JSPTL* (N.S.) 85.

scant attention paid to Savigny and Sumner is rather surprising given the renewed interest in the role of law in society.'[4]

As the reference to Savigny suggests, historical jurisprudence is understood as being concerned with theories of legal evolution.[5] These theories sought to explain legal change and their characteristic was the assumption that changes in the law followed a predetermined sequence of stages parallel to stages of social evolution.

Theories of historical jurisprudence of this kind had a universalist flavour. Their authors admitted that the schemes they proposed did not apply to all legal systems but nevertheless insisted that they applied to those systems that were worthy of study, systems which they designated by such titles as 'progressive'. The explanation for this insistence on generality must be sought, at least in part, in the fact that the theories were a reaction against a natural-law theory, which was of its nature general. Natural-law theorists had argued that in any society men had a similar nature, rational and social (which, in the view of some, was delineated by the finger of God). Consequently there were certain basic principles of conduct, such as repairing damage caused by one's wrongdoing, or respecting what was due to another, which were applicable in any society of men irrespective of its circumstances. Earlier natural lawyers had been modest about laying down too many such principles, and recognized that there was considerable scope in each society for positive law, which would, for example, indicate precisely what was considered to be 'wrongdoing', or what was 'due' to another. In the eighteenth century, however, the confident publicists of the Enlightenment greatly extended the scope of natural-law principles, and built them into systems that purported to have a general validity in any type of society.

About the middle of the eighteenth century it was pointed out (principally by Montesquieu) that although laws have a necessary relation to the nature of things, yet the nature of things is not the same in every society. There are significant social and economic differences between one society and another and so different laws are required. Montesquieu recognized that these differences often reflected the fact that some societies were more developed than others and therefore required more sophisticated laws, but he did not speculate about the ways in which some societies and their laws become more developed than others. He imposed no scheme of historical progression on his material. However, his immediate successors stressed the connection between the principal mode of subsistence of a society and its law. A society based on agriculture needed a different set of laws from one based on pastoralism or one based on commerce. It was a short step to the

[4] H. A. Barnett and D. M. Yach, 'The Teaching of Jurisprudence and Legal Theory in British Universities and Polytechnics', a paper presented to the W. G. Hart Legal Workshop, July 1984, 9.

[5] Generally, P. G. Stein, *Legal Evolution: the Story of an Idea* (Cambridge, 1980).

idea that societies move through a series of stages based on different modes of subsistence.[6] But it was left to nineteenth-century theorists to put forward theories that societies' laws develop according to predetermined stages, conceived by some as cyclical and by others as linear. We may briefly consider, as examples, the ideas of Savigny and of Maine.

Savigny's theory[7] was worked out in a polemic against the proposal to codify German law. The proponents of codes had cleverly managed to harness both the natural-lawyers and the positivists to their side. Eighteenth-century projects for codes were closely modelled on the systems developed by the leading publicists of natural law. These systems had usually been presented as blueprints for enlightened rulers who would ensure the prosperity of their subjects by enacting them as codes. Thus what would make them law was the fact that they were the product of legislation, but their substance would be dictated by what was found to be congruous with the nature of man. An opposing theory, therefore, had to stress, first, that law was not the product of legislation and, secondly, that its content was governed not by the universal nature of man but by the particular character of the society to which it was applied. But this was not enough; reform and restatement of the law were in the air and a convincing theory also had to explain legal change. It had to be demonstrated that such change was possible without the resort to wholesale legislative restatement. This required historical study of the development of influential legal systems.

Savigny's historical school engendered a ferment of studies of pure legal history, both in the field of Roman law and in the German law, many of which have stood the test of time. But brooding over such studies was a continuous felt need to transcend the purely particular and relative and attain some objective truth, which could have some of the mathematical certainty claimed by natural law. When in a famous phrase Leopold Ranke, the leader of German historical studies in the nineteenth century, appealed to historians to describe the past 'wie es eigentlich gewesen', as it really, or essentially, was, he was not asking for concentration on specific circumstances. Rather he was asking them 'to rise from the investigation and contemplation of the particular to a general view of events and to a recognition

[6] This was the basis of the legal theory of Adam Smith: *Lectures on Jurisprudence*, ed. R. L. Meek, D. D. Raphael and P. G. Stein (Oxford, 1978); cf. Stein, *Legal Evolution*, pp. 33 ff.

[7] *Legal Evolution*, pp. 56 ff. I take the opportunity of correcting an error on pp. 73–7. The Comte, whom William Empson and James Reddie compared with Savigny, was not Auguste Comte, whose positivism influenced Grote, but Charles Comte (1782–1837). His *Traité de Législation, ou exposition des lois générales suivant lesquelles les peuples prospèrent, dépérissent ou restent stationnaires* (4 vols., Paris, 1827) used similar, although more recent, sources to those used by Montesquieu, whom he purported to correct. Comte discussed particularly geographical and racial factors as the causes of the progress of some societies and lack of progress of others. He also identified utility or promotion of the happiness of mankind as a principal foundation of law from ancient times.

of their objectively existing relatedness.'[8] This meant that a historical study was incomplete unless it sought a pattern behind the events it described, although Ranke rejected the creation of models of the past as lessons for the future.

The German historical school of law thus demanded a theory that would show a pattern or scheme of legal evolution. Similarly Maine was concerned to provide a theory of law[9] which would provide an alternative description of law to that offered by Bentham and Austin, and he started with the advantage that there were obvious difficulties in seeing the common law as the command of the sovereign. But he was even more concerned to rebut the claims of the proponents of a priori abstractions, such as the law of nature, and to offer an explanation of law based on the facts of legal life. Such an explanation would be empirical and true in the same sense that natural science was true, and that meant universally true.

> If it be truth at all, it must be scientific truth. There can be no essential difference between the truths of the Astronomer, of the Physiologist, and of the Historian. The great principle which underlies all our knowledge of the physical world, that Nature is ever consistent with herself, must also be true of human nature and human society which is made up of human nature ... if indeed history be true, it must teach that which every other science teaches—continuous sequence, inflexible order, and eternal law.[10]

It may be suggested that in thus linking historical jurisprudence to the claims of scientific truth, Maine was endangering its survival. We no longer think of scientific knowledge as the exemplar of all knowledge. Scientific certainties seem less secure today than they did in the nineteenth century. But science goes on and scientific research is supported by increasing resources, so the tarnishing of the image of science cannot fully explain the eclipse of historical jurisprudence. A more plausible explanation may be that some of the most valuable parts of the subjects are studied under other labels; some areas of historical jurisprudence have been replaced by autonomous disciplines, which are in some sense its descendants. We may instance legal anthropology, sociological jurisprudence and legal history.

The schemes of Savigny and Maine were alike in being based on certain legal systems, of which Roman law was the most prominent, which were documented over long periods by written records. In the second half of the nineteenth century anthropologists began to study 'simple' societies that lacked such records. Their investigations revealed a different picture of 'early law' from that proposed by Maine and other evolutionists. With

[8] L. von Ranke, *The Theory and Practice of History*, ed. and tr. G. G. Iggers and K. von Moltke (Indianapolis, 1971), p. 30.

[9] *Legal Evolution*, pp. 86 ff.

[10] *Village Communities in the East and West* (1895 edn.), pp. 265–6.

some notable exceptions,[11] legal anthropologists have tended to distance themselves from historical jurisprudence and to emphasize the distinctive character of their own studies.

Sociological jurisprudence was founded on the recognition of the truth, revealed by historical jurisprudence, that the character of the law of any society is inextricably related to the social and economic circumstances of that society. But it has found its most fruitful areas of study in contemporary law and has concentrated on relatively narrow problems which have not involved studies over long periods of time.

The schemes of historical jurisprudence were shown by the detailed studies of late nineteenth-century legal historians to have been based on over-simplification of the history of the legal systems which were used to illustrate them. Legal historians tended to concentrate their energies on showing how particular systems developed and felt no need to relate those developments to any general principles of legal change. Legal history has spawned its own subdisciplines, such as the history of particular legal doctrines (*Dogmengeschichte*) and the history of legal thought (*storia del pensiero giuridico*), but these tend to be based on the experience of particular systems of law.

The best legal historians have insisted that meaningful historical study must be based on an awareness of what is happening in areas cognate to those studied. As Maitland put it, 'History involves comparison and the English lawyer who knew nothing and cared nothing for any system but his own hardly came in sight of the idea of legal history.' 'English lawyers', he added, 'have for the last six centuries exaggerated the uniqueness of our legal history ... I know just enough to say this with confidence, that there are great masses of medieval law very comparable with our own.'[12]

Maitland's mention of comparison referred to the perspective which the legal historian of one system can gain from an acquaintance with other systems. Some familiarity with other systems can show him what to look out for in the legal history of his own system. But there can also, of course, be comparative legal history. When a doctrine or institution in one system has been shown to have an analogue in another, it may be that further investigation will reveal that although they appear to be similar they function differently. To trace the reasons for this difference may require a historical study of the procedural assumptions of the systems in question. An explanation of current differences may thus involve a parallel historical study of two distinct legal traditions. This is comparative legal history

[11] Especially Max Gluckman, e.g., in *Ideas in Barotse Jurisprudence*, (New Haven, 1965), p. xvi.

[12] F. W. Maitland, 'Why the History of English Law is not written', *Collected Papers*, ed. H. A. L. Fisher (Cambridge, 1911), vol. I, p. 488.

rather than historical jurisprudence, because it is concerned with specific legal systems in particular historical contexts. The enquiry is still focused on the particular.

But we can ground an enquiry with a question about a type of institution in general, without reference to any particular system. This is what analytical jurisprudence purports to do. It analyses the nature of 'right', 'possession', etc. in general. The analysis of course utilizes illustrations from Roman law, English law and any other particular law whose data are ready to hand. But they are adduced to support a general argument. Can we do something similar on the historical plane?

Our starting-point would be a jurisprudential question, such as, what is the relationship of procedural law to substantive law? An adequate answer to such a question would necessarily involve a historical study of a number of systems, but the study would be focused not on the process of development of each system but on the extent to which the development of the various systems studied could throw light on the primary question.

If we study the development of the jury in England, that is English legal history. If we compare it with that of the professional procedure in France, that is comparative legal history. If we ask how the substantive law in England was affected by the jury system and how the substantive law in France was affected by the wholly professional courts, that is still comparative legal history. We are comparing the development of the substantive law in two legal systems, with roughly similar social and economic circumstances but with different kinds of procedure. But if we take the typical features of the English procedure and the typical features of the French procedure and out of them build two model types, we are moving out of the field of history and into that of jurisprudence.

Such models, 'ideal' in the sense of 'not actually exemplified in reality',[13] have been generally used by social theorists ever since their value was demonstrated by Max Weber. They may never be found in their pure form in any actual system but they bring similarities and differences into relief. They may show that the more an actual system approximates to the model type, the more certain consequences are likely to happen. Whether they will happen or not will usually depend on circumstances not included in the model. One can only use the language of the probable.

This approach may not only be interesting in itself; it may also throw light on historical problems in actual legal systems. For example, if one asks why the only remedy available in the common-law courts was damages, it may be difficult to find the answer from the history of the common law alone. If one turns to the experience of other legal systems which used lay judges, one finds that in classical Roman law the decision in a litigated

[13] D. G. MacRae, *Weber* (Fontana Modern Masters, London, 1974), p. 65.

case was given by a single lay juryman, or *iudex*, chosen for that particular case alone, and he also could only award damages.

If, then, out of the common features of the English jury and the Roman *iudex*, one builds a 'lay' model of procedure and compares it with a model of wholly professional judges, certain features of the layman's involvement with the process of judging become apparent.[14] The layman's task must be finished when he has given the decision assigned to him, so that it is not possible for him to give a remedy that requires supervision and further hearings at a later date, or the exercise of a trained judgment based on particular experience. In practice the transient nature of the layman's participation restricts him to the remedy of money damages. This hypothesis is supported by the fact that both the Roman *iudex* and the English jury were so limited.

In both Roman law and English law it was found necessary to use professional judges when remedies other than damages were required. For example, there seems no reason in principle why a lay judge should not give *restitutio in integrum* of a transaction which, although formally valid, is suspect because the result is inequitable to the parties. But such a remedy, if granted without discrimination, could seriously undermine public faith in the law and its forms. If the law is to produce satisfactory results such a remedy must be available, but it can only be granted at the discretion of a judge who has some idea of the kind of cases in which it is appropriate and of those in which it is not, and such a judge must in some sense be professional.

Such speculations on the implications of the lay and professional models of procedure lead on to inquiries about other consequences of adopting one rather than the other. Where laymen are involved in judging, the tasks assigned to them and those retained by the professionals must be clearly defined. As a result a sharp distinction is likely to be drawn between their respective functions, and such a distinction then demands a theoretical justification. This leads to the simple and attractive idea that laymen are concerned with facts and professionals with law. When, however, this idea is tested against the experience of actual legal systems, it is found not to be supported.

It is true that some legal questions are unsuitable for decision by laymen, but so also are some factual questions, such as those that involve a detailed assessment of accounts over a period. On the other hand, there are some legal questions which, since they require no precise technical knowledge, are quite appropriate for decision by laymen. Whether a man's mind is so disturbed that he is insane and so lacks legal capacity is a question of law;

[14] P. G. Stein, *Legal Institutions: the Development of Dispute Settlement* (London, 1984), pp. 25 ff.

whether he was responsible for the damage suffered by another may also involve a question of law; yet both these questions may be entirely suitable for laymen to answer.

Again, speculation with procedural models can help to clarify the position of the professional judge. In the lay model, the lay judges' function is primarily to assess evidence, but what evidence is brought before them is a matter for the parties themselves. The lay judges have little incentive to prolong the proceedings by asking for additional evidence, and even if their curiosity has been aroused, they are hardly in a position to know what to ask for. Their decision is not justified by reasons, but is based on a general impression of the effect of the evidence the parties have thought fit to offer. Like the judgment of God, expressed in an ordeal, there can be no appeal from the judgment of a lay tribunal, unless it has been misled by a professional. *Vox populi vox Dei.* In this situation the professional judges can concentrate their attention wholly on questions of law and legal policy. Since the time-consuming hearing of proof is assigned to laymen, and appeals are very limited, the professional judges can be few in number. Their oracular pronouncements enhance their status as an èlite group. They become father-figures.

Where, on the other hand, the procedure is wholly in the hands of professionals, they have to spend a great deal of their time hearing evidence and establishing facts, and there is a natural tendency for them to emphasize the importance of this activity. They are not satisfied merely with assessing the quality of the evidence submitted to them by the parties. They want to probe more deeply, to get at the truth of the matter, and so they initiate lines of enquiry of their own. Thus the whole business of fact-investigation becomes more professionalized. Furthermore, since the decision of a professional judge can be challenged on technical grounds, appeals become prominent and appeal structures must be set up. This all takes up much professional time and so more judges are required. Although they are arranged in a hierarchy, their very number means that their status is lessened. They appear to be parts of a bureaucratic machine rather than independent figures.

In some cases a model has been imposed on a legal system and has then seeped into the popular consciousness and become generally accepted as fundamental, with the result that the model itself has affected legal development. Changes in the structure of the legal system, unless they are very dramatic, are not accompanied by a corresponding adjustment of the model, so that even though it is increasingly remote from reality it continues to exert its influence.

The notions of 'written law' and 'unwritten law'[15] have acquired something of this mythical status. The essence of written law is that it is for-

[15] *Legal Institutions*, pp. 69 ff.

mulated in authoritative texts whose content is fixed, so that any adaptation of the law to fit new situations has to be within the terms of the rules so written; it has to take account of a particular verbal formulation. In unwritten law, on the other hand, the theory is that the rules themselves are fixed and unchanging, but no particular formulation of those rules is authoritative, however eminent the judge who was responsible for the formulation.

Roman law is a system that came to terms with the distinction. Roman law was originally unwritten, but substantial parts became written with the enactment of the Twelve Tables early in the Republic. Although the grant of new remedies by the praetor in the formative stage of the edict can be regarded as the formulation of unwritten law, there came a time when the edict itself became a fixed text, so that the *ius honorarium* became written law. Roman lawyers were conscious of the difference between the two forms of law and of the need for separate techniques in handling both forms of sources of law. The word *interpretatio* was properly applied to *interpretatio verborum*, whether in a statute, a contract or a testamentary document. In the application of the undeclared law, the immanent *logos* which was not yet incarnate in a formal declaration, the language of declaration was more appropriate. Yet the jurists were as innovative with one as with the other.

By contrast with Roman law, modern systems have tended to succumb to the myth of the models and to give precedence to one or the other. English law is characterized as essentially a system of unwritten law, in the sense that it is treated as the norm. Although they use the language of declaration, the judges have no scruples about reformulating the rules. They are conscious that their role is a creative one, although they have to operate within certain limits. Ronald Dworkin has recently characterized their activity as a special form of interpretation, and has suggested that it is like that of a group of novelists engaged to write a joint novel. Number one writes the opening chapter and sends it to number two, who adds a chapter of his own, but with the understanding that he is adding it to that novel rather than beginning a new one. Number two then sends the two chapters to number three and so on. Each one, except number one, has the dual responsibility of interpreting and creating because 'each must read all that has gone before to establish, in the interpretivist sense, what the novel so far created is ... what the characters are "really" like ... what the point or theme of the developing novel is ... This must be interpretation in the non-intention-bound style, because, at least for all novelists after the second, there is no single author whose intentions any interpreter can, by the rules of the project, regard as decisive.'[16]

The problem is that today relatively little English law applicable to the

[16] 'Law as Interpretation' (1982) 60 *Texas Law Rev.* 541–2.

man in the street is unwritten law of this kind. The bulk of it is statutory written law. When confronted by a statute, however, the judges are reluctant to apply its aim and purpose as their measure. They prefer to give effect to the intention of the legislature insofar as it can be discovered from the text of the statute itself. It is therefore vital that the drafting should reflect that intention. Sometimes, even in recent years, the judges have taken an almost perverse delight in catching out the draftsman. Much mutual suspicion has been created between Parliament and the courts, one accusing the other of twisting its clear statement and the other replying that in the face of slovenly expressions of intention it is impossible to know what Parliament would have intended. For the point may not have been thought of at all, or even if each member of Parliament had an ascertainable intention, the overall group intention may be indeterminate because there is no majority for any one view.

Explanations for this judicial attitude abound. The judge who refuses to apply a statutory rule to a set of facts is not perceived to be leaving a gap in the law. He can always claim to be falling back on the unwritten common law which provides a kind of safety net of rules with which he feels more at home. The fact that English law has recognized no formal distinction between public and private law means that there can be no difference between the interpretation of public and private statutes. But in the case of those which confer powers on public officials to intervene in the citizens' affairs or which impose penalties for deviant behaviour, there is a public interest in strict attention to detail.

Recently it has been argued that the issue of statutory interpretation is one which raises a constitutional question of the relationship of Parliament and the courts. Detailed legislation, says Lord Hailsham, is something 'we have come to accept as part of our constitutional liberty.'[17] We have certainly come to accept it, but it may be questioned whether the public see it as the price of liberty or would prefer the views of the Renton Committee[18] and Lord Denning[19] that statutes should lay down principles and that the judges should be trusted to fill in gaps in statute law as they do in the unwritten law.

The mesmerizing effect of mythical models is not confined to the common law. The attitudes of civil lawyers are equally influenced by a different model. In codified law all the law is written law, and the judges are expected to derive a rule applicable to every case that comes before them from the code and its satellite statutes. In theory case-law merely illustrates the application of the written law, which forms a complete and logical whole, so that no rule can be derived from any other source.

[17] House of Lords debate, 15 Dec. 1982.
[18] *The Preparation of Legislation* (1975) Cmnd. 6053.
[19] *The Closing Chapter* (London, 1983), p. 112.

This has the consequence that the rules of the code must be expressed in general terms, and paradoxically, since one of the purposes of introducing a code was to curb judicial licence, this generality gives the judges a wide discretion. So much was understood by the principal draftsman of the French *Code Civil*, Portalis. In his preliminary discourse, he described the function of the judge in the face of the *Code* in terms that recall the common-law approach to unwritten law: 'It is for the judge and jurist imbued with the general spirit of the *Code* to direct the application' of its rules, and 'to fill in the gaps that we leave. People's codes are made in time; but strictly speaking they are not made at all.'[20] Portalis expected that what was written in the *Code* should be capable of being moulded into something he could not foresee. The legislature has created it, and there are limits to how far its language can be stretched, but once it has come into being it must be treated as independent of its maker. Yet openly to admit that there is case-law in France would imply that the *Code* is not the only source. The judgments of courts are couched in language which suggests that solutions to all problems that may arise are lurking in the language of the *Code*.

In both the common law and the civil law, therefore, the acceptance of a single historical form as a model for law has led to an unrealistic attitude to other forms.

So far we have considered only models built from materials of Western legal systems. If in constructing new models or recognizing established models we take into account the history of non-Western systems of law, we may recognize even more fundamental stereotypes that threaten to become myths.

For example, we tend to assume that in any developed system of law, all the private law should be defined, so that its application to particular fact-situations should be readily ascertainable. From that we infer that the decision of any dispute by legal means should appear to be as inevitable as possible. It is thought that a court of law, *any* court, should identify the issue between the parties in legal terms, and then give judgment solely on the basis of the application of known rules to ascertained facts relevant to that issue.[21] All other facts, such as the relations of the parties to each other or their status in the community, are irrelevant to the issue and so must be ignored by the court.

If, however, we look at non-Western systems, such as Chinese imperial law or Muslim law, a different picture emerges. Courts may regard it as

[20] Portalis' *Discours préliminaire* is printed in Fenet, *Recueil complet des travaux préparatoires du Code Civil*, (Paris 1827) vol. i, pp. 463 ff., and Locré, *Legislation civile, commerciale et criminelle de la France*, (Paris 1827) vol. i, pp. 243 ff. (quotations in Fenet, pp. 470 and 476, Locré, 258 and 265). Cf. A. Tunc, 'The Grand Outlines of the Code' in B. Schwartz (ed.), *The Code Napoleon and the Common Law World* (New York, 1956).

[21] Stein, *Legal Institutions*, pp. 13 ff.

their function in certain situations to reconcile the parties rather than impose a decision on them. The rules are still important (and I am concerned only with societies that are sufficiently developed to have some form of court established by the state, rules written or unwritten, and an acceptance by the public of an obligation to obey those rules).[22] The point is that they are not considered all-important. Mediation and compromise may admittedly be preferred to adjudication where the court is not confident that its judgments can be enforced. This was the case in many medieval courts. But reconciliation may be regarded as desirable in itself. In Imperial China all law seems to have been regarded as essentially penal in character.[23] Notions of property and contract existed but normally community pressures were sufficient to persuade those in dispute to carry out their obligations to each other. Only in the last resort did the matter come to the magistrate who then punished the obstinate citizen who had resisted the social pressures to conformity.

It is not suggested that a procedure that allows for mediation as an alternative to adjudication is therefore better than one which requires an imposed solution. But recognition of alternative models which do not fit our system makes us aware that there are areas of law in which the parties themselves prefer compromise or arbitration to adjudication.

Nineteenth-century historical jurisprudence was founded on the connection between law and social and economic circumstances. It fell into disrepute because it distorted that connection by advancing theories that law moved through stages of development parallel with stages in the development of societies. However, there can be historical jurisprudence which is independent of social and economic data, and which concentrates on more strictly legal phenomena. Although we reject the idea that law moves inexorably in parallel with society, that does not mean that we cannot study the mechanisms of legal change at a certain level of generality. It means that we have to consider middle-order questions relating to the nature of the judicial process and study how different legal traditions tend to produce certain kinds of legal institutions and how they develop in certain ways and not in others.

The method I have advocated involves the building of ideal models as instruments for the production of hypotheses, which are then tested by reference to actual legal systems. Obviously the models will be more sophisticated and the testing more effective if account is taken at both stages of non-Western systems of law, past and present. But the argument that the study is not jurisprudence unless it takes account of such systems must

[22] G. MacCormack, 'On the Problem of Law in Primitive Societies', in W. Krawietz, T. Mayer-Maly, and O. Weinberger (edd.), *Objectivierung des Rechtsdenkens: Gedächtnisschrift für I. Tammelo* (Berlin, 1984), pp. 667 ff.

[23] D. Bodde and C. Morris, *Law in Imperial China* (Cambridge, Mass., 1967), pp. 3 ff.

be rejected. A study can be jurisprudential even if its generalizations are based on a limited range of systems, so long, of course, as its limitations are recognized. It is jurisprudence, rather than, say, a form of legal history, by virtue of its aims and methods. It seeks to elucidate institutions and processes in legal systems generally, rather than in particular systems. However widely based the study and however many legal systems are taken into consideration, it will never be possible to claim universal validity for the results. The latter will always be tentative, but they may provide new perspectives and relate particular enquiries to general structures.

There is always a danger that the enquirer may become the prisoner of his own model and adopt an uncritical historicism, but it can be resisted, and the risk is worth taking. Studies of this kind are admittedly modest when compared with the grand schemes of the theorists of legal evolution. They produce tentative hypotheses; they postulate what may happen. Yet they can be explanatory, predictive, and critical. They may provide an historical explanation for a certain development in a particular legal system, or they may suggest what is likely to happen if counter-measures are not taken. They may point to an enquiry into why a development that would have been expected has not taken place. They can also offer a critique of contemporary law from a historical standpoint. They enable the observer to stand back and judge aspects of a legal system not against an ideal ethical system, nor in terms of its effectiveness, but according to its resemblance to, or deviation from, a historical model.[24]

[24] These reflections, dedicated with affection to a scholar who has illuminated so many jurisprudential problems from an historical perspective, grew out of participation in the W. G. Hart Legal Workshop, July 1984, and owe much to the other contributors.

18

The Publications of Tony Honoré 1950–1985

BARBARA TEARLE

BOOKS

1950 (with R. W. Lee and others) *The South African Law of Obligations*. Durban: Butterworth & Co. (Africa) Ltd., 1950. lii, 250, [24] pp.

1954 (with R. W. Lee and T. W. Price) *The South African Law of Property, family relations and succession*. Durban: Butterworth & Co. (Africa) Ltd., 1954. lxx, 268, [12] pp.

1959 (with H. L. A. Hart) *Causation in the Law*. Oxford: Clarendon Press, 1959. xxxii, 454 pp.

1962 *Gaius*. Oxford: Clarendon Press, 1962. xviii, 183 pp.: tables.

1966 *The South African Law of Trusts*. Cape Town: Juta, 1966. lii, 512 pp.

1971 *Justinian's Digest: Work in Progress; An Inaugural lecture delivered before the University of Oxford on 12 May 1971*. Oxford: Clarendon Press, 1971. 35 pp. ISBN 0 19 951288 4. Reprinted Aalen: Scientia, 1983.

1976 *The South African Law of Trusts*. 2nd edn. Cape Town: Juta, 1976. lviii, 508 pp. ISBN 0 7021 0722 0.

1978 *Sex Law*. London: Duckworth, 1978. vi, 200 pp. ISBN 0 7156 1170 4.

The South African Law of Obligations. 2nd edn. by E. Newman and D. J. McQuoid-Mason. Durban: Butterworths, 1978. xciii, 419 pp. ISBN 0 409 04000 2.

Tribonian. London: Duckworth, 1978. xvii, 314 pp. ISBN 0 7156 1131 3.

1980 (with Josef Menner) *Concordance to the Digest jurists*. Oxford: Clarendon Press, Oxford Microform Publications, 1980. Booklet: ix, 65 pp. ISBN 0 19 825354 0. Microfiche: 84 sheets.

1981 *Emperors and Lawyers*. London: Duckworth, 1981. xv, 190 pp. ISBN 0 7156 1449 5.

1982 *The Quest for Security: Employees, Tenants, Wives*. London: Stevens, 1982. xiv, 128 pp. The Hamlyn lectures, 34th series. ISBN 0 420 46410 7.

Ulpian. Oxford: Clarendon Press, 1982. ix, 303 pp. ISBN 0 19 825358 3.

1983 *Family, Things and Succession*. 2nd edn. by H. J. Erasmus, C. G. van der

Merwe and A. H. van Wyk. Durban: Butterworths, 1983. xvii, 615 pp. ISBN 0 409 04053 3.

1985 (with H. L. A. Hart) *Causation in the law.* 2nd edn. Oxford: Clarendon Press, 1985. 544 pp. ISBN 0 19 825475 X.

The South African Law of Trusts. 3rd edn. Cape Town, Wetton, and Johannesberg: Juta, 1985. 618pp. ISBN 0 7021 1532 0.

ARTICLES, ETC.

1956 (with H. L. A. Hart) 'Causation in the Law', (1956) 72 *LQR* 58–90, 260–81, 398–417.

1957 'Die Kausalitätslehre im anglo-amerikanischen Recht im Vergleich zum deutschen Recht', (1957) 69 *Zeitschrift für die gesamte Strafrechtswissenschaft* 463–74.

1958 '*Condictio* and Payment', [1958] *Acta Juridica* 135–40.

'Degrees of Invalidity', (1958) 75 *South African Law Journal* 32–8.

1959 'The History of Aedilitian Actions from Roman to Roman-Dutch Law'. In David Daube (ed.), *Studies in the Roman Law of Sale Dedicated to the Memory of Francis de Zulueta.* Oxford: Clarendon Press, 1959. pp. 132–59.

1960 'Rights of Exclusion and Immunities against Divesting', (1959–1960) 34 *Tulane Law Review* 453–68.

'Third Party Enrichment', [1960] *Acta Juridica* 236–53.

1961 '*Arra* as you were', (1961) 77 *LQR* 172–5.

'Ownership'. In A. G. Guest (ed.), *Oxford Essays in Jurisprudence.* Oxford: Clarendon Press, 1961. pp. 107–47.

1962 'Proculus', (1962) 30 *Tijdschrift voor Rechtsgeschiedenis* 472–509.

'The Severan Lawyers: A Preliminary Survey', (1962) 28 *Studia et Documenta Historiae et Iuris* 162–232.

'Social Justice', (1961–1962) 8 *McGill LJ* 77–105.

1963 'Textual Chains in the Digest', (1963) 80 *ZSS Rom. Abt.* 362–78.

'Can and can't', (1964) 73 *Mind* N.S. 463–79.

'Julian's Circle', (1964) 32 *Tijdschrift voor Rechtsgeschiedenis* 1–44.

'Remoteness of Damage', (1964) 81 *South African Law Journal* 410–14.

1965 'The *"Fragmentum Dositheanum"*', (1965) 12 *Revue Internationale des Droits de l'Antiquité*, 3e. série 301–23.

'Hedley Byrne & Co., Ltd. v *Heller & Partners, Ltd.'*, (1964–1965) 8 *JSPTL* N.S. 284–300.

1966 'Law, Morals and Rescue'. In James M. Ratcliffe (ed.), *The Good Samaritan and the Law.* New York: Doubleday, 1966. pp. 225–42. Reprinted in Joel Feinberg and Hyman Gross (eds.), *Philosophy of law.* Encino, Calif.: Dickenson Publishing Company Inc., 1975; pp. 424–32. and 2nd edn., Belmont, Calif.: Wadsworth Publishing Company, 1980. pp. 440–7.

1967 'Allegiance and the Usurper', [1967] *Cambridge Law Journal* 214–23.

'Reflections on Revolutions', (1967) 2 *Irish Jurist*, N.S. 268–78.

1968 'Social Justice'. In Robert S. Summers, ed. *Essays in legal philosophy*. Oxford: Blackwell, 1968. ISBN 0 631 11380 0. pp. 61–94. Summary on p. 94. [Revision of article of same title previously published in 1962.]

'A Statistical Study of the Synoptic Problem', (1968) 10 *Novum Testamentum* 95–147.

1969 'Honoré's Views on Trust Law: a Reply', (1969) 32 *Tydskrif vir Hedendaagse Romeins-Hollandse Reg* 126–33.

1970 (with Alan Rodger) 'How the Digest Commissioners worked', (1970) 87 *ZSS Rom. Abt.* 246–314.

1971 'Causation and remoteness of damage', In *International Encyclopedia of Comparative Law*. Vol. 11, Torts, Ch. 7. Tübingen: J. C. B. Mohr; The Hague: Mouton: New York: Oceana, 1971. 156 pp. Reprinted as Vol. 11, Part 1. Tübingen: J. C. B. Mohr; The Hague: Nijhoff, 1983. ISBN 3 16 644542 0 (Mohr). Ch. 7, pp. 1–156.

'Reference to the Non-existent', (1971) 46 *Philosophy* 302–8.

1972 (with Alan Rodger) 'The Distribution of Digest Texts into Titles', (1972) 89 *ZSS Rom. Abt.* 351–62.

'Justinian's Digest: Following the Trail', (1972) 88 *LQR* 530–42.

'Justinian's Digest: Work in Progress', (1972) 88 *LQR* 30–56. Inaugural lecture previously published in 1971.

'Linguistic and social context of the *Lex Aquilia*', (1972) 7 *Irish Jurist*, N.S. 138–50.

'Word Frequencies and the Study of Roman Law,' [1972 A] *Cambridge Law Journal* 280–93.

1973 'The Editing of the Digest Titles', (1973) 90 *ZSS Rom. Abt.* 262–304.

'Groups, laws, and obedience'. In A. W. B. Simpson (ed.), *Oxford Essays in Jurisprudence* (*second series*). Oxford: Clarendon Press, 1973. pp. 1–21.

'Kodifikationstanker i England i dag', (1973) 86 *Tidsskrift for Rettsvitenskap* 341–57. ['Thoughts on codification in England today'.]

'Legal reasoning in Rome and today', (1973) 4 *Cambrian Law Review* 58–67. Reprinted (1974) 91 *South African Law Journal* 84–94. That issue reprinted in Ellison Kahn and David Zeffertt, eds. *Select South African legal problems: essays in memory of R. G. McKerron*. Cape Town: Juta, 1974. pp. 84–94.

'Romerretten og den moderne retstænkning', (1973) 86 *Tidsskrift for Rettsvitenskap* 219–40. ['Roman law and modern legal thought.']

1974 'The Background to Justinian's Codification', (1973–1974) 48 *Tulane Law Review* 859–93.

(with Alan Rodger) 'Citations in the Edictal Commentaries', (1974) 42 *Tijdschrift voor Rechtsgeschiedenis* 57–70.

'Labeo's *Posteriora* and the Digest Commission'. In Alan Watson (ed.), *Daube Noster: Essays in Legal History for David Daube*. Edinburgh: Scottish Academic Press, 1974. pp. 161–81.

'Law of Donations and Trusts', [1974] *Annual Survey of South African Law* 145–51.

1975 (with H. L. A. Hart) 'Causation and Responsibility'. In Joel Feinberg and Hyman Gross (eds.), *Philosophy of Law*. Encino, Calif.: Dickenson Publishing Company Inc., 1975. pp. 339–50; and 2nd edn. Belmont. Calif.: Wadsworth Publishing Company, 1980; pp. 404–14. Reprinted from *Causation in the Law*. 1959.

'Law of Donations and Trusts', [1975] *Annual Survey of South African Law* 158–61.

'Some Constitutions Composed by Justinian', (1975) 65 *JRS* 107–23.

'A Study of Neratius and a Reflection on Method. On Reinhold Greiner. *Opera Neratii, drei Textgeschichten*', (1975) 43 *Tijdschrift voor Rechtsgeschiedenis* 223–40.

'What is a group?' (1975) 61 *Archiv für Rechts- und Sozialphilosophie*, 161–80. Summary in French and German.

1977 'Property, Title and Redistribution'. In Carl Wellman (ed.) *Equality and Freedom: Past, Present and Future*. Wiesbaden: Franz Steiner, 1977. *ARSP* Beiheft N.F. 10. ISBN 3 515 02624 X. pp. 107–15. Summary in English, French and German. Reprinted in Virginia Held (ed.), *Property, profits and economic justice*. Belmont, Calif.: Wadsworth Publishing Company, 1980, pp. 84–92.

'Real laws'. In P M. S. Hacker and J. Raz (eds), *Law, morality and society: essays in honour of H. L. A. Hart*. Oxford: Clarendon Press, 1977. pp. 99–118.

1978 'Die menschliche Gemeinschaft und das Prinzip der Mehrheitsregel'. In Friedrich Kaulbach and Werner Krawietz, (eds), *Recht und Gesellschaft: Festschrift für Helmut Schelsky zum 65. Geburtstag*. Berlin: Duncker und Humblot, 1978. pp. 229–47. Reprinted as 'The Human Community and the Principle of Majority Rule', (1976–1979) 8 *Sydney Law Review* 599–612; and in Eugene Kamenka (ed.), *Community as a Social Ideal*. London: Edward Arnold, 1982. pp. 147–60.

1979 '"Imperial Rescripts" A.D. 193–305: Authorship and Authenticity', (1979) 69 *JRS* 51–64.

'The Rights of the Rightless'. In F. C. Huntley (ed.) *Law and the Future of Society*. Wiesbaden: Franz Steiner, 1979. *ARSP* Beiheft NF 11. pp. 173–86. Summary in English, French and German.

'Some simple measures of richness of vocabulary', (1979) 7 *Association for Literary and Linguistic Computing Bulletin* 172–7.

1981 'Alfred Rupert Neale Cross 1912–1980'. In *Crime, Proof and Punishment: Essays in Memory of Sir Rupert Cross*. London: Butterworths, 1981. pp. xxi–xxvi.

'Must we obey? Necessity as a Ground of Obligation', (1981) 67 *Virginia Law Review* 39–61.

'The Primacy of Oral Evidence?' In *Crime, Proof, and Punishment: Essays in Memory of Sir Rupert Cross*. London: Butterworths, 1981. pp. 172–92.

'Some suggestions for the study of Interpolations', (1981) 49 *Tijdschrift voor Rechtsgeschiedenis* 225–49.

1983 'Sale and the Transfer of Ownership: the Compilers' Point of View'. In P. G. Stein and A. D. E. Lewis (eds.), *Studies in Justinian's Institutes in Memory of J. A. C. Thomas*. London: Sweet & Maxwell, 1983. pp. 56–72.

1984 'New Methods in Roman law', (1984) 3 *Rechtshistorisches Journal* 290–305.

'Techniques of Interpolation: D.33.4.15–17'. In *Sodalitas: scritti in onore di Antonio Guarino*. Naples: Jovene, 1984. Volume 6, pp. 2723–38.

BOOK REVIEWS

1960 *Verrykingsaanspreeklikheid in die Suid-Afrikaanse Reg*, by W. de Vos. Cape Town, 1958. (1960) 9 *International and Comparative Law Quarterly* 160–3.

1961 *Acta Juridica 1959*. Cape Town and Amsterdam, 1959. (1961) 10 *International and Comparative Law Quarterly* 202–4.

1966 *Hermogenians Iuris Epitomae, zum Stand der römischen Jurisprudenz im Zeitalter Diokletians*, by D. Liebs. Göttingen, 1964. (1966) 34 *Tijdschrift voor Rechtsgeschiedenis* 266–9.

1969 *Gaio nel suo tempo: Atti del simposio romanistico*, by A. Guarino and L. Bove. Naples, 1966. (1969) 35 *Studia et Documenta Historiae et Iuris* 418–25.

1971 *The Law of Delict*, 7th edn. by R. G. McKerron. Cape Town, 1970. (1971) 88 *South African Law Journal* 369–72.

1972 *Proculi Epistulae, eine frühklassische Juristenschrift*, by C. Krampe. Karlsruhe, 1970. (1972) 40 *Tijdschrift voor Rechtsgeschiedenis* 561–5.

1974 *Handbuch der Quellen und Literatur der neueren Europäischen Privatrechtsgeschichte. Band 1. Mittelalter*, H. Coing, ed. Munich, 1973. (1974) 90 *LQR* 427–9.

From Personal to Territorial Law: Aspects of the History and Structure of the Western Legal-constitutional Traditions, by S. L. Guterman. Metuchen, NJ, 1972. (1974) 89 *English Historical Review* 143–4.

1976 *Das römische Privatrecht, zweiter Abschnitt: die nachklassischen Entwicklungen*, 2nd edn. by M. Kaser. Munich, 1975. (1976) 92 *LQR* 632–3.

1978 'Brutal Assaults', *Understanding Sexual Attacks*, by D. J. West and others. London, 197 (1978) 46 *New Society* 224.

'Confidentiality', *Privacy*, J. B. Young, ed. Chichester, 1978. (1978) 45 *New Society* 30.

Censorship and Obscenity, by R. Dhavan and C. Davies. London, 1978. (1978) 45 *New Society* 526.

1979 'Cop porn', *Obscenity: an Account of Censorship Laws and Their Enforcement in England and Wales*, by G. Robertson. London, 1979. (1979) 48 *New Society* 726–7.

1980 *Causes and Damages*, by A. Peczenik. Lund, 1979. (1980) 29 *International and Comparative Law Quarterly* 544.

Iavoleni Epistulae, by B. Eckhardt. Berlin, 1978. (1980) 48 *Tijdschrift voor Rechtsgeschiedenis* 264–6.

Reskripte der Soldatenkaiser: ein Beitrag zur römischen Rechtsgeschichte des dritten nachchristlichen Jahrhunderts, by G. Schnebelt. Karlsruhe, 1974. (1980) 70 *JRS* 210–11.

Studien zur allgemeinen Rechtslehre des Gaius: Ius gentium und ius naturale im ihrem Verhältnis zum ius civile, by H. Wagner. Zutphen, 1978. (1980) 52 *Gnomon* 276–80.

1983 *Giuristi adrianei, con note di prosopografia e bibliografia su giuristi del II sec olo d.c. di G. De Cristofaro*, by F. Casavola. Naples, 1980. (1983) 55 *Gnomon* 368–70.

Landlords and Tenants in Imperial Rome, by B.W. Frier. Princeton, N.J., 1980. (1983) 31 *American Journal of Comparative Law* 388–90.

LETTERS

1968 'Strict liability', (1968) 85 *South African Law Journal* 210.

1983 'Ulpian', *Times Literary Supplement*, 4 March 1983, 215.

'Ulpian', *Times Literary Supplement*, 8 April 1983, 355.

Index

This is an index of citations, in four parts. Part 1 lists names and, where the name is that of an author whose work is cited by its title, works. Part 2 lists cases. Part 3 lists statutes. Part 4 lists texts.

PART 1: NAMES AND WORKS

PART 2: CASES

PART 3: STATUTES

(i) *Modern*

(ii) *Ancient*

PART 4: TEXTS

(i) *Juristic Texts*

(ii) *Non-Juristic Texts*